The Hannah Whitall Smith

Collection

Three Books in One
The Christian's Secret of a Happy Life
The God of All Comfort
The Unselfishness of God

A BARBOUR BOOK

THE HANNAH WHITALL SMITH COLLECTION

ISBN 1-55748-637-9

Hannah Whitall Smith

The Christian's
Secret of a Happy Life

CONTENTS

PART I   THE LIFE

CHAPTER ONE

Is It Scriptural?

No THOUGHTFUL PERSON CAN QUESTION THE FACT that, for the most part, the Christian life, as it is generally lived, is not entirely a happy life. A keen observer once said to me, "You Christians seem to have a religion that makes you miserable. You are like a man with a headache. He does not want to get rid of his head, but it hurts him to keep it. You cannot expect outsiders to seek very earnestly for anything so uncomfortable." Then for the first time I saw, as in a flash, that the religion of Christ ought to be, and was meant to be, to its possessors, not something to make them miserable, but something to make them happy; and I began then and there to ask the Lord to show me the secret of a happy Christian life.

It is this secret, so far as I have learned it, that I shall try to tell in the following pages.

All of God's children, I am convinced, feel instinctively, in their moments of divine illumination, that a life of inward rest and outward victory is their inalienable birthright. Can you not remember, some of you, the shout of triumph your souls gave when you first became acquainted with the Lord Jesus, and had a glimpse of His mighty saving power? How sure you were of victory, then! How easy it seemed to be more than conquerors, through Him that loved you! Under the leadership of a Captain, who had never been foiled in battle, how could you dream of defeat? And yet, to many of you, how different has been your real experience! Your victories have been few and fleeting, your defeats many and disastrous. You have not lived as you feel children of God ought to live. You have had perhaps a clear understanding of doctrinal truths, but you have not come into possession of their life and power. You have rejoiced in your knowledge of the things revealed in the Scriptures, but have not had a living realization of the things themselves, consciously felt in the soul. Christ is believed in, talked about, and served, but He is not known as the soul's actual and very life, abiding there forever, and revealing Himself there continually in His beauty. You have found Jesus as your Saviour from the penalty of sin, but you have not found Him as your Saviour from its power. You have carefully studied the Holy Scriptures, and have gathered much precious truth therefrom, which you have trusted would feed and nourish your spiritual life, but in spite of it all, your souls are starving and dying within you, and you cry out in secret, again and again, for that bread and water of life which you see promised in the Scriptures to all believers. In the very depths of your hearts, you know that your experience is not a Scriptural experience; that, as an old writer said, your religion is "but a *talk* to what the early Christians enjoyed, possessed, and lived in." And your hearts have sunk within you, as, day after day, and year after year, your early visions of triumph have seemed to grow more and more dim, and you have been forced to settle down to the conviction, that the best you can expect from your religion is a life of alternate failure and victory, one hour sinning, and the next repenting, and then beginning again, only to fail again, and again to repent.

But *is* this all? Had the Lord Jesus only this in His mind when He laid down His precious life to deliver you from your sore and cruel bondage to sin? Did He propose to Himself only this partial deliverance? Did He intend to leave you thus struggling under a weary consciousness of defeat and discouragement? Did He fear that a continuous victory would dishonor Him, and bring reproach on His name? When all those declarations were made concerning His coming, and the work He was to accomplish, did they mean only this that you have experienced? Was there a hidden reserve in each promise that was meant to deprive it of its complete fulfilment? Did "delivering us out of the hand of our enemies" mean that they should still have dominion over us? Did "enabling us always to triumph" mean that we were only to triumph sometimes? Did being made "more than conquerors through Him that loved us" mean constant defeat and failure? Does being "saved to the uttermost" mean the meager salvation we see manifested among us now? Can we dream that the Saviour, who was wounded for our transgressions and bruised for our iniquities, could possibly see of the travail of His soul and be satisfied in such Christian lives as fill the Church to-day? The Bible tells us that "for this purpose the Son of God was manifested, that he might destroy the works of the devil"; and can we imagine for a moment that this is beyond His power, and that He finds Himself unable to accomplish the thing He was manifested to do?

In the very outset, then, settle down on this one thing, that Jesus came to save you now, in this life, from the power and dominion of sin, and to make you more than conquerors through His power. If you doubt this, search your Bible, and collect together every announcement or declaration concerning the purposes and object of His death on the cross. You will be astonished to find how full they are. Everywhere and always, His work is said to be to deliver us from our sins, from our bondage, from our defilement; and not a hint is given, anywhere, that this deliverance was to be only the limited and partial one with which Christians so continually try to be satisfied.

Let me give you the teaching of Scripture on this subject. When the angel of the Lord appeared unto Joseph in a dream, and announced the coming birth of the Saviour, he said, "And thou shalt call his name Jesus, for he shall save his people from their sins."

When Zacharias was "filled with the Holy Ghost" at the birth of his son, and "prophesied," he declared that God had visited His people in order to fulfil the promise and the oath He had made them; which promise was, "that he would grant unto us, that we, being delivered out of the hand of our enemies, might serve him without fear, in holiness and righteousness before him, all the days of our life."

When Peter was preaching in the porch of the temple to the wondering Jews, he said, "Unto you first, God, having raised up his Son Jesus, sent him to bless you in turning away every one of you from his iniquities."

When Paul was telling to the Ephesian Church the wondrous truth that Christ had so loved them as to give Himself for them, he went on to declare that His purpose in thus doing was "that he might sanctify and cleanse it by the washing of water by the word, that he might present it to himself a glorious church, not having spot or wrinkle, or any such thing; but that it should be holy and without blemish."

When Paul was seeking to instruct Titus, his own son after the common faith, concerning the grace of God, he declared that the object of that grace was to teach us "that, denying ungodliness and worldly lusts, we should live soberly, righteously, and godly in this present world"; and adds, as the reason of this, that Christ "gave himself for us that he might redeem us from all iniquity, and purify us unto himself a peculiar people, zealous of good works."

When Peter was urging upon the Christians to whom he was writing a holy and Christlike walk, he tells them that "even hereunto were ye called: because Christ also suffered for us, leaving us an example that ye should follow his steps: who did no sin, neither was guile found in his mouth"; and adds, "Who his own self bare our sins in his own body on the tree, that we, being dead to sins, should live unto righteousness: by whose stripes ye were healed."

When Paul was contrasting in the Ephesians the walk suitable for a Christian with the walk of an unbeliever, he sets before them the truth in Jesus as being this, "that ye put off concerning the former conversation the old man, which is corrupt according to the deceitful lusts; and be renewed in the spirit of your mind; and that ye put on the new man, which after God is created in righteousness and true holiness."

And when, in Romans 6, he was answering forever the question as to a child of God continuing in sin, and showing how utterly foreign it was to the whole spirit and aim of the salvation of Jesus, he brings up the fact of our judicial death and resurrection with Christ as an unanswerable argument for our practical deliverance from it, and says, "God forbid. How shall we, that are dead to sin, live any longer therein? Know ye not, that so many of us as were baptized into Jesus Christ were baptized into his death? Therefore we are buried with him by baptism into death: that like as Christ was raised up from the dead by the glory of the Father, even so we also should walk in newness of life"; and adds, "Knowing this, that our old man is crucified with him, that the body of sin might be destroyed, that henceforth we should not serve sin."

It is a fact sometimes overlooked that, in the declarations concerning the object of the death of Christ, far more mention is made of a present salvation from sin, than of a future salvation in a heaven beyond, showing plainly God's estimate of the relative importance of these two things.

Dear Christians, will you receive the testimony of the Scripture on this matter? The same crucial questions that troubled the Church in Paul's day are troubling it now: first, "Shall we continue in sin that grace may abound?" and second, "Do we then make void the law through faith?" Shall our answer to these be Paul's emphatic "God forbid," and his triumphant assertions that, instead of making it void, "we establish the law"; and that "what the law could not do, in that it was weak through the flesh, God sending his own Son in the likeness of sinful flesh, and for sin, condemned sin in the flesh: that the righteousness of the law might be fulfilled in us, who walk not after the flesh, but after the Spirit?"

Can we, for a moment, suppose that the holy God, who hates sin in the sinner, is willing to tolerate it in the Christian, and that He has even arranged the plan of salvation in such a way as to make it impossible for those who are saved from the guilt of sin to find deliverance from its power?

As Dr. Chalmers well says, "Sin is that scandal which must be rooted out from the great spiritual household over which the Divinity rejoices . . . . Strange administration, indeed, for sin to be so hateful to God as to lay all who had incurred it under death, and yet, when readmitted into life, that sin should be permitted; and that what was before the object of destroying vengeance should now become the object of an upheld and protected toleration. Now that the penalty is taken off, think you it is possible that the unchangeable God has so given up His antipathy to sin as that man, ruined and redeemed man, may now perseveringly indulge, under the new arrangement, in that which under the old destroyed him? Does not the God who loved righteousness and hated iniquity six thousand years ago bear the same love to righteousness and hatred to iniquity still? . . . I now breathe the air of loving-kindness from heaven, and can walk before God in peace and graciousness; shall I again attempt the incompatible alliance of two principles so adverse as that of an approving God and a persevering sinner? How shall we, recovered from so awful a catastrophe, continue that which first involved us in it? The cross of Christ, by the same mighty and decisive stroke wherewith it moved the curse of sin away from us, also surely moves away the power and the love of it from over us."

And not Dr. Chalmers only, but many other holy men of his generation, and of our own, as well as of generations long past, have united in declaring that the redemption accomplished for us by our Lord Jesus Christ on the cross at Calvary is a redemption from the power of sin as well as from its guilt, and that He *is* able to save to the uttermost all who come unto God by Him.

A quaint old Quaker divine of the seventeenth century says: "There is nothing so contrary to God as sin, and God will not suffer sin always to rule His masterpiece, man. When we consider the infiniteness of God's power for destroying that which is contrary to Him, who can believe that the devil must always stand and prevail? I believe it is inconsistent and disagreeable with true faith for people to be Christians and yet to believe that Christ, the eternal Son of God, to whom all power in heaven and earth is given, will suffer sin and the devil to have dominion over them.

"But you will say no man by all the power he hath can redeem himself, and no man can live without sin. We will say Amen to it. But if men tell us that when God's power comes to help us and to redeem us out of sin, it cannot be effected, then this doctrine we cannot away with; nor I hope you neither.

"Would you approve of it if I should tell you that God puts forth His power to do such a thing, but the devil hinders Him? That it is impossible for God to do it, because the devil does not like it? That it is impossible that any one should be free from sin, because the devil hath got such a power in them that God cannot cast him out? This is lamentable doctrine, yet hath not this been preached? It doth in plain terms say, though God doth interpose His power, it is impossible, because the devil hath so rooted sin in the nature of man. Is not man God's creature, and cannot He new make him, and cast sin out of him? If you say sin is deeply rooted in man, I say so, too; yet not so deeply rooted but Christ Jesus hath entered so deeply into the root of the nature of man, that He hath received power to destroy the devil and his works, and to recover and redeem man into righteousness and holiness. Or else it is false that 'He is able to save to the uttermost all that come unto God by Him.' We must throw away the Bible if we say that it is impossible for God to deliver man out of sin.

"We know," he continues, "when our friends are in captivity, as in Turkey or elsewhere, we pay our money for their redemption; but we will not pay our money if they be kept in their fetters still. Would not any one think himself cheated to pay so much money for their redemption, and the bargain he made so that he shall be *said* to be redeemed, and be *called* a redeemed captive, but he must wear his fetters still? How long? As long as he hath a day to live. This is for bodies, but now I am speaking of souls. Christ must be made to me redemption, and rescue me from captivity. Am I a prisoner anywhere? Yes, verily, verily, he that committeth sin, saith Christ, he is a servant of sin, he is a slave of sin. If thou hast sinned, thou art a slave, a captive that must be redeemed out of captivity. Who will pay a price for me? I am poor; I have nothing; I cannot redeem myself: who will pay a price for me? There is One come who hath paid a price for me. That is well; that is good news; then I hope I shall come out of my captivity. What is His name? Is He called a Redeemer? So, then, I do expect the benefit of my redemption and that I shall go out of my captivity. No, say they, you must abide in sin as long as you live. What! must we never be delivered? Must this crooked heart and perverse will always remain? Must I be a believer, and yet have no faith that reacheth to sanctification and holy living? Is there no mastery to be had, no getting victory over sin? Must it prevail over me as long as I live? What sort of a Redeemer, then, is this, or what benefit have I in this life, of my redemption?"

Similar extracts might be quoted from Marshall and Romaine, and many others, to show that this doctrine is no new one in the Church, however much it may have been lost sight of by the present generation of believers. It is the same old story that has filled with songs of triumph the daily lives of many saints of God, both Catholic and Protestant, throughout all ages; and it is now being sounded forth afresh to the unspeakable joy of weary and burdened souls.

Do not reject it, then, dear reader, until you have prayerfully searched the Scriptures to see whether these things be indeed so. Ask God to open the eyes of your understanding by His Spirit, that you may know "what is the exceeding greatness of his power to us-ward who believe, according to the working of his mighty power, which he wrought in Christ, when he raised him from the dead, and set him at his own right hand in the heavenly places." And when you have begun to have some faint glimpses of this power, learn to look away utterly from your own weakness, and, putting your case into His hands, trust Him to deliver you.

"When thou goest out to battle against thine enemies, and seest horses, and chariots, and a people more than thou, be not afraid of them: for the Lord thy God is with thee, which brought thee up out of the land of Egypt. And it shall be, when ye are come nigh unto the battle, that the priest shall approach and speak unto the people, and shall say unto them, Hear, O Israel, ye approach this day unto battle against your enemies: let not your hearts faint, fear not, and do not tremble, neither be ye terrified because of them; for the Lord your God is he that goeth with you, to fight for you against your enemies to save you."

CHAPTER TWO

God's Side and Man's Side

MUCH MISUNDERSTANDING ARISES, IN REFERENCE TO this subject of the life and walk of faith, from the fact that its two sides are not clearly seen. People are apt to think that there is only one side to it, and, dwelling exclusively upon the one they happen to see the most clearly, without even a thought of any other, it is no wonder that distorted views of the whole matter are the legitimate consequence.

Now, there are two very decided and distinct sides to this subject, and, like all other subjects, it cannot be fully understood unless both of these sides are kept constantly in view. I refer of course to God's side and man's side; or, in other words, to God's part in the work of sanctification, and man's part. These are very distinct and even contrasting, but, although to a cursory observer they may sometimes so appear, they are not really contradictory.

At one time this was very strikingly illustrated to me. There were two teachers of this interior life holding meetings in the same place, at alternate hours. One spoke only of God's part in the work, and the other dwelt exclusively upon man's part. They were both in perfect sympathy with each other, and realized fully that they were each teaching different sides of the same great truth; and this also was understood by a large proportion of their hearers. But with some of the hearers it was different, and one lady said to me in the greatest perplexity, "I cannot understand it at all. Here are two preachers undertaking to teach just the same truth, and yet to me they seem flatly to contradict each other." And I felt at the time that she expressed a puzzle that, very often, causes great difficulty in the minds of many honest inquirers after this truth.

Suppose two friends go to see some celebrated building, and return home to describe it. One has seen only the north side, and the other only the south. The first says: "The building was built in such a manner, and has such and such stories and ornaments." "Oh, no," says the other, interrupting him, "you are altogether mistaken; I saw the building, and it was built in quite a different manner, and its ornaments and stories were so and so." A lively dispute might follow upon the truth of the respective descriptions, until the two friends should discover that they had been describing different *sides* of the building, and then all would be reconciled at once.

I would like to state, as clearly as I can, what I judge to be the two distinct sides in this matter; and to show how looking at one, without seeing the other, will be sure to create wrong impressions and views of the truth.

To state it in brief, I would say, that man's part is

to trust, and God's part is to work; and it can be seen at a glance how these two parts contrast with each other, and yet are not necessarily contradictory. I mean this: there is a certain *work* to be accomplished. We are to be delivered from the power of sin, and are to be made perfect in every good work to do the will of God. "Beholding as in a glass the glory of the Lord," we are to be actually "changed into the same image from glory to glory, even as by the Spirit of the Lord." We are to be transformed by the renewing of our minds, that we may prove what is that good, and acceptable, and perfect will of God. A real work is to be wrought in us and upon us. Besetting sins are to be conquered; evil habits are to be overcome; wrong dispositions and feelings are to be rooted out, and holy tempers and emotions are to be begotten. A positive transformation is to take place. So at least the Bible teaches. Now, somebody must do this. Either we must do it for ourselves, or another must do it for us. We have most of us tried to do it for ourselves at first, and have grievously failed; then we discover, from the Scriptures and from our own experience, that it is something we are unable to do, but that the Lord Jesus Christ has come on purpose to do it, and that He will do it for all who put themselves wholly into His hands and trust Him without reserve. Now, under these circumstances, what is the part of the believer, and what is the part of the Lord? Plainly the believer can do nothing but trust; while the Lord, in whom he trusts, actually does the work entrusted to Him. *Trusting* and *doing* are certainly contrasted things, often indeed contradictory; but are they contradictory in this case? Manifestly not, because it is two different parties that are concerned. If we should say of one party in a transaction that he trusted his case to another, and yet attended to it himself, we should state a contradiction and an impossibility, but, when we say of two parties in a transaction that one trusts the other to do something, and that the other goes to work and does it, we are stating something that is perfectly simple and harmonious. When we say, therefore, that, in this higher life, man's part is to trust, and God's part is to do the thing entrusted to Him, we do not surely present any very difficult or puzzling problem.

The preacher who is speaking on man's part in the matter cannot speak of anything but surrender and trust, because this is positively all the man can do. We all agree about this. And yet such preachers are constantly criticised as though, in saying this, they had meant to imply there *was* no other part, and that therefore nothing but trusting is to be done. And the cry goes out that this doctrine of faith does away with all realities, that souls are just told to trust, and there is the end of it, and that they sit down thenceforward in a sort of religious easy-chair, dreaming away a life fruitless of any actual result. All this misapprehension arises, of course, from the fact that either the preacher has neglected to state, or the hearer has failed to hear the other side of the matter, which is that when we trust, the Lord works, and that a great deal is done, not by us, but by Him. Actual results are reached by our trusting, because our Lord undertakes the thing entrusted to Him, and accomplishes it.

We do not do anything, but *He* does it, and it is all the more effectually done because of this. As soon as this is clearly seen, the difficulty as to the preaching of faith disappears entirely.

On the other hand, the preacher who dwells on God's part in the matter is criticised on a totally different ground. He does not speak of trust, for the Lord's part is not to trust, but to work. The Lord's part is to *do* the thing entrusted to Him. He disciplines and trains by inward exercises and outward providences. He brings to bear upon us all the refining and purifying resources of His wisdom and His love. He makes everything in our lives and circumstances subservient to the one great purpose of causing us to grow in grace, and of conforming us, day by day and hour by hour, to the image of Christ. He carries us through a process of transformation, longer or shorter as our peculiar case may require, making actual and experimental the results for which we have trusted. We have dared, for instance, according to the command in Rom. 6:11, by faith to reckon ourselves dead unto sin. The Lord makes this a reality and puts us to death by a thousand little mortifications and crosses to the natural man. Our reckoning is available only because God thus makes it real. And yet the preacher who dwells upon this practical side of the matter, and tells of God's processes for making faith's reckonings experimental realities, may be accused of contradicting the preaching of faith altogether, and of declaring only a process of gradual sanctification by works, and of setting before the soul an impossible and hopeless task.

Now, sanctification is both a step of faith, and a process of works. It is a step of surrender and trust on our part, and it is a process of development on God's part. By a step of faith we get into Christ; by a process we are made to "grow up into him in all things." By a step of faith we put ourselves into the hands of the Divine Potter; by a gradual process He makes us into a vessel unto His own honor, meet for His use, and prepared to every good work.

To illustrate this, suppose I were to describe to a person who was entirely ignorant of the subject the way in which a lump of clay is made into a beautiful vessel. I tell him first the part of the clay in the matter; and all I can say about this is that the clay is put into the potter's hands, and then lies passive there, submitting itself to all the turnings and overturnings of the potter's hands upon it. There is really nothing else to be said about the clay's part. But could my hearer argue from this that nothing else is done because I say that this is all the clay can do? If he is an intelligent hearer he will not dream of doing so, but will say, "I understand; this is what the clay must do. But what must the potter do?" "Ah," I answer, "now we come to the important part. The potter takes the clay thus abandoned to his working, and begins to mold and fashion it according to his own will. He kneads and works it; he tears it apart and presses it together again; he wets it and then suffers it to dry. Sometimes he works at it for hours together; sometimes he lays it aside for days, and does not touch it. And then, when by all these processes he has made it perfectly pliable in his hands, he proceeds to make it up into the vessel he has proposed. He turns it upon the wheel, planes it and smooths it, and dries it in the sun, bakes it in the oven, and finally turns it out of his workshop, a vessel to his honor and fit for his use."

Will my reader be likely now to say that I am contradicting myself, that a little while ago I had said the clay had nothing to do but to lie passive in the potter's hands, and that now I am putting upon it a great work, which it is not able to perform, and that to make itself into such a vessel is an impossible and hopeless undertaking? Surely not. For he will see that while before I was speaking of the clay's part in the matter, I am now speaking of the potter's part, and that these two are necessarily contrasted, but not in the least contradictory, and that the clay is not expected to do the potter's work, but only to yield itself up to his working.

Nothing, it seems to me, could be clearer than the perfect harmony between these two *apparently* contradictory sorts of teaching.

What *can* be said about man's part in this great work but that he must continually surrender himself and continually trust? But when we come to God's side of the question, what is there that may not be said as to the manifold and wonderful ways, in which He accomplishes the ork entrusted to Him? It is here that the growing comes in. The lump of clay could never grow into a beautiful vessel if it stayed in the clay pit for thousands of years; but when it is put into the hands of a skillful potter it grows rapidly, under his fashioning, into the vessel he intends it to be. And in the same way the soul, abandoned to the working of the Heavenly Potter, is made into a vessel unto honor, sanctified, and meet for the Master's use.

Having, therefore, taken the step of faith by which you have put yourself wholly and absolutely into His hands, you must now expect Him to begin to work. His way of accomplishing that which you have entrusted to Him may be different from your way; but He knows, and you must be satisfied.

I knew a lady who had entered into this life of faith with a great outpouring of the Spirit, and a wonderful flood of light and joy. She supposed, of course, this was a preparation for some great service, and expected to be put forth immediately into the Lord's harvest field. Instead of this, almost at once her husband lost all his money, and she was shut up in her own house to attend to all sorts of domestic duties, with no time or strength left for any Gospel work at all. She accepted the discipline, and yielded herself up as heartily to sweep, and dust, and bake, and sew, as she would have done to preach, or pray, or write for the Lord. And the result was that, through this very training, He made her into a vessel "meet for the master's use, and prepared unto every good work."

Another lady, who had entered this life of faith under similar circumstances of wondrous blessing, and who also expected to be sent out to do some great work, was shut up with two peevish invalid children to nurse, and humor, and amuse all day long. Unlike the first one, this lady did not accept the training, but chafed and fretted, and finally rebelled, lost all her blessing, and went back into a state of sad coldness and misery. She had understood her part of trusting to begin with, but, not understanding the Divine process of accomplishing that for which she had trusted, she took herself out of the hands of the Heavenly Potter, and the vessel was marred on the wheel.

I believe many a vessel has been similarly marred by a want of understanding these things. The maturity of a Christian experience cannot be reached in a moment, but is the result of the work of God's Holy Spirit, who, by His energizing and transforming power, causes us to grow up into Christ in all things. And we cannot hope to reach this maturity in any way other than by yielding ourselves up, utterly and willingly, to His mighty working. But the sanctification the Scriptures urge, as a present experience upon all believers, does not consist in maturity of growth, but in purity of heart; and this may be as complete in the early as in our later experiences.

The lump of clay, from the moment it comes under the transforming hand of the potter is, during each day and each hour of the process, just what the potter wants it to be at that hour or on that day, and therefore pleases him; but it is very far from being matured into the vessel he intends in the future to make it.

The little babe may be all that a babe could be, or ought to be, and may therefore perfectly please its mother; and yet it is very far from being what that mother would wish it to be when the years of maturity shall come.

The apple in June is a perfect apple for June; it is the best apple that June can produce: but it is very different from the apple in October, which is a perfected apple.

God's works are perfect in every stage of their growth. Man's works are never perfect until they are in every respect complete.

All that we claim, then, in this life of sanctification is that by an act of faith we put ourselves into the hands of the Lord, for Him to work in us all the good pleasure of His will, and then, by a continuous exercise of faith, keep ourselves there. This is our part in the matter. And when we do it, and while we do it, we are, in the Scripture sense, truly pleasing to God, although it may require years of training and discipline to mature us into a vessel that shall be in all respects to His honor, and fitted to every good work.

Our part is the trusting; it is His to accomplish the results. And when we do our part, He never fails to do His, for no one ever trusted in the Lord and was confounded. Do not be afraid, then, that, if you trust, or tell others to trust, the matter will end there. Trust is the beginning and the continuing foundation; but when we trust, the Lord works, and His work is the important part of the whole matter. And this explains that apparent paradox which puzzles so many. They say, "In one breath you tell us to do nothing but trust, and in the next you tell us to do impossible things. How can you reconcile such contradictory statements?" They are to be reconciled, just as we reconcile the statements concerning a saw in a carpenter's shop when we say, at one moment, that the saw has sawn asunder a log, and the next moment declare that the carpenter has done it. The saw is the instrument used; the power that uses it is the carpenter's. And so we, yielding ourselves unto God, and our members as instruments of righteousness unto Him, find that He works in us to will and to do of His good pleasure, and we can say with Paul, "I labored; yet not I, but the grace of God which was with me."

In the divine order, God's working depends upon our co-operation. Of our Lord it was declared that at a certain place He could do there no mighty work because of their unbelief. It was not that He would not, but He could not. I believe we often think of God that He will not, when the real truth is that He cannot. Just as the potter, however skilful, cannot make a beautiful vessel out of a lump of clay that is never put into his hands, so neither can God make out of me a vessel unto His honor unless I put myself into His hands. My part is the essential correlation of God's part in the matter of my salvation; and as God is *sure* to do His part all right, the vital thing for me is to find out what my part is, and then do it.

In this book, therefore, I shall of course dwell mostly upon man's side, as I am writing for human beings and in the hope of making it plain how we are to fulfil our part of this great work. But I wish it to be distinctly understood all through that, unless I believed with all my heart in God's effectual working on His side, not one word of this book would ever have been written.

CHAPTER THREE

The Life Defined

IN THE FIRST CHAPTER I HAVE TRIED TO SETTLE THE question as to the scripturalness of the experience sometimes called the Higher Christian Life but which is the only true Christian life, and which to my own mind is best described in the words, the "life hid with Christ in God." In the second, I have sought to reconcile the two distinct sides of this life; that is, the part to be done by the Lord, and the part necessarily to be done by ourselves. I shall now, therefore, consider it as a settled point that the Scriptures do set before the believer in the Lord Jesus a life of abiding rest and of continual victory, which is very far beyond the ordinary run of Christian experience; and that in the Bible we have presented to us a Saviour able to save us from the power of our sins as really as He saves us from their guilt.

The point to be next considered is as to what are the chief characteristics of this life hid with Christ in God, and how it differs from much in the ordinary Christian experience.

Its chief characteristics are an entire surrender to

the Lord, and a perfect trust in Him, resulting in victory over sin and inward rest of soul; and it differs from the lower range of Christian experience in that it causes us to let the Lord carry our burdens and manage our affairs for us instead of trying to do it ourselves.

Most Christians are like a man who was toiling along the road, bending under a heavy burden, when a wagon overtook him, and the driver kindly offered to help him on his journey. He joyfully accepted the offer but when seated in the wagon, continued to bend beneath his burden, which he still kept on his shoulders. "Why do you not lay down your burden?" asked the kind-hearted driver. "Oh!" replied the man, "I feel that it is almost too much to ask you to carry me, and I could not think of letting you carry my burden too." And so Christians, who have given themselves into the care and keeping of the Lord Jesus still continue to bend beneath the weight of their burdens, and often go weary and heavy-laden throughout the whole length of their journey.

When I speak of burdens, I mean everything that troubles us, whether spiritual or temporal.

I mean, first of all, ourselves. The greatest burden we have to carry in life is self; the most difficult thing we have to manage is self. Our own daily living, our frames and feelings, our especial weaknesses and temptations, our peculiar temperaments, our inward affairs of every kind,—these are the things that perplex and worry us more than anything else, and that bring us most frequently into bondage and darkness. In laying off your burdens, therefore, the first one you must get rid of is yourself. You must hand yourself, with your temptations, your temperament, your frames and feelings, and all your inward and outward experiences, over into the care and keeping of your God, and leave it all there. He made you, and therefore He understands you, and knows how to manage you; and you must trust Him to do it. Say to Him, "Here, Lord, I abandon myself to thee. I have tried in every way I could think of to manage myself, and to make myself what I know I ought to be, but have always failed. Now I give it up to thee. Do thou take entire possession of me. Work in me all the good pleasure of thy will. Mold and fashion me into such a vessel as seemeth good to thee. I leave myself in thy hands, and I believe thou wilt, according to thy promise, make me into a vessel unto thy own honor, 'sanctified, and meet for the master's use, and prepared unto every good work.'" And here you must rest, trusting yourself thus to Him, continually and absolutely.

Next, you must lay off every other burden,— your health, your reputation, your Christian work, your houses, your children, your business, your servants; everything, in short, that concerns you, whether inward or outward.

It is generally much less difficult for us to commit the keeping of our future to the Lord than it is to commit our present. We know we are helpless as regards the future, but we feel as if the present was in our own hands, and must be carried on our own shoulders; and most of us have an unconfessed idea that it is a great deal to ask the Lord to carry ourselves, and that we cannot think of asking Him to carry our burdens too.

I knew a Christian lady who had a very heavy temporal burden. It took away her sleep and her appetite, and there was danger of her health breaking down under it. One day, when it seemed especially heavy, she noticed lying on the table near her a little tract called "Hannah's Faith." Attracted by the title, she picked it up and began to read it, little knowing, however, that it was to create a revolution in her whole experience. The story was of a poor woman who had been carried triumphantly through a life of unusual sorrow. She was giving the history of her life to a kind visitor on one occasion, and at the close the visitor said feelingly, "Oh, Hannah, I do not see how you could bear so much sorrow!" "I did not bear it," was the quick reply; "the Lord bore it for me." "Yes," said the visitor, "that is the right way. We must take our troubles to the Lord." "Yes," replied Hannah, "but we must do more than that: we must *leave* them there. Most people," she continued, "take their burdens to Him, but they bring them away with them again, and are just as worried and unhappy as ever. But I take mine, and I leave them with Him, and come away and forget them. If the worry comes back, I take it to Him again; and I do this over and over, until at last I just forget I have any worries, and am at perfect rest."

My friend was very much struck with this plan, and resolved to try it. The circumstances of her life she could not alter, but she took them to the Lord, and handed them over into His management; and then she believed that He took it, and she left all the responsibility and the worry and anxiety with Him. As often as the anxieties returned, she took them back, and the result was that, although the circumstances remained unchanged, her soul was kept in perfect peace in the midst of them. She felt that she had found out a practical secret; and from that time she sought never to carry her own burdens, nor to manage her own affairs, but to hand them over, as fast as they arose, to the Divine Burden-bearer.

This same secret, also, which she had found to be so effectual in her outward life, proved to be still more effectual in her inward life, which was in truth ever more utterly unmanageable. She abandoned her whole self to the Lord, with all that she was and all that she had, and, believing that He took that which she had committed to Him, she ceased to fret and worry, and her life became all sunshine in the gladness of belonging to Him. It was a very simple secret she found out: only this, that it was possible to obey God's commandment contained in those words, "Be careful for nothing; but in everything by prayer and supplication, with thanksgiving, let your requests be made known unto God"; and that, in obeying it, the result would inevitably be, according to the promise, that the "peace of God which passeth all understanding shall keep your hearts and minds through Christ Jesus."

There are many other things to be said about this life hid with Christ in God, many details as to what the Lord Jesus does for those who thus abandon themselves to Him. But the gist of the whole matter is here stated; and the soul that has discovered this secret of simple faith has found the key that will unlock the whole treasure-house of God.

I am sure these pages will fall into the hands of some child of God who is hungering for just such a life as I have been describing. You long unspeakably to get rid of your weary burdens. You would be delighted to hand over the management of your unmanageable self into the hands of one who is able to manage you. You are tired and weary, and the rest I speak of looks unutterably sweet to you.

Do you recollect the delicious sense of rest with which you have sometimes gone to bed at night after a day of great exertion and weariness? How delightful was the sensation of relaxing every muscle, and letting your body go in a perfect abandonment of ease and comfort! The strain of the day had ceased, for a few hours at least, and the work of the day had been laid off. You no longer had to hold up an aching head or a weary back. You trusted yourself to the bed in an absolute confidence, and it held you up, without effort, or strain, or even thought, on your part. You rested!

But suppose you had doubted the strength or the stability of your bed, and had dreaded each moment to find it giving way beneath you and landing you on the floor; could you have rested then? Would not every muscle have been strained in a fruitless effort to hold yourself up, and would not the weariness have been greater than if you had not gone to bed at all?

Let this analogy teach you what it means to rest in the Lord. Let your souls lie down upon the couch of

His sweet will, as your bodies lie down in their beds at night. Relax every strain, and lay off every burden: Let yourself go in a perfect abandonment of ease and comfort, sure that, since He holds you up, you are perfectly safe. Your part is simply to rest. His part is to sustain you; and He cannot fail.

Or take another analogy, which our Lord Himself has abundantly sanctioned,—that of the child-life. For "Jesus called a little child unto him, and set him in the midst of them, and said, Except ye be converted and become as little children, ye shall not enter into the kingdom of heaven."

Now, what are the characteristics of a little child, and how does it live? It lives by faith, and its chief characteristic is freedom from care. Its life is one long trust from year's end to year's end. It trusts its parents, it trusts its caretakers, it trusts its teachers; it even trusts people sometimes who are utterly unworthy of trust, out of the abounding trustfulness of its nature. And this trust is abundantly answered. The child provides nothing for itself, and yet everything is provided. It takes no thought for the morrow, and forms no plans, and yet all its life is planned out for it, and it finds its paths made ready, opening out as it comes to them day by day and hour by hour. It goes in and out of its father's house with an unspeakable ease and abandonment, enjoying all the good things therein, without having spent a penny in procuring them. Pestilence may walk through the streets of its city, but the child regards it not. Famine and fire and war may rage around it, but under its father's tender care the child abides in utter unconcern and perfect rest. It lives in the present moment, and receives its life unquestioningly as it comes to it day by day from its father's hands.

I was visiting once in a wealthy home, where there was a little adopted child, upon whom was lavished all the love and tenderness and care that human hearts could bestow, or human means procure. And as I watched that child running in and out day by day, free and light-hearted, with the happy carelessness of childhood, I thought what a picture it was of our wonderful position as children in the house of our Heavenly Father. And I said to myself, If nothing would so grieve and wound the loving hearts around her as to see this little child beginning to be worried or anxious about herself in any way,— about whether her food and clothes would be provided, or how she was to get her education or her future support,—how much more must the great, loving heart of our God and Father be grieved and wounded at seeing His children taking so much anxious care and thought! And I understood why it was that our Lord had said to us so emphatically, "Take no thought for yourselves."

Who is the best cared for in every household? Is it not the little children? And does not the least of all, the helpless baby, receive the largest share? We all know that the baby toils not, neither does it spin; and yet it is fed, and clothed, and loved, and rejoiced in more tenderly than the hardest worker of them all.

This life of faith, then, about which I am writing, consists in just this,—being a child in the Father's house. And when this is said, enough is said to transform every weary, burdened life into one of blessedness and rest.

Let the ways of childish confidence and freedom from care, which so please you and win your hearts in your own little ones, teach you what should be your ways with God; and, leaving yourselves in His hands, learn to be literally "careful for nothing"; and you shall find it to be a fact that the peace of God, which passeth all understanding, shall keep (as with a garrison) your hearts and minds through Christ Jesus.

"Thou wilt keep him in perfect peace, whose mind is stayed on thee: because he trusteth in thee." This is the Divine description of the life of faith about which I am writing. It is no speculative theory, neither is it a dream of romance. There *is* such a thing as having one's soul kept in perfect peace, now and here in this life; and childlike trust in God is the key to its attainment.

CHAPTER FOUR

How to Enter In

HAVING SOUGHT TO SETTLE THE QUESTION AS TO THE scripturalness of an actual living of this life hid with Christ in God, and having also shown a little of what it is, the next point is as to how it is to be reached and realized.

I would say, first of all, that this blessed life must not be looked upon in any sense as an attainment, but as an obtainment. We cannot earn it, we cannot climb up to it, we cannot win it; we can do nothing but ask for it and receive it. It is the gift of God in Christ Jesus. And where a thing is a gift, the only course left for the receiver is to take it and thank the giver. We never say of a gift, "See to what I have attained," and boast of our skill and wisdom in having attained it; but we say, "See what has been given me," and boast of the love and wealth and generosity of the giver. And everything in our salvation is a gift. From beginning to end, God is the giver and we are the receivers; and it is not to those who do great things, but to those who "receive abundance of grace and of the gift of righteousness," that the richest promises are made.

In order, therefore, to enter into a practical experience of this interior life, the soul must be in a recep-

tive attitude, fully recognizing the fact that it is God's
gift in Christ Jesus, and that it cannot be gained by
any efforts or works of our own. This will simplify the
matter exceedingly; and the only thing left to be considered then will be to discover upon whom God bestows this gift, and how they are to receive it. To this I
would answer, in short, that He can bestow it only
upon the fully consecrated soul, and that it is to be
received by faith.

Consecration is the first thing,—not in any legal
sense, not in order to purchase or deserve the blessing, but to remove the difficulties out of the way and
make it possible for God to bestow it. In order for a
lump of clay to be made into a beautiful vessel, it must
be entirely abandoned to the potter, and must lie passive in his hands. And similarly, in order for a soul to
be made into a vessel unto God's honor, "sanctified
and meet for the master's use, and prepared unto
every good work," it must be utterly abandoned to
Him, and must lie passive in His hands. This is manifest at the first glance.

I was once trying to explain to a physician who
had charge of a large hospital the necessity and meaning of consecration, but he seemed unable to understand. At last I said to him, "Suppose, in going your
rounds among your patients, you should meet with
one man who entreated you earnestly to take his case
under your especial care in order to cure him, but
who should at the same time refuse to tell you all his
symptoms or to take all your prescribed remedies,
and should say to you, 'I am quite willing to follow
your directions as to certain things, because they
commend themselves to my mind as good, but in

other matters I prefer judging for myself, and following my own directions.' What would you do in such a case?" I asked. "Do!" he replied with indignation,— "Do! I would soon leave such a man as that to his own care. For, of course," he added, "I could do nothing for him unless he would put his whole case into my hands without any reserves, and would obey my directions implicitly." "It is necessary, then," I said, "for doctors to be obeyed if they are to have any chance to cure their patient?" *"Implicitly obeyed!"* was his emphatic reply. "And that is consecration," I continued. "God must have the whole case put into His hands without any reserves, and His directions must be implicitly followed." "I see it," he exclaimed, "I see it! And I will do it. God shall have His own way with me from henceforth."

To some minds perhaps the word "abandonment" might express this idea better than the word "consecration." But whatever word we use, we mean an entire surrender of the whole being to God,— spirit, soul, and body placed under His absolute control, for Him to do with us just what He pleases. We mean that the language of our hearts, under all circumstances and in view of every act, is to be "Thy will be done." We mean the giving up of all liberty of choice. We mean a life of inevitable obedience.

To a soul ignorant of God, this may look hard; but to those who know Him it is the happiest and most restful of lives. He is our Father, and He loves us, and He knows just what is best, and therefore, of course, His will is the very most blessed thing that can come to us under any circumstances. I do not understand how it is that the eyes of so many Christians have been blinded to this fact. But it really would seem as if God's own children were more afraid of His will than of anything else in life,—His lovely, lovable will, which only means loving-kindnesses and tender mercies, and blessings unspeakable to their souls! I wish only I could show to every one the unfathomable sweetness of the will of God. Heaven is a place of infinite bliss because His will is perfectly done there, and our lives share in this bliss just in proportion as His will is perfectly done in them. He loves us,—*loves us*, I say,—and the will of love is always blessing for its loved one. Some of us know what it is to love, and we know that could we only have our way, our beloved ones would be overwhelmed with blessings. All that is good and sweet and lovely in life would be poured out upon them from our lavish hands, had we but the power to carry out our will for them. And if this is the way of love with us, how much more must it be so with our God, who is love itself! Could we but for one moment get a glimpse into the mighty depths of His love, our hearts would spring out to meet His will and embrace it as our richest treasure; and we would abandon ourselves to it with an enthusiasm of gratitude and joy that such a wondrous privilege could be ours.

A great many Christians seem practically to think that all their Father in heaven wants is a chance to make them miserable and to take away all their blessings; and they imagine, poor souls, that if they hold on to things in their own will they can hinder Him from doing this. I am ashamed to write the words, yet we must face a fact which is making wretched hundreds of lives.

A Christian who was in a great deal of trouble was recounting to another Christian the various efforts he had made to find deliverance, and concluded by saying, "But it has all been in vain, and there is literally nothing left for me to do now but to trust the Lord."

"Alas!" exclaimed his friend in a tone of the deepest commiseration, as though no greater risk were possible,—"Alas! has it come to *that?*"

A Christian lady who had this feeling was once expressing to a friend how impossible she found it to say, "Thy will be done," and how afraid she should be to do it. She was the mother of an only little boy, who was the heir to a great fortune, and the idol of her heart. After she had stated her difficulties fully, her friend said, "Suppose your little Charley should come running to you to-morrow and say, 'Mother, I have made up my mind to let you have your own way with me from this time forward. I am always going to obey you, and I want you to do just whatever you think best with me. I will trust your love.' How would you feel towards him? Would you say to yourself, 'Ah, now I shall have a chance to make Charley miserable. I will take away all his pleasures, and fill his life with every hard and disagreeable thing that I can find. I will compel him to do just the things that are the most difficult for him to do, and will give him all sorts of impossible commands.'" "Oh, no, no, no!" exclaimed the indignant mother. "You know I would not. You know I would hug him to my heart and cover him with kisses, and would hasten to fill his life with all that was sweetest and best." "And are you more tender and more loving than God?" asked her friend.

"Ah, no!" was the reply; "I see my mistake. Of course I must not be any more afraid of saying, 'Thy will be done,' to my Heavenly Father than I would want my Charley to be of saying it to me."

Better and sweeter than health, or friends, or money, or fame, or ease, or prosperity, is the adorable will of our God. It gilds the darkest hours with a divine halo, and sheds brightest sunshine on the gloomiest paths. He always reigns who has made it his kingdom, and nothing can go amiss to him. Surely, then, it is only a glorious privilege that is opening before you when I tell you that the first step you must take in order to enter into the life hid with Christ in God is that of entire consecration. I beg of you not to look at it as a hard and stern demand. You must do it gladly, thankfully, enthusiastically. You must go in on what I call the privilege side of consecration; and I can assure you, from the universal testimony of all who have tried it, that you will find it the happiest place you have ever entered yet.

Faith is the next thing after surrender. Faith is an absolutely necessary element in the reception of any gift; for let our friends give a thing to us ever so fully, it is not really ours until we believe it has been given, and claim it as our own. Above all, this is true in gifts which are purely mental or spiritual. Love may be lavished upon us by another without stint or measure, but until we believe that we are loved, it never really becomes ours.

I suppose most Christians understand this principle in reference to the matter of their forgiveness. They know that the forgiveness of sins through Jesus might have been preached to them forever, but it

would never really have become theirs until they believed this preaching, and claimed the forgiveness as
their own. But when it comes to living the Christian
life, they lose sight of this principle, and think that,
having been saved by faith, they are now to live by
works and efforts; and instead of continuing to *receive*
they are now to begin to *do*. This makes our declaration, that the life hid with Christ in God is to be entered by faith, seem perfectly unintelligible to them.
And yet it is plainly declared, that, "*as* we have received Christ Jesus the Lord, *so* we are to walk in
him." We received Him by faith, and by faith alone;
therefore we are to walk in Him by faith, and by faith
alone. And the faith by which we enter into this hidden life is just the same as the faith by which we were
translated out of the kingdom of darkness into the
kingdom of God's dear Son, only it lays hold of a
different thing. *Then* we believed that Jesus was our
Saviour from the guilt of sin, and according to our
faith it was unto us; *now* we must believe that He is
our Saviour from the power of sin, and according to
our faith it shall be unto us. *Then* we trusted Him for
forgiveness, and it became ours; *now* we must trust
Him for righteousness, and it shall become ours also.
Then we took Him as a Saviour in the future from the
penalties of our sins; *now* we must take Him as a
Saviour in the present from the bondage of our sins.
Then He was our Redeemer; *now* He is to be our Life.
Then He lifted us out of the pit; *now* He is to seat us in
heavenly places with Himself.

I mean all this, of course, experimentally and
practically. Theologically and judicially I know that
every believer has everything as soon as he is con-

verted; but experimentally nothing is his until by faith he claims it. "Every place that the sole of your foot shall tread upon, that have I given unto you." God "hath blessed us with all spiritual blessings in heavenly places in Christ"; but until we set the foot of faith upon them, they do not practically become ours. "According to our faith," is always the limit and the rule.

But this faith of which I am speaking must be a present faith. No faith that is exercised in the future tense amounts to anything. A man may believe forever that his sins will be forgiven at some future time, and he will never find peace. He has to come to the *now* belief, and say by a present appropriating faith, "My sins are now forgiven," before his soul can be at rest. And, similarly, no faith that looks for a future deliverance from the power of sin will ever lead a soul into the life we are describing. The enemy delights in this future faith, for he knows it is powerless to accomplish any practical results. But he trembles and flees when the soul of the believer dares to claim a present deliverance, and to reckon itself *now* to be free from his power.

Perhaps no four words in the language have more meaning in them than the following, which I would have you repeat over and over with your voice and with your soul, emphasizing each time a different word:—

Jesus saves me now.—It is He.
Jesus *saves* me now.—It is His work to save.
Jesus saves *me* now.—I am the one to be saved.
Jesus saves me *now*.—He is doing it every moment.

To sum up, then, in order to enter into this blessed interior life of rest and triumph, you have two steps to take,—first, entire abandonment; and second, absolute faith. No matter what may be the complications of your peculiar experience, no matter what your difficulties, or your surroundings, or your "peculiar temperament," these two steps, definitely taken and unwaveringly persevered in, will certainly bring you out sooner or later into the green pastures and still waters of this life hid with Christ in God. You may be perfectly sure of this. And if you will let every other consideration go, and simply devote your attention to these two points, and be very clear and definite about them, your progress will be rapid, and your soul will reach its desired haven far sooner than you can now think possible.

Shall I repeat the steps, that there may be no mistake? You are a child of God, and long to please Him. You love your divine Master, and are sick and weary of the sin that grieves Him. You long to be delivered from its power. Everything you have hitherto tried has failed to deliver you: and now, in your despair, you are asking if it can indeed be, as these happy people say, that Jesus is able and willing to deliver you. Surely you must know in your very soul that He is,—that to save you out of the hand of all your enemies is, in fact, just the very thing He came to do. Then trust Him. Commit your case to Him in an absolute unreserve, and believe that He undertakes it; and at once, knowing what He is and what He has said, claim that He does even now save you. Just as you believed at first that He delivered you from the guilt of sin because He said it, so now believe that He delivers you from the power of sin because He says it. Let your faith now lay hold of a new power in Christ. You have trusted Him as your dying Saviour; now trust Him as your living Saviour. Just as much as He came to deliver you from future punishment did He also come to deliver you from present bondage. Just as truly as He came to bear your stripes for you has He come to live your life for you. You are as utterly powerless in the one case as in the other. You could as easily have got yourself rid of your own sins, as you could now accomplish for yourself practical righteousness. Christ, and Christ only, must do both for you; and your part in both cases is simply to give the thing to Him to do, and then believe that He does it.

A lady, now very eminent in this life of trust, when she was seeking in great darkness and perplexity to enter in, said to the friend who was trying to help her, "You all say, 'Abandon yourself and trust, abandon yourself and trust.' But I do not know how. I wish you would just do it out loud, so that I may see how you do it."

Shall I do it out loud for you?

"Lord Jesus, I believe that thou art able and willing to deliver me from all the care and unrest and bondage of my Christian life. I believe thou didst die to set me free, not only in the future, but now and here. I believe thou art stronger than sin, and that thou canst keep me, even me, in my extreme of weakness, from falling into its snares or yielding obedience to its commands. And, Lord, I am going to trust thee to keep me. I have tried keeping myself, and have failed, and failed most grievously. I am absolutely

helpless. So now I will trust thee. I give myself to thee.
I keep back no reserves. Body, soul, and spirit, I present myself to thee as a piece of clay, to be fashioned
into anything thy love and thy wisdom shall choose.
And now I *am* thine. I believe thou dost accept that
which I present to thee; I believe that this poor, weak,
foolish heart has been taken possession of by thee,
and that thou hast even at this very moment begun to
work in me to will and to do of thy good pleasure. I
trust thee *utterly,* and I trust thee *now.*"

A man was obliged to descend into a deep well by
sliding down a fixed rope which was supposed to be of
ample length. But to his dismay he came to the end of
it before his feet had touched the bottom. He had not
the strength to climb up again, and to let go and drop
seemed to him but to be dashed to pieces in the
depths below. He held on until his strength was utterly exhausted, and then dropped, as he thought, to
his death. He fell—just three inches—and found himself safe on the rock bottom.

Are you afraid to take this step? Does it seem too
sudden, too much like a leap in the dark? Do you not
know that the step of faith always "falls on the seeming void, but finds the rock beneath"? If ever you are
to enter this glorious land, flowing with milk and
honey, you must sooner or later step into the brimming waters, for there is no other path; and to do it
now may save you months and even years of disappointment and grief. Hear the word of the Lord,—

"Have not I commanded thee? Be strong and of a
good courage; be not afraid, neither be thou dismayed: for the Lord thy God is with thee, whithersoever thou goest."

PART II   DIFFICULTIES

CHAPTER FIVE

Difficulties Concerning Consecration

IT IS VERY IMPORTANT THAT CHRISTIANS SHOULD NOT be ignorant of the temptations that seem to stand ready to oppose every onward step of their progress heavenward, and that are especially active when the soul is awakened to a hunger and thirst after righteousness, and begins to reach out after the fulness that is ours in Christ.

One of the greatest of these temptations is a difficulty concerning consecration. The seeker after holiness is told that he must consecrate himself, and he endeavors to do so. But at once he meets with a difficulty. He has done it as he thinks, and yet he finds no difference in his experience; nothing seems changed, as he has been led to expect it would be, and he is completely baffled, and asks the question almost despairingly, "How am I to know when I am consecrated?"

The one chief temptation that meets the soul at this juncture is the same that assaults it all along the pathway, at every step of its progress; namely, the question as to *feelings*. We cannot believe we are con-

59

secrated until we *feel* that we are: and because we do not feel that God has taken us in hand, we cannot believe that He has. As usual, we put feeling first, and faith second, and the fact last of all. No, God's invariable rule in everything is, fact first, faith second, and feeling last of all; and it is striving against the inevitable when we seek to change this order.

The way, then, to meet this temptation in reference to consecration, is simply to take God's side in the matter, and to adopt His order, by putting faith before feeling. Give yourself to the Lord definitely and fully, according to your present light, asking the Holy Spirit to show you all that is contrary to Him, either in your heart or life. If He shows you anything, give it to the Lord immediately, and say in reference to it, "Thy will be done." If he shows you nothing, then you must believe that there is nothing and must conclude that you have given Him all. Then recognize that it must be the fact, that, when you give yourself to God He accepts you; and at once let your faith take hold of this fact. Begin to believe, and hold on to it steadfastly, that He has taken that which you have surrendered to Him. You positively must not wait to feel either that you have given yourself, or that God has taken you. You must simply believe it, and reckon it to be the case. And if you are steadfast in this reckoning, sooner or later the feeling will come, and you will realize that it is indeed a blessed fact that you are wholly the Lord's.

If you were to give an estate to a friend, you would have to give it, and he would have to receive it, by faith. An estate is not a thing that can be picked up and handed over to another; the gift of it and its reception are altogether a transaction by word and on paper, and therefore one of faith. Now, if you should give an estate one day to a friend, and then should go away and wonder whether you really had given it, and whether he actually had taken it and considered it his own, and should feel it necessary to go the next day and renew the gift; and if on the third day you should still feel a similar uncertainty about it, and should again go and renew the gift; and on the fourth day go through a like process, and so on, day after day, for months and years,—what would your friend think, and what at last would be the condition of your own mind in reference to it? Your friend would certainly begin to doubt whether you ever had intended to give it to him at all, and you yourself would be in such hopeless perplexity about it, that you would not know whether the estate was yours or his, or whose it was.

Now, is not this very much the way in which you have been acting toward God in this matter of consecration? You have given yourself to Him over and over daily, perhaps for months, but you have invariably come away from your seasons of consecration wondering whether you really have given yourself after all, and whether He has taken you; and because you have not *felt* any change, you have concluded at last, after many painful tossings, that the thing has not been done. Do you know, dear believer, that this sort of perplexity will last forever, unless you cut it short by faith? You must come to the point of reckoning the matter to be an accomplished and settled thing, and must leave it there before you can possibly expect any change of feeling whatever.

The Levitical law of offerings to the Lord settles this as a primary fact, that everything which is given to Him becomes, by that very act, something holy, set apart from all other things, something that cannot without sacrilege be put to any other uses. "Notwithstanding, no devoted thing that a man shall devote unto the Lord of all that he hath, both of man and beast, and of the field of his possession, shall be sold or redeemed; every devoted thing is most holy unto the Lord." Having once given it to the Lord, the devoted thing henceforth was reckoned by all Israel as being the Lord's, and no one dared to stretch forth a hand to retake it. The giver might have made his offering very grudgingly and halfheartedly, but, having made it, the matter was taken out of his hands altogether, and the devoted thing, by God's own law, became "most holy unto the Lord." It was not made holy by the state of mind of the giver, but by the holiness of the Divine receiver. "The altar sanctifies the gift"; and an offering, once laid upon the altar, from that moment belonged to the Lord. I can imagine an offerer, after he had deposited a gift, beginning to search his heart as to his sincerity and honesty in doing it, and coming back to the priest to say that he was afraid, after all, he had not given it rightly, or had not been perfectly sincere in giving it. I feel sure the priest would have silenced him at once, saying, "As to how you gave your offering, or what were your motives in giving it, I do not know. The facts are that you did give it, and that it is the Lord's, for every devoted thing is most holy unto Him. It is too late to recall the transaction now." And not only the priest, but all Israel, would have been aghast at the man, who, having once given his offering, should have reached out his hand to take it back. Yet, day after day, earnest-hearted Christians, with no thought of the sacrilege they are committing, are guilty in their own experience of a similar act by giving themselves to the Lord in solemn consecration, and then, through unbelief, taking back that which they have given.

Because God is not visibly present to the eye, it is difficult to feel that a transaction with Him is real. I suppose that if, when we made our acts of consecration, we could actually see Him present with us, we should feel it to be a very real thing, and would realize that we had given our word to Him, and could not dare to take it back, no matter how much we might wish to do so. Such a transaction would have to us the binding power that a spoken promise to an earthly friend always has to a man of honor. What we need, therefore, is to see that God's presence is a certain fact always, and that every act of our soul is done before Him, and that a word spoken in prayer is as really spoken to Him as if our eyes could see Him and our hands could touch Him. Then we shall cease to have such vague conceptions of our relations with Him, and shall feel the binding force of every word we say in His presence.

I know some will say here, "Ah, yes; but if He would only speak to me, and say that He took me when I gave myself to Him, I would have no trouble then in believing it." No, of course you would not; but then where would be the room for faith? Sight is not faith, and hearing is not faith, neither is feeling faith; but believing when we can neither see, hear, nor feel, *is* faith; and everywhere the Bible tells us our salvation is to be by faith. Therefore we must believe before we feel, and often against our feelings, if we would honor God by our faith. It is always he that believeth who has the witness, not he that doubteth. But how can we doubt, since, by His very command to us to present ourselves to Him a living sacrifice, He has pledged Himself to receive us? I cannot conceive of an honorable man asking another to give him a thing which, after all, he was doubtful about taking; still less can I conceive of a loving parent acting so toward a beloved child. "My son, give me thy heart," is a sure warrant for knowing that the moment the heart is given, it will be taken by the One who has commanded the gift. We may, nay, we must, feel the utmost confidence, then, that when we surrender ourselves to the Lord, according to His own command, He does then and there receive us, and from that moment we are His. A real transaction has taken place, which cannot be violated without dishonor on our part, and which we know will not be violated by Him.

In Deuteronomy 26:17–19, we see God's way of working under these circumstances: "Thou hast avouched the Lord this day to be thy God, and to walk in his ways, and to keep his statutes, and his commandments, and his judgments, and to hearken unto his voice; and the Lord hath avouched thee this day to be his peculiar people, as he hath promised thee, and

that thou shouldst keep all his commandments; . . .
and that thou mayest be an holy people unto the Lord
thy God, as he hath spoken."

When we avouch the Lord to be our God, and
that we will walk in His ways and keep His commandments, He avouches us to be His, and that we
shall keep all His commandments. And from that
moment He takes possession of us. This has always
been His principle of working, and it continues to be
so. "Every devoted thing is most holy to the Lord."
This is so plain as not to admit of a question.

But if the soul still feels in doubt or difficulty, let
me refer you to a New Testament declaration which
approaches the subject from a different side, but
which settles it, I think, quite as definitely. It is in I
John 5:14, 15, and reads, "And this is the confidence
that we have in him, that, if we ask anything according to his will, he heareth us; and if we know that he
hear us, whatsoever we ask, we know that we *have* the
petitions that we desired of Him." Is it according to
His will that you should be entirely surrendered to
Him? There can be, of course, but one answer to this,
for He has *commanded* it. Is it not also according to His
will that He should work in you to will and to do of
His good pleasure? This question also can have but
one answer, for He has declared it to be His purpose.
You know, then, that these things are according to
His will; therefore, on God's own word, you are
obliged to know that He hears you. And knowing this
much, you are compelled to go farther, and know that
you have the petitions that you have desired of Him.
That you *have*, I say,—not will have, or may have, but

have now in actual possession. It is thus that we "obtain promises" by faith. It is thus that we have "access by faith" into the grace that is given us in our Lord Jesus Christ. It is thus, and thus only, that we come to know our hearts "purified by faith," and are enabled to live by faith, to stand by faith, to walk by faith.

I desire to make this subject so plain and practical that no one need have any further difficulty about it, and therefore I will repeat again just what must be the acts of your soul, in order to bring you out of this difficulty about consecration.

I suppose that you have trusted the Lord Jesus for the forgiveness of your sins, and know something of what it is to belong to the family of God, and to be made an heir of God through faith in Christ. And now you feel springing up in your heart the longing to be conformed to the image of your Lord. In order for this, you know there must be an entire surrender of yourself to Him, that He may work in you all the good pleasure of His will; and you have tried over and over to do it, but hitherto without any apparent success. At this point it is that I desire to help you. What you must do now is to come once more to Him, in a surrender of your whole self to His will, as complete as you know how to make it. You must ask Him to reveal to you, by His Spirit, any hidden rebellion; and if He reveals nothing, then you must believe that there is nothing, and that the surrender is complete. This must, then, be considered a settled matter; you have wholly yielded yourself to the Lord, and from henceforth you do not in any sense belong to yourself; you must never even so much as listen to a suggestion to the contrary. If the temptation comes to wonder whether you really have completely surrendered yourself, meet it with an assertion that you have. Do not even argue the matter. Repel any such idea instantly, and with decision. You meant it then, you mean it now, you have really done it. Your emotions may clamor against the surrender, but your will must hold firm. It is your purpose God looks at, not your feelings about that purpose; and your purpose, or will, is therefore the only thing you need to attend to.

The surrender, then, having been made, never to be questioned or recalled, the next point is to believe that God takes that which you have surrendered, and to reckon that it is His. Not that it will be His at some future time, but that it is now; and that He has begun to work in you to will and to do of His good pleasure. And here you must rest. There is nothing more for you to do except to be henceforth an obedient child; for you are the Lord's now, absolutely and entirely in His hands, and He has undertaken the whole care and management and forming of you, and will, according to His word, "work in you that which is well-pleasing in His sight through Jesus Christ." But you must hold steadily here. If you begin to question your surrender, or God's acceptance of it, then your wavering faith will produce a wavering experience, and He cannot work in you to do His will. But while you trust, He works; and the result of His working always is to change you into the image of Christ, from glory to glory, by His mighty Spirit.

Do you, then, now at this moment, surrender

yourself wholly to Him. You answer, Yes. Then, my dear friend, begin at once to reckon that you are His, that He has taken you, and that He is working in you to will and to do of His good pleasure. And keep on reckoning this. You will find it a great help to put your reckoning into words, and say over and over to yourself and to your God, "Lord, I am thine; I do yield myself up entirely to thee, and I believe that thou dost take me. I leave myself with thee. Work in me all the good pleasure of thy will, and I will only lie still in thy hands and trust thee."

Make this a daily, definite act of your will, and many times a day recur to it, as being your continual attitude before the Lord. Confess it to yourself. Confess it to your God. Confess it to your friends. Avouch the Lord to be your God, continually and unwaveringly, and declare your purpose of walking in His ways and keeping His statutes; and sooner or later, you will find in practical experience that He has avouched you to be one of His peculiar people, and will enable you to keep all His commandments, and that you are being made into "an holy people unto the Lord, as he hath spoken."

"For Thou art making me, I thank Thee Sire.
What Thou hast done and doest, Thou knowest well;
And I will help Thee, gently in Thy fire
I will lie burning; on Thy potter's wheel
I will whirl patient, though my brain should reel;
Thy grace shall be enough my grief to quell,
And growing strength perfect through weakness dire."

CHAPTER SIX

Difficulties Concerning Faith

THE NEXT STEP AFTER CONSECRATION, IN THE SOUL'S progress out of the wilderness of a failing Christian experience into the land that floweth with milk and honey, is that of faith. And here, as in the first step, the soul encounters at once certain forms of difficulty and hindrance.

The child of God, whose eyes have been opened to see the fulness there is in Jesus for him, and whose heart has been made hungry to appropriate that fulness, is met with the assertion, on the part of every teacher to whom he applies, that this fulness is only to be received by faith. But the subject of faith is involved in such a hopeless mystery to his mind that this assertion, instead of throwing light upon the way of entrance, seems only to make it more difficult and involved than ever.

"Of course it is to be by faith," he says, "for I know that everything in the Christian life is by faith. But that is just what makes it so hard, for I have no faith, and I do not even know what it is, nor how to get it." And, thus, baffled at the very outset by this insuperable difficulty, he is plunged into darkness, and almost despair.

This trouble arises from the fact that the subject of faith is very generally misunderstood; for, in reality, faith is the simplest and plainest thing in the world, and the most easy of exercise.

Your idea of faith, I suppose, has been something like this. You have looked upon it as in some way a sort of *thing*, —either a religious exercise of soul, or an inward, gracious disposition of heart; something tangible, in fact, which, when you have secured it, you can look at and rejoice over, and use as a passport to God's favor, or a coin with which to purchase His gifts. And you have been praying for faith, expecting all the while to get something like this; and never having received any such thing, you are insisting upon it that you have no faith. Now, faith, in fact, is not in the least like this. It is nothing at all tangible. It is simply believing God; and, like sight, it is nothing apart from its object. You might as well shut your eyes and look inside, and see whether you have sight, as to look inside to discover whether you have faith. You see something, and thus know that you have sight; you believe something, and thus know that you have faith. For as sight is only seeing, so faith is only believing. And as the only necessary thing about sight is that you see the thing as it is, so the only necessary thing about belief is that you believe the thing as it is. The virtue does not lie in your believing, but in the thing you believe. If you believe the truth, you are saved; if you believe a lie, you are lost. The act of believing in both cases is the same; the things believed are exactly opposite, and this it is which makes the mighty difference. Your salvation comes, not because your faith saves you, but because it links you to the Saviour who saves; and your believing is really nothing but the link.

I do beg of you to recognize, then, the extreme simplicity of faith; namely, that it is nothing more nor less than just believing God when He says He either has done something for us, or will do it; and then trusting Him to keep His word. It is so simple that it is hard to explain. If anyone asks me what it means to trust another to do a piece of work for me, I can answer only that it means committing the work to that other, and leaving it without anxiety in his hands. All of us have many times trusted very important affairs to others in this way, and have felt perfect rest in thus trusting because of the confidence we have had in those who have undertaken them. How constantly do mothers trust their most precious infants to the care of nurses, and feel no shadow of anxiety! How continually we are all of us trusting our health and our lives, without a thought of fear, to cooks and coachmen, engine-drivers, railway-conductors, and all sorts of paid servants, who have us completely at their mercy, and who could, if they chose to do so, or even if they failed in the necessary carefulness, plunge us into misery or death in a moment. All this we do, and make no demur about it. Upon the slightest acquaintance, often, we thus put our trust in people, requiring only the general knowledge of human nature and the common rules of human intercourse as the foundation of our trust, and we never feel as if we were doing anything in the least remarkable.

You have done this yourself, dear reader, and are doing it continually. You could not live among your fellow men and go through the customary routine of life a single day if you were unable to trust your fellow men, and it never enters into your head to say you cannot. But yet you do not hesitate to say, continually, that you cannot trust your God! And you excuse yourself by the plea that you are "a poor weak creature" and "have no faith."

I wish you would try to imagine yourself acting in your human relations as you do in your spiritual relations. Suppose you should begin to-morrow with the notion in your head that you could not trust anybody because you had no faith. When you sat down to breakfast you would say, "I cannot eat anything on this table, for I have no faith, and I cannot believe the cook has not put poison in the coffee, or that the butcher has not sent home diseased or unhealthy meat"; so you would go away starving. When you went out to your daily avocations, you would say, "I cannot ride in the railway train, for I have no faith, and therefore I cannot trust the engineer, nor the conductor, nor the builders of the carriages, nor the managers of the road." And you would be compelled to walk everywhere, and would grow unutterably weary in the effort, besides being actually unable to reach the places you could have reached in the train. When your friends met you with any statements, or your business agent with any accounts, you would say, "I am very sorry that I cannot believe you, but I have no faith, and never can believe anybody." If you opened a newspaper, you would be forced to lay it down again, saying, "I really cannot believe a word this paper says, for I have no faith; I do not believe there is any such person as the Queen, for I never saw her; nor any such country as Ireland, for I was never there. I have no faith, so of course I cannot believe anything that I have not actually felt and touched myself. It is a great trial, but I cannot help it, for I have no faith."

Just picture such a day as this, and see how disastrous it would be to yourself, and what utter folly it would appear to anyone who should watch you through the whole of it. Realize how your friends would feel insulted, and how your servants would refuse to serve you another day. And then ask yourself the question, if this want of faith in your fellow men would be so dreadful, and such utter folly, what must it be when you tell God that you have no power to trust Him, nor to believe His word; that it is a great trial, but you cannot help it, "for you have no faith."

Is it possible that you can trust your fellow men, and cannot trust your God; that you can receive the "witness of msn," and cannot receive the "witness of God"; that you can believe man's records, and cannot believe God's record; that you can commit your dearest earthly interests to your weak, failing fellow creatures without a fear, and are afraid to commit your spiritual interests to the Saviour who laid down His life for you, and of whom it is declared that He is "able to save to the uttermost all who came unto God by him"?

Surely, surely, dear believer, you, whose very name of believer implies that you can believe, you will never again dare to excuse yourself on the plea of having no faith. For when you say this, you mean of course that you have no faith in God, since you are not asked to have faith in yourself, and would be in a very wrong condition of soul if you had. Let me beg of you, then, when you think or say these things, always to complete the sentence, and say, "I have no faith in—God! I cannot believe—God!" and this I am sure will soon become so dreadful to you that you will not dare to continue it.

But, you say, I cannot believe without the Holy Spirit. Very well; will you conclude, then, that your want of faith is because of the failure of the Holy Spirit to do His work? For if it is, then surely you are not to blame, and need feel no condemnation; and all exhortations to you to believe are useless.

But no! Do you not see, that, in taking up the position that you have no faith and cannot believe, you are not only "making God a liar," but you are also showing an utter want of confidence in the Holy Spirit.

For He is always ready to help our infirmities. We never have to wait for Him, He is always waiting for us. And I for my part have such absolute confidence in the Holy Ghost, and in His being always ready to do His work, that I dare to say to every one of you, that you *can* believe now, at this very moment; and that if you do not, it is not the Spirit's fault, but your own. Put your will, then, over on the believing side. Say, "Lord, I will believe, I do believe," and continue to say it. Insist upon believing, in the face of every suggestion of doubt that intrudes itself. Out of your very unbelief, throw yourself unreservedly on the word and promises of God, and dare to abandon yourself to the keeping and saving power of the Lord Jesus. If you have ever trusted a precious interest in the hands of an earthly friend, I entreat you, trust yourself and all your spiritual interests now, in the hands of your Heavenly Friend, and never, *never*, NEVER, allow yourself to doubt again.

Remember always that there are two things which are more utterly incompatible even than oil and water, and these two are trust and worry. Would you call it trust if you should give something into the hands of a friend to attend to for you, and then should spend your nights and days in anxious thought and worry as to whether it would be rightly and successfully done? And can you call it trust, when you have given the saving and keeping of your soul into the hands of the Lord, if day after day, and night after night, you are spending hours of anxious thought and questionings about the matter? When a believer really trusts anything, he ceases to worry about the thing he has trusted. And when he worries, it is a plain proof that he does not trust. Tested by this rule, how little real trust there is in the Church of Christ! No wonder our Lord asked the pathetic question, "When the Son of man cometh, shall he find faith on the earth?" He will find plenty of work, a great deal of earnestness, and doubtless many consecrated hearts; but shall He find faith, the one thing He values more than all the rest? Every child of God, in his own case, will know how to answer this question. Should the answer, for any of you, be a sorrowful No, let me entreat you to let this be the last time for such an answer; and if you have ever known anything of the trustworthiness of our Lord, may you henceforth set to your seal that He is true, by the generous recklessness of your trust in Him!

I remember, very clearly in my Christian life, having every tender and loyal impulse within me stirred to the depths of an appeal I met with in a volume of old sermons to all who loved the Lord Jesus, that they should show to others how worthy He was of being trusted by the steadfastness of their own faith in Him. As I read the inspiring words, there came to me a sudden glimpse of the privilege and the glory of being called to walk in paths so dark that only an utter recklessness of trust would be possible!

"Ye have not passed this way heretofore," it may be; but to-day it is your happy privilege to prove, as never before, your loyal confidence in Jesus by starting out with Him on a life and walk of faith, lived, moment by moment, in absolute and childlike trust in Him.

You have trusted Him in a few things, and He has not failed you. Trust Him now for everything, and see if He does not do for you exceedingly abundantly, above all that you could ever have asked or even thought, not according to your power or capacity, but according to His own mighty power, working in you all the good pleasure of His most blessed will.

It is not hard, you find, to trust the management of the universe, and of all the outward creation, to the Lord. Can your case then be so much more complex and difficult than these, that you need to be anxious or troubled about His management of you? Away with such unworthy doubtings! Take your stand on the power and trustworthiness of your God, and see how quickly all difficulties will vanish before a steadfast determination to believe. Trust in the dark, trust in the light, trust at night and trust in the morning, and you will find that the faith that many begin, perhaps by a mighty effort will end, sooner or later, by becoming the easy and natural habit of the soul. It is a law of the spiritual life that every act of trust makes the next act less difficult, until at length, if these acts are persisted in, trusting becomes, like breathing, the natural unconscious action of the redeemed soul.

You must therefore put your will into your believing. Your faith must not be a passive imbecility, but an active energy. You may have to believe against every seeming; but no matter. Set your face like a flint to say, "I will believe, and I know I shall not be confounded." We are made "partakers of Christ if we hold the beginning of our faith steadfast unto the end." Hundreds fail just here. They have a little beginning of faith, but discouragements come, the "seemings" are all against it, their doubts clamor louder and louder, and at last they let them in; and when doubt comes in at the door, trust always flies out of the window.

We are told that all things are possible to God, and that all things are possible also to him that believeth. Faith has in times past "subdued kingdoms, wrought righteousness, obtained promises, stopped the mouths of lions, quenched the violence of fire, escaped the edge of the sword, waxed valiant in fight, turned to flight the armies of the aliens"; and faith can do it again. For our Lord Himself says unto us, "If ye have faith as a grain of mustard seed, ye shall say unto this mountain, Remove hence to yonder place;

and it shall remove; and nothing shall be impossible unto you."

If you are a child of God at all, you must have at least as much faith as a grain of mustard seed, and therefore you dare not say again that you "cannot trust because you have no faith." Say rather, "I can trust my Lord, and I will trust Him; and not all the powers of earth or hell shall be able to make me doubt my wonderful, glorious, faithful Redeemer!"

"Faith is sweetest of worships to Him, who so loves
  His unbearable splendors in darkness to hide;
And to trust to Thy word, dearest Lord! is true love,
  For those prayers are most granted which seem most denied.

"Our faith throws her arms around all Thou hast told her,
And, able to hold as much more, can but grieve.
She could hold Thy grand self, Lord! if Thou wouldst reveal it,
  And love makes her long to have more to believe."

Let your faith, then, "throw its arms around all God has told you," and in every dark hour remember that "though now for a season, if need be, ye are in heaviness through manifold temptations," it is only like going through a tunnel. The sun has not ceased shining because the traveler through the tunnel has ceased to see it; and the Sun of righteousness is still shining, although you in your dark tunnel do not see Him. Be patient and trustful, and wait. This time of darkness is only permitted that "the trial of your faith, being much more precious than of gold that perisheth, though it be tried with fire, might be found unto praise and honor and glory at the appearing of Jesus Christ."

CHAPTER SEVEN

Difficulties Concerning the Will

WHEN THE CHILD OF GOD HAS, BY ENTIRE ABANDON-
ment and absolute trust, stepped out of himself into
Christ, and has begun to know something of the
blessedness of the life hid with Christ in God, there is
one form of difficulty which is especially likely to start
up in his path. After the first emotions of peace and
rest have somewhat subsided, or if, as is sometimes
the case, they have never seemed to come at all, he
begins to feel such an utter unreality in the things he
has been passing through that he seems to himself
like a hypocrite when he says or even thinks they are
real. It seems to him that his belief does not go below
the surface; that it is a mere lip-belief, and therefore
of no account, and that his surrender is not a surrender of the heart, and therefore cannot be acceptable
to God. He is afraid to say he is altogether the Lord's,
for fear he will be telling an untruth; and yet he cannot bring himself to say he is not, because he longs for
it so intensely. The difficulty is real and very disheartening.

But there is nothing here which will not be very

easily overcome when the Christian once thoroughly understands the principles of the new life, and has learned *how* to live it. The common thought is that this life hid with Christ in God is to be lived in the emotions, and consequently all the attention of the soul is directed toward them, and as they are satisfactory or otherwise, the soul rests or is troubled. Now, the truth is, that this life is not to be lived in the emotions at all, but in the will; and therefore, if only the will is kept steadfastly abiding in its center, God's will, the varying states of emotion do not in the least disturb or affect the reality of the life.

To make this plain, I must enlarge a little. Fenelon says, somewhere, that "pure religion resides in the will alone." By this he means that, as the will is the governing power in the man's nature, if the will is set right, all the rest of the nature must come into harmony. By the will, I do not mean the wish of the man, or even his purpose, but the deliberate choice, the deciding power, the king, to which all that is in the man must yield obedience. It is the man, in short, the "*Ego,*" that which we feel to be ourselves.

It is sometimes thought that the emotions are the governing power in our nature. But I think we all of us know, as a matter of practical experience, that there is something within us, behind our emotions and behind our wishes, an independent self, that, after all, decides everything and controls everything. Our emotions belong to us, and are suffered and enjoyed by us, but they are not ourselves; and if God is to take possession of us, it must be into this central will or personality that He enters. If, then, He is reigning there by the power of His Spirit, all the rest of our nature must come under His sway; and as the will is, so is the man.

The practical bearing of his truth upon the difficulty I am considering is very great. For the decisions of our will are often so directly opposed to the decisions of our emotions, that, if we are in the habit of considering our emotions as the test, we shall be very apt to feel like hypocrites in declaring those things to be real which our will alone has decided. But the moment we see that the will is king, we shall utterly disregard anything that clamors against it, and shall claim as real its decisions, let the emotions rebel as they may.

I am aware that this is a difficult subject to deal with; but it is so exceedingly practical in its bearing upon the life of faith, that I beg of you, dear reader, not to turn from it until you have mastered it.

Perhaps an illustration will help you. A young man of great intelligence, seeking to enter into this new life, was utterly discouraged at finding himself the slave to an inveterate habit of doubting. To his emotions nothing seemed real; and the more he struggled, the more unreal did it all become. He was told this secret concerning the will, that if he would only put his will over on the believing side, if he would choose to believe, if, in short, he would in this Ego of his nature say, "I will believe! I do believe!" he need not then trouble about his emotions, for they would find themselves compelled, sooner or later, to come into harmony. "What!" he said. "Do you mean to tell me that I can *choose* to believe in that bald way, when nothing seems true to me? And will that kind of believing be real?" "Yes," was the answer; "it will. Fenelon says that true religion resides in the will alone; and he means that, since a man's will is really the man's self, of course, what his will does, he does. Your part then is simply to put your will, in this matter of believing, over on God's side, making up your mind that you will believe what He says because He says it, and that you will not pay any regard to the feelings that make it seem so unreal. God will not fail to respond, sooner or later, with His revelation to such a faith."

The young man paused a moment, and then said solemnly, "I understand, and will do what you say. I cannot control my emotions, but I can control my will; and the new life begins to look possible to me if it is only my will that needs to be set straight in the matter. I can give my will to God, and I do."

From that moment, disregarding all the pitiful clamoring of his emotions, which continually accused him of being a wretched hypocrite, this young man held on steadily to the decision of his will, answering every accusation with the continued assertion that he chose to believe, he meant to believe, he did believe; until at the end of a few days he found himself triumphant, with every emotion and every thought brought into captivity to the power of the Spirit of God, who had taken possession of the will thus put into His hands. He had held fast the *profession* of his faith without wavering, although it had seemed to him that, as to real faith itself, he had none to hold fast. At

times it had drained all the will power he possessed to
his lips to say that he believed, so contrary was it to all
the evidence of his senses or of his emotions. But he
had caught the idea that his will was, after all, himself,
and that if he kept that on God's side, he was doing all
he could do, and that God alone could change his
emotions or control his being. The result has been
one of the grandest Christian lives I know of, in its
marvelous simplicity, directness, and power over sin.

The secret lies just here,—that our will, which is
the spring of all our actions, has been in the past
under the control of sin and self, and these have
worked in us all their own good pleasure. But now
God calls upon us to yield our wills up unto Him, that
He may take the control of them, and may work in us
to will and to do of His good pleasure. If we will obey
this call, and present ourselves to Him as a living sacrifice, He will take possession of our surrendered
wills, and will begin at once to work in us "that which
is well pleasing in His sight, through Jesus Christ,"
giving us the mind that was in Christ, and transforming us into His image (see Rom. 12:1, 2).

Let us take another illustration. A lady who had
entered into this life hid with Christ was confronted
by a great prospective trial. Every emotion she had
within her rose up in rebellion against it; and had she
considered her emotions to be her king, she would
have been in utter despair. But she had learned this
secret of the will, and knowing that, at the bottom, she
herself did really choose the will of God for her portion, she did not pay the slightest attention to her

emotions, but persisted in meeting every thought concerning the trial with the words, repeated over and over, "Thy will be done! Thy will be done!" asserting, in the face of all her rebelling feelings, that she did submit her will to God's, that she chose to submit it, and that His will should be and was her delight! The result was that in an incredibly short space of time every thought was brought into captivity, and she began to find even her very emotions rejoicing in the will of God.

Again, there was a lady who had a besetting sin, which in her emotions she dearly loved, but which in her will she hated. Believing herself to be necessarily under the control of her emotions, she had fully supposed she was unable to conquer it, unless her emotions should first be changed. But she learned this secret concerning the will, and going to her closet she said, "Lord, thou seest that with my emotions I love this sin, but in my real central self I hate it. Until now my emotions have had the mastery; but now I put my will into thy hands, and give it up to thy working. I will never again consent in my will to yield to this sin. Take possession of my will, and work in me to will and to do of thy good pleasure."

Immediately she began to find deliverance. The Lord took possession of the will thus surrendered to Himself, and began to work in her by His own power, so that His will in the matter gained the mastery over her emotions, and she found herself delivered, not by the power of an outward commandment, but by the inward power of the Spirit of God, "working in her that which was well pleasing in his sight."

And now, dear Christian, let me show you how to apply this principle to your difficulties. Cease to consider your emotions, for they are only the servants; and regard simply your will, which is the real king in your being. Is that given up to God? Is that put into His hands? Does your will decide to believe? Does your will choose to obey? If this is the case, then *you* are in the Lord's hands, and you decide to believe, and you choose to obey; for your will is yourself. And the thing is done. The transaction with God is as real, when only your will acts, as where every emotion coincides. It does not seem as real to you; but in God's sight it is as real. And when you have got hold of this secret, and have discovered that you need not attend to your emotions but simply to the state of your will, all the Scripture commands to yield yourself to God, to present yourself a living sacrifice to Him, to abide in Christ, to walk in the light, to die to self, become possible to you; for you are conscious that in all these your will can act, and can take God's side; whereas, if it had been your emotions that must do it, you would, knowing them to be utterly uncontrollable, sink down in helpless despair.

When, then, this feeling of unreality or hypocrisy comes, do not be troubled by it. It is only in your emotions, and is not worth a moment's thought. Only see to it that your will is in God's hands, that your inward self is abandoned to His working, that your choice, your decision, is on His side; and there leave it. Your surging emotions, like a tossing vessel at anchor, which by degrees yields to the steady pull of the cable, finding themselves attached to the mighty power of God by the choice of your will, must inevitably come into captivity, and give in their allegiance to Him; and you will sooner or later verify the truth of the saying that "if any man will do his will, he shall know of the doctrine."

The will is like a wise mother in a nursery; the feelings are like a set of clamoring, crying children. The mother makes up her mind to a certain course of action which she believes to be right and best. The children clamor against it and declare it shall not be. But the mother, knowing that she is mistress and not they, pursues her course lovingly and calmly in spite of all their clamors; and the result is that the children are sooner or later won over to the mother's course of action, and fall in with her decisions, and all is harmonious and happy. But if that mother should for a moment let in the thought that the children were the masters instead of herself, confusion would reign unchecked. And in how many souls at this very moment is there nothing but confusion, simply because the feelings are allowed to govern, instead of the will.

Remember, then, that the real thing in your experience is what your will decides, and not the verdict of your emotions; and that you are far more in danger of hypocrisy and untruth in yielding to the assertions of your feelings than in holding fast to the decision of your will. So that, if your will is on God's side, you are no hypocrite at this moment in claiming as your own the blessed reality of belonging altogether to Him, even though your emotions may all declare the contrary.

I am convinced that throughout the Bible the expressions concerning the "heart" do not mean the emotions, that which we now understand by the word "heart," but they mean the will, the personality of the man, the man's own central self; and that the object of God's dealings with man is that this "I" may be yielded up to Him, and this central life abandoned to His entire control. It is not the feelings of the man God wants, but the man himself.

But do not let us make a mistake here. I say we must "give up" our wills, but I do not mean we are to be left will-less. We are not so to give up our wills as to be left like limp nerveless creatures, without any will at all. We are simply to substitute for our foolish, misdirected wills of ignorance and immaturity the higher, divine, mature will of God. If we lay the emphasis on the word "our," we shall understand it better. The will we are to give up is our will, as it is misdirected, and so parted off from God's will, not our will when it is one with God's will; for when our will is in harmony with His will, when it has the stamp of oneness with Him, it would be wrong for us to give it up.

The child is required to give up the misdirected will that belongs to it *as a child,* and we cannot let it say, "I will" or "I will not"; but when its will is in harmony with ours, we want it to say, "I will" or "I will not," with all the force of which it is capable.

When God is "working in us to will," we must set

our faces like a flint to carry out this will, and must respond with an emphatic "I will" to every "Thou shalt" of His. For God can only carry out His own will with us as we consent to it, and will in harmony with Him.

Have you thus consented, dear reader, and is your face set as a flint to will what God wills? He wills that you should be entirely surrendered to Him, and that you should trust Him perfectly. Do you will the same?

Again I repeat, it is all in the will. Fenelon says, "The will to love God is the whole of religion." If, therefore, you have in your will taken the steps of surrender and faith, it is your right to believe even now, no matter how much your feelings may clamor against it, that you *are* all the Lord's, and that He *has* begun to "work in you to will and to do of His good pleasure."

After this chapter was first written some years ago, the following remarkable practical illustration of its teaching was handed to me by Pastor Theodore Monod, of Paris. It is the experience of a Presbyterian minister, which this pastor had carefully kept for many years:—

NEWBURGH, Sept. 26, 1842

DEAR BROTHER,—I take a few moments of that time which I have devoted to the Lord, in writing a short epistle to you, His servant. It is sweet to feel we are wholly the Lord's, that He has received us and called us His. This is religion, a relinquishment of the principle of self-

ownership, and the adoption in full of the abiding sentiment, "I am not my own, I am bought with a price." Since I
last saw you I have been pressing forward, and yet there
has been nothing remarkable in my experience, of which I
can speak; indeed, I do not know that it is best to look for
remarkable things; but strive to be holy, as God is holy,
pressing right on toward the mark of the prize.

I do not feel myself qualified to instruct you: I can only
tell you the way in which I was led. The Lord deals differently with different souls, and we ought not to attempt to
copy the experience of others; yet there are certain things
which must be attended to by every one who is seeking
after a clean heart.

There must be a personal consecration of all to God; a
covenant made with God that we will be wholly and forever
His. This I made intellectually, without any change in my
feelings, with a heart full of hardness and darkness, unbelief and sin and insensibility.

I covenanted to be the Lord's, and laid all upon the
altar, a living sacrifice, to the best of my ability. And after I
rose from my knees I was conscious of no change in my
feelings. I was painfully conscious that there was no
change. But yet I was sure that I did, with all the sincerity
and honesty of purpose of which I was capable, make an
entire and eternal consecration of myself to God. I did not
then consider the work as done by any means, but I engaged to abide in a state of entire devotion to God, a living
perpetual sacrifice. And now came the effort to do this.

I knew also that I must believe that God did accept me,
and did come to dwell in my heart. I was conscious I did
not believe this and yet I desired to do so. I read with much
prayer John's first epistle, and endeavored to assure my
heart of God's love to me as an individual. I was sensible

that my heart was full of evil. I seemed to have no power to overcome pride, or to repel evil thoughts which I abhorred. But Christ was manifested to destroy the works of the devil, and it was clear that the sin in my heart was the work of the devil. I was enabled, therefore, to believe that God was working *in* me to will and to do, while I was working *out* my own salvation with fear and trembling.

I was convinced of unbelief, that it made the faithful God a liar. The Lord brought before me my besetting sins which had dominion over me, especially preaching myself instead of Christ, and indulging in self-complacent thoughts after preaching. I was enabled to make myself of no reputation, and to seek the honor which cometh from God only. Satan struggled hard to beat me back from the Rock of Ages; but thanks to God, I finally hit upon the method of living by the moment, and then I found rest.

. . . .

I felt shut up to a momentary dependence upon the grace of Christ. I would not permit the adversary to trouble me about the past or future, for I each moment looked for the supply for that moment. I agreed that I would be a child of Abraham, and walk by naked faith in the word of God, and not by inward feelings and emotions; I would seek to be a Bible Christian. *Since that time the Lord has given me a steady victory over sins which before enslaved me.* I delight in the Lord and in His word. I delight in my work as a minister; my fellowship is with the Father and with His Son Jesus Christ. I am a babe in Christ; I know my progress has been small, compared with that made by many. My feelings vary; but when I have feelings I praise God and trust in His word; and when I am empty and my feelings are gone, I do the same. I have covenanted to walk by faith, and not by feelings.

The Lord, I think, is beginning to revive His work among my people. "Praise the Lord!" May the Lord fill you with all His fulness, and give you all the mind of Christ. Oh, be faithful! Walk before God and be perfect. Preach the Word. Be instant in season and out of season. The Lord loves you. He works with you. Rest your soul fully upon that promise, "Lo, I am with you always, even unto the end of the world."

Your fellow-soldier,

WILLIAM HILL

CHAPTER EIGHT

Difficulties Concerning Guidance

YOU HAVE NOW BEGUN, DEAR READER, THE LIFE OF faith. You have given yourself to the Lord to be His wholly and altogether, and you are now entirely in His hands to be molded and fashioned according to His own divine purpose into a vessel unto His honor. Your one most earnest desire is to follow Him whithersoever He may lead you, and to be very pliable in His hands; and you are trusting Him to "work in you to will and to do of his good pleasure." But you find a great difficulty here. You have not learned yet to know the voice of the Good Shepherd, and are therefore in great doubt and perplexity as to what really is His will concerning you.

Perhaps there are certain paths into which God seems to be calling you, of which your friends disapprove. And these friends, it may be, are older than yourself in the Christian life, and seem to you also to be much farther advanced. You can scarcely bear to differ from them or to distress them; and you feel also very diffident of yielding to any seeming impressions of duty of which they do not approve. And yet you cannot get rid of these impressions, and you find yourself therefore plunged into great doubt and uneasiness.

There is a way out of all these difficulties to the fully surrendered soul. I would repeat *fully* surrendered, because, if there is any reserve of will upon any point, it becomes almost impossible to find out the mind of God in reference to that point; and therefore the first thing is to be sure that you really do *purpose* to obey the Lord in every respect. If however this is your purpose, and your soul only needs to know the will of God in order to consent to it, then you surely cannot doubt His willingness to make His will known, and to guide you in the right paths. There are many very clear promises in reference to this. Take, for instance, John 10:3, 4, "He calleth his own sheep by name, and leadeth them out. And when he putteth forth his own sheep he goeth before them, and the sheep follow him, for they know his voice." Or John 14:26: "But the Comforter, which is the Holy Ghost, whom the Father will send in my name, he shall teach you all things and bring all things to your remembrance, whatsoever I have said unto you." Or James 1:5, 6: "If any of you lack wisdom, let him ask of God, that giveth to all liberally, and upbraideth not; and it shall be given him."

With such declarations as these, and many more like them, we must believe that Divine guidance is promised to us, and our faith must therefore confidently look for and expect it. This is essential, for in James 1:6, 7, we are told, "Let him ask in faith, nothing wavering. For he that wavereth is like a wave of the sea, driven with the wind and tossed. For let not that man think that he shall receive anything of the Lord."

Settle this point then, first of all, and let no suggestion of doubt turn you from a steadfast faith in regard to it, that Divine guidance has been promised, and that, if you seek it, you are sure to receive it.

Next, you must remember that our God has all knowledge and all wisdom, and that therefore it is very possible He may guide you into paths wherein *He* knows great blessings are awaiting you, but which, to the short-sighted human eyes around you, seem sure to result in confusion and loss. You must recognize· the fact that God's thoughts are not as man's thoughts, nor His ways as man's ways; and that He alone, who knows the end of things from the beginning, can judge of what the results of any course of action may be. You must therefore realize that His very love for you may perhaps lead you to run counter to the loving wishes of even your dearest friends. You must learn, from Luke 14:26–33, and similar passages, that in order to be a disciple and follower of your Lord, you may perhaps be called upon to forsake inwardly all that you have, even father or mother, or brother or sister, or husband or wife, or it may be your own life also. Unless the possibility of this is clearly recognized, you will be very likely to get into difficulty, because it often happens that the child of God who enters upon this life of obedience is sooner or later led into paths which meet with the disapproval of those he best loves; and unless he is prepared for this, and can trust the Lord through it all, he will scarcely know what to do.

But, these points having all been settled, we come now to the question as to how God's guidance is to come to us, and how we shall be able to know His voice. There are four ways in which He reveals His will to us, —through the Scriptures, through providential circumstances, through the convictions of our own higher judgment, and through the inward impressions of the Holy Spirit on our minds. Where thsse four harmonize, it is safe to say that God speaks. For I lay it down as a foundation principle, which no one can gainsay, that of course His voice will always be in harmony with itself, no matter in how many different ways He may speak. The voices may be many, the message can be but one. If God tells me in one voice to do or to leave undone anything, He cannot possibly tell me the opposite in another voice. If there is a contradiction in the voices, the speakers cannot be the same. Therefore my rule for distinguishing the voice of God would be to bring it to the test of this harmony.

The Scriptures come first. If you are in doubt upon any subject, you must, first of all, consult the Bible about it, and see whether there is any law there to direct you. Until you have found and obeyed God's will as it is there revealed, you must not ask nor expect a separate, direct, personal revelation. A great many fatal mistakes are made in the matter of guidance by the overlooking of this simple rule. Where our Father has written out for us a plain direction about anything, He will not of course make an especial revelation to us about that thing. And if we fail to search out and obey the Scripture rule, where there is one, and look instead for an inward voice, we shall open ourselves to delusions, and shall almost indvitably get into error. No man, for instance, needs or could expect any direct personal revelation to tell him not to steal, because God has already in the Scriptures plainly declared His will about stealing. This seems such an obvious thing that I would not speak of it, but that I have frequently met with Christians who have altogether overlooked it, and who have, as the result, gone off into fanaticism. I knew one earnest Christian who had the text "All things are yours" so strongly impressed upon her mind in reference to some money belonging to a friend, that she felt it was a direct command to her to steal that money; and after a great struggle she obeyed this apparent guidance, with of course most grievous after-results. Had she submitted her "leading" to the plain teaching of Scripture in reference to stealing, she would have been saved.

The Bible, it is true, does not always give a rule for every particular course of action, and in these cases we need and must expect guidance in other ways. But the Scriptures are far more explicit, even about details, than most people think, and there are not many important affairs in life for which a clear direction may not be found in God's book. Take the matter of dress and we have I Peter 3:3, 4, and I Timothy 2:9. Take the matter of conversation, and we have Ephesians 4:29, and 5:4. Take the matter of avenging injuries and standing up for our rights, and we have Romans 12:19–21, and Matthew 5:38–48, and I Peter 2:19–21. Take the matter of forgiving one another, and we have Ephesians 4:32, and Mark 11:25, 26. Take the matter of conformity to the world, and we have Romans 12:2, and I John 2:15–17, and James 4:4. Take the matter of anxieties of every kind, and we have Matthew 6:25–34, and Philippians 4:6, 7.

I only give these as examples to show how very full and practical the Bible guidance is. If, therefore, you find yourself in perplexity, first of all search and see whether the Bible speaks on the point in question, asking God to make plain to you, by the power of His Spirit, through the Scriptures, what is His mind. And whatever shall seem to you to be plainly taught there, that you must obey. No especial guidance will ever be given about a point on which the Scriptures are explicit, nor could any guidance ever be contrary to the Scriptures.

It is essential, however, in this connection to remember that the Bible is a book of principles, and not a book of disjointed aphorisms. Isolated texts may often be made to sanction things to which the principles of Scripture are totally opposed. I believe all fanaticism comes in this way. An isolated text is so impressed upon the mind that it seems a necessity to obey it, no matter into what wrong thing it may lead; and thus the principles of Scripture are violated, under the very plea of obedience to the Scriptures. In Luke 4 the enemy is represented as using isolated texts to endorse his temptations, while Christ repelled him by announcing principles.

If, however, upon searching the Bible you do not

find any principles that will settle your especial point of difficulty, you must then seek guidance in the other ways mentioned; and God will surely voice Himself to you, either by a conviction of your judgment, or by providential circumstances, or by a clear inward impression. In all true guidance these four voices will, as I have said, necessarily harmonize, for God cannot say in one voice that which He contradicts in another. Therefore, if you have an impression of duty, you must see whether it is in accordance with Scripture, and whether it commends itself to your own higher judgment, and also whether, as we Quakers say, the "way opens" for its carrying out. If any one of these tests fail, it is not safe to proceed, but you must wait in quiet trust until the Lord shows you the point of harmony, which He surely will, sooner or later, if it is His voice that is speaking. Anything which is out of this divine harmony must be rejected, therefore, as not coming from God. For we must never forget that "impressions" can come from other sources as well as from the Holy Spirit. The strong personalities of those around us are the source of a great many of our impressions. Impressions also arise often from our wrong physical conditions, which color things far more than we dream. And finally, impressions come from those spiritual enemies which seem to lie in wait for every traveler who seeks to enter the higher regions of the spiritual life. In the same epistle which tells us that we are seated in "heavenly places in Christ" (Eph. 2:6), we are also told that we shall have to fight there with spiritual enemies (Eph. 6:12). These spiritual enemies, whoever or whatever they may be, must necessarily communicate with us by means of our spiritual faculties; and their voices therefore will be, as the voice of God is, an inward impression made upon our spirits. Consequently, just as the Holy Spirit may tell us by impressions what is the will of God concerning us, so also will these spiritual enemies tell us by impressions what is their will concerning us, disguising themselves, of course, as "angels of light" who have come to lead us closer to God.

Many earnest and honest-hearted children of God have been thus deluded into paths of extreme fanaticism, while all the while thinking they were closely following the Lord. God, who sees the sincerity of their hearts, can and does, I am sure, pity and forgive; but the consequences as to this life are often very sad. It is not enough to have a "leading"; we must find out the source of that leading before we give ourselves up to follow it. It is not enough, either, for the leading to be very "remarkable," or the coincidences to be very striking, to stamp it as being surely from God. In all ages of the world evil and deceiving agencies have been able to work miracles, foretell events, reveal secrets, and give "signs"; and God's people have always been emphatically warned about being deceived thereby.

It is essential, therefore, that our "leadings" should all be tested by the teachings of Scripture. But this alone is not enough. They must be tested as well by our own spiritually enlightened judgment, or what is familiarly called "common sense."

So far as I can see, the Scriptures everywhere make it an essential thing for the children of God, in their journey through this world, to use all the faculties that have been given them. They are to use their outward faculties for their outward walk, and their inward faculties for their inward walk; and they might as well expect to be "kept" from dashing their feet against a stone in the outward, if they walk blindfold, as to be "kept" from spiritual stumbling if they put aside their judgment and common sense in their interior life.

Some, however, may say here, "But I thought we were not to depend on our human understanding in Divine things." I answer to this that we are not to depend on our unenlightened human understanding, but upon our human judgment and common sense enlightened by the Spirit of God. That is, God will speak to us through the faculties He has Himself given us, and not independently of them; so that just as we are to use our outward eyes in our outward walk, no matter how full of faith we may be, so also we are to use the interior "eyes of our understanding" in our interior walk with God.

The third test to which our impressions must be brought is that of providential circumstances. If a "leading" is of God, the way will always open for it. Our Lord assures us of this when He says, in John 10: 4, "And when he putteth forth his own sheep, *he goeth before them,* and the sheep *follow* him; for they know his voice," Notice here the expressions "goeth before" and "follow." He goes before to open a way, and we are to follow in the way thus opened. It is never a sign of a Divine leading when the Christian insists on opening his own way, and riding roughshod over all opposing things. If the Lord "goes before" us, He will open the door for us, and we shall not need to batter down doors for ourselves.

The fourth point I would make is this,—that, just as our impressions must be tested, as I have shown, by the other three voices, so must these other voices be tested by our inward impressions; and if we feel a "stop in our minds" about anything, we must wait until that is removed before acting. A Christian who had advanced with unusual rapidity in the Divine life gave me, as her secret, this simple receipt: "I always mind the checks." We must not ignore the voice of our inward impressions, nor ride roughshod over them, any more than we must the other three voices of which I have spoken.

Every peculiarly precious spiritual gift is always necessarily linked with some peculiar danger. When the spiritual world is opened to a soul, both the good and the evil there will meet it. But we must not be discouraged by this. Who would not rather take manhood with all its risks and dangers than remain forever in the ignorance and innocence of childhood; and who would not rather grow up into the stature of Christ, even if it shall involve new and more subtle forms of temptation?

Therefore we must not be deterred from embracing the blessed privilege of Divine guidance by a dread of the dangers that environ it. With the four tests I have mentioned, and a divine sense of "oughtness," derived from the harmony of all of God's voices, there need be nothing to fear. And to me it seems that the blessedness and joy of this direct communication of God's will to us is one of our grandest privileges. That God *cares* enough about us to desire to regulate the details of our lives is the strongest proof of love He could give; and that He should condescend to tell us all about it, and to let us know just how to live and walk so as perfectly to please Him seems almost too good to be true. We never care about the little details of people's lives unless we love them. It is a matter of indifference to us what the majority of people we meet do, or how they spend their time. But as soon as we begin to love any one we begin at once to care. God's law, therefore, is only another name for God's love; and the more minutely that law descends into the details of our lives, the more sure we are made of the depth and reality of the love. We can never know the full joy and privileges of the life hid with Christ in God until we have learned the lesson of a daily and hourly guidance.

God's promise is that He will work in us to *will* as well as to do of His good pleasure. This means, of course, that He will take possession of our will, and work it for us; and that His suggestions will come to us, not so much commands from the outside as desires springing up within. They will originate in our will; we shall feel as though we *desired* to do so and so, not as though we *must*. And this makes it a service of perfect liberty; for it is always easy to do what we desire to do, let the accompanying circumstances be as difficult as they may. Every mother knows that she could secure perfect and easy obedience in her child if she could only get into that child's will and work it for him, making him want himself to do the things she willed he should. And this is what our Father, in the new dispensation, does for His children; He "writes his laws on our hearts and on our minds," so that our affection and our understanding embrace them, and we are *drawn* to obey instead of being *driven* to it.

The way in which the Holy Spirit, therefore, usually works, in a fully obedient soul, in regard to this direct guidance, is to impress upon the mind a wish or desire to do or to leave undone certain things.

The child of God when engaged in prayer feels, perhaps, a sudden suggestion made to his inmost consciousness in reference to a certain point of duty. "I would like to do this or the other," he thinks; "I wish I could." At once this matter should be committed to the Lord, with an instant consent of the will to obey Him, should the suggestion prove to be really from Him. And then the tests I have mentioned should be intelligently applied, namely, as to whether the suggestion is in accordance with the teaching of Scripture, with a sanctified judgment, and with providential circumstances. Often no distinct consciousness of this process is necessary, as our spiritual intelligence can see at a glance the right or wrong of the matter. But, however it may come, when the divine harmony is reached, and the divine sense of "oughtness" settles down on the heart, then an immediate obedience is the safest and easiest course. The first moment that we clearly see a thing to be right is always the moment when it is easy to do it. If we "let in the reasoner," as the Quakers express it, the golden opportunity is lost, and obedience becomes more and more difficult with every moment's delay. The old self-will wakens into life; and the energies that should have been occupied with obeying are absorbed instead in the struggle with doubts and reasonings.

It sometimes happens, however, that, in spite of all our efforts to discover the truth, the divine sense of "oughtness" does not seem to come, and our doubts and perplexities continue unenlightened. In addition to this our friends differ from us, and would, we know, oppose our course. In such a case there is nothing to do but to wait until the light comes. But we must wait in faith, and in an attitude of entire surrender, saying a continual "Yes" to the will of our Lord, let it be what it may. If the suggestion is from Him, it will continue and strengthen; if it is not from Him, it will disappear, and we shall almost forget we ever had it. If it continues, if every time we are brought into near communion with the Lord it seems to return, if it troubles us in our moments of prayer, and disturbs all our peace, and if finally it conforms to the test of the divine harmony of which I have spoken, we may then feel sure it is from God, and we must yield to it, or suffer an unspeakable loss.

The Apostle gives us a rule in reference to doubtful things which seems to me very explicit. He is speaking about certain kinds of meat-eating which were ceremonially unclean, and after declaring his own liberty says, "I know, and am persuaded by the Lord Jesus, that there is nothing unclean of itself; but to him that esteemeth anything to be unclean, to him it is unclean." And in summing up the whole subject he writes: "Hast thou faith? have it to thyself before

God. Happy is he that condemneth not himself in that thing which he alloweth. And he that doubteth is damned [condemned] if he eat, because he eateth not of faith: for whatsoever is not of faith is sin." In all doubtful things you must stand still and refrain from action until God gives you light to know more clearly His mind concerning them. Very often you will find that the doubt has been His voice calling upon you to come into more perfect conformity to His will; but sometimes these doubtful things are only temptations, or morbid feelings, to which it would be most unwise for you to yield, and the only safe way is to wait until you can act in faith, for "whatsoever is not of faith is sin."

Take all your present perplexities, then, to the Lord. Tell Him you only want to know and obey His voice, and ask Him to make it plain to you. Promise Him that you will obey, whatever it may be. Believe implicitly that He is guiding you, according to His word. In all doubtful things, wait for clear light. Look and listen for His voice continually; and the moment you are sure of it, then, but not until then, yield an immediate obedience. Trust Him to make you forget the impression if it is not His will; and if it continues, and is in harmony with all His other voices, do not be afraid to obey.

Above everything else, trust Him. Nowhere is faith more needed than here. He has promised to guide. You have asked Him to do it. And now you must believe that He does, and must take what comes as being His guidance. No earthly parent or master could guide his children or servants if they should refuse to take his commands as being really the expression of his will; and God *cannot* guide those souls who never trust Him enough to believe that He is doing it.

Above all, do not be afraid of this blessed life, lived hour by hour and day by day under the guidance of thy Lord! If He seeks to bring thee out of the world and into very close conformity to Himself, do not shrink from it. It is thy most blessed privilege. Rejoice in it. Embrace it eagerly. Let everything go that it may be thine.

"God only is the creature's home,
    Though rough and strait the road;
Yet nothing else can satisfy
    The love that longs for God.

"How little of that road, my soul!
    How little hast thou gone!
Take heart, and let the thought of God
    Allure thee further on.

"Dole not thy duties out to God,
    But let thy hand be free;
Look long at Jesus,—His sweet love
    How was it dealt to thee?

"The perfect way is hard to flesh,
    It is not hard to love;
If thou wert sick for want of God,
    How swiftly wouldst thou move!

"And only this perfection needs
    A heart kept calm all day.
To catch the words the Spirit there
    From hour to hour may say.

"Then keep thy conscience sensitive,
No inward token miss;
And go where grace entices thee,—
Perfection lies in this.

"Be docile to thine unseen Guide,
Love Him as He loves thee;
Time and obedience are enough,
And thou a saint shall be."

CHAPTER NINE

Difficulties Concerning Doubts

A GREAT MANY CHRISTIANS ARE SLAVES TO AN INVETerate habit of doubting. I do not mean doubts as to the existence of God or the truths of the Bible, but doubts as to their own personal relations with the God in whom they profess to believe, doubts as to the forgiveness of their sins, doubts as to their hopes of heaven, and doubts about their own inward experience. No drunkard was ever more in bondage to his habit of drink than they are to their habit of doubting. Every step of their spiritual progress is taken against the fearful odds of an army of doubts that are forever lying in wait to assail them at each favorable moment. Their lives are made wretched, their usefulness is effectually hindered, and their communion with God is continually broken, by their doubts. And although the entrance of the soul upon the life of faith does, in many cases, take it altogether out of the region where these doubts live and flourish, yet even here it sometimes happens that the old tyrant will rise up and reassert his sway, and will cause the feet to stumble and the heart to fail, even when he cannot succeed in utterly turning the believer back into the dreary wilderness again.

We all of us remember, doubtless, our childish fascination, and yet horror, in the story of Christian's imprisonment in Doubting Castle by the wicked giant Despair, and our exultant sympathy in his escape through those massive gates and from that cruel tyrant. Little did we suspect then that we should ever find ourselves taken prisoner by the same giant, and imprisoned in the same castle. But I fear that each one of us, if we were perfectly honest, would have to confess to at least one such experience, and some of us perhaps to a great many.

It seems strange that people whose very name of Believers implies that their one chiefest characteristic is that they believe, should have to confess that they havs doubts. And yet it is such a universal habit, that I feel, if the name were to be given over again, the only fitting and descriptive name that could be given to many of God's children would have to be that of Doubters. In fact, most Christians have settled down under their doubts, as to a sort of inevitable malady, from which they suffer acutely, but to which they must try to be resigned as a part of the necessary discipline of this earthly life; and they lament over their doubts as a man might lament over his rheumatism, making themselves out as "interesting cases" of especial and peculiar trial which require the tenderest sympathy and the utmost consideration.

This is too often true even of believers who are earnestly longing to enter upon the life and walk of faith, and who have made, perhaps, many steps towards it. They have got rid, it may be, of the old doubts that once tormented them, as to whether their sins are really forgiven, and whether they shall, after all, get safe to heaven; but they have not got rid of doubting. They have simply shifted the habit to a higher platform. They are saying, perhaps, "Yes, I believe my sins are forgiven, and I am a child of God through faith in Jesus Christ. I dare not doubt this any more. But then—" and this "but then" includes an interminable array of doubts concerning most of the declarations and promises our Father has made to His children. One after another they fight with these promises, and refuse to believe them until they can have some more reliable proof of their being true than the simple word of their God; and then they wonder why they are permitted to walk in such darkness, and look upon themselves almost in the light of martyrs, and groan under the peculiar spiritual conflicts they are compelled to endure.

Spirtual conflicts! Far better would they be named did we call them spiritual rebellions! Our fight is to be a fight of faith; and the moment we let in doubts, our fight ceases, and our rebellion begins.

I desire to put forth, if possible, a vigorous protest against this whole thing.

Just as well might I join in with the laments of a drunkard, and unite with him in prayer for grace to endure the discipline of his fatal appetite, as to give way for one instant to the weak complaints of these enslaved souls, and try to console them under their slavery. To one and to the other I would dare to do nothing else but proclaim the perfect deliverance which the Lord Jesus Christ has in store for them, and beseech, entreat, and importune them, with all the power at my command, to avail themselves of it and be free. Not for one moment would I listen to their despairing excuses. You ought to be free, you can be free, you must be free!

Will you undertake to tell me that it is an inevitable necessity for God to be doubted by His children? Is it an inevitable necessity for your children to doubt you? Would you tolerate their doubts a single hour? Would you pity your son, and condole with him, and feel that he was an "interesting case" if he should come to you and say, "Father, I am such a doubter that I cannot believe I am your child, or that you really love me"? And yet how often we hear a child of God excuse himself for his doubts by saying, "Oh, but I am such a doubter that I cannot believe in God's love and forgiveness"; and no one seems shocked at it. You might just as well say, with a like complacency, "Oh, but I am such a liar that I cannot help telling lies," and expect people to consider it a sufficient excuse. In the sight of God, I verily believe doubting is in some cases as displeasing as lying. It certainly is more dishonoring to Him, for it impugns His truthfulness and defames His character. John says that "he that believeth not God hath made him a liar," and it seems to me that hardly anything could be worse than thus to fasten on God the character of being a liar! Have you ever thought of *this* as the result of your doubting?

I remember seeing once the indignation and sorrow of a mother's heart deeply stirred by a little doubting on the part of one of her children. She had brought two little girls to my house, to leave them while she did some errands. One of them, with the happy confidence of childhood, abandoned herself to all the pleasures she could find in my nursery, and sang and played until her mother's return. The other one, with the wretched caution and mistrust of maturity, sat down alone in a corner, to wonder, first, whether her mother would remember to come back for her, and to fear she would be forgotten, and then to imagine her mother would be glad of the chance to get rid of her anyhow, because she was such a naughty girl; and ended with working herself up into a perfect frenzy of despair. The look on that mother's face, when upon her return the weeping little girl told what was the matter with her, I shall not easily forget. Grief, wounded love, indignation, and pity all strove together for mastery; and the mother hardly knew who was most at fault, herself or the child, that such doubts should be possible.

Perhaps such doubts might be possible with an earthly mother, but never, never with God; and a hundred times in my life since, has that scene come up before me with deepest teaching, and has compelled me, peremptorily, to refuse admittance to the doubts about my Heavenly Father's love and care and remembrance of me that have clamored at the door of my heart for entrance.

Doubting is, I am convinced, to many people a real luxury, and to deny themselves this luxury would be the hardest piece of self-denial they have ever known. It is a luxury which, like the indulgence in some other luxuries, brings very sorrowful results; and perhaps, looking at the sadness and misery it has brought into your own Christian experience, you may be inclined to say, "Alas! it is no luxury to me, but only a fearful trial." But pause for a moment. Try giving it up, and you will soon find out whether it is a luxury or not. Do not your doubts come trooping to your door like a company of sympathizing friends who appreciate your hard case and have come to condole with you? And is it no luxury to sit down with them, and entertain them, and listen to their arguments, and join in with their condolences? Would it be no self-denial to turn resolutely from them, and refuse to hear a word they have to say? If you do not know, try it and see.

Have you never tasted the luxury of indulging in hard thoughts against those who have, as you think, injured you? Have you never known what a positive fascination it is to brood over their unkindnesses, and to pry into their malice, and to imagine all sorts of wrong and uncomfortable things about them? It has made you wretched, of course; but it has been a fascinating sort of wretchedness, that you could not easily give up.

Just like this is the luxury of doubting. Things have gone wrong with you in your experience. Dispensations have been mysterious, temptations have been peculiar, your "case" has seemed different from others. What more natural than to conclude that for some reason God has forsaken you, and does not love you, and is indifferent to your welfare? How irresistible is the conviction that you are too wicked for Him to care for, or too difficult for Him to manage!

You do not mean to blame Him, or accuse Him of injustice, for you feel that His indifference and rejection of you are, because of your unworthiness, fully deserved; and this very subterfuge leaves you at liberty, under the guise of a just and true appreciation of your own shortcomings, to indulge in your dishonoring doubts. Although you think it is yourself you are doubting, you are really doubting the Lord, and are indulging in as hard and wrong thoughts of Him as ever you did of a human enemy. For He declares that He came to save, not the righteous, but sinners; and your very sinfulness and unworthiness, instead of being a reason why He should not love you and care for you, are really your chiefest claim upon His love and His care.

As well might the poor little lamb that has wandered from the flock and got lost in the wilderness say, "I am lost, and therefore the Shepherd cannot love me, nor care for me, nor remember me; he only loves and cares for the lambs that never wander." As well might the ill man say, "I am ill, and therefore the doctor will not come to see me, nor give me any medicine; he only cares for and visits well people." Jesus says, "They that are whole need not a physician, but they that are sick." And again He says, "What man of you, having an hundred sheep, if he lose one of them, doth not leave the ninety and nine in the wilderness, and go after that which is lost until he find it?" Any thoughts of Him, therefore, that are different from this which He Himself has said, are hard thoughts; and to indulge in them is far worse than to indulge in hard thoughts of any earthly friend or foe. From beginning to end of your Christian life it is always sinful to indulge in doubts. Doubts and discouragements are all from an evil source, and are always untrue. A direct and emphatic denial is the only way to meet them.

This brings me to the practical part of the whole subject, as to how to get deliverance from this fatal habit. My answer would be that the deliverance from this must be by the same means as the deliverance from any other sin. It is to be found in Christ, and in Him only. You must hand your doubting over to Him as you have learned to hand your other temptations. You must do with it just what you do with your temper or your pride; that is, you must give it up to the Lord. I believe myself the only effectual remedy is to take a pledge against it as you would urge a drunkard to do against drink, trusting in the Lord alone to keep you steadfast.

Like any other sin, the stronghold is in the will, and the will or purpose to doubt must be surrendered exactly as you surrender the will or purpose to yield to any other temptation. God always takes possession of a surrendered will; and if we come to the point of saying that we will not doubt, and surrender this central fortress of our nature to Him, His blessed Spirit will begin at once to "work in us all the good pleasure of his will," and we shall find ourselves kept from doubting by His mighty and overcoming power.

The trouble is, that in this matter of doubting the Christian does not always make a full surrender, but is apt to reserve a little secret liberty to doubt, looking upon it as being sometimes a necessity.

"I do not want to doubt any more," we will say, or, "I hope I shall not"; but it is hard to come to the point of saying, "I *will* not doubt again," and no surrender is effectual until it reaches the point of saying, "I will not." The liberty to doubt must be given up forever; and we must consent to a continuous life of inevitable trust. It is often necessary, I think, to make a definite transaction of this surrender of doubting, and come to a point about it. I believe it is quite as necessary in the case of a doubter as in the case of a drunkard. It will not do to give it up by degrees. The total-abstinence principle is the only effectual one here.

Then, the surrender once made, we must rest absolutely upon the Lord for deliverance in each time of temptation. The moment the assault comes, we must lift up the shield of faith against it. We must hand the very first suggestion of doubt over to the Lord, and must let Him manage it. We must refuse to entertain the doubt a single moment. Let it come ever so plausibly, or under whatever guise of humility, we must simply say, "I dare not doubt; I must trust. God *is* my Father, and He does love me. Jesus saves me; He saves me now." Those three little words, repeated over and over, "Jesus saves me, Jesus saves me," will put to flight the greatest army of doubts that ever assaulted any soul. I have tried it times without number, and have never known it to fail. Do not stop to argue out the matter with yourself or with your doubts. Pay no attention to them whatever, but treat them with the utmost contempt. Shut your door in their very face, and emphatically deny every word they say to you. Bring up some "It is written," and hurl it after them. Look right at Jesus, and tell Him that you do trust Him, and that you intend to go on trusting Him. Then let the doubts clamor as they may, they cannot hurt you if you will not let them in.

I know it will look to you sometimes as though you were shutting your door against your best friends, and your hearts wipl long after your doubts more than ever the Israelites longed after the flesh-pots of Egypt. But deny yourself; take up your cross in this matter, and quietly but firmly refuse ever to listen to a single word.

Often has it happened to me to find, on awaking in the morning, a perfect army of doubts clamoring at my door for admittance. Nothing has seemed real, nothing has seemed true; and least of all has it seemed possible that I—miserable, wretched I—could be the object of the Lord's love, or care, or notice. If I only had been at liberty to let these doubts in, and invite them to take seats and make themselves at home, what a luxury I should many times have felt it to be! But years ago I made a pledge against doubt-ing, and I would as soon think of violating my pledge against intoxicating liquor as of violating this one. I have never dared to admit the first doubt. At such times, therefore, I have been compelled to lift up the "shield of faith" the moment I have become conscious of these suggestions of doubt; and handing the whole army over to the Lord to conquer, I have begun to assert, over and over, my faith in Him, in the simple words, "God *is* my Father; I *am* His forgiven child; He *does* love me; Jesus saves me; Jesus saves me now!" The victory has always been complete. The enemy has come in like a flood, but the "Spirit of the Lord has lifted up a standard against him," and my doubts have been put to flight. And I have been able to join in the song of Moses and the children of Israel, saying, "I will sing unto the Lord, for he hath triumphed gloriously: the horse and his rider hath he thrown into the sea. The Lord is my strength and song, and he is become my salvation."

Dear doubting souls, go and do likewise, and a similar victory shall be yours. You may think, perhaps, that doubts are a necessity in your case, owing to the peculiarity of your temperament; but I assure you most emphatically that this is not so. You are no more under a necessity to be doubtful as to your relationships to your Heavenly Father than you are to be doubtful as to your relationships to your earthly father. In both cases the thing you must depend on is their word, not your feelings; and no earthly father has ever declared or manifested his fatherhood one thousandth part as unmistakably or as lovingly as your Heavenly Father has declared and manifested His. If you would not "make God a liar," therefore, you must make your believing as inevitable and necessary a thing as your obedience. You would obey God, I believe, even though you should die in the act. Believe Him, also, even though the effort to believe should cost you your life. The conflict may be very severe; it may seem at times unendurable. But let your unchanging declaration be from henceforth, "Though he slay me, yet will I trust in him." When doubts come, meet them, not with arguments, but with assertions of faith. All doubts are an attack of the enemy; the Holy Spirit never suggests them, never. He is the Comforter, not the Accuser; and He never shows us our need without at the same time revealing the Divine supply.

Do not give heed to your doubts, therefore, for a moment. Turn from them with horror, as you would from blasphemy; for they *are* blasphemy. You cannot perhaps hinder the suggestions of doubt from coming to you any more than you can hinder the boys in the street from swearing as you go by; and consequently you are not sinning in the one case any more than in the other. But just as you can refuse to listen to the boys or join in their oaths, so can you also refuse to listen to the doubts or join in with them. They are not *your* doubts until you consent to them and adopt them as true. When they come you must at once turn from them as you would from swearing. Often a very good practical way of getting rid of them is to go at once and confess your faith, in the strongest language possible, somewhere or to someone. If you cannot do this by word of mouth, write it in a letter, or repeat it over and over in your heart to the Lord.

As you lay down this book, therefore, take up your pen and write out your determination never to doubt again. Make it a real transaction between your soul and the Lord. Give up your liberty to doubt forever. Put your will in this matter over on the Lord's side, and trust Him to keep you from falling. Tell Him all about your utter weakness and your long-encouraged habits of doubt, and how helpless you are before it, and commit the whole battle to Him. Tell Him you *will* not doubt again, putting forth all your will power on His side, and against His enemy and yours; and then, henceforward, keep your face steadfastly "looking unto Jesus," away from yourself and away from your doubts, holding fast the profession of your faith without wavering, because "he is faithful who hath promised." Rely on *His* faithfulness, not on your own. You have committed the keeping of your soul to Him as unto a "faithful Creator," and you must never again admit the possibility of His being unfaithful. Believe He is faithful, not because you feel it, or see it, but because He says He is. Believe it, whether you feel it or not. Believe it, even when it seems to you that you are believing something that is absolutely untrue. Believe it actively, and believe it persistently. Cultivate a continuous habit of believing, and never let your faith waver for any "seeming," however plausible it may be. The result will be that sooner or later you will come to *know* that it is true, and all doubts will vanish in the blaze of the glory of the absolute faithfulness of God!

It is an inexorable rule in the spiritual life according to our faith it is to be unto us; and of course this rule must work both ways, and therefore we may fairly expect that it will be also unto us according to our doubts.

Doubts and discouragements are, I believe, inlets by which evil enters, while faith is an impregnable wall against all evil.

Dear doubting souls, my heart yearns over you with a tender sympathy! I know your sincerity and your earnestness, and your struggles after an abiding experience of peace with God, through the Lord Jesus Christ: and I know also how effectually your fatal habit of doubting has held you back. I would that my words might open your eyes to see the deliverance that lies at your very door. Try my plan, I beseech of you, and see if it will not be true, that "according to your faith" it shall inevitably be unto you.

CHAPTER TEN

Difficulties Concerning Temptation

CERTAIN VERY GREAT MISTAKES ARE MADE CONCERNING this matter of temptation in the practical working out of the life of faith.

First of all, people seem to expect, that, after the soul has entered into rest in the Lord, temptations will cease; and they think that the promised deliverance is to be not only from yielding to temptation, but even also from being tempted. Consequently, when they find the "Canaanite still in the land," and see the "cities great and walled up to heaven," they are utterly discouraged, and think they must have gone wrong in some way, and that this cannot be the true land, after all.

Then, next, they make the mistake of looking upon temptation as sin, and of blaming themselves for suggestions of evil, even while they abhor them. This brings them into condemnation and discouragement; and discouragement, if continued in, always ends at last in actual sin. Sin makes an easy prey of a discouraged soul; so that we fall often from the very fear of having fallen.

To meet the first of these difficulties, it is only necessary to refer to the Scripture declarations which state that the Christian life is to be throughout a warfare; .and that it is to be especially so when we are "seated in heavenly places in Christ Jesus," and are called to wrestle against spiritual enemies, whose power and skill to tempt us must doubtless be far superior to any we have heretofore encountered. As a fact, temptations generally increase in strength tenfold, after we have entered into the interior life, rather than decrease; and no amount or sort of them must ever for a moment lead us to suppose we have not really found the true abiding place. Strong temptations are often more a sign of great grace than of little grace. When the children of Israel had first left Egypt, the Lord did not lead them through the country of the Philistines, although that was the nearest way; "for God said, Lest peradventure the people repent when they see war, and they return to Egypt." But afterwards, when they had learned how to trust Him better, He permitted their enemies to attack them. Moreover, even in their wilderness journey they met with but few enemies, and fought but few battles, compared to those they encountered in the land of Canaan, where they found seven great nations and thirty-one kings to be conquered, besides walled cities to be taken, and giants to be overcome.

They could not have fought with the "Canaanites, and the Hittites, and the Amorites, and the Perizzites, and the Hivites, and the Jebusites," until they had gone into the land where these enemies were. The very power of your temptations, dear Christian, therefore, may perhaps be one of the strongest proofs that you really are in the land of promise you have been seeking to enter, because they are temptations peculiar to that land; consequently you must never allow them to cause you to question the fact of your having entered it.

The second mistake is not quite so easy to deal with. It seems hardly worth while to say that temptation is not sin, and yet much distress arises from not understanding this fact. The very suggestion of wrong seems to bring pollution with it; and the poor tempted soul begins to feel as if it must be very bad indeed, and very far off from God, to have had such thoughts and suggestions. It is as though a burglar should break into a man's house to steal, and, when the master of the house begins to resist him and drive him out, should turn round and accuse the owner of being himself the thief. It is the enemy's grand ruse for entrapping us. He comes and whispers suggestions of evil to us,—doubts, blasphemies, jealousies, envyings, and pride,—and then turns round and says, "Oh, how wicked you must be to think such things! It is very plain that you are not trusting the Lord; for if you had been, it would be impossible for these things to have entered your heart." This reasoning sounds so very plausible that we often accept it as true, and so come under condemnation, and are filled with discouragement; and then it is easy for temptation to develop into actual sin. One of the most fatal things in the life of faith is discouragement; one of the most helpful is confidence. A very wise man once said that in overcoming temptations confidence was the first thing, confidence the second, and confidence the third. We must *expect* to conquer. That is why the Lord said so often to Joshua, "Be strong and of a good courage"; "Be not afraid, neither be thou dismayed"; "Only be thou strong and very courageous." And it is also the reason He says to us, "Let not your heart be troubled, neither let it be afraid." The power of temptation is in the fainting of our own hearts. The enemy knows this well, and he always begins his assaults by discouraging us, if he can in any way accomplish it.

This discouragement arises sometimes from what we think is a righteous grief and disgust at ourselves that such things *could* be any temptation to us, but which is really mortification coming from the fact that we have been indulging in a secret self-congratulation that our tastes were too pure, or our separation from the world was too complete, for such things to tempt us. We are discouraged because we have expected something from ourselves, and have been sorely disappointed not to find that something there. This mortification and discouragement, though they present an appearance of true humility, are really a far worse condition than the temptation itself, for they are nothing but the results of wounded self-love. True humility can bear to see its own utter weakness and foolishness revealed, because it never expected anything from itself, and knows that its only hope and expectation must be in God. Therefore, instead of discouraging the humble soul from trusting, such revelations drive it to a deeper and more utter trust. But the counterfeit humility that self-love produces plunges the soul into the depths of a faithless discouragement, and drives it into the very sin with which it is so distressed.

There is an allegory that illustrates this to me wonderfully. Satan called together a council of his servants to consult how they might make a good man sin. One evil spirit started up and said, "I will make him sin." "How will you do it?" asked Satan. "I will set before him the pleasures of sin," was the reply; "I will tell him of its delights, and the rich rewards it brings." "Ah," said Satan, "that will not do; he has tried it, and knows better than that." Then another imp started up and said, "I will make him sin." "What will you do?" asked Satan. "I will tell him of the pains and sorrows of virtue. I will show him that virtue has no delights, and brings no rewards." "Ah, no!" exclaimed Satan, "that will not do at all; for he has tried it, and knows that 'Wisdom's ways *are* ways of pleasantness, and all her paths are peace.'" "Well," said another imp, starting up, "I will undertake to make him sin." "And what will you do?" asked Satan, again. "I will discourage his soul," was the short reply. "Ah, that will do!" cried Satan; "that will do! We shall conquer him now."

An old writer says, "All discouragement is from the devil"; and I wish every Christian would take this as a motto, and would realize that he must fly from discouragement as he would from sin.

But if we fail to recognize the truth about temptation, this is impossible; for if the temptations are our own fault, we cannot help being discouraged. But they are not. The Bible says, "Blessed is the man that endureth temptation"; and we are exhorted to "count it all joy when we fall into divers temptations." Temptation, therefore, cannot be sin; and the truth is, it is no more a sin to hear these whispers and suggestions of evil in our souls than it is for us to hear the wicked talk of bad men as we pass along the street. The sin comes, in either case, only by our stopping and joining in with them. If, when the wicked suggestions come, we turn from them at once, as we would from wicked talk, and pay no more attention to them than we would to the talk, we do not sin. But if we carry them on in our minds, and roll them under our tongues, and dwell on them with a half consent of our will to them as true, then we sin. We may be enticed by temptations a thousand times a day without sin, and we cannot help these enticings, and are not to blame for them. But if we begin to think that these enticings are actual sin on our part, then the battle is half lost already, and the sin can hardly fail to gain a complete victory.

A dear lady once came to me under great darkness, simply from not understanding this. She had been living very happily in the life of faith for some time, and had been so free from temptations as almost to begin to think she would never be tempted again. But suddenly a very peculiar form of temptation had assailed her, which had horrified her. She found that the moment she began to pray, dreadful thoughts of all kinds would rush into her mind. She had lived a very sheltered, innocent life; and these thoughts seemed so awful to her that she felt she must be one of the most wicked of sinners to be capable of having them. She began by thinking that she could not possibly have entered into the rest of faith, and ended by concluding that she had never even been born again. Her soul was in an agony of distress. I told her that these dreadful thoughts were purely and simply temptations, and that she herself was not to blame for them at all; that she could not help them any more than she could help hearing if a wicked man should pour out his blasphemies in her presence. And I urged her to recognize and treat them as temptations only, and not to blame herself or be discouraged, but rather to turn at once to the Lord and commit them to Him. I showed her how great an advantage the enemy had gained by making her think these thoughts were originated by herself, and by plunging her into condemnation and discouragement on account of them. And I assured her she would find a speedy victory if she would pay no attention to them; but, ignoring their presence, would simply turn her back on them and look to the Lord.

She grasped the truth, and the next time these blasphemous thoughts came, she said inwardly to the enemy, "I have found you out now. It is you who are suggesting these dreadful thoughts to me, and I hate them, and will have nothing to do with them. The Lord is my helper; take them to Him, and settle them in His presence." Immediately the baffled enemy, finding himself discovered, fled in confusion, and her soul was perfectly delivered.

Another thing also. Our spiritual enemies know that if a Christian recognizes a suggestion of evil as coming from them, he will recoil from it far more quickly than if it seems to be the suggestion of his own mind. If the devil prefaced each temptation with the words "I am the devil, your relentless enemy; I have come to make you sin," I suppose we would hardly feel any desire at all to yield to his suggestions. He has to hide himself in order to make his baits attractive. And our victory will be far more easily gained if we are not ignorant of his devices, but recognize them at his very first approach.

We also make another great mistake about temptations in thinking that all time spent in combating them is lost. Hours pass, and we seem to have made no progress, because we have been so beset with temptations. But it often happens that we have been serving God far more truly during these hours than in our times of comparative freedom from temptation. For we are fighting our Lord's battles when we are fighting temptation, and hours are often worth days to us under these circumstances. We read, "Blessed is the man that *endureth* temptation," and I am sure this means enduring the continuance of it and its frequent recurrence. Nothing so cultivates the grace of patience as the endurance of temptation, and nothing so drives the soul to an utter dependence upon the Lord Jesus as its continuance. And finally, nothing brings more praise and honor and glory to our Lord Himself than the trial of our faith that comes through manifold temptations. We are told that it is "more precious than gold, though it be tried with fire," and that we, who patiently endure the trial, shall receive for our reward "the crown of life which the Lord hath promised to them that love him."

We cannot wonder, therefore, any longer at the

exhortation with which the Holy Ghost opens the Book of James: "Count it all joy when ye fall into divers temptations; knowing this, that the trying of your faith worketh patience. But let patience have her perfect work, that ye may be perfect and entire, wanting nothing."

Temptation is plainly one of the instruments used by God to complete our perfection; and thus sin's own weapons are turned against itself, and we see how it is that all things, even temptations, can work together for good to them that love God.

As to the way of victory over temptation, it seems hardly necessary to say to those whom I am at this time especially addressing, that it is to be by faith; for this is, of course, the foundation upon which the whole interior life rests. Our one great motto is throughout, "We are nothing: Christ is all"; and always and everywhere we have started to stand, and walk, and overcome, and live by faith. We have discovered our own utter helplessness, and know that we cannot do anything for ourselves; and we have learned that our only way, therefore, is to hand the temptation over to our Lord, and trust Him to conquer it for us. But when we put it into His hands we must *leave* it there. The greatest difficulty of all is, I think, this *leaving*. It seems impossible to believe that the Lord can or will manage our temptations without our help, especially if they do not immediately disappear. To go on patiently "enduring" the continuance of a temptation without yielding to it, and also without snatching ourselves out of the Lord's hands in regard to it, is a wonderful victory for our impatient natures; but it is a victory we must gain, if we would do what will please God.

We must then commit ourselves as really to the Lord for victory over our temptations, as we committed ourselves at first for forgiveness; and we must leave ourselves just as utterly in His hands for one as for the other.

Thousands of God's children have done this, and can testify to-day that marvelous victories have been gained for them over numberless temptations, and that they have in very truth been made "more than conquerors" through Him who loves them.

But into this part of the subject I cannot go at present, as my object has been rather to present temptation in its true light than to develop the way of victory over it. I desire greatly that conscientious, faithful souls should be delivered from the bondage into which they are sure to be brought if they fail to understand the true nature and use of temptation, and confound it with sin. When temptation is recognized *as* temptation, we shall be able to say at once, "Get thee behind me," and shall walk even through the midst of the fiercest assaults with unclouded and triumphant peace; knowing that, "when the enemy shall come in like a flood, the Spirit of the Lord shall lift up a standard against him."

CHAPTER ELEVEN

Difficulties Concerning Failures

THE VERY TITLE OF THIS CHAPTER MAY PERHAPS STAR-
tle some. "Failures!" they will say; "we thought there
were no failures in this life of faith."

To this I would answer that there ought not to
be, and need not be; but, as a fact, there sometimes
are, and we must deal with facts, and not with
theories. No safe teacher of this interior life ever says
that it becomes impossible to sin; they only insist that
sin ceases to be a necessity, and that a possibility of
continual victory is opened before us. And there are
very few, if any, who do not confess that, as to their
own actual experience, they have at times been overcome by at least a momentary temptation.

Of course, in speaking of sin here, I mean conscious, known sin. I do not touch on the subject of sins
of ignorance, or what are called the inevitable sins of
our nature, which are all met by the provisions of
Christ, and do not disturb our fellowship with God.
I have no desire or ability to treat of the doctrines
concerning sin; these I will leave with the theolo-
gians to discuss and settle, while I speak only of the

believer's experience in the matter.

There are many things which we do innocently enough until an increasing light shows them to be wrong, and these may all be classed under sins of ignorance; but because they are done in ignorance they do not bring us under condemnation, and do not come within the range of the present discussion.

An illustration of this occurred once in my presence. A little baby girl was playing about the library one warm summer afternoon, while her father was resting on the lounge. A pretty inkstand on the table took the child's fancy, and, unnoticed by any one, she climbed on a chair and secured it. Then, walking over to her father with an air of childish triumph, she turned it upside down on the white expanse of his shirt bosom, and laughed with glee as she saw the black streams trickling down on every side.

This was a very wrong thing for the child to do, but it could not be called sin, for she knew no better. Had she been older, and been made to understand that inkstands were not playthings, it would have been sin. "To him that knoweth to do good and doeth it not, to him it is sin"; and in all I shall say concerning sin in this chapter I desire it to be fully understood that I have reference simply to that which comes within the range of our consciousness.

Misunderstanding, then, on this point of known or conscious sin, opens the way for great dangers in the life of faith. When a believer who has, as he trusts, entered upon the highway of holiness, finds himself surprised into sin, he is tempted either to be utterly discouraged, and to give everything up as lost; or else in order to preserve the doctrines untouched, he feels it necessary to cover his sin up, calling it infirmity, and refusing to be candid and aboveboard about it. Either of these courses is equally fatal to any real growth and progress in the life of holiness. The only way is to face the sad fact at once, call the thing by its right name, and discover, if possible, the reason and the remedy. This life of union with God requires the utmost honesty with Him and with ourselves. The blessing that the sin itself would only momentarily disturb, is sure to be lost by any dishonest dealing with it. A sudden failure is no reason for being discouraged and giving up all as lost. Neither is the integrity of our doctrine touched by it. We are not preaching a *state*, but a *walk*. The highway of holiness is not a *place*, but a *way*. Sanctification is not a thing to be picked up at a certain stage of our experience, and forever after possessed, but it is a life to be lived day by day, and hour by hour. We may for a moment turn aside from a path, but the path is not obliterated by our wandering, and can be instantly regained. And in this life and walk of faith, there may be momentary failures that, although very sad and greatly to be deplored, need not, if rightly met, disturb the attitude of the soul as to entire consecration and perfect trust, nor interrupt, for more than the passing moment, its happy communion with its Lord.

The great point is an instant return to God. Our sin is no reason for ceasing to trust, but only an unanswerable argument why we must trust more fully than ever. From whatever cause we have been betrayed into failure, it is very certain that there is no remedy to be found in discouragement. As well might a child who is learning to walk, lie down in despair when he has fallen, and refuse to take another step, as a believer, who is seeking to learn how to live and walk by faith, give up in despair because of having fallen into sin. The only way in both cases is to get right up and try again. When the children of Israel had met with that disastrous defeat, soon after their entrance into the land, before the little city of Ai, they were all so utterly discouraged that we read: "Wherefore the hearts of the people melted, and became as water. And Joshua rent his clothes, and fell to the earth upon his face before the ark of the Lord until the eventide, he and the elders of Israel, and put dust upon their heads. And Joshua said, Alas, O Lord God, wherefore hast thou at all brought this people over Jordan, to deliver us into the hand of the Amorites, to destroy us? Would to God we had been content, and dwelt on the other side Jordan! O Lord, what shall I say, when Israel turneth their backs before their enemies! For the Canaanites and all the inhabitants of the land shall hear of it, and shall environ us round, and cut off our name from the earth: and what wilt thou do unto thy great name?"

What a wail of despair this was! And how exactly it is repeated by many a child of God in the present day, whose heart, because of a defeat, melts and becomes as water, and who cries out, "Would to God we had been content and dwelt on the other side Jordan!" and predicts for itself further failures and even utter discomfiture before its enemies. No doubt Joshua thought then, as we are apt to think now, that discouragement and despair were the only proper and safe condition after such a failure. But God thought otherwise. "And the Lord said unto Joshua, Get thee up; wherefore liest thou upon thy face?" The proper thing to do, was not to abandon themselves thus to utter discouragement, humble as it might look, but at once to face the evil and get rid of it, and afresh and immediately to "sanctify themselves."

"Up, sanctify the people," is always God's command. "Lie down and be discouraged," is always our temptation. Our feeling is that it is presumptuous, and even almost impertinent, to go at once to the Lord, after having sinned against Him. It seems as if we ought to suffer the consequences of our sin first for a little while, and endure the accusings of our conscience; and we can hardly believe that the Lord *can* be willing at once to receive us back into loving fellowship with Himself.

A little girl once expressed this feeling to me, with a child's outspoken candor. She had asked whether the Lord Jesus always forgave us for our sins as soon as we asked Him, and I had said, "Yes, of course He does." "*Just* as soon?" she repeated doubtingly. "Yes," I replied, "the very minute we ask, He forgives us." "Well," she said deliberately, "I cannot believe that. I should think He would make us feel sorry for two or three days first. And then I should think He would make us ask Him a great many times, and in a very pretty way too, not just in common talk. And I believe that *is* the way He does, and you need not try to make me think He forgives me right at once, no matter what the Bible says." She only *said* what most Christians *think*, and what is worse, what most Christians act on, making their discouragement and their very remorse separate them infinitely further off from God than their sin would have done. Yet it is so totally contrary to the way we like our children to act toward us, that I wonder how we ever could have conceived such an idea of God. How a mother grieves when a naughty child goes off alone in despairing remorse, and doubts her willingness to forgive; and how, on the other hand, her whole heart goes out in welcoming love to the repentant little one who runs to her at once and begs her forgiveness! Surely our God felt this yearning love when He said to us, "Return, ye backsliding children, and I will heal your backslidings."

The fact is, that the same moment which brings the consciousness of sin ought to bring also the confession and the consciousness of forgiveness. This is especially essential to an unwavering walk in the "life hid with Christ in God," for no separation from Him can be tolerated here for an instant.

We can only walk this path by "looking continually unto Jesus," moment by moment; and if our eyes are turned away from Him to look upon our own sin and our own weakness, we shall leave the path at once. The believer, therefore, who has, as he trusts, entered upon this highway, if he finds himself overcome by sin, must flee with it instantly to the Lord. He must act on I John 1:9, "If we confess our sins, He is faithful and just to forgive us our sins, and to cleanse us from all unrighteousness." He must not hide his sin, and seek to salve it over with excuses, or to push it out of his memory by the lapse of time. But he must do as the children of Israel did, rise up "*early* in the morning," and "*run*" to the place where the evil thing is hidden, and take it out of its hiding-place, and lay it "out before the Lord." He must confess his sin. And then he must stone it with stones, and burn it with fire, and utterly put it away from him, and raise over it a great heap of stones, that it may be forever hidden from his sight. And he must believe, then and there, that God *is*, according to His word, faithful and just to forgive him his sin, and that He does do it; and further, that He also cleanses him from all unrighteousness. He must claim by faith an immediate forgiveness and an immediate cleansing, and must go on trusting harder and more absolutely than ever.

As soon as Israel's sin had been brought to light and put away, at once God's word came again in a message of glorious encouragement: "Fear not, neither be thou dismayed . . . . See, I have given into thy hand the king of Ai, and his people, and his city, and his land." Our courage must rise higher than ever, and we must abandon ourselves more completely to the Lord, that His mighty power may the more perfectly "work in us all the good pleasure of His will." Moreover, we must forget our sin as soon as it is thus confessed and forgiven. We must not dwell on it, and examine it, and indulge in a luxury of distress and remorse. We must not put it on a pedestal, and then walk around it and view it on every side, and so magnify it into a mountain that hides God from our eyes. We must follow the example of Paul, and, "forgetting those things which are behind, and reaching forth unto those things which are before," we must "press toward the mark for the prize of the high calling of God in Christ Jesus."

Let me recall two contrasting illustrations of these things. One was an earnest Christian man, an active worker in the Church, who had been living for several months in an experience of great peace and joy. He was suddenly overcome by a temptation to treat a brother unkindly. Having supposed it to be an impossibility that he could ever so sin again, he was plunged at once into the deepest discouragement, and concluded he had been altogether mistaken, and had never entered into the life of full trust at all. Day by day his discouragement increased until it became despair, and he concluded at last that he had never even been born again, and gave himself up for lost. He spent three years of utter misery, going farther and farther away from God, and being gradually drawn off into one sin after another, until his life was a curse to himself and to all around him. His health failed under the terrible burden, and fears were entertained for his reason. At the end of three years he met a Christian lady, who understood this truth about sin that I have been trying to explain. In a few moments' conversation she found out his trouble, and at once said, "You sinned in that act, there is no doubt about it, and I do not want you to try to excuse it. But have you never confessed it to the Lord and asked Him to forgive you?" "Confessed it!" he exclaimed. "Why, it seems to me I have done nothing but confess it, and entreat God to forgive me, night and day, for all these three dreadful years." "And you have never believed He did forgive you?" asked the lady. "No," said the poor man, "how could I, for I never *felt* as if He did?" "But suppose He had said He forgave you, would not that have done as well as for you to feel it?" "Oh, yes," replied the man; "if God said it, of course I would believe it." "Very well, He does say so," was the lady's answer; and she turned to the verse we have taken above (I John 1:9) and read it aloud. "Now," she continued, "you have been all these three years confessing and confessing your sin, and all the while God's record has been declaring that He was faithful and just to forgive it and to cleanse you, and yet you have never once believed it. You have been 'making God a liar' all this while by refusing to believe His record."

The poor man saw the whole thing, and was dumb with amazement and consternation; and when the lady proposed that they should kneel down, and that he should confess his past unbelief and sin, and should claim, then and there, a present forgiveness and a present cleansing, he obeyed like one in a maze. But the result was glorious. The light broke in, his darkness vanished, and he began aloud to praise God for the wonderful deliverance. In a few minutes his soul was enabled to traverse back by faith the whole long, weary journey that he had been three years in making, and he found himself once more resting in the Lord, and rejoicing in the fulness of His Salvation.

The other illustration was the case of a Christian lady, who had been living in the land of promise a few weeks, and who had had a very bright and victorious experience. Suddenly at the end of that time, she was overcome by a violent burst of anger. For a moment a flood of discouragement swept over her soul. The temptation came, "There now, that shows it was all a mistake. Of course you have been deceived about the whole thing, and have never entered into the life of faith at all. And now you may as well give up altogether, for you never can consecrate yourself any more entirely nor trust any more fully than you did this time; so it is very plain this life of holiness is not for you!" These thoughts flashed through her mind in a moment; but she was well taught in the ways of God, and she said at once, "Yes, I have sinned, and it is very sad. But the Bible says that, if we confess our sins, God is faithful and just to forgive us our sins, and to cleanse us from all unrighteousness; and I believe He will do it." She did not delay a moment, but, while still boiling over with anger, she ran (for she could not walk) into a room where she could be alone, and kneeling down beside the bed she said, "Lord, I confess my sin. I have sinned; I am even at this very moment sinning. I hate it, but I cannot get rid of it. I confess it with shame and confusion of face to thee. And now I believe that, according to thy word, thou dost forgive and thou dost cleanse." She said it out loud, for the inward turmoil was too great for it to be said inside. As the words, "Thou dost forgive and thou dost cleanse," passed her lips, the deliverance came. The Lord said, "Peace, be still!" and there was a great calm. A flood of light and joy burst on her soul, the enemy fled, and she was more than conquered through Him that loved her. The whole thing, the sin and the recovery from it, had occupied not five minutes, and her feet trod more firmly than ever in the blessed highway of holiness. Thus the "valley of Achor" became to her a "door of hope," and she sang afresh and with deeper meaning her song of deliverance, "I will sing unto the Lord, for he hath triumphed gloriously."

The truth is, the only remedy, after all, in every emergency is to trust in the Lord. And if this is all we ought to do, and all we can do, is it not better to do it at once? I have often been brought to a stand by the question, "Well, what *can* I do but trust?" And I have realized at once the folly of seeking for deliverance in any other way by saying to myself, "I shall have to come to simple trusting in the end, and why not come to it at once, now in the beginning." It is a life and walk of *faith* we have entered upon; and if we fail in it, our only recovery must lie in an increase of faith, not in a lessening of it.

Let every failure, then, if any occur, drive you instantly to the Lord, with a more complete abandonment and a more perfect trust; and if you do this, you will find that, sad as it is, your failure has not taken you out of the land of rest, nor broken for long your sweet communion with Him.

Where failure is thus met, a recurrence is far more likely to be prevented than where the soul allows itself to pass through a season of despair and remorse. If it should however sometimes recur, and is always similarly treated, it is sure to become less and less frequent, until finally it ceases altogether. There are some happy souls who learn the whole lesson at once; but the blessing is also upon those who take slower steps and gain a more gradual victory.

Having shown the way of deliverance from failure, I would now say a little as to the causes of failure in this life of full salvation. The causes do not lie in the strength of the temptation, nor in our own weakness, nor above all in any lack in the power or willingness of our Saviour to save us. The promise to Israel was positive: "There shall not any man be able to stand before thee all the days of thy life." And the promise to us is equally positive: "God is faithful, who will not suffer you to be tempted above that ye are able; but will with the temptation also make a way to escape, that ye may be able to bear it." The men of Ai were "but few," and yet the people who had conquered the mighty Jericho "fled before the men of Ai." It was not the strength of their enemy, neither had God failed them. The cause of their defeat lay somewhere else, and the Lord Himself declares it: "Israel hath sinned, and they have also transgressed my covenant which I commanded them: for they have even taken of the accursed thing, and have also stolen, and dissembled also, and they have put it even among their own stuff. Therefore the children of Israel could not stand before their enemies, but turned their backs before their enemies." It was a hidden evil that conquered them. Buried under the earth, in an obscure tent in that vast army, was hidden something against which God had a controversy; and this little hidden thing made the whole army helpless before their enemies. "There is an accursed thing in the midst of thee, O Israel: thou canst not stand before thine enemies until ye take away the accursed thing from among you."

The lesson here is simply this, that anything cherished in the heart which is contrary to the will of God, let it seem ever so insignificant, or be ever so deeply hidden, will cause us to fall before our enemies. Any conscious root of bitterness cherished toward another, any self-seeking, any harsh judgments, any slackness in obeying the voice of the Lord, any doubtful habits or surroundings,—these things or any one of them, consciously indulged, will effectually cripple and paralyze our spiritual life. We may have hidden the evil in the most remote corner of our hearts, and may have covered it over from our sight, refusing even to recognize its existence, although we cannot help being all the time secretly aware that it is there. We may steadily ignore it, and persist in declarations of consecration and full trust; we may be more earnest than ever in our religious duties, and have the eyes of our understanding opened more and more to the truth and the beauty of the life and walk of faith. We may seem to ourselves and to others to have reached an almost impregnable position of victory, and yet we may find ourselves suffering bitter defeats. We may wonder, and question, and despair, and pray. Nothing will do any good until the wrong thing is dug up from its hiding-place, brought out to the light, and laid before God.

The moment, therefore, that a believer who is walking in this interior life meets with a defeat, he must at once seek for the cause, not in the strength of that particular enemy, but in something behind,—

some hidden want of consecration lying at the very center of his being. Just as a headache is not the disease itself, but only a symptom of a disease, situated in some other part of the body, so the failure in such a Christian is only the symptom of an evil, hidden in probably a very different part of his nature.

Sometimes the evil may be hidden even in what at a cursory glance would look like good. Beneath apparent zeal for the truth, may be hidden a judging spirit, or a subtle leaning to our own understanding. Beneath apparent Christian faithfulness may be hidden an absence of Christian love. Beneath an apparently rightful care for our affairs, may be hidden a great want of trust in God. I believe our blessed Guide, the indwelling Holy Spirit, is always secretly discovering these things to us by continual little checks and pangs of conscience, so that we are left without excuse. But it is very easy to disregard His gentle voice, and insist upon it to ourselves that all is right, while the fatal evil continues hidden in our midst, causing defeat in most unexpected quarters.

A capital illustration of this occurred to me once in my housekeeping. We had moved into a new house, and in looking it over to see if it was all ready for occupancy, I noticed in the cellar a very clean-looking cider-cask headed up at both ends. I debated with myself whether I should have it taken out of the cellar and opened to see what was in it, but concluded, as it seemed empty and looked clean, to leave it undisturbed, especially as it would have been quite a piece of work to get it up the stairs. I did not feel quite easy, but reasoned away my scruples and left it. Every spring and fall, when housecleaning time came on, I would remember that cask with a little twinge of my housewifely conscience, feeling I could not quite rest in the thought of a perfectly clean house while it remained unopened, as how did I know but under its fair exterior it contained some hidden evil? Still I managed to quiet my scruples on the subject, thinking always of the trouble it would involve to investigate it; and for two or three years the innocent-looking cask stood quietly in our cellar. Then, most unaccountably, moths began to fill our house. I used every possible precaution against them, and made every effort to eradicate them, but in vain. They increased rapidly, and threatened to ruin everything we had. I suspected our carpets as being the cause, and subjected them to a thorough cleaning. I suspected our furniture, and had it newly upholstered. I suspected all sorts of impossible things. At last the thought of the cask flashed on me. At once I had it brought up out of the cellar and the head knocked in, and I think it safe to say that thousands of moths poured out. The previous occupant of the house must have headed it up with something in it which bred moths, and this was the cause of all my trouble.

Now, I believe that in the same way, some innocent-looking habit or indulgence, some apparently unimportant and safe thing, about which, however, we have now and then little twinges of conscience,—something which is not brought out fairly into the light, and investigated under the searching eye of God,—lies at the root of most of the failure in this interior life. *All* is not given up. Some secret corner is kept locked against the entrance of the Lord. Some evil thing is hidden in the recesses of our hearts, and therefore we cannot stand before our enemies, but find ourselves smitten down in their presence.

In order to prevent failure, or to discover its cause, if we find we have failed, it is necessary to keep continually before us this prayer: "Search me, O God, and know my heart; try me and know my thoughts; and see if there be any wicked way in me, and lead me in the way everlasting."

Let me beg of you, however, dear Christians, do not think, because I have said all this about failure, that I believe in it. There is no necessity for it whatever. The Lord Jesus *is* able, according to the declaration concerning Him, to deliver us out of the hands of our enemies, that we may "serve him without fear, in holiness and righteousness before him all the days of our life." Let us then pray, every one of us, day and night, "Lord, keep us from sinning, and make us living witnesses of Thy mighty power to save to the uttermost"; and let us never be satisfied until we are so pliable in His hands, and have learned so to trust Him, that He will be able to "make us perfect in every good work to do his will, working in us that which is well pleasing in his sight, through Jesus Christ; to whom be glory for ever and ever. Amen!"

CHAPTER TWELVE

Is God in Everything?

ONE OF THE GREATEST OBSTACLES TO AN UNWAVERING experience in the interior life is the difficulty of seeing God in everything. People say, "I can easily submit to things that come from God; but I cannot submit to man, and most of my trials and crosses come through human instrumentality." Or they say, "It is all well enough to talk of trusting; but when I commit a matter to God, man is sure to come in and disarrange it all; and while I have no difficulty in trusting God, I do see serious difficulties in the way of trusting men."

This is no imaginary trouble, but is of vital importance; and if it cannot be met, it does really make the life of faith an impossible and visionary theory. For nearly everything in life comes to us through human instrumentalities, and most of our trials are the result of somebody's failure, or ignorance, or carelessness, or sin. We know God cannot be the author of these things; and yet, unless He is the agent in the matter, how can we say to Him about it, "Thy will be done"?

Besides, what good is there in trusting our affairs

to God, if, after all, man is to be allowed to come in and disarrange them; and how is it possible to live by faith, if human agencies, in which it would be wrong and foolish to trust, are to have a prevailing influence in moulding our lives?

Moreover, things in which we can see God's hand always have a sweetness in them that consoles while it wounds; but the trials inflicted by man are full of nothing but bitterness.

What is needed, then, is to see God in everything, and to receive everything directly from His hands, with no intervention of second causes; and it is to just this that we must be brought before we can know an abiding experience of entire abandonment and perfect trust. Our abandonment must be to God, not to man; and our trust must be in Him, not in any arm of flesh, or we shall fail at the first trial.

The question here confronts us at once, "But is God in everything, and have we any warrant from the Scripture for receiving everything from His hands without regarding the second causes that may have been instrumental in bringing them about?" I answer to this, unhesitatingly, Yes. To the children of God, everything comes directly from their Father's hand, no matter who or what may have been the apparent agents. There are no "second causes" for them.

The whole teaching of Scripture asserts and implies this. Not a sparrow falls to the ground without our Father. The very hairs of our head are all numbered. We are not to be careful about anything, because our Father cares for us. We are not to avenge ourselves, because our Father has charged Himself with our defense. We are not to fear, for the Lord is on our side. No one can be against us, because He is for us. We shall not want, for He is our Shepherd. When we pass through the rivers they shall not overflow us, and when we walk through the fire we shall not be burned, because He will be with us. He shuts the mouths of lions, that they cannot hurt us. "He delivereth and rescueth." "He changeth the times and the seasons; he removeth kings and setteth up kings." A man's heart is in His hand, and, "as the rivers of water, he turneth it whithersoever he will." He ruleth over all the kingdoms of the heathen; and in His hand there is power and might, "so that none is able to withstand" Him. "He ruleth the raging of the sea; when the waves thereof arise, he stilleth them." He "bringeth the counsel of the heathen to naught; he maketh the devices of the people of none effect." "Whatsoever the Lord pleaseth, that doeth he, in heaven and in earth, in the seas and all deep places." "Lo, these are parts of his ways: but how little a portion is heard of him? But the thunder of his power who can understand?" "Hast thou not known? hast thou not heard, that the everlasting God, the Lord, the Creator of the ends of the earth, fainteth not, neither is weary? There is no searching of his understanding."

And it is this very God who is declared to be "our refuge and strength, a very present help in trouble. Therefore will not we fear, though the earth be removed, and though the mountains be carried into the midst of the sea; though the waters thereof roar and be troubled, though the mountains shake with the swelling thereof." "I will say of the Lord, he is my refuge and my fortress: my God; in him will I trust. Surely he shall deliver thee from the snare of the fowler, and from the noisome pestilence. He shall cover thee with his feathers, and under his wings shalt thou trust: his truth shall be thy shield and buckler. Thou shalt not be afraid for the terror by night; nor for the arrow that flieth by day; nor for the pestilence that walketh in darkness; nor for the destruction that wasteth at noonday. A thousand shall fall at thy side, and ten thousand at thy right hand; but it shall not come nigh thee . . . . Because thou hast made the Lord, which is my refuge, even the most High, thy habitation; there shall no evil befall thee, neither shall any plague come nigh thy dwelling. For he shall give his angels charge over thee, to keep thee in all thy ways." "Be content, therefore, with such things as ye have: for he hath said, I will never leave thee nor forsake thee. So that we may boldly say, The Lord is my helper, and I will not fear what man shall do unto me."

To my own mind, these scriptures, and many others like them, settle forever the question as to the power of "second causes" in the life of the children of God. Second causes must all be under the control of our Father, and not one of them can touch us except with His knowledge and by His permission. It may be the sin of man that originates the action, and therefore the thing itself cannot be said to be the will of God; but by the time it reaches us it has become God's will for us, and must be accepted as directly from His hands. No man or company of men, no power in earth or heaven, can touch that soul which is abiding in Christ, without first passing through His encircling presence, and receiving the seal of His permission. If God be for us, it matters not who may be against us; nothing can disturb or harm us, except He shall see that it is best for us, and shall stand aside to let it pass.

An earthly parent's care for his helpless child is a feeble illustration of this. If the child is in its father's arms, nothing can touch it without that father's consent, unless he is too weak to prevent it. And even if this should be the case, he suffers the harm first in his own person before he allows it to reach his child. If an earthly parent would thus care for his little helpless one, how much more will our Heavenly Father, whose love is infinitely greater, and whose strength and wisdom can never be baffled, care for us! I am afraid there are some, even of God's own children, who scarcely think that He is equal to themselves in tenderness, and love, and thoughtful care; and who, in their secret thoughts, charge Him with a neglect and indifference of which they would feel themselves incapable. The truth really is that His care is infinitely superior to any possibilities of human care; and that He, who counts the very hairs of our heads, and suffers not a sparrow to fall without Him, takes note of the minutest matters that can affect the lives of His children, and regulates them all according to His own perfect will, let their origin be what they may.

The instances of this are numberless. Take Joseph. What could have seemed more apparently on the face of it to be the result of sin, and utterly contrary to the will of God, than the action of his brethren in selling him into slavery? And yet Joseph, in speaking of it said, "As for you, ye thought evil against me; but God meant it unto good." "Now therefore be not grieved, nor angry with yourselves, that ye sold me hither: for God did send me before you to preserve life." It was undoubtedly sin in Joseph's brethren, but by the time it had reached Joseph it had become God's will for him, and was, in truth, though he did not see it then, the greatest blessing of his whole life. And thus we see how God can make even "the wrath of man to praise Him," and how all things, even the sins of others, "shall work together for good to them that love him."

I learned this lesson practically and experimentally, long years before I knew the scriptural truth concerning it. I was attending a prayer-meeting held in the interests of the life of faith, when a strange lady rose to speak, and I looked at her, wondering who she could be, little thinking she was to bring a message to my soul which would teach me a grand practical lesson. She said she had great difficulty in living the life of faith, on account of the second causes that seemed to her to control nearly everything that concerned her. Her perplexity became so great that at last she began to ask God to teach her the truth about it, whether He really was in everything or not. After praying this for a few days, she had what she described as a vision. She thought she was in a perfectly dark place, and that there advanced toward her, from a distance, a body of light which gradually surrounded and enveloped her and everything around her. As it approached, a voice seemed to say, "This is

the presence of God! This is the presence of God!"
While surrounded with this presence, all the great
and awful things in life seemed to pass before her,—
fighting armies, wicked men, raging beasts, storms
and pestilences, sin and suffering of every kind. She
shrank back at first in terror; but she soon saw that
the presence of God so surrounded and enveloped
herself and each one of these things that not a lion
could reach out its paw, nor a bullet fly through the
air, except as the presence of God moved out of the
way to permit it. And she saw that if there were ever
so thin a film, as it were, of this glorious Presence
between herself and the most terrible violence, not a
hair of her head could be ruffled, nor anything touch
her, except as the Presence divided to let the evil
through. Then all the small and annoying things of
life passed before her; and equally she saw that there
also she was so enveloped in this presence of God that
not a cross look, nor a harsh word, nor petty trial of
any kind could affect her, unless God's encircling
presence moved out of the way to let it.

Her difficulty vanished. Her question was answered forever. God *was* in everything; and to her
henceforth there were no second causes. She saw that
her life came to her, day by day and hour by hour,
directly from the hand of God, let the agencies which
should seem to control it be what they might. And
never again had she found any difficulty in an abiding
consent to His will and an unwavering trust in His
care.

Would that it were only possible to make every
Christian see this truth as plainly as I see it! For I am

convinced it is the only clue to a completely restful life. Nothing else will enable a soul to live only in the present moment, as we are commanded to do, and to take no thought for the morrow. Nothing else will take all the risks and "supposes" out of a Christian's life, and enable him to say, "Surely goodness and mercy shall follow me all the days of my life." Under God's care we run no risks. I once heard of a poor colored woman who earned a precarious living by daily labor, but who was a joyous, triumphant Christian. "Ah, Nancy," said a gloomy Christian lady to her one day, who almost disapproved of her constant cheerfulness, and yet envied it,—"Ah, Nancy, it is all well enough to be happy now, but I should think the thoughts of your future would sober you. Only suppose, for instance, that you should have a spell of sickness, and be unable to work; or suppose your present employers should move away, and no one else should give you anything to do; or suppose—" "Stop!" cried Nancy, "I never supposes. De Lord is my Shepherd, and I knows I shall not want. And, honey," she added to her gloomy friend, "it's all dem *supposes* as is makin' you so mis'able. You'd better give dem all up, and just trust de Lord."

Nothing else but this seeing God in everything will make us loving and patient with those who annoy and trouble us. They will be to us then only the instruments for accomplishing His tender and wise purposes toward us, and we shall even find ourselves at last inwardly thanking them for the blessings they bring.

Nothing else will completely put an end to all

murmuring or rebelling thoughts. Christians often feel at liberty to murmur against man, when they would not dare to murmur against God. Therefore this way of receiving things would make it impossible ever to murmur. If our Father permits a trial to come, it must be because the trial is the sweetest and best thing that could happen to us, and we must accept it with thanks from His dear hand. This does not mean, however, that we must like or enjoy the trial itself, but that we must like God's will in the trial; and it is not hard to do this when we have learned to know that His will is the will of love, and is therefore always lovely.

A very good illustration of this may be found in the familiar fact of a mother giving medicine to her dearly loved child. The bottle *holds* the medicine, but the mother *gives* it; and the bottle is not responsible, but the mother. No matter how full her closet may be of bottles of medicine, the mother will not allow one drop to be given to the child unless she believes it will be good for it; but when she does believe it will be good for her darling, the very depth of her love compels her to force it on the child, no matter how bitter may be its taste.

The human beings around us are often the bottles that hold our medicine, but it is our Father's hand of love that pours out the medicine, and compels us to drink it. The human bottle is the "second cause" of our trial; but it has no real agency in it, for the medicine that these human "bottles" hold is prescribed for us and given to us by the Great Physician of our souls, who is seeking thereby to heal all our spiritual diseases.

For instance, I know no better medicine to cure the disease of irritability than to be compelled to live with a human "bottle" of sensitiveness whom we are bound to consider and yield to.

Shall we rebel against the human bottles then? Shall we not rather take thankfully from our Father's hand the medicine they contain, and, losing sight of the second cause, say joyfully, "Thy will be done," in everything that comes to us, no matter what its source may be?

This way of seeing our Father in everything makes life one long thanksgiving, and gives a rest of heart, and, more than that, a gayety of spirit that is unspeakable.

Faber says, in his wonderful hymn on the Will of God,—

> "I know not what it is to doubt,
>   My heart is always gay;
> I run no risks, for, come what will,
>   Thou always hast Thy way."

Since, therefore, God is sure to have His own way concerning those who abandon themselves to Him in perfect trust, into what wonderful green pastures of inward rest, and beside what blessedly still waters of inward refreshment, will He lead all such!

If the will of God is our will, and if He always has His way, then we always have our way also, and we reign in a perpetual kingdom. He who sides with God cannot fail to win in every encounter; and whether the result shall be joy or sorrow, failure or success, death or life, we may under all circumstances join in the Apostle's shout of victory, "Thanks be unto God, which always causeth us to triumph in Christ!"

THE WILL OF GOD *

Thou sweet, beloved Will of God,
　My anchor ground, my fortress hill,
My spirit's silent, fair abode,
　In Thee I hide me, and am still.

O Will, that willest good alone,
　Lead Thou the way, Thou guidest best;
A little child I follow on,
　And trusting lean upon Thy breast.

Thy beautiful, sweet Will, my God,
　Holds fast in Its sublime embrace
My captive will, a gladsome bird,
　Prisoned in such a realm of grace.

Within this place of certain good,
　Love ever more expands her wings;
Or, nestling in Thy perfect choice,
　Abides content with what it brings.

Oh, sweetest burden, lightest yoke,
　It lifts, it bears my happy soul,
It giveth wings to this poor heart:
　My freedom is Thy grand control.

Upon God's Will I lay me down,
　As child upon its mother's breast;
No silken couch, nor softest bed,
　Could ever give me such sweet rest.

Thy wonderful, grand Will, my God
　With triumph now I make It mine,
And Love shall cry a jealous *Yes,*
　To every dear command of Thine.

* From "Hymns of Consecration."

PART III RESULTS

CHAPTER THIRTEEN

Bondage or Liberty

IT IS A FACT BEYOND QUESTION THAT THERE ARE two kinds of Christian experience, one of which is an experience of bondage, and the other an experience of liberty.

In the first case the soul is controlled by a stern sense of duty, and obeys the law of God, either from fear of punishment or from expectation of wages. In the other case the controlling power is an inward life-principle that works out, by the force of its own motions or instincts, the will of the Divine Life-giver, without fear of punishment or hope of reward. In the first the Christian is a servant, and works for hire; in the second he is a son, and works for love.

There ought not, it is true, to be this contrast in the experience of Christians, for to "walk at liberty" is plainly their only right and normal condition; but as we have to deal with what is rather than with what ought to be we cannot shut our eyes to the sad condition of bondage in which so many of God's children pass a large part of their Christian lives. The reason of this, and the remedy for it are not difficult to find.

The reason is legality, and the remedy is Christ.

Nowhere do we find those two forms or stages of Christian life more fully developed and contrasted than in the Epistle to the Galatians. The occasion of its being written was that some Jewish brethren had come among the churches in Galatia, and, by representing that certain forms and ceremonies were necessary to their salvation, had tried to draw them away from the liberty of the gospel. And with these teachers Peter had allowed himself to unite. Therefore Paul reproves, not only the Galatians, but also Peter himself.

Neither Peter nor the Galatians had committed any moral sin; but they had committed a spiritual sin. They had got into a wrong attitude of soul toward God,—a legal attitude. They had begun, as Christians generally do, in the right attitude; that is, they had entered by the "hearing of faith" into the spiritual life. But when it came to a question of how they were to live in this life, they had changed their ground. They had sought to substitute works for faith. Having "begun in the Spirit," they were now seeking to be "made perfect by the flesh." They had, in short, descended, in their Christian living, from the plane of life to the plane of law.

An illustration will help us to understand this. Here are two men neither of whom steals. Outwardly their actions are equally honest; but inwardly there is a vital difference. One man has a dishonest nature that wants to steal, and is only deterred by the fear of a penalty; while the other possesses an honest nature that hates thieving, and could not be induced to steal, even by the hope of a reward. The one is honest in the spirit; the other is honest only in the flesh. No words are needed to say of which sort the Christian life is meant to be.

We are, however, continually tempted to forget that it is not what men *do* that is the vital matter, but rather what they *are*. In Christ Jesus neither legal observances nor the omission of legal observances avails anything, "but a new creature." God is a great deal more concerned about our really *being* "new creatures" than about anything else; because He knows that if we *are* right as to our inward being, we shall certainly *do* right as to our outward actions. We may, in fact, sometimes even *do* right without *being* right at all; and it is very evident that no doing of this kind has any vitality in it, nor is of any real account. The essential thing, therefore, is character; and *doing* is valuable only as it is an indication of *being*.

Paul was grieved with the Galatian Christians because they seemed to have lost sight of this vital truth, that the inward life, the "new creature," was the only thing that availed. They had begun on this plane, but they had "fallen from grace" to a lower plane, where the "oldness of the letter" was put in place of the "newness of the spirit." "Christ is become of no effect unto you, whosoever of you are justified by the law; ye are fallen from grace."

This passage is the only one in which the expression "fallen from grace" is used in the New Testament; and it means that the Galatians had made the mistake of thinking that something else besides Christ was necessary for their right Christian living. The

Jewish brethren who had come among them had taught them that Christ alone was not enough, but that obedience to the ceremonial law must be added.

They had therefore imported, as being necessary for salvation, some ceremonies out of the Jewish ritual, and had tried to compel the "Gentiles to live as do the Jews." Modern Christians are greatly surprised at them, and wonder how they could have been so legal. But is there not the same temptation to legality, under a different form, among these same modern Christians? *They* added the ceremonial law; *we* add resolutions, or agonizings, or Christian work, or churchgoing, or religious ceremonies of one sort or another; and what is there, therefore, to choose between us and them? It does not make much difference what you add; the wrong thing is to add anything at all.

We are full of condemnation of the "Jew's religion," because it "frustrates the grace of God," and makes Christ to be "dead in vain" by depending upon outward deeds and outward ceremonies to bring salvation. But I fear there is a great deal of the "Jew's religion" mixed up with the Christian religion now, just as there was among these Galatian Christians, and that the grace of God is as much frustrated by our legality as it was by theirs; although ours may manifest itself in a slightly different form.

The following contrasts may help some to understand the difference between these two kinds of religion, and may also enable them to discover where the secret of their own experience of legal bondage lies:

The law says, This *do* and thou shalt live.

The law says, *Pay* me that thou owest.

The law says, *Make* you a new heart and a new spirit.

The law says, Thou shalt love the Lord thy God with all thy heart, and with all thy soul, and with all thy mind.

The law says, *Cursed* is every one who continueth not in all things written in the book of the law to do them.

The law says, The *wages* of sin is death.

The law *demands* holiness.

The law says, *Do.*

The law *extorts* the unwilling service of a bondman.

The law makes blessings the result of *obedience.*

The law places the day of rest at the end of the week's work.

The law says, *If.*

The gospel says, *Live*, and then thou shalt do.

The gospel says, I frankly *forgive* thee all.

The gospel says, A new heart will I *give* you, and a new spirit will I put within you.

The gospel says, Herein is love, not that we loved God, but that He loved us and sent His son to be the propitiation for our sins.

The gospel says, *Blessed* is the man whose iniquities are forgiven, and whose sins are covered.

The gospel says, The *gift* of God is eternal life through Jesus Christ our Lord.

The gospel *gives* holiness.

The gospel says, *Done.*

The gospel *wins* the loving service of a son and freeman.

The gospel makes obedience the result of *blessings.*

The gospel places it at its beginning.

The gospel says, *Therefore.*

| The law was given for the restraint of the old man. | The gospel was given to bring liberty to the new man. |
| Under the law, salvation was *wages*. | Under the gospel, salvation is a *gift*. |

These two forms of the religious life began at exactly opposite ends. The religion of legality is as though a man should decide to have an apple orchard, and should try to make one by first getting some apples of the kind desired, and then getting a tree and fastening the apples on its branches, and then getting roots to fasten to the trunk, and finally purchasing a field in which to plant his manufactured tree. That is, first the fruit, second the branches, third the root, fourth the field. But the religion of grace follows a different order. It begins at the root, and grows up, and blossoms out into flowers and fruit.

Paul tells us that the law "is our schoolmaster," not our saviour; and he emphasizes the fact that it is our schoolmaster only for the purpose of bringing us to Christ, for, after faith in Christ is come, he declares, we are no longer to be under a schoolmaster. He uses the contrast between a servant and a son as an illustration of his meaning. "Wherefore," he says, "thou art no more a servant, but a son," and he entreats us, because of this, to "stand fast in the liberty wherewith Christ hath made us free, and be not entangled again with the yoke of bondage."

It is as if a woman had been a servant in a house, paid for her work in weekly wages, and under the law of her master, whom she had tried to please, but towards whom her service had been one of duty only. Finally, however, the master offers her his love, and lifts her up from the place of a servant to be his bride and to share his fortunes. At once the whole spirit of her service is changed. She may perhaps continue to do the same things that she did before, but she does them now altogether from a different motive. The old sense of duty is lost in the new sense of love. The cold word "master" is transformed into the loving word "husband." "And it shall be at that day, saith the Lord, that thou shalt call me Ishi [my husband], and shalt call me no more Baali [my lord]."

But imagine this bride beginning after a while to look back upon her low estate, and to be so overwhelmed by the retrospect as to feel unworthy of union with her husband, and to lose consequently the inward sense of this union. Who can doubt that very soon the old sense of working for wages would drive out the new sense of working for love, and in spirit the old name of "my master" would again take the place of the new name of "my husband"?

We exclaim at the folly of such a course. But is not this just what happens to many Christians now? The servitude of duty takes the place of the service of love; and God is looked upon as the stern taskmaster who demands our obedience, instead of the loving Father who wins it.

We all know that nothing so destroys the sweetness of any relation as the creeping in of this legal spirit. The moment a husband and wife cease to per-

form their services to each other out of a heart of love
and union, and begin to perform them from a sense
of duty alone, that moment the sweetness of the
union is lost, and the marriage tie becomes a bondage,
and things that were a joy before are turned into
crosses. This lies at the bottom, I think, of the current
idea of "taking up the cross" in the Christian Church.
We think it means doing something we ought to do,
but dislike to do. And such service is thought to be
very meritorious toward God; although we all know
very well that we would not endure it a moment as
toward ourselves. What wife could endure it if her
husband should use toward her the language that
Christians are continually using toward the Lord; if
he should say, for instance, every morning, as he went
out to business, "I am going to work for you to-day,
but I wish you to know that it is a very great cross, and
I hardly know how to bear it." O what husband would
like such language from his wife? No wonder Paul
was alarmed when he found there was danger of a
legal spirit such as this creeping into the Church of
Christ.

Legal Christians do not deny Christ; they only
seek to add something to Christ. Their idea is, Christ
and—something besides. Perhaps it is Christ and
good works, or Christ and earnest feelings, or Christ
and clear doctrines, or Christ and certain religious
performances. All these are good in themselves, and
good as the results of fruits of salvation; but to add
anything to Christ, no matter how good it may be, as
the procuring cause of salvation, is to deny His completeness, and to exalt self. Men will undergo many

painful self-sacrifices rather than take the place of utter helplessness and worthlessness. A man will gladly be a Saint Simeon Stylites or even a fakir, if only it is self that does it, so that self may share the glory. And a religion of bondage always exalts self. It is what *I* do,—*my* efforts, *my* wrestlings, *my* faithfulness. But a religion of liberty leaves self nothing to glory in; it is all Christ, and what He does, and what He is, and how wonderfully He saves. The child does not boast of itself, but of its father and mother; and our souls can "make their boast in the Lord," when, in this life of liberty, we have learned to know that He and He alone is the sufficient supply for our every need.

We are the children of God, and therefore of course His heirs; and our possessions come to us, not by working for them, but by inheritance from our Father. Ah, dear friends, how little some of you act like the "heirs of God"! How poverty-stricken you are, and how hard you work for the little you do possess!

You may perhaps point to the results of your legal working or your asceticism, which, it is true, do seem to have a "show of wisdom in will worship, and humility, and neglecting of the body," as being a proof of the rightness of your course. But I am convinced that whatever really good results there are, have come in spite of, and not because of, your legal working.

I had a friend once whose Christian life was a life of bondage. She worked for her salvation harder than any slave ever worked to purchase his freedom. Among other things, she never felt as if the day could go right for herself or any of her family unless she started it with a long season of wrestling, and agonizing, and conflict; "winding up her machine," I called it. One day we were talking about it together, and she was telling me of the hardness and bondage of her Christian life, and was wondering what the Bible *could* mean when it said Christ's yoke was easy and His burden light. I told her that I thought she must have got things wrong somehow, that the Bible always expressed the truth of our relationships with God by using figures that did not admit of any such wrestlings and agonizings as she described. "What would you think," I asked, "of children that had to wrestle and agonize with their parents every morning for their necessary food and clothing, or of sheep that had to wrestle with their shepherd before they could secure the necessary care?" "Of course I see that would be all wrong," she said; "but, then, why do I have such good times after I have gone through these conflicts?" This puzzled me for a moment, but then I asked, "what brings about those good times finally?" "Why, finally," she replied, "I come to the point of trusting the Lord." "Suppose you should come to that point to begin with?" I asked. "Oh," she replied, with a sudden illumination, "I never until this minute thought that I might!"

Christ says that except we "become as little children" we cannot enter into the kingdom of Heaven. But it is impossible to get the child-spirit until the servant-spirit has disappeared. Notice, I do not say the spirit of service, but the servant-spirit. Every good child is filled with the spirit of service, but ought not to have anything of the servant-spirit. The child serves from love; the servant works for wages.

If a child of loving parents should get the idea that its parents would not give it food and clothing unless it earned them in some way, all the sweetness of the relationship between parent and child would be destroyed. I knew a little girl who did get this idea, and who went around the neighborhood asking at the doors for work, that she might earn a little money to buy herself some clothes. It nearly broke the hearts of her parents when they discovered it. Legal Christians grieve the heart of their Heavenly Father far more than they dream by letting the servant-spirit creep into their relations with Him. As soon as we begin to "work for our living" in spiritual things, we have stepped out of the son's place into the servant's, and have "fallen from grace."

One servant, of whom we read in the Bible, thought his lord was a "hard master," and the spirit of bondage makes us think the same now. How many Christians there are who have bowed their necks to the yoke of Christ as to a "yoke of bondage," and have read His declaration that His yoke is easy as though it were a fairy tale, and gone on their way, never dreaming that it was meant to be actually realized as a fact! In truth, so deeply is the idea that the Christian life is a species of bondage ingrained in the Church that whenever any of the children of God find themselves "walking at liberty" they at once begin to think there must be something wrong in their experience, because they no longer find anything to be a "cross" to them. As well might the wife think there must be something wrong in her love for her husband when she finds all her services for him are a pleasure instead of a trial!

Sometimes I think that the whole secret of the Christian life that I have been trying to describe, is revealed in the child relationship. Nothing more is needed than just to believe that God is as good a Father as the best ideal earthly father, and that the relationship of a Christian to Him is just the same as that of a child to its parent in this world. Children do not need to carry about in their own pockets the money for their support. If the father has plenty, that satisfies them, and is a great deal better than if it were in the child's own possession, since in that case it might get lost. In the same way it is not necessary for Christians to have all their spiritual possessions in their own keeping. It is far better that their riches should be stored up for them in Christ, and that when they want anything they should receive it direct from His hands. He of God is "made unto us wisdom, and righteousness, and sanctification, and redemption," and apart from Him we have nothing.

When people are comparative strangers to one another they cannot with any comfort receive great gifts from each other. But when they are united in spirit, with a bond of true love between them, then, no matter how great the gifts may be that pass from one to the other, they can be accepted without any feeling of embarrassment of obligation on either side.

This principle holds good in the spiritual life. When Christians are living far off from God they cannot be brought to accept any great gifts from Him. They feel as if they were too unworthy, and did not deserve such gifts; and, even when He puts the blessing into their very laps, as it were, their false humility prevents them from seeing it, and they go on their way without it.

But when Christians get near enough to the Lord to feel the true spirit of adoption, they are ready to accept with delight all the blessings He has in store for them, and never think anything too much to receive. For then they discover that He is only eager, as parents are, to pour out every good gift upon His children, and that, in fact, all things are theirs, because they are Christ's, and Christ is God's.

Sometimes a great mystery is made out of the life hid with Christ in God, as though it were a strange mystical thing that ordinary people could not understand. But this contrast between bondage and liberty makes it very plain. It is only to find out that we really are "no more servants, but sons," and practically to enter into the blessed privileges of this relationship. All can understand what it is to be a little child; there is no mystery about that. God did not use the figure of Father and children without knowing all that this relationship implies; and those, therefore, who know Him as their Father know the whole secret. They are their Father's heirs, and may enter now into possession of all that is necessary for their present needs. They will therefore be very simple in their prayers. "Lord," they will say, "I am Thy child, and I need such and such things." "My child," He answers, "all things are thine in Christ; come and take just what thou needest."

Where the executors are honorable men, the heirs to an estate are not obliged to "wrestle" for their inheritance. The executors are appointed, not to keep them out of it, but to help them into possession of it. I sometimes think Christians look upon our Lord as someone appointed to keep them out of their possessions instead of the one who has come to bring them in. They little know how such an implication grieves and dishonors Him.

It is because legal Christians do not know the truth of their relationship to God, as children to a father, and do not recognize His fatherly heart toward them, that they are in bondage. When they do recognize it, the spirit of bondage becomes impossible to them.

Our liberty must come, therefore, from an understanding of the mind and thoughts of God towards us.

What are the facts of the case? If He has called us only to the servants' place, then the Christians whose lives are lives of weary bondage are right. But if He has called us to be children and heirs, if we are His friends, His brethren, His bride, how sadly and grievously wrong we are in being entangled under any yoke of bondage whatever, no matter how pious a yoke it may seem to be!

The thought of bondage is utterly abhorrent to any of earth's true relationships, and surely it must be more repugnant to heavenly relationship. It will not, of course, hinder the final entrance of the poor enslaved soul into its heavenly rest, but it will, I am sure, put it into the sad condition of those who are described in I Corinthians 3:11–15. Their work shall be burned, and they shall suffer loss; yet they themselves shall be saved, but so as by fire.

"Against such there is no law," is the Divine sentence concerning all who love and walk in the Spirit; and you shall find it most blessedly true in your own experience if you will but lay aside all self-effort and self-dependence of every kind, and will consent to let Christ live in you, and work in you, and be your indwelling life.

The man who lives by the power of an inward righteous nature is not under bondage to the outward law of righteousness; but he who is restrained by the outward law alone, without the inward restraint of a righteous nature, is a slave to the law. The one fulfils the law in his soul, and is therefore free. The other rebels against the law in his soul, and is therefore bound.

I would that every child of God did but know the deliverance from bondage which I have tried to set forth!

Let me entreat of you, my readers, to abandon yourselves so utterly to the Lord Jesus Christ that He may be able to "work in you all the good pleasure of his will," and may, by the law of the Spirit of Life in Himself, deliver you from every other law that could possibly enslave you.

CHAPTER FOURTEEN

Growth

ONE GREAT OBJECTION MADE AGAINST THOSE WHO AD-
vocate this life of faith is that they do not teach a
growth in grace. They are supposed to teach that the
soul arrives in one moment at a state of perfection,
beyond which there is no advance, and that all the
exhortations in the Scriptures that point towards
growth and development are rendered void by this
teaching.

Since exactly the opposite of this is true, I will try,
if possible, to answer these objections, and to show
what seems to me the Scriptural way of growing, and
in what place the soul must be in order to grow.

The text which is most frequently quoted, is II
Peter 3:18: "But grow in grace, and in the knowledge
of our Lord and Saviour Jesus Christ." Now, this text
expresses exactly what we who teach this life of faith
believe to be God's will for us, and what we also believe He has made it possible for us to experience. We
accept, in their very fullest meaning, all the commands and promises concerning our being no more
children, and our growing up into Christ in all things,

176

until we come unto a perfect man, unto the "measure of the stature of the fulness of Christ." We rejoice that we need not continue always to be babes, needing milk; but that we may, by reason of use and development, become such as have need of strong meat, skilful in the word of righteousness, and able to discern both good and evil. And none would grieve more than we ourselves at the thought of any finality in the Christian life beyond which there could be no advance.

But, then, we believe in a growing that does really produce continually progressing maturity, and in a development that, as a fact, does bring forth ripe fruit. We expect to reach the aim set before us; and if we do not find ourselves on the way towards it we feel sure there must be some fault in our growing. No parent would be satisfied with the growth of his child if day after day, and year after year, it remained the same helpless babe it was in the first months of its life. And no farmer would feel comfortable under such growing of his grain as should stop short at the blade, and never produce the ear, or the full corn in the ear. Growth, to be real, must be progressive, and the days and weeks and months should bring a development and increase of maturity in the thing growing. But is this the case with a large part of that which is called growth in grace? Does not the very Christian who is the most strenuous in his longings and his efforts after this growth too often find that, at the end of the year, he is not as far on in his Christian experience as at the beginning, and that his zeal, and his devotedness, and his separation from the world, are not as whole-souled or complete as when his Christian life first began?

I was once urging upon a company of Christians the duty and privilege of an immediate and definite step into the "land of promise," when a lady of great intelligence interrupted me with what she evidently felt to be a complete rebuttal of all I had been saying by exclaiming, "Ah! but, Mrs. Smith, I believe in *growing* in grace." "How long have *you* been growing?" I asked. "About twenty-five years," was her answer. "And how much more unworldly and devoted to the Lord are you now, than when your Christian life began?" I continued. "Alas!" was the answer, "I fear I am not nearly so much so." And with this answer her eyes were opened to see that at all events her way of growing had not been successful, but quite the reverse.

The trouble with her, and with every other such case, is simply this: they are trying to grow *into* grace instead of *in* it. They are like a rosebush planted by a gardener in the hard, stony path with a view to its growing *into* the flower-bed, and which has of course dwindled and withered in consequence instead of flourishing and maturing. The children of Israel, wandering in the wilderness, are a perfect picture of this sort of growing. They were traveling about for forty years, taking many weary steps, and finding but little rest from their wanderings; and yet, at the end of it all, were no nearer the promised land than they were at the beginning. When they started on their wanderings at Kadesh Barnea, they were at the borders of the land, and a few steps would have taken them into it. When they ended their wanderings in the plains of Moab, they were also at its borders; only with this difference, that now there was a river to cross, which at first there would not have been. All their wanderings and fightings in the wilderness had not put them in possession of one inch of the promised land. In order to get possession of this land it was necessary first to be in it; and in order to grow in grace it is necessary first to be planted in grace. When once in the land, however, their conquest was rapid; and when once planted in grace, the growth of the spiritual life becomes vigorous and rapid beyond all conceiving. For grace is a most fruitful soil, and the plants that grow therein are plants of a marvelous growth. They are tended by a Divine Husbandman, and are warmed by the Sun of Righteousness, and watered by the dew from Heaven. Surely it is no wonder that they bring forth fruit, "some an hundred-fold, some sixty-fold, some thirty-fold."

But, it will be asked, what is meant by growing in grace? It is difficult to answer this question, because so few people have any conception of what the grace of God really is. To say that it is free unmerited favor only expresses a little of its meaning. It is the unhindered, wondrous, boundless love of God, poured out upon us in an infinite variety of ways, without stint or measure, not according to our deserving, but according to His measureless heart of love, which passeth knowledge, so unfathomable are its heights and depths. I sometimes think a totally different meaning is given to the word "love" when it is associated with God from that which we so well understand in its human application. We seem to consider that Divine love is hard and self-seeking and distant, concerned about its own glory, and indifferent to the fate of others. But if ever human love was tender and self-sacrificing and devoted, if ever it could bear and forbear, if ever it could suffer gladly for its loved one, if ever it was willing to pour itself out in a lavish abandonment for the comfort or pleasure of its objects, then infinitely more is Divine love tender and self-sacrificing and devoted, and glad to bear and forbear, and suffer, and eager to lavish its best of gifts and blessings upon the objects of its love. Put together all the tenderest love you know of, dear reader, the deepest you have ever felt, and the strongest that has ever been poured out upon you, and heap upon it all the love of all the loving human hearts in the world, and then multiply it by infinity, and you will begin perhaps to have some faint glimpses of the love and grace of God!

In order to "grow in grace," therefore, the soul must be planted in the very heart of this Divine love, be enveloped by it, steeped in it. It must let itself out to the joy of it, and must refuse to know anything else. It must grow in the apprehension of it, day by day, it must entrust everything to its care, and must have no shadow of doubt but that it will surely order all things well.

To grow in grace is opposed to all growth in self-dependence or self-effort,—to all legality, in fact, of every kind. It is to put our growing, as well as everything else, into the hands of the Lord and leave it with him. It is to be so satisfied with our Husbandman, and with His skill and wisdom, that not a question will cross our minds as to His mode of treatment or His plan of cultivation. It is to grow as the lilies grow, or as the babies grow, without care and without anxiety; to grow by the power of an inward life-principle that cannot help but grow; to grow because we live, and therefore must grow; to grow because He who has planted us has planted a growing thing, and has made us on purpose to grow.

Surely this is what our Lord meant when He said, "Consider the lilies, how they grow: they toil not, neither do they spin: and yet I say unto you, that even Solomon in all his glory was not arrayed like one of these." Or, when He says again, "Which of you by taking thought can add one cubit unto his stature?" There is no effort in the growing of a babe or of a lily. The lily does not toil nor spin, it does not stretch nor strain, it does not make any effort of any kind to grow, it is not conscious even that it is growing; but by an inward life-principle, and through the nurturing care of God's providence and the fostering of caretaker or gardener, by the heat of the sun and the falling of the rain, it grows and buds and blossoms into the beautiful plant God meant it to be.

The result of this sort of growing in the Christian life is sure. Even Solomon in all his glory, our Lord says, was not arrayed like one of God's lilies. Solomon's array cost much toiling and spinning, and gold and silver in abundance: but the lily's array costs none of these. And though we may toil and spin to make for ourselves beautiful spiritual garments, and may strain and stretch in our efforts after spiritual growth, we shall accomplish nothing; for no man by taking thought *can* add one cubit to his stature, and no array of ours can ever equal the beautiful dress with which the great Husbandman clothes the plants that grow in His garden of grace and under His fostering care.

Could I but make each one of my readers realize how utterly helpless we are in this matter of growing, I am convinced a large part of the strain would be taken out of many lives at once.

Imagine a child possessed of the monomania that he would not grow unless he made some personal effort after it, and who should insist upon a combination of ropes and pulleys whereby to stretch himself up to the desired height. He might, it is true, spend his days and years in a weary strain, but after all there would be no change in the inexorable fiat, "No man by taking thought can add one cubit unto his stature," and his weary efforts would be only wasted, if they did not actually hinder the longed-for end.

Imagine a lily trying to clothe itself in beautful colors and graceful lines, and drawing to its aid, as so many of God's children try to do, the wisdom and strength of all the lilies around it! I think such a lily would very soon become a chronic "case" of spiritual perplexities and difficulties, similar to some that are familiar to every Christian worker.

Neither child nor lily is ever found doing such a vain and foolish thing as *trying* to grow. But I fear many of God's children are doing exactly this foolish thing. They know that they ought to grow, and they feel within them an instinct that longs for growth;

but, instead of letting the Divine Husbandman care for their growing, as it is surely His business to do, they think to accomplish it by their own toiling and spinning, and stretching and straining; and in consequence they pass their lives in a round of wearisome self-efforts that exhausts their energies, while all the time they find themselves, to their infinite grief, growing backward rather than forward.

> " 'Ye flowrets of the field,' Siddartha said,
> 'Who turn your tender faces to the sun,
> What secret know ye, that ye grow content?' "

What we all need is to "consider the flowers of the field," and learn their secret. Grow, by all means, dear Christians; but grow, I beseech you, in God's way, which is the only effectual way. See to it that you are planted in grace, and then let the Divine Husbandman cultivate you in His own way and by His own means. Put yourselves out in the sunshine of His presence, and let the dew of heaven come down upon you, and see what will be the result. Leaves and flowers and fruit must surely come in their season; for your Husbandman is skilful, and He never fails in His harvesting. Only see to it that you oppose no hindrance to the shining of the Sun of Righteousness, or the falling of the dew from Heaven. The thinnest covering may serve to keep off the sunshine and the dew, and the plant may wither, even where these are most abundant. And so also the slightest barrier between your soul and Christ may cause you to dwindle and fade, as a plant in a cellar or under a bushel.

Keep the sky clear. Open wide every avenue of your being to receive the blessed influences your Divine Husbandman may bring to bear upon you. Bask in the sunshine of His love. Drink of the waters of His goodness. Keep your face upturned to Him as the flowers do to the sun. Look, and your soul shall live and grow.

But it may be objected here that we are not inanimate flowers, but intelligent human beings, with personal powers and personal responsibilities. This is true; and it makes this important difference, that what the flower is by nature we must be by an intelligent and free surrender. To be one of God's lilies means an interior abandonment of the rarest kind. It means that we are to be infinitely passive, and yet infinitely active also: passive as regards self and its workings, active as regards attention and response to God. It is very hard to explain this so as to be understood. But it means that we must lay down all the activity of the creature as such, and must let only the activities of God work in us, and through us, and by us. Self must step aside to let God work.

You need make no efforts to grow, therefore; but let your efforts instead be all concentrated on this, that you abide in the Vine. The Divine Husbandman who has the care of the Vine, will care also for you who are His branches, and will so prune and purge and water and tend you that you will grow and bring forth fruit, and your fruit shall remain, and, like the lily, you shall find yourself arrayed in apparel so glorious, that the apparel of Solomon will be as nothing to it.

What if you seem to yourselves to be planted at this moment in a desert soil, where nothing can grow. Put yourselves absolutely into the hands of the good Husbandman, and He will at once begin to make that very desert blossom as the rose, and will cause springs and fountains of water to start up out of its sandy wastes. For the promise is sure, that the man who trusts in the Lord "shall be as a tree planted by the waters, and that spreadeth out her roots by the river, and shall not see when heat cometh, but her leaf shall be green; and shall not be careful in the year of drought, neither shall cease from yielding fruit."

It is the great prerogative of our Divine Husbandman that He is able to turn any soil, whatever it may be like, into the soil of grace the moment we put our growing into His hands. He does not need to transplant us into a different field, but right where we are, with just the circumstances that surround us, He makes His sun to shine and His dew to fall upon us, and transforms the very things that were before our greatest hindrances into the chiefest and most blessed means of our growth. I care not what the circumstances may be, His wonder-working power can accomplish this; and we must trust Him with it all. Surely He is a Husbandman we *can* trust; and if He sends storms, or winds, or rains, or sunshine, all must be accepted at His hands with the most unwavering confidence that He who has undertaken to cultivate us, and to bring us to maturity, knows the very best way of accomplishing His end, and regulates the elements, which are all at His disposal, expressly with a view to our most rapid growth.

Let me entreat of you, then, to give up all your efforts after growing, and simply to *let* yourselves grow. Leave it all to the Husbandman whose care it is, and who alone is able to manage it. No difficulties in your case can baffle Him. If you will only put yourselves absolutely into His hands, and let Him have His own way with you, no dwarfing of your growth in the years that are past, no apparent dryness of your inward springs of life, no crookedness or deformity in your development, can in the least mar the perfect work that He will accomplish. His own gracious promise to His backsliding children assures you of this. "I will heal their backslidings," He says, "I will love them freely: for mine anger is turned away from him. I will be as the dew unto Israel; he shall grow as the lily, and cast forth his roots as Lebanon. His branches shall spread and his beauty shall be as the olive-tree, and his smell as Lebanon. They that dwell under his shadow shall return; they shall revive as the corn, and grow as the vine: the scent thereof shall be as the wine of Lebanon." And again He says: "Be not afraid: for the pastures of the wilderness do spring, for the tree beareth her fruit, the fig-tree and the vine do yield their strength . . . . And the floors shall be full of wheat, and the vats shall overflow with wine and oil. And I will restore to you the years that the locust hath eaten . . . . And ye shall eat in plenty, and be satisfied, and praise the name of the Lord your God, that hath dealt wondrously with you: and my people shall never be ashamed."

Oh that you could but know just what your Lord

meant when He said, "Consider the lilies of the field, *how they grow;* they toil not, neither do they spin!" Surely these words give us the picture of a life and growth far different from the ordinary life and growth of Christians,—a life of rest, and a growth without effort; and yet a life and a growth crowned with glorious results. And to every soul that will thus become a lily in the garden of the Lord, and will grow as the lilies grow, the same glorious array will be as surely given as was given to them; and they will know the fulfilment of that wonderful mystical passage concerning their Beloved, that "He feedeth among the lilies."

> "I feel as weak as a violet
> Alone with the awful sky:
> Winds wander, and dews drop earthward,
> Rains fall, suns rise and set,
> Earth whirls; and all but to prosper
>   A poor little violet!"

We may rest assured of this, that all the resources of God's infinite grace will be brought to bear on the growing of the tiniest flower in His spiritual garden, as certainly as they are in His earthly creation; and as the violet abides peacefully in its little place, content to receive its daily portion without concerning itself about the wandering of the winds, or the falling of the rain, so must we repose in the present moment as it comes to us from God, contented with our daily portion, and without anxious thought as to anything that may be whirling around us in God's glorious universe, sure that all things will be made to "prosper" for us.

This is the kind of "growth in grace" in which we who have entered into the life of full trust believe; a growth without care or anxiety on our part, but a growth which does actually grow, which blossoms out into flower and fruit, and becomes like a "tree planted by the rivers of water, that bringeth forth his fruit in his season"; whose leaf also does not wither, and who prospers in whatsoever he doeth. And we rejoice to know that there are growing up now in the Lord's heritage many such plants, who, as the lilies behold the face of the sun and grow thereby, are, by "beholding as in a glass the glory of the Lord," being changed into the same image from glory to glory, even as by the Spirit of the Lord.

Should you ask such how it is that they grow so rapidly and with such success, their answer would be that they are not concerned about their growing, and are hardly conscious that they do grow. That their Lord has told them to abide in Him, and has promised that, if they do thus abide, they shall certainly bring forth much fruit; and that they are concerned, therefore, only about the abiding, which is their part, and are content to leave the cultivating, and the growing, and the training, and the pruning, to their good Husbandman, who alone is able to manage these things or to bring them about. You will find that such souls are not engaged in watching self, but in "looking unto Jesus." They do not "toil and spin" for their spiritual garments, but leave themselves in the hands of the Lord, to be arrayed as it may please Him. Self-effort and self-dependence are at an end with them. Formerly they tried to be not only the garden but the gardener also as well, and undertook to fulfil the duties of both. Now they are content to *be* what they *are*,—willing to leave the gardener's duties to the Divine Husbandman, who alone is responsible for their rightful performance. Their interest in self is gone, transferred over into the hands of another; and self in consequence has become nothing to them more and more, and Christ alone is seen to be all in all. And the blessed result is that not even Solomon in all his glory was arrayed as these shall be.

Let us look at the subject practically. We all know that growing is not a thing of effort, but is the result of an inward life-principle of growth. All the stretching and pulling in the world could not make a dead oak grow; but a live oak grows without stretching. It is plain, therefore, that the essential thing is to get within you the growing life, and then you cannot help but grow. And this life is the "life hid with Christ in God," the wonderful divine life of an indwelling Holy Ghost. Be filled with this, dear believer, and, whether you are conscious of it or not, you must grow, you cannot help growing. Do not trouble about your growing, but see to it that you have the growing life. Abide in the Vine. Let the life from Him flow through all your spiritual veins. Interpose no barrier to His mighty life-giving power, "working in you all the good pleasure of his will." Yield yourself up utterly to His lovely control. Put your growing into His hands as completely as you have put all your other affairs. Suffer Him to manage it as He will. Do not concern yourself about it, nor even think of it. Do not, as children do, keep digging your plants to see if they are growing. Trust the Divine Husbandman absolutely, and always. Accept each moment's dispensation as it comes to you from His dear hands as being the needed sunshine or dew for that moment's growth. Say a continual "Yes" to your Father's will. And finally, in this, as in all the other cares of your life, "be careful for nothing; but in everything, by prayer and supplication, with thanksgiving, let your requests be made known unto God. And the peace of God that passeth all understanding shall keep your hearts and minds through Christ Jesus."

If your "growth in grace" is of this sort, dear reader, you will surely know, sooner or later, a wonderful growing, and you will come to understand, as you cannot now, it may be, what the Psalmist meant when he said, "The righteous shall flourish like the palm-tree: he shall grow like a cedar in Lebanon. Those that be planted in the house of the Lord shall flourish in the courts of our God. They shall bring forth fruit in old age; they shall be fat and flourishing."

CHAPTER FIFTEEN

Service

THERE IS, PERHAPS, NO PART OF CHRISTIAN EXPERIENCE where a greater change is known, upon entering into this life hid with Christ in God, than in the matter of service.

In all the ordinary forms of Christian life, service is apt to have more or less of bondage in it; that is, it is done purely as a matter of duty, and often as a trial and a cross. Certain things, which at the first may have been a joy and a delight, become after a while weary tasks, performed faithfully, perhaps, but with much secret disinclination, and many confessed or unconfessed wishes that they need not be done at all, or at least that they need not be done so often. The soul finds itself saying, instead of the "May I?" of love, the "Must I?" of duty. The yoke, which was at first easy, begins to gall, and the burden feels heavy instead of light.

One dear Christian expressed it once to me in this way: "When I was first converted," she said, "I was so full of joy and love that I was only too glad and thankful to be allowed to do anything for my Lord, and I eagerly entered every open door. But after a while, as my early joy faded away, and my love burned less fervently, I began to wish I had not been quite so eager; for I found myself involved in lines of service that were gradually becoming very distasteful and burdensome to me. Since I had begun them, I could not very well give them up without exciting great remark, and yet I longed to do so increasingly. I was expected to visit the sick, and pray beside their beds. I was expected to attend prayer-meetings, and speak at them. I was expected, in short, to be always read for every effort in Christian work, and the sense of these expectations bowed me down continually. At last it became so unspeakably burdensome to me to live the sort of Christian life I had entered upon, and was expected by all around me to live, that I felt as if any kind of manual labor would have been easier; and I would have infinitely preferred scrubbing all day on my hands and knees to being compelled to go through the treadmill of my daily Christian work. I envied," she said, "the servants in the kitchen, and the women at the washtubs."

This may seem to some like a strong statement; but does it not present a vivid picture of some of your own experiences, dear Christian? Have you never gone to your work as a slave to his daily task, believing it to be your duty and that therefore you must do it, but rebounding like an India-rubber ball back into your real interests and pleasures the moment your work was over?

You have known of course that this was the wrong way to feel, and have been thoroughly ashamed of it, but still you have seen no way to help it. You have not *loved* your work; and, could you have done so with an easy conscience, you would have been glad to give it up altogether.

Or, if this does not describe your case, perhaps another picture will. You do love your work in the abstract, but in the doing of it you find so many cares and responsibilities connected with it, and feel so many misgivings and doubts as to your own capacity or fitness, that it becomes a very heavy burden, and you go to it bowed down and weary before the labor has even begun. Then also you are continually distressing yourself about the results of your work, and greatly troubled if they are not just what you would like; and this of itself is a constant burden.

Now, from all these forms of bondage the soul that enters fully into the blessed life of faith is entirely delivered. In the first place, service of any sort becomes delightful to it, because, having surrendered its will into the keeping of the Lord, He works in it to will and to do of His good pleasure, and the soul finds itself really *wanting* to do the things God wants it to do. It is always very pleasant to do the things we *want* to do, let them be ever so difficult of accomplishment, or involve ever so much of bodily weariness. If a man's *will* is really set on a thing he regards with a sublime indifference the obstacles that lie in the way of his reaching it, and laughs to himself at the idea of any opposition or difficulties hindering him. How many men have gone gladly and thankfully to the ends of the world in search of worldly fortunes, or to fulfil worldly ambitions, and have scorned the thought of any "cross" connected with it! How many mothers have congratulated themselves, and rejoiced over the honor done their sons in seeing them promoted to some place of power and usefulness in their country's service, although it has involved perhaps years of separation, and a life of hardship for their dear ones! And yet these same men, and these very mothers, would have felt and said that they were taking up crosses too heavy almost to be borne, had the service of Christ required the same sacrifice of home, and friends, and worldly ease.

It is altogether the way we look at things, whether we think they are crosses or not. And I am ashamed to think that any Christian should ever put on a long face and shed tears over doing a thing for Christ which a worldly man would be only too glad to do for money.

What we need in the Christian life is to get believers to *want* to do God's will as much as other people want to do their own will. And this is the idea of the Gospel. It is what God intended for us; and it is what He has promised. In describing the new covenant in Hebrews 8:6–13, He says it shall no more be the old covenant made on Sinai,—that is, a law given from the outside, controlling a man by force,—but it shall be a law written *within*, constraining a man by love. "I will put my laws," He says, "into their mind, and write them in their hearts." This can mean nothing but that we shall *love* His law; for anything written in our hearts we must love. "And putting it into our minds" is surely the same as God working in us to "will and to do of his good pleasure," and means that we shall will what God wills, and shall obey His sweet commands, not because it is our duty to do so, but because we ourselves want to do what He wants us to do.

Nothing could possibly be conceived more effectual than this. How often have we thought, when dealing with our children, "Oh, if I could only get inside of them, and make them *want* to do just what I want, how easy it would be to manage them then!" How often in practical experience we have found that to deal with cross-grained people we most carefully avoid suggesting our wishes to them, but must in some way induce them to suggest the thing themselves, sure that there will then be no opposition to contend with. And we, who are by nature a stiff-necked people, always rebel more or less against a law from outside of us, while we joyfully embrace the same law springing up within.

God's way of working, therefore, is to get possession of the inside of a man, to take the control and management of his will, and to work it for him. Then obedience is easy and a delight, and service becomes perfect freedom, until the Christian is forced to explain, "This happy service! who could dream earth had such liberty?"

What you need to do, then, dear Christian, if you are in bondage in the matter of service, is to put your will over completely into the hands of your Lord, surrendering to Him the entire control of it. Say, "Yes, Lord, YES!" to everything, and trust Him so to work in you to will as to bring your whole wishes and affections into conformity with His own sweet, and lovable, and most lovely will. I have seen this done often in cases where it looked beforehand an utterly impossible thing. In one case, where a lady had been for years rebelling fearfully against a little act of service which she knew was right, but which she hated, I saw her, out of the depths of despair, and without any feeling whatever, give her will in that matter up into the hands of her Lord, and begin to say to Him, "Thy will be done; *Thy will be done!*" And in one short hour that very thing began to look sweet and precious to her.

It is wonderful what miracles God works in wills that are utterly surrendered to Him. He turns hard things into easy, and bitter things into sweet. It is not that He puts easy things in the place of the hard, but He actually changes the hard thing into an easy one, and makes us love to do the thing we before so hated. While we rebel against the yoke, and try to avoid it, we find it hard and galling. But when we "take the yoke upon us" with a consenting will, we find it easy and comfortable. It is said of Ephraim that at one time he was like "a bullock unaccustomed to the yoke," but that afterwards, when he had submitted to the yoke, he was "as an heifer that is taught, and *loveth* to tread out the corn."

Many Christians, as I have said, love God's will in the abstract, but carry great burdens in connection with it. From this also there is deliverance in the wonderful life of faith. For in this life no burdens are carried, no anxieties felt. The Lord is our burden-bearer, and upon Him we must lay off every care. He says, in effect, "Be careful for nothing, but make your requests known to me, and I will attend to them all."

Be careful for *nothing*, He says, not even your service. Above all, I should think, our service, because we know ourselves to be so utterly helpless in regard to it, that, even if we were careful, it would not amount to anything. What have we to do with thinking whether we are fit or not? The Master-workman surely has a right to use any tool He pleases for His own work, and it is plainly not the business of the tool to decide whether it is the right one to be used or not. He knows; and if He chooses to use us, of course we must be fit. And in truth, if we only knew it, our chief fitness is in our utter helplessness. His strength is made perfect, not in our strength, but in our weakness. Our strength is only a hindrance.

I was once visiting an idiot asylum, and saw the children going through dumbbell exercises. Now, we all know that it is a very difficult thing for idiots to manage their movements. They have strength enough, generally, but no skill to use this strength, and as a consequence cannot do much. And in these dumbbell exercises this deficiency was very apparent. They made all sorts of awkward movements. Now and then, by a happy chance, they would make a movement in harmony with the music and the teacher's directions, but for the most part all was out of harmony. One little girl, however, I noticed, who made perfect movements. Not a jar or a break disturbed the harmony of her exercises. And the reason was not that she had more strength than the others, but that she had no strength at all. She could not so much as close her hands over the dumbbells, nor lift her arms, and the master had to stand behind her, and do it all. She yielded up her members as instruments to him, and his "strength was made perfect" in her weakness. He knew how to go through those exercises, for he himself had planned them; and therefore when he did it, it was done right. She did nothing but yield herself up utterly into his hands, and he did it all. The yielding was her part; the responsibility was all his. It was not her skill that was needed to make harmonious movements, but only his. The question was not of her capacity, but of his. Her utter weakness was her greatest strength.

To me this is a very striking picture of our Christian life, and it is no wonder therefore that Paul could say, "Most gladly therefore will I rather *glory* in my infirmities, that the power of Christ may rest upon me." Who would not glory in being so utterly weak and helpless that the Lord Jesus Christ should find no hindrance to the perfect working of His mighty power through us and in us?

Then, too, if the work is His, the responsibility is His, also, and we have no room left for worrying about results. Everything in reference to it is known to Him, and He can manage it all. Why not leave it all with Him, then, and consent to be "treated like a child and guided where to go"? It is a fact that the most effectual workers I know, are those who do not feel the least care or anxiety about their work, but who commit it all to their dear Master, and, asking Him to guide them moment by moment in reference to it, trust Him implicitly for each moment's needed supplies of wisdom and of strength. To look at them, you would almost think, perhaps, that they were too free from care where such mighty interests were at stake. But when you have learned God's secret of trusting, and see the beauty and the power of the life that is yielded up to His working, you will cease to condemn, and will begin to wonder how any of God's workers can dare to carry the burdens, or assume the responsibilities, which He alone is able to bear.

Some may object that the Apostle Paul spoke of the "care of the churches" coming upon him. But we must not fail to remember that it was the constant habit of the Apostle to roll every care off on the Lord, and thus, while full of care, to be "without carefulness."

There are one or two other bonds in service from which this life of trust delivers us. We find out that no one individual is responsible for all the work in the world, but only for a small share. Our duty ceases to be universal, and becomes personal and individual. The Master does not say to us, "Go and do everything," but He marks out an especial path for each one of us, and gives to each one of us an especial duty. There are "diversities of gifts" in the kingdom of God, and these gifts are divided to "every man according to his ability." I may have five talents, or two, or only one; I may be called to do twenty things, or only one. My responsibility is simply to do that which I am called to do, and nothing more. "The *steps* of a good man are ordered of the Lord," not his way only, but each separate step in that way.

Many Christians make the further mistake of looking upon every act of service as of perpetual obligation. They think because it was right for them to give a tract to one person in a railway train, for instance, that therefore they are always to give tracts to everybody, and in this way they burden themselves with an impossible duty.

There was a young Christian once, who, because she had been sent to speak a message to one soul whom she met in a walk, supposed it was a perpetual obligation, and thought she must speak about his soul to every one she met in her walks. This was of course impossible, and as a consequence she was soon in hopeless bondage about it. She became absolutely afraid to go outside of her own door, and lived in perpetual condemnation. At last she disclosed her distress to a friend who was instructed in the ways of God with His servants; and this friend told her she was making a great mistake; that the Lord had His own especial work for each especial workman, and that the servants in a well-regulated household might as well each one take it upon himself to try to do the work of all the rest as for the Lord's servants to think they were each one under obligation to do everything. He told her just to put herself under the Lord's personal guidance as to her work, and trust Him to point out to her each particular person to whom He would have her speak, assuring her that He never puts forth His own sheep without going before them, and making a way for them Himself. She followed this advice, and laid the burden of her work on the Lord, and the result was a happy pathway of daily guidance, in which she was led into much blessed work for her Master, and was able to do it all without a care or a burden, because He led her out and prepared the way before her.

I have been very much instructed myself by thinking of the arrangements of our own households. When we appoint a servant for an especial part of the work of the household, we want him to attend to that alone, and not run all over the house trying to attend to the work of all the other servants. It would make endless confusion in any earthly household if the servants were to act in this fashion, and it makes no less confusion in the Divine household.

Our part in the matter of service seems to me just like making the junction between the machinery and the steam-engine. The power is not in the machinery, but in the steam. Disconnected from the engine, the machinery is perfectly useless. But let the connection be made, and the machinery goes easily and without effort because of the mighty power there is behind it. Thus the Christian life, when it is the development of the Divine life working within, becomes an easy and natural life. Most Christians live in a strain, because their wills are not fully in harmony with the will of God, the connection is not perfectly made at every point, and it requires an effort to move the machinery. But when once the connection is fully made, and the "law of the Spirit of life in Christ Jesus" can work in us with all its mighty power, we are then indeed made "free from the law of sin and death," and shall know the glorious liberty of the children of God.

Another form of bondage as to service, from which the life of faith delivers the soul, is in reference to the after-reflections which always follow any Christian work. These after-reflections are of two sorts:

either the soul congratulates itself upon its success, and is lifted up; or it is distressed over its failure, and is utterly cast down. One of these is *sure* to come; and of the two I think the former is the more to be dreaded, although the latter causes at the time the greater suffering. But in the life of trust neither will trouble us; for, having committed ourselves in our work to the Lord, we shall be satisfied to leave it to Him, and shall not think about ourselves in the matter at all.

Years ago I came across this sentence in an old book: "Never indulge, at the close of an action, in any self-reflective acts of any kind, whether of self-congratulation or of self-despair. Forget the things that are behind, the moment they are past, leaving them with God." This has been of unspeakable value to me. When the temptation comes, as it mostly does to every worker after the performance of any service, to indulge in these reflections, either of one sort or the other, I turn from them at once and positively refuse to think about my work at all, leaving it with the Lord to overrule the mistakes, and to bless it as He chooses. I believe there would be far fewer "blue Mondays" for ministers of the Gospel than there are now if they would adopt this plan; and I am sure all workers would find their work far less wearing.

To sum it all up, then, what is needed for happy and effectual service is simply to put your work into the Lord's hands, and leave it there. Do not take it to Him in prayer, saying, "Lord, guide me; Lord, give me wisdom; Lord, arrange for me," and then rise from your knees, and take the burden all back and try to guide and arrange for yourself. *Leave* it with the Lord; and remember that what you trust to Him you must not worry over nor feel anxious about. Trust and worry cannot go together. If your work is a burden it is because you are not trusting it to Him. But if you do trust it to Him you will surely find that the yoke He puts upon you is easy, and the burden He gives you to carry is light: and even in the midst of a life of ceaseless activity you shall "find rest to your soul."

If the Divine Master only had a band of such workers as this, there is no limit to what He might do with them. Truly, one such would "chase a thousand, and two would put ten thousand to flight," and nothing would be impossible to them. For it is nothing with the Lord "to help, whether with many, or with them that have no power," if only He can find instruments that are fully abandoned to His working.

May God raise up such an army speedily! And may you, my dear reader, enroll your name among this band, and, yielding yourself unto God as one who is "alive from the dead," may every one of your members be also yielded unto Him as "instruments of righteousness," to be used by Him as He pleases!

CHAPTER SIXTEEN

Practical Results in Daily Use

IF ALL THAT HAS BEEN WRITTEN IN THE FOREGOING chapters on the life hid with Christ be true, its results in the practical daily walk and conversation ought to be very marked, and the people who have entered into the enjoyment of it ought to be, in very truth, a peculiar people, zealous of good works.

My son, now with God, once wrote to a friend something to this effect: that we are God's witnesses necessarily, because the world will not read the Bible, but they will read our lives; and that upon the report these give will very much depend their belief in the divine nature of the religion we possess. This age is essentialy an age of facts, and all scientific inquiries are being increasingly turned from theories to realities. If, therefore, our religion is to make any headway in the present time, it must be proved to be more than a theory; and we must present to the investigation of the critical minds of our age the realities of lives transformed by the mighty power of God, "working in them all the good pleasure of His will."

I desire, therefore, to speak very solemnly of

what I conceive to be the necessary fruits of a life of faith such as I have been describing, and to press home to the hearts of every one of my readers their personal responsibility to "walk worthy of the high calling" wherewith they have been called.

I think that I may speak to some of you at least as personal friends, for I feel sure we have not gone thus far together through these pages without there having grown in your hearts, as there has in mine, a tender personal interest and longing for one another, that we may in everything show forth the praises of Him who has "called us out of darkness into His marvelous light." As a friend to friends, then, I speak, and I am sure I shall be pardoned if I go into some details of our daily lives, which may seem of secondary importance, and which make up the largest part of them.

The standard of practical holy living has been so low among Christians that the least degree of real devotedness of life and walk is looked upon with surprise and often even with disapprobation by a large portion of the Church. And, for the most part, the followers of the Lord Jesus Christ are satisfied with a life so conformed to the world, and so like it in almost every respect, that, to a casual observer, no difference is discernible.

But we who have heard the call of our God to a life of entire consecration and perfect trust must do differently. We must come out from the world and be separate, and must not be conformed to it in our characters or in our lives. We must set our affections on heavenly things, not on earthly ones, and must seek first the kingdom of God and His righteousness; surrendering every thing that would interfere with this. We must walk through the world as Christ walked. We must have the mind that was in Him. As pilgrims and strangers, we must abstain from fleshly lusts that war against the soul. As good soldiers of Jesus Christ, we must disentangle ourselves inwardly from the affairs of this life, that we may please Him who hath chosen us to be soldiers. We must abstain from all appearance of evil. We must be kind to one another, tender-hearted, forgiving one another, even as God, for Christ's sake, hath forgiven us. We must not resent injuries or unkindness, but must return good for evil, and turn the other cheek to the hand that smites us. We must take always the lowest place among our fellow men; and seek, not our own honor, but the honor of others. We must be gentle, and meek, and yielding; not standing up for our own rights, but for the rights of others. We must do everything, not for our own glory, but for the glory of God. And, to sum it all up, since He who hath called us is holy, so we must be holy in all manner of conversation; because it is written, "Be ye holy, for I am holy."

Some Christians seem to think that all the requirements of a holy life are met when there is very active and successful Christian work; and because they do so much for the Lord in public they feel a liberty to be cross and ugly and un-Christlike in private. But this is not the sort of Christian life I am depicting. If we are to walk as Christ walked, it must be in private as well as in public, at home as well as abroad; and it must be every hour all day long, and not at stated periods or on certain fixed occasions. We must be just as Christlike to our servants as we are to our minister, and just as "good" in our countinghouse as we are in our prayer-meeting.

It is in daily homely living, indeed, that practical piety can best show itself, and we may well question any "professions" that fail under this test of daily life.

A cross Christian, or an anxious Christian, a discouraged, gloomy Christian, a doubting Christian, a complaining Christian, an exacting Christian, a selfish Christian, a cruel, hard-hearted Christian, a self-indulgent Christian, a Christian with a sharp tongue or bitter spirit, all these may be very earnest in their work, and may have honorable places in the Church; but they are *not* Christlike Christians, and they know nothing of the realities of which this book treats, no matter how loud their professions may be.

The life hid with Christ in God is a hidden life, as to its source, but it must not be hidden as to its practical results. People must see that we walk as Christ walked, if we say that we are abiding in Him. We must prove that we "possess" that which we "profess." We must, in short, be real followers of Christ, and not theoretical ones only. And this means a great deal. It means that we must really and absolutely turn our backs on everything that is contrary to the perfect will of God. It means that we are to be a "peculiar people," not only in the eyes of God, but in the eyes of the world around us; and that, wherever we go, it will be known from our habits, our tempers, our conversation and our pursuits, that we are followers of the Lord Jesus Christ, and are not of the world, even as

He was not of the world. We must no longer look upon our money as our own, but as belonging to the Lord, to be used in His service. We must not feel at liberty to use our energies in the pursuit of worldly means, but must recognize, that, if we seek first the kingdom of God and His righteousness, all needful things shall be added unto us. We shall find ourselves forbidden to seek the highest places, or to strain after worldly advantages. We shall not be permitted to make self, as heretofore, the center of all our thoughts and all our aims. Our days will have to be spent, not in serving ourselves, but in serving the Lord; and we shall find ourselves called upon to bear one another's burdens, and so fulfil the law of Christ. And all our daily homely duties will be more perfectly performed than ever, because whatever we do will be done, "not with eye-service, as men-pleasers, but as the servants of Christ, doing the will of God from the heart."

Into all this we shall undoubtedly be led by the Spirit of God if we give ourselves up to His guidance. But unless we have the right standard of Christian life set before us, we may be hindered by our ignorance from recognizing His voice; and it is for this reason I desire to be very plain and definite in my statements.

I have noticed that wherever there has been a faithful following of the Lord in a consecrated soul, several things have, sooner or later, inevitably followed.

Meekness and quietness of spirit become in time the characteristics of the daily life. A submissive acceptance of the will of God, as it comes in the hourly events of each day, is manifested; pliability in the hands of God to do or to suffer all the good pleasure of His will; sweetness under provocation; calmness in the midst of turmoil and bustle; a yielding to the wishes of others, and an insensibility to slights and affronts; absence of worry or anxiety; deliverance from care and fear,—all these, and many other similar graces, are invariably found to be the natural outward development of that inward life which is hid with Christ in God. Then as to the habits of life: we always see such Christians sooner of later laying aside thoughts of self, and becoming full of consideration for others; they dress and live in simple, healthful ways; they renounce self-indulgent habits, and surrender all purely fleshly gratifications. Some helpful work for others is taken up, and useless occupations are dropped out of the life. God's glory and the welfare of His creatures become the absorbing delight of the soul. The voice is dedicated to Him, to be used in singing His praises. The purse is placed at His disposal. The pen is dedicated to write for Him, the lips to speak for Him, the hands and the feet to do His bidding. Year after year such Christians are seen to grow more unworldly, more serene, more heavenly-minded, more transformed, more like Christ, until even their faces express so much of the beautiful inward divine life, that all who look at them cannot but take knowledge of them that they live with Jesus, and are abiding in Him.

I feel sure that to each one of you have come some divine intimations or foreshadowings of the life I here describe. Have you not begun to feel dimly conscious of the voice of God speaking to you, in the depths of your soul, about these things? Has it not been a pain and a distress to you of late to discover how full your lives are of self? Has not your soul been plunged into inward trouble and doubt about certain dispositions or pursuits in which you have been formerly accustomed to indulge? Have you not begun to feel uneasy with some of your habits of life, and to wish that you could do differently in certain respects? Have not paths of devotedness and of service begun to open out before you, with the longing thought, "Oh that I could walk in them!" All these questions and doubts and this inward yearning are the voice of the Good Shepherd in your heart, seeking to call you out of that which is contrary to His will. Let me entreat of you not to turn away from His gentle pleadings! You little know the sweet paths into which He means to lead you by these very steps, not the wonderful stories of blessedness that lie at their end, or you would spring forward with an eager joy to yield to every one of His requirements. The heights of Christian perfection can only be reached by each moment faithfully following the Guide who is to lead you there; and He reveals the way to us one step at a time, in the little things of our daily lives, asking only on our part that we yield ourselves up to His guidance. Be perfectly pliable then in His dear hands, to go where He entices you, and to turn away from all from which He makes you shrink. Obey Him perfectly the moment you are sure of His will; and you will soon find that He is leading you out swiftly and easily into such a wonderful life of conformity to Himself that it will be a testimony to all around you, beyond what you yourself will ever know.

I knew a soul thus given up to follow the Lord whithersoever He might lead her, who in a very little while traveled from the depths of darkness and despair, into the realization and actual experience of a most blessed union with the Lord Jesus Christ. Out of the midst of her darkness she consecrated herself to the Lord, surrendering her will up altogether to Him, that He might work in her to will and to do of His own good pleasure. Immediately He began to speak to her by His Spirit in her heart, suggesting to her some little acts of service for Him, and troubling her about certain things in her habits and her life, showing her where she was selfish and un-Christlike, and how she could be transformed. She recognized His voice, and yielded to Him each thing He asked for the moment she was sure of His will. Her swift obedience was rewarded by a rapid progress, and day by day she was conformed more and more to the image of Christ, until very soon her life became such a testimony to those around her that some even who had begun by opposing and disbelieving were forced to acknowledge that it was of God, and were won to a similar surrender. And, finally, in a little while it came to pass, so swiftly had she gone, that her Lord was able to reveal to her wondering soul some of the deepest secrets of His love, and to fulfil to her the marvelous promise of Acts 1:5 by giving her to realize the baptism of the Holy Ghost. Think you she has ever regretted her whole-hearted following of Him? Or that aught but thankfulness and joy can ever fill her soul when she reviews the steps by which her feet have been led to this place of wondrous blessedness, even though some of them may have seemed at the time hard to take? Ah, dear soul, if thou wouldst know a like blessing abandon thyself, like her, to the guidance of thy divine Master, and shrink from no surrender for which He may call.

> "The perfect way is hard to flesh,
>   It is not hard to love;
> If thou wert sick for want of God,
>   How swiftly wouldst thou move!"

Surely thou canst trust Him! And if some things may be called for that look to thee of but little moment, and not worthy thy Lord's attention, remember that He sees not as man seeth, and that things small to thee may be in His eyes the key and the clue to the deepest springs of thy being. No life can be complete that fails in its little things. A look, a word, a tone of voice even, however small they may seem to human judgment, are often of vital importance in the eyes of God. Thy one great desire is to follow Him fully; canst thou not say, then, a continual "Yes" to all His sweet commands, whether small or great, and trust Him to lead thee by the shortest road to thy fullest blessedness?

My dear friend, whether thou knew it or not, this, and nothing less than this, is what thy consecration meant. It meant inevitable obedience. It meant that the will of thy God was henceforth to be thy will, under all circumstances and at all times. It meant that from that moment thou didst surrender thy liberty of choice, and gave thyself up utterly into the control of thy Lord. It meant an hourly following of Him, whithersoever He might lead thee, without any turning back.

All this and far more was involved in thy surrender to God, and now I appeal to thee to make good thy word. Let everything else go, that thou mayst live out, in a practical daily walk and conversation, the Christ-life thou hast dwelling within thee. Thou art united to thy Lord by a wondrous tie; walk, then, as He walked, and show to the unbelieving world the blessed reality of His mighty power to save, by letting Him save thee to the very uttermost. Thou needst not fear to consent to this, for He is thy Saviour, and His power is to do it all. He is not asking thee, in thy poor weakness, to do it thyself; He only asks thee to yield thyself to Him, that He may work in thee and through thee by His own mighty power. Thy part is to yield thyself, His part is to work; and never, never will He give thee any command that is not accompanied by ample power to obey it. Take no thought for the morrow in this matter; but abandon thyself with a generous trust to the good Shepherd, who has promised never to call His own sheep out into any path, without Himself going before them to make the way easy and safe. Take each little step as He makes it plain to thee. Bring all thy life, in each of its details, to Him to regulate and guide. Follow gladly and quickly the sweet suggestions of His Spirit in thy soul. And day by day thou wilt find Him bringing thee more and more into conformity with His will in all things; molding thee and fashioning thee, as thou art able to bear it, into a "vessel unto his honor, sanctified and meet for his use, and fitted to every good work." So shall be given to thee the sweet joy of being an "epistle of Christ, known and read of all men"; and thy light shall shine so brightly that men seeing, not thee, but thy good works, shall glorify, not thee, but thy Father which is in heaven.

"But Thou art making me, I thank Thee, Sire.
    What Thou hast done and doest, Thou knowest well,
And I will help Thee: gently in Thy fire
    I will lie burning; on Thy potter's wheel
    I will whirl patient, though my brain should reel;
    Thy grace shall be enough to quell,
And growing strength perfect, through weakness dire.

"I have not knowledge, wisdom, insight, thought,
    Nor understanding, fit to justify
Thee in Thy work, O Perfect! Thou hast brought
Me up to this; and lo! what Thou hast wrought,
    I cannot comprehend. But I can cry,
'O enemy, the Maker hath not done;
One day thou shalt behold, and from the sight shalt run!'

"Thou workest perfectly. And if it seem
    Some things are not so well, 'tis but because
    They are too loving deep, too lofty wise,
    For me, poor child, to understand their laws.
My highest wisdom, half is but a dream;
My love runs helpless like a falling stream;
    Thy good embraces ill, and lo! its illness dies." *

* George Macdonald.

CHAPTER SEVENTEEN

The Joy of Obedience

HAVING SPOKEN OF SOME OF THE DIFFICULTIES IN THIS life of faith, let me now speak of some of its joys. And foremost among these stands the joy of obedience.

Long ago I met somewhere with this sentence, "Perfect obedience would be perfect happiness if only we had perfect confidence in the power we were obeying." I remember being struck with the saying as the revelation of a possible although hitherto undreamed-of, way of happiness; and often afterwards, even when full of inward rebellion, did that saying recur to me as the vision of a rest, and yet of a possible development, that would soothe, and at the same time satisfy all my yearnings.

Need I say that this rest has been revealed to me now, not as a vision, but as a reality; and that I have seen in the Lord Jesus the Master to whom we may yield up our implicit obedience, and, taking His yoke upon us, may find our perfect rest?

You little know, dear hesitating soul, of the joy you are missing. The Master has revealed Himself to you, and is calling for your complete surrender, and you shrink and hesitate. A measure of surrender you are willing to make, and think indeed it is fit and proper that you should. But an *utter* abandonment, without any reserves, seems to you too much to be asked for. You are afraid of it. It involves too much, you think, and is too great a risk. To be measurably obedient you desire; to be perfectly obedient appalls you.

Then, too, you see other souls who seem able to walk with easy consciences in a far wider path than that which appears to be marked out for you, and you ask yourself why this need be. It seems strange, and perhaps hard to you, that you must do what they need not, and must leave undone what they have liberty to do.

Ah, dear Christian, this very difference between you is your privilege, though you do not yet know it. Your Lord says, "He that *hath* my commandments, and keepeth them, he it is that loveth me; and he that loveth me shall be loved of my Father, and I will love him, and will manifest myself to him." You *have* His commandments; those you envy have them not. *You* know the mind of your Lord about many things, in which, as yet, *they* are walking in darkness. Is not this a privilege? Is it a cause for regret that your soul is brought into such near and intimate relations with your Master that He is able to tell you things which those who are farther off may not know? Do you not realize what a tender degree of intimacy is implied in this?

There are many relations in life that require from the different parties only very moderate degrees of devotion. We may have really pleasant friendships with one another, and yet spend a large part of our lives in separate interests and widely differing pursuits. When together, we may greatly enjoy one another's society, and find many congenial points; but separation is not any especial distress to us, and other and more intimate friendships do not interfere. There is not enough love between us to give us either the right or the desire to enter into and share one another's most private affairs. A certain degree of reserve and distance seems to be the suitable thing in such relations as these. But there are other relations in life where all this is changed. The friendship becomes love. The two hearts give themselves to each other, to be no longer two, but one. A union of soul takes place, which makes all that belongs to one the property of the other. Separate interests and separate paths in life are no longer possible. Things that were lawful before become unlawful now because of the nearness of the tie that binds. The reserve and distance suitable to mere friendship become fatal in love. Love gives all, and must have all in return. The wishes of one become binding obligations to the other, and the deepest desire of each heart is that it may know every secret wish or longing of the other in order that it may fly on the wings of the wind to gratify it.

Do such as these chafe under this yoke which love imposes? Do they envy the cool, calm, reasonable friendships they see around them, and regret the nearness into which their souls are brought to their beloved one because of the obligations it creates? Do they not rather glory in these very obligations, and inwardly pity, with a tender yet exulting joy, the poor far-off ones who dare not come so near? Is not every fresh revelation of the wishes of the loved one a fresh delight and privilege, and is any path found hard which their love compels them to travel?

Ah, dear soul, if you have ever known this, even for a few hours, in any earthly relation; if you have ever loved any of your fellow human beings enough to find sacrifice and service on their behalf a joy; if a whole-souled abandonment of your will to the will of another has ever gleamed across you as a blessed and longed-for privilege, or as a sweet and precious reality, then by all the tender longing love of your Heavenly Lover would I entreat you to let it be so towards Christ!

He loves you with more than the love of friendship. As a bridegroom rejoices over his bride, so does He rejoice over you, and nothing but the bride's surrender will satisfy Him. He has given you all, and He asks for all in return. The slightest reserve will grieve Him to the heart. He spared not Himself, and how can you spare yourself? For your sake He poured out in a lavish abandonment all that He had, and for His sake you must pour out all that you have, without stint or measure.

Oh, be generous in your self-surrender! Meet His measureless devotion for you with a measureless devotion to Him. Be glad and eager to throw yourself unreservedly into His loving arms, and to hand over the reins of government to Him. Whatever there is of you, let Him have it all. Give up forever everything that is separate from Him. Consent to resign, from this time forward, all liberty of choice, and glory in the blessed nearness of union which makes this enthusiasm of devotedness not only possible but necessary.

Have you never longed to lavish your love and attentions upon someone far off from you in position or circumstances, with whom you were not intimate enough for any closer approach? Have you not felt a capacity for self-surrender and devotedness that has seemed to burn within you like a fire, and yet had no object upon which it dared to lavish itself? Have not your hands been full of "alabaster boxes of ointment, very precious," which you have never been near enough to any heart to pour out? If, then, you are hearing the loving voice of your Lord calling you out into a place of nearness to Himself that will require a separation from all else, and that will make an enthusiasm of devotedness not only possible but necessary, will you shrink or hesitate? Will you think it hard that He reveals to you more of His mind than He does to others, and that He will not allow you to be happy in anything that separates you from Himself? Do you *want* to go where He cannot go with you, or to have pursuits which He cannot share?

No! no, a thousand times no! You will spring out to meet His lovely will with an eager joy. Even His slightest wish will become a binding law to you that it would fairly break your heart to disobey. You will glory in the very narrowness of the path He marks out for you, and will pity, with an infinite pity, the poor far-off ones who have missed this precious joy. The obligations of love will be to you its sweetest privileges; and the right you have acquired to lavish the uttermost wealth of abandonment of all that you have upon your Lord will seem to lift you into a region of unspeakable glory. The perfect happiness of perfect obedience will dawn upon your soul, and you will begin to know something of what Jesus meant when He said, "I *delight* to do thy will, O my God."

But do you think the joy in this will be all on your side? Has the Lord no joy in those who have thus surrendered themselves to Him, and who love to obey Him? Ah, my friends, we are not able to understand this; but surely the Scriptures reveal to us glimpses of the delight, the satisfaction, the joy our Lord has in us, which rejoice our souls with their marvelous suggestions of blessedness. That *we* should need Him is easy to comprehend; that *He* should need us seems incomprehensible. That our desire should be toward Him is a matter of course; but that His desire should be toward us passes the bounds of human belief. And yet He says it, and what can we do but believe Him? He has made our hearts capable of this supreme overmastering affection, and has offered Himself as the object of it. It is infinitely precious to Him. So much does He value it that He has made it the first and chiefest of all His commandments that we should love Him with all our might and with all our strength. Continually at every heart He is knocking, asking to be taken in as the supreme object of love. "Wilt thou have me," He says to the believer, "to be thy Beloved? Wilt thou follow me into suffering and loneliness, and endure hardness for my sake, and ask for no reward but my smile of approval and my word of praise? Wilt thou throw thyself, with a passion of abandonment, into my will? Wilt thou give up to me the absolute control of thyself and of all that thou hast? Wilt thou be content with pleasing me, and me only? May I have my way with thee in all things? Wilt thou come into so close a union with me as to make a separation from the world necessary? Wilt thou accept me for thy heavenly Bridegroom, and leave all others to cleave only unto me?"

In a thousand ways He makes this offer of union with Himself to every believer. But all do not say "Yes" to Him. Other loves and other interests seem to them too precious to be cast aside. They do not miss of Heaven because of this. But they miss an unspeakable present joy.

You, however, are not one of these. From the very first your soul has cried out eagerly and gladly to all His offers, "Yes, Lord, yes!" You are more than ready to pour out upon Him all your richest treasures of love and devotedness. You have brought to Him an enthusiasm of self-surrender that perhaps may disturb and distress the so-called prudent and moderate Christians around you. Your love makes necessary a separation from the world, of which a lower love cannot even conceive. Sacrifices and services are possible and sweet to you that could not come into the grasp of a more half-hearted devotedness. The life of love upon which you have entered gives you the right to a lavish outpouring of your *all* upon your beloved One. An intimacy and friendship, which more distant souls cannot enter upon become now not only your privilege, but your duty. Your Lord claims from you, because of your union with Him, far more than He claims of them. What to them is lawful love has made unlawful for you. To you He can make known His secrets, and to you He looks for an instant response to every requirement of His love.

Oh, it is wonderful, the glorious unspeakable privilege upon which you have entered! How little it will matter to you if men shall hate you, and shall separate you from their company, and shall reproach you and cast out your name as evil for His dear sake! You may well "rejoice in that day, and leap for joy," for, behold, your reward is great in heaven; for if you are a partaker of His suffering, you shall also be of His glory.

In you He is seeing of the "travail of his soul," and is satisfied. Your love and devotedness are His precious reward for all He has done for you. It is unspeakably sweet to Him. Do not be afraid, then, to let yourself go in a heart-whole devotedness to your Lord that can brook no reserves. Others may not approve, but He will; and that is enough. Do not stint or measure your obedience or your service. Let your heart and your hand be as free to serve Him as His heart and hand were to serve you. Let Him have all there is of you, body, soul, mind, spirit, time, talents, voice, everything. Lay your whole life open before Him, that He may control it. Say to Him each day, "Lord, enable me to regulate this day so as to please Thee! Give me spiritual insight to discover what is Thy will in all the relations of my life. Guide me as to my pursuits, my friendships, my reading, my dress, my Christian work." Do not let there be a day nor an hour in which you are not consciously doing His will and following Him wholly.

A personal service to your Lord, such as this, will give a halo to the poorest life, and gild the most monotonous existence with a heavenly glow. Have you ever grieved that the romance of youth is so soon lost in the hard realities of the world? Bring Christ thus into your life and into all its details, and a romance, far grander than the brightest days of youth could ever know, will thrill your soul, and nothing will seem hard or stern again. The meanest life will be glorified by this. Often, as I have watched a poor woman at her washtub, and have thought of all the disheartening accessories of such a life, and have been tempted to wonder why such lives need to be, there has come over me, with a thrill of joy, the recollection of this possible glorification of it, and I have realized that even this homely life lived in Christ, and with Christ, following Him whithersoever He might lead, would be filled with a spiritual romance that would make every hour of it grand; while to the most wealthy or most powerful of earthly lives, nothing more glorious could be possible.

Christ Himself, when He was on earth, declared the truth that there was no blessedness equal to the blessedness of obedience. "And it came to pass, as he spake these things, a certain woman of the company lifted up her voice, and said unto him, Blessed is the womb that bare thee, and the paps which thou hast sucked. But he said, Yea rather, blessed are they that hear the word of God, and keep it."

More blessed even than to have been the earthly mother of our Lord, or to have carried Him in our arms and nourished Him in our bosoms (and who could ever measure the bliss of that?), is it to hear and obey His will!

May our surrendered hearts reach out with an eager delight to discover and embrace the lovely will of our loving God!

CHAPTER EIGHTEEN

Divine Union

ALL THE DEALINGS OF GOD WITH THE SOUL OF THE believer are in order to bring it into oneness with Himself, that the prayer of our Lord may be fulfilled: "That they all may be one; as thou, Father, art in me, and I in thee, that they also may be one in us . . . I in them, and thou in me, that they may be made perfect in one; and that the world may know that thou hast sent me, and hast loved them, as thou hast loved me."

This Divine union was the glorious purpose in the heart of God for His people before the foundation of the world. It was the mystery hid from ages and generations. It was accomplished in the death of Christ. It has been made known by the Scriptures; and it is realized as an actual experience by many of God's dear children.

But not by all. It is true of all, and God has not hidden it or made it hard; but the eyes of many are too dim, and their hearts too unbelieving for them to grasp it. It is therefore for the purpose of bringing His people into the personal and actual realization of this that the Lord calls upon them so earnestly and so repeatedly to abandon themselves to Him, that He may work in them all the good pleasure of His will.

All the previous steps in the Christian life lead up to this. The Lord has made us for it; and until we have intelligently apprehended it, and have voluntarily consented to embrace it, the "travail of His soul" for us is not satisfied, nor have our hearts found their destined and real rest.

The usual course of Christian experience is pictured in the history of the disciples. First they were awakened to see their condition and their need, and they came to Christ, and gave their allegiance to Him. Then they followed Him, worked for Him, believed in Him, and yet how unlike Him! Seeking to be set up one above the other; running away from the cross; misunderstanding His mission and His words; forsaking their Lord in time of danger; but still sent out to preach, recognized by Him as His disciples, possessing power to work for Him. They knew Christ only "after the flesh," as outside of them, their Lord and Master, but not yet their life.

Then came Pentecost, and these same disciples came to know Him as inwardly revealed, as one with them in actual union, their very indwelling life. Henceforth He was to them Christ within, working in them to will and to do of His good pleasure, delivering them, by the law of the Spirit of His life, from the bondage to the law of sin and death under which they had been held. No longer was it between themselves and Him a war of wills and a clashing of interests. One will alone animated them, and that was His will. One interest alone was dear to them, and that was

His. They were made *one* with Him.

And surely all can recognize this picture, though perhaps as yet the final stage of it has not been fully reached. You may have left much to follow Christ, dear reader; you may have believed on Him, and worked for Him, and loved Him, and yet may not be like Him. Allegiance you know, and confidence you know, but not yet union. There are two wills, two interests, two lives. You have not yet lost your own life that you may live only in His. Once it was "I and not Christ." Next it was "I and Christ." Perhaps now it is even "Christ and I." But has it come yet to be Christ only, and not I at all?

If not, shall I tell you how it may? If you have followed me through all the previous chapters in this book, you will surely now be ready to take the definite step of faith which will lead your soul out of self and into Christ, and you will be prepared to abide in Him forever, and to know no life but His.

All you need, therefore, is to understand what the Scriptures teach about this marvelous union that you may be sure it is really intended for you.

If you read such passages as I Corinthians 3:16, "Know ye not that ye are the temple of God, and that the Spirit of God dwelleth in you?" and then look at the opening of the chapter and see to whom these wonderful words are spoken, even to "babes in Christ" who were "yet carnal," and walked according to men, you will see that this soul-union of which I speak, this unspeakably glorious mystery of an indwelling God, is the possession of even the weakest and most failing believer in Christ; so that it is not a new thing you are to ask for, but only to realize that which you already have. Of every believer in the Lord Jesus it is absolutely true, that his "body is the temple of the Holy Ghost, which is in him, which he has of God."

But although this is true, it is also equally true that unless the believer knows it, and lives in the power of it, it is to him as though it were not. Like the treasures under a man's field, which existed there before they were known or used by him, so does the life of Christ dwell in each believer as really before he knows it and lives in it as it does afterward, although its power is not manifested until, intelligently and voluntarily, the believer ceases from his own life, and accepts Christ's life in its place.

But it is very important not to make any mistakes here. This union with Christ is not a matter of emotions, but of character. It is not something we are to *feel*, but something we are to *be*. We may feel it very blessedly, and probably shall; but the vital thing is not the feeling, but the reality.

No one can be one with Christ who is not Christlike. This is a manifest truth, yet I fear it is often too much overlooked and very strong emotions of love and joy are taken as signs and proofs of Divine union in cases where the absolutely essential proofs of a Christlike life and character are conspicuously wanting. This is entirely contrary to the Scripture declaration that "he that *saith* he abideth in him ought himself also to *walk*, even as he walked." There is no escape from this, for it is not only a Divine declaration, but is in the very nature of things as well.

We speak of being one with a friend, and we mean that we have a union of purposes and thoughts and desires. No matter how enthusiastic our friends may be in their expressions of love and unity, there can be no real oneness between us unless there are, at least in some degree, the same likes and dislikes, the same thoughts and purposes and ideals. Oneness with Christ means being made a "partaker of his nature," as well as of His life; for nature and life are, of course, one.

If we are really one with Christ, therefore, it will not be contrary to our nature to be Christlike and to walk as He walked, but it will be in accordance with our nature. Sweetness, gentleness, meekness, patience, long-suffering, charity, kindness, will all be natural to the Christian, who is a partaker of the nature of Christ. It could not be otherwise.

But people who live in their emotions do not always see this. They *feel* so at one with Christ that they look no farther than this feeling, and often delude themselves with thinking they have come into the Divine union, when all the while their nature and dispositions are still under the sway of self-love.

Now, we all know that our emotions are most untrustworthy, and are largely the result of our physical condition or our natural temperaments. It is a fatal mistake, therefore, to make them the test of our oneness with Christ. This mistake works both ways. If I have very joyous emotions, I may be deluded by thinking I have entered into the Divine union when I have not; and if I have no emotions, I may grieve over my failure to enter, when I really have entered.

Character is the only real test. God is holy and those who are one with Him will be holy also. Our Lord Himself expressed His oneness with the Father in such words as these: "The Son can do nothing of himself, but what he seeth the Father do: for what things soever he doeth, these also doeth the Son likewise." "If I do not the works of my Father, believe me not. But if I do, though ye believe not me, believe the works; that ye may know, and believe, that the Father is in me, and I in him."

The test Christ gave, then, by which the reality of His oneness with the Father was to be known, was the fact that He did the works of the Father; and I know no other test for us now.

It is forever true in the nature of things that a tree is to be known by its fruits; and if we have entered into the Divine union we shall bear the Divine fruits of a Christlike life and conversation: for "he that saith, I know him, and keepeth not his commandments, is a liar, and the truth is not in him. But whoso keepeth his word, in him verily is the love of God perfected; hereby know we that we are in him."

"Hereby know we," that is, by the "keeping of his word." Pay no regard to your feelings, therefore, in this matter of oneness with Christ, but see to it that you have the really vital fruits of a oneness in character and walk and mind. Your emotions may be very delightful, or they may be very depressing. In neither case are they any real indications of your spiritual state. Very undeveloped Christians often have very powerful emotional experiences. I knew one who was kept awake often by the "waves of salvation," as she expressed it, which swept over her all night long, but who yet did not tell the truth in her intercourse with others, and was very far from honest in her business dealings. No one could possibly believe that she knew anything about a real Divine union, in spite of all her fervent emotions in regard to it.

Your joy in the Lord is to be a far deeper thing than a mere emotion. It is to be the joy of knowledge, of perception, of actual existence. It is a far gladder thing to *be* a bird, with all the actual realities of flying, than only to *feel* as if you were a bird, with no actual power of flying at all. Reality is always the vital thing.

But now, having guarded against this danger of an emotional experience of Divine union, let us consider how the reality is to be reached. And first I would say that it is not a new attitude to be taken by God, but only a new attitude to be taken by us. If I am really a child of God, then of necessity my heart is already the temple of God, and Christ is already within me. What is needed, therefore, is only that I shall recognize His presence and yield fully to His control.

It seems to me just in this way: as though Christ were living in a house, shut up in a far-off closet, unknown and unnoticed by the dwellers in the house, longing to make Himself known to them, and to be one with them in all their daily lives, and share in all their interests, but unwilling to force Himself upon their notice, because nothing but a voluntary companionship could meet or satisfy the needs of His love. The days pass by over that favored household, and they remain in ignorance of their marvelous privilege. They come and go about all their daily affairs, with no thought of their wonderful Guest. Their plans are laid without reference to Him. His wisdom to guide and His strength to protect are all lost to them. Lonely days and weeks are spent in sadness which might have been full of the sweetness of His presence.

But suddenly the announcement is made, "The Lord is in the house!" How will its owner receive the intelligence? Will he call out an eager thanksgiving, and throw wide open every door for the entrance of his glorious Guest? Or will he shrink and hesitate, afraid of His presence, and seek to reserve some private corner for a refuge from His all-seeing eye?

Dear friend, I make the glad announcement to thee that the Lord is in thy heart. Since the day of thy conversion He has been dwelling there, but thou hast lived on in ignorance of it. Every moment during all that time might have been passed in the sunshine of His sweet presence, and every step have been taken under His advice. But because thou knew it not, and did not look for Him there, thy life has been lonely and full of failure. But now that I make the announcement to thee, how wilt thou receive it? Art thou glad to have Him? Wilt thou throw wide open every door to welcome Him in? Wilt thou joyfully and thankfully give up the government of thy life into His hands? Wilt thou consult Him about everything, and let Him decide each step for thee, and mark out every path? Wilt thou invite Him into thy innermost chambers, and make Him the sharer in thy most hidden life? Wilt thou say "Yes" to all His longing for union with thee, and with a glad and eager abandonment hand thyself and all that concerns thee over into His hands? If thou wilt, then shall thy soul begin to know something of the joy of union with Christ.

But words fail me here! All that I can say is but a faint picture of the blessed reality. For far more glorious than it would be to have Christ a dweller in the house or in the heart is it to be brought into such a real and actual union with Him as to be one with Him—one will, one purpose, one interest, one life. Human words cannot express such a glory as this. And yet it ought to be expressed, and our souls ought to be made so unutterably hungry to realize it, that day or night we shall not be able to rest without it. Do you understand the words "one with Christ"? Do you catch the slightest glimpse of their marvelous meaning? Does not your whole soul begin to exult over such a wondrous destiny? It seems too wonderful to be true that such poor, weak, foolish beings as we are should be created for such an end as this; and yet it is a blessed reality. We are even *commanded* to enter into it. We are exhorted to lay down our own life that His life may be lived in us; we are asked to have no interests but His interests, to share His riches, to enter into His joys, to partake of His sorrows, to manifest His likeness, to have the same mind as He had, to think and feel and act and walk as He did.

Shall we consent to all this? The Lord will not force it on us, for He wants us as His companions and His friends, and a forced union would be incompatible with this. It must be voluntary on our part. The bride must say a willing "Yes" to the bridegroom, or the joy of their union is wanting. Can we not say a willing "Yes" to our Lord?

It is a very simple transaction, and yet very real. The steps are but three: first, we must be convinced that the Scriptures teach this glorious indwelling of God; then we must surrender our whole selves to Him to be possessed by Him; and, finally, we must believe that He *has* taken possession, and *is* dwelling in us. We must begin to reckon ourselves dead, and to reckon Christ as our only life. We must maintain this attitude of soul unwaveringly. It will help us to say, "I am crucified with Christ: nevertheless I live, yet not I, but Christ liveth in me," over and over, day and night, until it becomes the habitual breathing of our souls. We must put off our self-life by faith continually, and put on the life of Christ; and we must do this not only by faith, but practically as well. We must continually put self to death in all the details of daily life, and must let Christ instead live and work in us. I mean we must never do the selfish thing, but always the Christ-like thing. We must let this become, by its constant repetition, the attitude of our whole being. And as surely as we do, we shall come at last to understand something of what it means to be made one with Christ as He and the Father are one. Christ left all to be joined to us; shall we not also leave all to be joined to Him in this Divine union which transcends words, but for which our Lord prayed when He said, "Neither pray I for these alone, but for them also which shall believe on me through their word: that they all may be one; as thou, Father, art in me, and I in thee, that they also may be one in us"?

CHAPTER NINETEEN

The Chariots of God

IT HAS BEEN WELL SAID THAT "EARTHLY CARES ARE A heavenly discipline." But they are even something better than discipline,—they are God's chariots, sent to take the soul to its high places of triumph.

They do not look like chariots. They look instead like enemies, sufferings, trials, defeats, misunderstandings, disappointments, unkindnesses. They look like Juggernaut cars of misery and wretchedness, which are only waiting to roll over us and crush us into the earth. But could we see them as they really are, we should recognize them as chariots of triumph in which we may ride to those very heights of victory for which our souls have been longing and praying. The Juggernaut car is the visible thing; the chariot of God is the invisible. The King of Syria came up against the man of God with horses and chariots that could be seen by every eye, but God had chariots that could be seen by none save the eye of faith. The servant of the Prophet could only see the outward and visible; and he cried, as so many have done since, "Alas, my master! how shall we do?" But the Prophet himself sat calmly within his house without fear, because his eyes were opened to see the invisible; and all he asked for his servant was, "Lord, I pray thee open his eyes that he may see."

This is the prayer we need to pray for ourselves and for one another, "Lord, open our eyes that we may see"; for the world all around us, as well as around the Prophet, is full of God's horses and chariots, waiting to carry us to places of glorious victory. And when our eyes are thus opened, we shall see in all the events of life, whether great or small, whether joyful or sad, a "chariot" for our souls.

Everything that comes to us becomes a chariot the moment we treat it as such; and on the other hand, even the smallest trials may be a Juggernaut car to crush us into misery or despair if we so consider them. It lies with each of us to choose which they shall be. It all depends, not upon what these events are, but upon how we take them. If we lie down under them and let them roll over us and crush us, they become Juggernaut cars, but if we climb up into them, as into a car of victory, and make them carry us triumphantly onward and upward, they become the chariots of God.

Whenever we mount into God's chariots the same thing happens to us spiritually that happened to Elijah. We shall have a translation. Not into the heavens above us, as Elijah did, but into the heaven within us; and this, after all, is almost a grander translation than his. We shall be carried away from the low, earthly, groveling plane of life, where everything hurts and everything is unhappy, up into the "heavenly places in Christ Jesus," where we can ride in triumph over all below.

These "heavenly places" are interior, not exterior; and the road that leads to them is interior also. But the chariot that carries the soul over this road is generally some outward loss or trial or disappointment, some chastening that does not indeed seem for the present to be joyous, but grievous, but that nevertheless afterward "yieldeth the peaceable fruits of righteousness to them that are exercised thereby."

In the Canticles we are told of "chariots paved with love." We cannot always see the love-lining to our own particular chariot. It often looks very unlovely. It may be a cross-grained relative or friend; it may be the result of human malice or cruelty or neglect; but every chariot sent by God must necessarily be paved with love, since God is love; and God's love is the sweetest, softest, tenderest thing to rest one's self upon that was ever found by any soul anywhere. It is His love, indeed, that sends the chariot.

Look upon your chastenings then, no matter how grievous they may be for the present, as God's chariots sent to carry your souls into the "high places" of spiritual achievement and uplifting, and you will find that they are, after all, "paved with love."

The Bible tells us that when God went forth for the salvation of His people, then He "did ride upon His horses and chariots of salvation." And it is the same now. Everything becomes a "chariot of salvation" when God rides upon it. He maketh even the "clouds his chariot," we are told, and "rideth on the wings of the wind." Therefore the clouds and storms that darken our skies and seem to shut out the shining of the sun of righteousness are really only God's chariots, into which we may mount with Him, and "ride prosperously" over all the darkness. Dear reader, have you made the clouds in your life the chariots? Are you "riding prosperously" with God on top of them all?

I knew a lady who had a very slow servant. She was an excellent girl in every other respect, and very valuable in the household; but her slowness was a constant source of irritation to her mistress, who was naturally quick, and who always chafed at slowness. This lady would consequently get out of temper with the girl twenty times a day, and twenty times a day would repent of her anger and resolve to conquer it, but in vain. Her life was made miserable by the conflict. One day it occurred to her that she had for a long while been praying for patience, and that perhaps this slow servant was the very chariot the Lord had sent to carry her soul over into patience. She immediately accepted it as such, and from that time used the slowness of her servant as a chariot for her soul; and the result was a victory of patience that no slowness of anybody was ever after able to disturb.

I knew another lady, at a crowded convention, who was put to sleep in a room with two others on account of the crowd. *She* wanted to sleep, but *they* wanted to talk; and the first night she was greatly disturbed, and lay there fretting and fuming long after the others had hushed and she might have slept. But the next day she heard something about God's chariots, and at night she accepted these talking friends as her chariots to carry her over into sweetness and patience, and was kept in undisturbed calm. When, however, it grew very late, and she knew they all ought to be sleeping, she ventured to say quietly, "Friends, I am lying here riding in a chariot!" The effect was instantaneous, and perfect quiet reigned! Her chariot had carried her over to victory, not only inwardly, but at last outwardly as well.

If we would ride in God's chariot instead of our own we should find this to be the case continually.

Our constant temptation is to trust in the "chariots of Egypt," or, in other words, in earthly resources. We can *see* them; they are tangible, and real, and look substantial, while God's chariots are invisible and intangible, and it is hard to believe they are there.

We try to reach high spiritual places with the "multitude of our chariots." We depend first on one thing and then on another to advance our spiritual condition, and to gain our spiritual victories, We "go down to Egypt for help." And God is obliged often to destroy all our own earthly chariots before He can bring us to the point of mounting into His.

We lean too much upon a dear friend to help us onward in the spiritual life, and the Lord is obliged to separate us from that friend. We feel that all our spiritual prosperity depends on our continuance under the ministry of a favorite preacher, and he is mysteriously removed. We look upon our prayer-meeting or our Bible-class as the chief source of our spiritual strength, and we are shut up from attending them. And the "chariot of God" which alone can carry us to the places where we hoped to be taken by the instrumentalities upon which we have been depending is to be found in the very deprivations we have so mourned over. God must burn up with the fire of His love every chariot of our own that stands in the way of our mounting into His.

We have to be brought to the place where all other refuges fail us before we can say, "He only." We say, "He and—something else," "He and my experiences," or "He and my church relationships," or "He and my Christian work"; and all that comes after the "and" must be taken away from us, or must be proved useless, before we can come to the "He only." As long as visible chariots are at hand the soul will not mount into the invisible ones.

Let us be thankful, then, for every trial that will help to destroy our earthly chariots, and that will compel us to take refuge in the chariot of God which stands ready and waiting beside us in every event and circumstance of life. We are told that "God rideth upon the heavens," and if we would ride with Him there we need to be brought to the end of all riding upon the earth.

When we mount into God's chariot our goings are "established," for no obstacles can hinder His triumphal course. All losses, therefore, are gains that bring us to this. Paul understood this, and he gloried in the losses which brought him such unspeakable rewards. "But what things were gain to me, those I counted loss for Christ. Yea doubtless, and I count all things but loss for the excellency of the knowledge of Christ Jesus my Lord: for whom I have suffered the loss of all things, and do count them but dung, that I may win Christ, and be found in him."

Even the "thorn in the flesh," the messenger of Satan sent to buffet him, became a "chariot of God" to his willing soul, and carried him to the heights of triumph which he could have reached in no other way. To "take pleasure" in one's trials, what is this but to turn them into the grandest of chariots?

Joseph had a revelation of his future triumphs and reigning, but the chariots that carried him there looked to the eye of sense like dreadful Juggernaut cars of failure and defeat. Slavery and imprisonment are strange chariots to take one to a kingdom, and yet by no other way could Joseph have reached his exaltation. And our exaltation to the spiritual throne that awaits us is often reached by similar chariots.

The great point, then, is to have our eyes opened to see in everything that comes to us a "chariot of God," and to learn how to mount into these chariots. We must recognize each thing that comes to us as being really God's chariot for us, and must accept it as from Him. He does not command or originate the thing, perhaps; but the moment we put it into His hands it becomes His, and He at once turns it into a chariot for us. He makes all things, even bad things, work together for good to all those who trust Him. All He needs is to have them entirely committed to Him.

When your trial comes, then, put it right into the will of God, and climb into that will as a little child climbs into its mother's arms. The baby carried in the chariot of its mother's arms rides triumphantly through the hardest places, and does not even know they are hard. And how much more we who are carried in the chariot of the "arms of God!"

Get into your chariot, then. Take each thing that is wrong in your lives as God's chariot for you. No matter who the builder of the wrong may be, whether men or devils, by the time it reaches your side it is God's chariot for you, and is meant to carry you to a heavenly place of triumph. Shut out all the second causes, and find the Lord in it. Say, "Lord, open my eyes that I may see, not the visible enemy, but thy unseen chariots of deliverance."

No doubt the enemy will try to turn your chariot into a Juggernaut car by taunting you with the suggestion that God is not in your trouble, and that there is no help for you in Him. But you must utterly disregard all such suggestions, and must overcome them with the assertion of a confident faith. "God *is* my refuge and strength, a very present help in time of trouble," must be your continual declaration, no matter what the seemings may be.

Moreover, you must not be half-hearted about it. You must climb wholly into your chariot, not with one foot dragging on the ground. There must be no "ifs," or "buts," or "supposings," or "questionings." You must accept God's will fully, and must hide yourself in the arms of His love, that are always underneath to receive you, in every circumstance and at every moment. Say, "Thy will be done, Thy will be done," over and over. Shut out every thought but the one thought of submission to His will and of trust in His love. There can be no trials in which God's will has not a place somewhere; and the soul has only to mount into His will as in a chariot, and it will find itself "riding upon the heavens" with God in a way it had never dreamed could be.

The soul that thus rides with God "on the sky" has views and sights of things that the soul which grovels on the earth can never have. The poor crushed and bleeding victim under the car of Juggernaut can see only the dust and stones and the grinding wheels, but the triumphant rider in the chariot sees far fairer sights.

Do any of you ask where your chariots are to be found? The Psalmist says, "The chariots of God are twenty thousand, even thousands of angels." There is never in any life a lack of chariots. One dear Christian said to me at the close of a meeting where I had been speaking about these chariots: "I am a poor woman, and have all my life long grieved that I could not drive in a carriage like some of my rich neighbors. But I have been looking over my life while you have been talking, and I find that it is so full of chariots on every side that I am sure I shall never need to walk again."

I have not a shadow of doubt, dear readers, that if all our eyes could be opened to-day we should see our homes, and our places of business, and the streets we traverse, filled with the "chariots of God." There is no need for any one of us to walk for lack of chariots. That cross inmate of your household, who has hitherto made life a burden to you, and who has been the Juggernaut car to crush your soul into the dust, may henceforth be a glorious chariot to carry you to the heights of heavenly patience and long-suffering. That misunderstanding, that mortification, that un-kindness, that disappointment, that loss, that defeat,—all these are chariots waiting to carry you to the very heights of victory you have so longed to reach.

Mount into them, then, with thankful hearts, and lose sight of all second causes in the shining of His love, who will "carry you in his arms" safely and triumphantly over it all.

CHAPTER TWENTY

The Life on Wings

THIS LIFE HID WITH CHRIST IN GOD HAS MANY ASPECTS, and can be considered under a great many different figures. There is one aspect which has been a great help and inspiration to me, and I think may be also to some other longing and hungry souls. It is what I call the life on wings.

Our Lord has not only told us to consider the "flowers of the field," but also the "birds of the air"; and I have found that these little winged creatures have some wonderful lessons for us. In one of the Psalms, the Psalmist, after enumerating the darkness and bitterness of his life in this earthly sphere of trial, cries out, "Oh that I had wings like a dove! for then would I fly away, and be at rest. Lo, then would I wander far off, and remain in the wilderness. I would hasten my escape from the windy storm and tempest" (Psalm 55:6–8).

This cry for "wings" is as old as humanity. Our souls were made to "mount up with wings," and they can never be satisfied with anything short of flying. Like the captive-born eagle that feels within it the instinct of flight, and chafes and frets at its imprison-ment, hardly knowing what it longs for, so do our souls chafe and fret, and cry out for freedom. We can never rest on earth, and we long to "fly away" from all that so holds and hampers and imprisons us here.

This restlessness and discontent develop them-selves generally in seeking an outward escape from our circumstances or from our miseries. We do not at first recognize the fact that our only way of escape is to "mount up with wings," and we try to "flee on horses," as the Israelites did, when oppressed by their trials (see Isaiah 30:16).

Our "horses" are the outward things upon which we depend for relief, some change of circumstances, or some help from man; and we mount on these and run east or west, or north or south, anywhere to get away from our trouble, thinking in our ignorance that a change of our environment is all that is necessary to give deliverance to our souls. But all such efforts to escape are unavailing, as we have each one proved hundreds of times; for the soul is not so made that it can "flee upon horses," but must make its flight always upon wings.

Moreover, these "horses" generally carry us, as they did the Israelites, out of one trouble only to land us in another. It is as the Prophet says, "As if a man did flee from a lion, and a bear met him; or went into the house, and leaned his hand on the wall, and a serpent bit him."

How often have we also run from some "lion" in our pathway only to be met by a "bear," or have hid-den ourselves in a place of supposed safety only to be bitten by a "serpent"! No; it is useless for the soul to hope to escape by running away from its troubles to any earthly refuge, for there is not one that can give it deliverance.

Is there, then, no way of escape for us when in trouble or distress? Must we just plod wearily through it all and look for no relief? I rejoice to answer that there is a glorious way of escape for every one of us if we will but mount up on wings and fly away from it all to God. It is not a way east or west, or north or south, but it is a way upwards. "They that wait upon the Lord shall renew their strength; they shall mount up with wings as eagles; they shall run, and not be weary; and they shall walk, and not faint."

All creatures that have wings can escape from every snare that is set for them if only they will fly high enough; and the soul that uses its wings can always find a sure "way to escape" from all that can hurt or trouble it.

What, then, are these wings? Their secret is contained in the words, "They that wait upon the Lord." The soul that waits upon the Lord is the soul that is entirely surrendered to Him, and that trusts Him perfectly. Therefore we might name our wings the wings of Surrender and of Trust. I mean by this, that if we will only surrender ourselves utterly to the Lord, and will trust Him perfectly, we shall find our souls "mounting up with wings as eagles" to the "heavenly places" in Christ Jesus, where earthly annoyances or sorrows have no power to disturb us.

The wings of the soul carry it up into a spiritual plane of life, into the "life hid with Christ in God," which is a life utterly independent of circumstances, one that no cage can imprison and no shackles bind.

The "things above" are the things the soul on wings cares about, not the "things on the earth," and it views life and all its experiences from the high altitude of "heavenly places in Christ Jesus." Things look very different according to the standpoint from which we view them. The caterpillar, as it creeps along the ground, must have a widely different "view" of the world around it from that which the same caterpillar will have when its wings are developed, and it soars in the air above the very places where once it crawled. And similarly the crawling soul must necessarily see things in a very different aspect from the soul that has "mounted up with wings." The mountain top may blaze with sunshine when all the valley below is shrouded in fogs, and the bird whose wings can carry him high enough may mount at will out of the gloom below into the joy of the sunlight above.

I was at one time spending a winter in London, and during three long months we did not once see any genuine sunshine because of the dense clouds of smoke that hung over the city like a pall. But many a time I saw that above the smoke the sun was shining, and once or twice through a rift I had a glimpse of a bird, with sunshine on its wings, sailing above the fog in the clear blue of the sunlit sky. Not all the brushes in London can sweep away the fog; but could we only mount high enough we should reach a region above it all.

And this is what the soul on wings does. It overcomes the world through faith. To overcome means to "come over," not to be crushed under; and the soul on wings flies over the world and the things of it. These lose their power to hold or bind the spirit that can "come over" them on the wings of Surrender and Trust. That spirit is made in very truth "more than conqueror."

Birds overcome the lower law of gravitation by the higher law of flight; and the soul on wings overcomes the lower law of sin and misery and bondage by the higher law of spiritual flying. The "law of the spirit of life in Christ Jesus" must necessarily be a higher and more dominant law than the law of sin and death; therefore the soul that has mounted into this upper region of the life in Christ cannot fail to conquer and triumph.

But it may be asked how it is, then, that all Christians do not always triumph. I answer that it is because a great many Christians do not "mount up with wings" into this higher plane of life at all. They live on the same low level with their circumstances; and instead of flying over them, they try to fight them on their own earthly plane. On this plane the soul is powerless; it has no weapons with which to conquer there; and instead of overcoming, or coming over, the trials and sorrows of the earthly life it is overcome by them and crushed under them.

We all know, as I have said, that things look differently to us according to our "point of view." Trials assume a very different aspect when looked down upon from above than when viewed from their own level. What seems like an impassable wall on its own level becomes an insignificant line to the eyes that see it from the top of a mountain; and the snares and sorrows that assume such immense proportion while we look at them on the earthly plane become insignificant little motes in the sunshine when the soul has mounted on wings to the heavenly places above them.

A friend once illustrated to me the difference between three of her friends in the following way. She said if they should all three come to a spiritual mountain which had to be crossed, the first one would tunnel through it with hard and wearisome labor; the second would meander around it in an indefinite fashion, hardly knowing where she was going, and yet, because her aim was right, getting around it at last; but the third, she said, would just flap her wings and fly right over. I think we must all know something of these different ways of locomotion; and I trust, if any of us in the past have tried to tunnel our way through the mountains that have stood across our pathway, or have been meandering around them, that we may from henceforth resolve to spread our wings and "mount up" into the clear atmosphere of God's presence, where it will be easy to overcome, or come over, the highest mountain of them all.

I say "spread our wings and mount up," because not the largest wings ever known can lift a bird one inch upward unless they are used. We must *use* our wings, or they avail us nothing.

It is not worth while to cry out, "Oh that I had wings and then I would flee," for we *have* the wings already, and what is needed is not more wings, but only that we should use those we have. The power to surrender and trust exists in every human soul, and only needs to be brought into exercise. With these two wings we *can* "flee" to God at any moment; but, in order really to reach Him, we must actively use them. We must not merely want to use them, but we must *do* it definitely and actively. A passive surrender or a passive trust will not do. I mean this very practically. We shall not "mount up" very high if we only surrender and trust in theory, or in our especially religious moments. We must do it definitely and practically about each detail of daily life as it comes to us. We must meet our disappointments, our thwartings, our persecutions, our malicious enemies, our provoking friends, our trials and temptations of every sort, with an active and experimental attitude of surrender and trust. We must spread our wings and "mount up" to the "heavenly places in Christ" above them all, where they will lose their power to harm or distress us. For from these high places we shall see things through the eye of Christ, and all earth will be glorified in the heavenly vision.

> "The dove hath neither claw nor sting,
>   Nor weapon for the fight,
> She owes her safety to the wing,
>   Her victory to flight.
> The bridegroom opes His arms of love,
>   And in them folds the panting dove."

How changed our lives would be if we could only fly through the days on these wings of surrender and trust! Instead of stirring up strife and bitterness by trying, metaphorically, to knock down and walk over our offending brothers and sisters, we should escape all strife by simply spreading our wings and mounting up to the heavenly region, where our eyes would see all things covered with a mantle of Christian love and pity.

Our souls were made to live in this upper atmosphere, and we stifle and choke on any lower level. Our eyes were made to look off from these heavenly heights, and our vision is distorted by any lower gazing. It is a great blessing, therefore, that our loving Father in heaven has mercifully arranged all the discipline of our lives with a view to teaching us to fly.

In Deuteronomy we have a picture of how this teaching is done: "As an eagle stirreth up her nest, fluttereth over her young, spreadeth abroad her wings, taketh them, beareth them on her wings: so the Lord alone did lead him, and there was no strange god with him."

The mother eagle teaches her little ones to fly by making their nest so uncomfortable that they are forced to leave it and commit themselves to the unknown world of air outside. And just so does our God to us. He stirs up our comfortable nests, and pushes us over the edge of them, and we are forced to use our wings to save ourselves from fatal falling. Read your trials in this light, and see if you cannot begin to get a glimpse of their meaning. Your wings are being developed.

I knew a lady whose life was one long strain of trial by a cruel, wicked, drunken husband. There was no possibility of human help, and in her despair she was driven to use her wings and fly to God. And during the long years of trial her wings grew so strong from constant flying that at last, as she told me, when the trials were at their hardest, it seemed to her as if her soul was carried over them on a beautiful rainbow and found itself in a peaceful resting-place on the other side.

With this end in view we can surely accept with thankfulness every trial that compels us to use our wings, for only so can they grow strong and large and fit for the highest flying. Unused wings gradually wither and shrink and lose their flying power; and if we had nothing in our lives that made flying necessary we might perhaps at last lose all capacity to fly.

But you may ask, Are there no hindrances to flying, even where the wings are strong, and the soul is trying hard to use them? I answer, Yes. A bird may be imprisoned in a cage, or it may be tethered to the ground with a cord, or it may be loaded with a weight that drags it down, or it may be entrapped in the "snare of the fowler," and hindrances which answer to all these in the spiritual realm may make it impossible for the soul to fly until it has been set free from them by the mighty power of God.

One "snare of the fowler" that entraps many souls is the snare of doubt. The doubts look so plausible and often so humble that Christians walk into their "snare" without dreaming for a moment that it is a snare at all, until they find themselves caught and unable to fly; for there is no more possibility of flying for the soul that doubts than there is for the bird caught in the fowler's snare.

The reason of this is evident. One of our wings, namely, the wing of trust, is entirely disabled by the slightest doubt; and just as it requires two wings to lift a bird in the air, so does it require two wings to lift the soul. A great many people do everything but trust. They spread the wing of surrender, and use it vigorously, and wonder why it is that they do not mount up, never dreaming that it is because all the while the wing of trust is hanging idle by their sides. It is because Christians use one wing only, that their efforts to fly are often so irregular and fruitless.

Look at a bird with a broken wing trying to fly, and you will get some idea of the kind of motion all one-sided flying must make. We must use both our wings, or not try to fly at all.

It may be that for some the "snare of the fowler" is some subtle form of sin, some hidden want of consecration. Where this is the case the wing of trust may seem to be all right, but the wing of surrender hangs idly down; and it is just as hopeless to try to fly with the wing of trust alone as with the wing of surrender alone. Both wings must be used, or no flying is possible.

Or perhaps the soul may feel as if it were in a prison from which it cannot escape, and consequently is debarred from mounting up on wings. No earthly bars can ever imprison the soul. No walls however high, or bolts however strong, can imprison an eagle so long as there is an open way upward; and earth's power can never hold the soul in prison while the upward way is kept open and free. Our enemies may build walls around us as high as they please, but they cannot build any barrier between us and God; and if we "mount up with wings" we can fly higher than any of their walls can ever reach.

If we find ourselves imprisoned, then, we may be sure of this, that it is not our earthly environment that constitutes our prison-house, for the soul's wings scorn all paltry bars and walls of earth's making. The only thing that can really imprison the soul is something that hinders its upward flight. The Prophet tells us that it is our iniquities that have separated between us and our God and our sins that have hid His face from us. Therefore, if our soul is imprisoned, it must be because some indulged sin has built a barrier between us and the Lord, and we cannot fly until this sin is given up and put out of the way.

But often where there is no conscious sin the soul is still unconsciously tethered to something of earth, and so struggles in vain to fly. A party of my friends once got into a boat in Norway to row around one of the fiords there. They took their seats and began to row vigorously, but the boat made no headway. They put out more strength and rowed harder than before, but all in vain, not an inch did the boat move. Then one of the party suddenly recollected that the boat had not been unmoored, and he exclaimed, "No wonder we could not get away when we were trying to pull the whole continent of Europe after us!" And just so our souls are often not unmoored from earthly things. We must cut ourselves loose. As well might an eagle try to fly with a hundred-ton weight tied fast to its feet as the soul try to "mount up with wings" while a weight of earthly cares and anxieties is holding it down to earth.

When our Lord was trying to teach His disciples concerning this danger, He told them a parable of a great supper to which many who were invited failed to come because they were hindered by their earthly cares. One had bought a piece of ground, another a yoke of oxen, and a third had married a wife; and they felt that all these things needed their care.

Wives, or oxen, or land, or even very much smaller things, may be the cords that tether the soul from flying, or the weights that hold it down. Let us, then, cut every cord, and remove every barrier, that our souls may find no hindrance to their mounting up with wings as eagles to heavenly places in Christ Jesus.

We are commanded to have our hearts filled with songs of rejoicing and to make inward melody to the Lord. But unless we mount up with wings this is impossible, for the only creature that can sing is the creature that flies. When the Prophet declared that though all the world should be desolate, yet he would rejoice in God and joy in the God of his salvation, his soul was surely on wings. Paul knew what it was to use his wings when he found himself to be "sorrowful, yet always rejoicing." On the earthly plane all was dark to both Paul and the Prophet, but on the heavenly plane all was brightest sunshine.

Do you know anything of this life on wings, dear reader? Do you "mount up" continually to God, out of and above earth's cares and trials, to that higher plane of life where all is peace and triumph, or do you plod wearily along on foot through the midst of your trials and let them overwhelm you at every turn?

Let us, however, guard against a mistake here. Do not think that by flying I mean necessarily any very joyous emotions or feelings of exhilaration. There is a great deal of emotional flying that is not real flying at all. It is such flying as a feather accomplishes which is driven upward by a strong puff of wind but flutters down again as soon as the wind ceases to blow. The flying I mean is a matter of *principle,* not a matter of *emotion.* It may be accompanied by very joyous emotions, but it does not depend on them. It depends only upon the facts of an entire surrender and an absolute trust. Every one who will honestly use these two wings, and will faithfully persist in using them, will find that they *have* mounted up with wings as an eagle, no matter how empty of all emotion they may have felt themselves to be before.

For the promise is sure: "They that wait upon the Lord SHALL mount up with wings as eagles." Not "may perhaps mount up," but "SHALL." It is the inevitable result. May we each one prove it for ourselves!

> "The lark soars singing from its nest,
>   And tells aloud
> His trust in God, and so is blest
>   Let come what cloud.
>
> "He has no store, he sows no seed,
> Yet sings aloud, and doth not heed.
> Through cloudy day or scanty feed,

He sings to shame
Men who forget in fear of need
A Father's name.

"The heart that trusts forever sings,
And feels as light as it has wings;
A well of peace within it springs.
Come good or ill,
Whate'er to-day or morrow bring,
It is His will."

Hannah Whitall Smith

The God
of All Comfort

CHAPTER 1
WHY THIS BOOK HAS BEEN WRITTEN

"My heart is inditing a good matter; I speak of the things which I have made touching the king."

I was once talking on the subject of religion with an intelligent agnostic, whom I very much wished to influence, and after listening to me politely for a little while, he said, "Well, madam, all I have to say is this. If you Christians want to make us agnostics inclined to look into your religion, you must try to be more comfortable in the possession of it yourselves. The Christians I meet seem to me to be the very most uncomfortable people anywhere around. They seem to carry their religion as a man carries a headache. He does not want to get rid of his head, but at the same time it is very uncomfortable to have it. And I for one do not care to have that sort of religion."

This was a lesson I have never forgotten, and it is the primary cause of my writing this book.

I was very young in the Christian life at the time of this conversation, and was still in the first joy of my entrance into it, so I could not believe that any of God's children could be as uncomfortable in their religious lives as my agnostic friend had asserted. But when the early glow of my conversion had passed, and I had come down to the dullness of everyday duties and responsibilities, I soon found from my own experience, and also from the similar experiences of most of the Christians around me, that there was far too much truth in his assertion, and that the religious life of most of us was full of discomfort and unrest. In fact, it seemed, as one of my Christian friends said to me one day when we were comparing our experiences, "as if we had just enough religion to make us miserable."

I confess that this was very disappointing, for I had expected something altogether different. It seemed to me exceedingly incongruous that a religion, whose fruits were declared in the Bible to be love, and joy, and peace should so often work out practically in an exactly opposite direction, and should develop the fruits of doubt, and fear, and unrest, and conflict, and discomforts of every kind; and I resolved if possible to find out what was the matter. Why, I asked myself, should the children of God lead such utterly uncomfortable religious lives when He has led us to believe that His yoke would be easy and His burden light? Why are we tormented with so many spiritual doubts, and such heavy spiritual anxieties? Why do we find it so hard to be sure that God really loves us, and why is it that we never seem able to believe long at a time in His kindness and His care? How is it that we can let ourselves suspect Him of forgetting us and forsaking us in times of need? We can trust our earthly friends, and can be comfortable in their companionship, and why is it then that we cannot trust our heavenly Friend, and that we seem unable to be comfortable in His service?

I believe I have found the answer to these questions, and I should like to state frankly that my object in writing this book is to try to bring into some troubled Christian lives around me a little real and genuine comfort. My own idea of the religion of the Lord Jesus Christ is that it was meant to be full of comfort. I feel sure any unprejudiced reader of the New Testament would say the same; and I believe that every newly converted soul, in the first joy of its conversion, fully expects it. And yet, as I have said, it seems as if, with a large proportion of Christians, their religious lives are the most uncomfortable part of their existence. Does the fault of this state of things lie with the Lord? Has He promised more than He is able to supply?

A writer has said, "We know what overadvertisement is.

It is a twentieth-century disease from which we all suffer. There are posters on every billboard, exaggerations on every blank wall, representations and misrepresentations without number. What visions we have seen of impossible fruits and flowers grown from Mr. So-and-So's seeds. Everything is overadvertised. Is it the same with the kingdom of God? Do the fruits which we raise from the good seed of the kingdom verify the description given by Him from whom we obtained that good seed? Has He played us false? There is a feeling abroad that Christ has offered in His Gospel more than He has to give. People think that they have not exactly realized what was predicted as the portion of the children of God. But why is this so? Has the kingdom of God been overadvertised, or is it only that it has been underbelieved; has the Lord Jesus Christ been overestimated, or has He only been undertrusted?"

What I want to do in this book is to show, in my small measure, what I firmly believe, that the kingdom of God could not possibly be overadvertised, nor the Lord Jesus Christ overestimated, for eye hath not seen, nor ear heard, neither have entered into the heart of man, the things which God hath prepared for them that love Him; and that all the difficulty arises from the fact that we have underbelieved and undertrusted.

I want, therefore, to show as best I can the grounds there are in the religion of the Lord Jesus Christ for that deep and lasting peace and comfort of soul, which nothing earthly can disturb, and which is declared to be the portion of those who embrace it. And I want further to tell, if this is indeed our rightful portion, how we are to avail ourselves of it, and what are the things that hinder. There is God's part in the matter, and there is man's part, and we must look carefully at both.

A wild young fellow, who was brought to the Lord at a mission meeting, and who became a rejoicing Christian and lived an exemplary life afterward, was asked by someone what he did to get converted. "Oh," he said, "I did my part, and the Lord did His."

"But what was your part," asked the inquirer, "and what was the Lord's part?"

"My part," was the prompt reply, "was to run away,

and the Lord's part was to run after me until He caught me." A most significant answer; but how few can understand it!

God's part is always to run after us. Christ came to seek and to save that which was lost. "What man of you," He says, "having a hundred sheep, if he lose one of them, doth not leave the ninety and nine in the wilderness, and go after that which is lost until he find it? And when he hath found it, he layeth it on his shoulders rejoicing." This is always the divine part; but in our foolishness we do not understand it, but think that the Lord is the the one who is lost, and that our part is to seek and find Him. The very expressions we use show this. We urge sinners to "seek the Lord," and we talk about having "found" Him. "Have you found the Saviour?" asked a too zealous mission worker of a happy, trusting little girl.

With a look of amazement, she replied in a tone of wonder, "Why, I did not know the Saviour was lost!"

It is our ignorance of God that does it all. Because we do not know Him, we naturally get all sorts of wrong ideas about Him. We think He is an angry Judge who is on the watch for our slightest faults, or a harsh Taskmaster determined to exact from us the uttermost service, or a self-absorbed Deity demanding His full measure of honor and glory, or a far-off Sovereign concerned only with His own affairs and indifferent to our welfare. Who can wonder that such a God can neither be loved nor trusted? And who could expect Christians, with such ideas concerning Him, to be anything but full of discomfort and misery?

But I can assert boldly, and without fear of contradiction, that it is impossible for anyone who really knows God to have such uncomfortable thoughts about Him. Plenty of outward discomforts there may be, and many earthly sorrows and trials, but through them all the soul that knows God cannot but dwell inwardly in a fortress of perfect peace. "Whoso hearkeneth unto me," He says, "shall dwell safely; and shall be quiet from fear of evil." And this is a statement that no one dare question. If we would really hearken unto God, which means not only hearing Him, but believing what we hear, we could not fail to know that, just because He is God, He cannot do other than care for us as

He cares for the apple of His eye; and that all that tender love and divine wisdom can do for our welfare, must be and will be unfailingly done. Not a single loophole for worry or fear is left to the soul that knows God.

"Ah, yes," you say, "but how am I to get to know Him? Other people seem to have some kind of inward revelation that makes them know Him, but I never do; and no matter how much I pray, everything seems dark to me. I want to know God, but I do not see how to manage it."

Your trouble is that you have got a wrong idea of what knowing God is, or at least the kind of knowing I mean. For I do not mean any mystical interior revelations of any kind. Such revelations are delightful when you can have them, but they are not always at your command, and they are often variable and uncertain. The kind of knowing I mean is just the plain matter-of-fact knowledge of God's nature and character that comes to us by believing what is revealed to us in the Bible concerning Him. The apostle John at the close of his Gospel says, regarding the things he had been recording: "And many other signs truly did Jesus in the presence of His disciples which are not written in this book: but these are written that ye might believe that Jesus is the Christ, the Son of God; and that, believing, ye might have life through his name." It is believing the thing that is written, not the thing that is inwardly revealed, that is to give life; and the kind of knowing I mean is the knowing that comes from believing the things that are written.

I mean, to be practical, that when I read in the Bible that God is love, I am to believe it, just because "it is written," and not because I have had any inward revelation that is true; and when the Bible says that He cares for us as He cares for the lilies of the field and the birds of the air, and that the very hairs of our head are all numbered, I am to believe it, just because it is written, no matter whether I have any inward revelation of it or not.

It is of vital importance for us to understand that the Bible is a statement, not of theories, but of actual facts; and that things are not true because they are in the Bible, but they are only in the Bible because they are true. A little boy, who had been studying at school about the discovery of America, said to his father one day, "Father, if I had been

Columbus, I would not have taken all that trouble to discover America."

"Why, what would you have done?" asked the father.

"Oh," replied the little boy, "I would have just gone to the map and found it." This little boy did not understand that maps are only pictures of already known places, and that America did not exist because it was on the map, but it could not be on the map until it was already known to exist. And similarly with the Bible. It is, like the map, a simple statement of facts; so that when it tells us that God loves us, it is only telling us something that is a fact, and that would not be in the Bible if it had not been already known to be a fact.

It was a great discovery to me when I grasped this idea. It seemed to take all uncertainty and all speculation out of the revelation given us in the Bible of the salvation of the Lord Jesus Christ, and to make all that is written concerning Him to be simply a statement of incontrovertible facts. And facts we can believe, and what is more, we do believe them as soon as we see that they are facts. Inward revelations we cannot manage, but anyone in his senses can believe the thing that is written. And although this may seem very dry and bare to start with, it will, if steadfastly persevered in, result in very blessed inward revelations, and will sooner or later lead us out into such a knowledge of God as will transform our lives. This kind of knowing brings us convictions; and to my mind convictions are far superior to any inward revelations, delightful as these last are. An inward revelation may be upset by the state of one's health, or by many other upsetting things, but a conviction is permanent. Once convince a man that two and two make four, and no amount of dyspepsia, or liver complaint, or east winds, or anything else, but actual lunacy, can upset his conviction. He knows it just as well when he has an attack of dyspepsia as he does when his digestion is in good working order. Convictions come from knowledge, and no amount of good feelings or bad feelings, of good health or ill health, can alter knowledge.

It is to try to help my readers to come to a knowledge of God in the plain matter-of-fact sort of way of which I have spoken, and to the convictions which result from this knowledge, that this book is written. I shall first try to show what God is, not theologically, nor doctrinally, but simply what He is in actual, practical reality, as the God and Father of each one of us. And I shall also point out some of the things that seem to me the principal hindrances to becoming really acquainted with Him.

I am so absolutely certain that coming to know Him as He really is will bring unfailing comfort and peace to every troubled heart that I long unspeakably to help everyone within my reach to this knowledge. One of Job's friends said, in his arguments against Job's bitter complaints, "Acquaint now thyself with God, and be at peace"; and our Lord in His last recorded prayer said: "This is life eternal, that they might know thee, the only true God, and Jesus Christ whom thou has sent." It is not a question of acquaintance with ourselves, or of knowing what we are, or what we do, or what we feel; it is simply and only a question of becoming acquainted with God, and getting to know what He is, and what He does, and what He feels. Comfort and peace can never come from anything we know about ourselves, but only and always from what we know about Him.

We may spend our days in what we call our religious duties, and we may fill our devotions with fervor, and still may be miserable. Nothing can set our hearts at rest but a real acquaintance with God; for, after all, everything in our salvation must depend upon Him in the last instance; and, according as He is worthy or not of our confidence, so must necessarily be our comfort. If we were planning to take a dangerous voyage, our first question would be as to the sort of captain we were to have. Our common sense would tell us that if the captain were untrustworthy, no amount of trustworthiness on our part would make the voyage safe; and it would be his character and not our own that would be the thing of paramount importance to us.

If I can only say this often enough and in enough different ways to bring conviction to some troubled hearts, and lift them out of their sad and uncomfortable religious lives into the kingdom of love, and joy, and peace, which is their undisputed inheritance, I shall feel that my object in writing this book has been accomplished. And I shall be able to say, Lord, now lettest Thou Thy servant depart in peace, for mine eyes have seen Thy salvation; and my pen has tried to tell it.

It must, however, be clearly understood that my book does not propose to touch on the critical or the theological aspects of our religion. It does not undertake to deal with any questions concerning the authenticity of the Bible. Other and far abler minds can deal with these matters. My book is written for people, who, like myself, profess to believe in the Lord Jesus Christ, and who accept the Bible simply as the revelation of Him.

Putting aside all critical questions, therefore, I seek only to tell such believers of what seems to me the necessary result of their belief, and how they can personally realize this result.

Mistakes in the telling there may be, and for these I ask the charity of my readers. But the thing I want to say, and to say in such a way that no one can fail to understand it, is not a mistake; and that thing is this, that our religious lives ought to be full of joy, and peace, and comfort, and that, if we become better acquainted with God, they will be.

CHAPTER 2
WHAT IS HIS NAME?

"And Moses said unto God, Behold, when I come un-
to the children of Israel, and shall say unto them, The
God of your fathers hath sent me unto you; and they
shall say to me, What is his name? what shall I say un-
to them?"

The vital question of all ages and of every human heart is
here expressed, "What is his name?"

The whole fate of humanity hangs on the answer to this
question.

As we all know, the condition of a country depends upon
the character of its rulers. The state of an army depends
upon the officers who command it. And the more absolute
the government, the more is this necessarily the case.

We can see how it must be, therefore, that everything in a
universe will depend upon the sort of creator and ruler who
has brought that universe into existence, and that the whole
welfare of the human beings who have been placed there is
of necessity bound up with the character of their Creator. If
the God who created us is a good God, then everything must
of necessity be all right for us, since a good God cannot or-
dain any but good things. But if He is a bad God, or a careless
God, or an unkind God, then we cannot be sure that anything
is right, and can have no peace or comfort anywhere.

The true ground for peace and comfort is only to be found

in the sort of God we have. Therefore, we need first of all to find out what is His name, or, in other words, what is His character — in short, what sort of a God He is.

In Bible language *name* always means character. Names are not given arbitrarily there, as with us, but are always given with reference to the character or work of the person named. Cruden in his Concordance says that the names of God signify that which He really is, and are used throughout the Bible to express His attributes, and His purposes, His glory, His grace, His mercy, and His love, His wisdom, and power, and goodness. A careful study of His names will make this plain.

When, therefore, the children of Israel asked, "What is his name?" they meant, "Who and what is this God of whom you speak? What is His character; what are His attributes; what does He do? In short, what sort of a being is He?"

The psalmist says, "They that know thy name will put their trust in thee: for thou, Lord, hast not forsaken them that seek thee." And again he says, "The name of the Lord is a strong tower, the righteous runneth into it and is safe." "They that know thy name will put their trust in thee." They cannot do anything else, because in knowing His name they know His character and His nature, that He is a God whom it is safe to trust to the uttermost. And there can be no doubt that a large part of the unrest and discomfort in so many Christian hearts comes simply from the fact that they do not yet know His name.

"Some trust in chariots and some in horses: but we will remember the name of the Lord our God. They are brought down and are fallen, but we are risen and stand upright." In all that we read concerning Israel of old we find this constant refrain, that all they were and all they had depended upon the fact that their God was the Lord. "Blessed is the nation whose God is the Lord; and the people whom he hath chosen for his own inheritance." "O Lord, there is none like thee, neither is there any God beside thee, according to all that we have heard with our ears. And what one nation in the earth is like thy people Israel, whom God went to redeem to be his own people: to make thee a name of greatness and terribleness, by driving out nations from before thy people, whom thou has redeemed out of Egypt?

For thy people Israel didst thou make thine own people forever, and thou, Lord, becamest their God." "Happy is that
people that is in such a case, yea, happy is that people
whose God is the Lord."

Blessed is that nation, happy is that people whose God is
the Lord! All the blessing and happiness of Israel arose
from the fact that their God was the Lord. Nothing else was
of sufficient importance to be mentioned in the recapitula-
tion of their advantages. The fact that their God was the
Lord Jehovah was enough to account for every good thing
they possessed.

The question of all questions for each one of us, therefore, is this one, "What is his name?" To the Israelites God
Himself answered this question. And God said unto Moses,
"I am that I am"; and He said, "Thus shalt thou say unto
the children of Israel, *I Am* hath sent me unto you." And
God said, moreover, unto Moses: "Thus shalt thou say unto the children of Israel, the Lord God of your fathers, the
God of Abraham, the God of Isaac, and the God of Jacob
hath sent me unto you; this is my name forever, and this is
my memorial unto all generations."

In the Gospel of John Christ adopts this name of "I am"
as His own. When the Jews were questioning Him as to His
authority, He said unto them: "Verily, verily, I say unto
you, before Abraham was I am." And in the Book of Revelation He again declares: "I am Alpha and Omega, the
beginning and the ending, saith the Lord, which is, and
which was, and which is to come, the Almighty."

These simple words, *I am,* express therefore eternity and
unchangeableness of existence, which is the very first element necessary in a God who is to be depended upon. No
dependence could be placed by any one of us upon a
changeable God. He must be the same yesterday, today,
and forever, if we are to have any peace or comfort.

But is this all His name implies, simply "I am"? I am
what? — we ask. What does this "I am" include?

I believe it includes everything the human heart longs for
and needs. This unfinished name of God seems to me like a
blank check signed by a rich friend given to us to be filled in
with whatever sum we may desire. The whole Bible tells us
what it means.

Every attribute of God, every revelation of His character, every proof of His undying love, every declaration of His watchful care, every assertion of His purposes of tender mercy, every manifestation of His loving kindness — all are the filling out of this unfinished "I am."

God tells us through all the pages of His Book what He is. "I am," He says, "all that my people need": "I am their strength"; "I am their wisdom"; "I am their righteousness"; "I am their peace"; "I am their salvation"; "I am their life"; "I am their all in all."

This apparently unfinished name, therefore, is the most comforting name the heart of man could devise, because it allows us to add to it, without any limitation, whatever we feel the need of, and even "exceeding abundantly" beyond all that we can ask or think.

But if our hearts are full of our own wretched "I ams" we will have no ears to hear His glorious, soul-satisfying "I am." We say, "Alas, I am such a poor weak creature," or "I am so foolish," or "I am so good-for-nothing," or "I am so helpless"; and we give these pitiful "I ams" of ours as the reason of the wretchedness and discomfort of our religious lives, and even feel that we are very much to be pitied that things are so hard for us. While all the time we entirely ignore the blank check of God's magnificent "I am," which authorizes us to draw upon Him for an abundant supply for every need.

If you are an uncomfortable Christian, then the only thing to give you a thoroughly comfortable religious life is to know God. The psalmist says that they that know God's name will put their trust in Him, and it is, I am convinced, impossible for anyone really to know Him and not to trust Him. A trustworthy person commands trust; not in the sense of ordering people to trust him, but by irresistibly winning their trust by his trustworthiness.

What our Lord declares is eternally true, "I, if I be lifted up, will draw all men unto me." When once you know Him, Christ is absolutely irresistible. You can no more help trusting Him than you can help breathing. And could the whole world but know Him as He is, the whole world, sinners and all, would fall at His feet in adoring worship. They simply could not help it. His surpassing loveliness would carry all before it.

How then can we become acquainted with God?

There are two things necessary: first, God must reveal Himself; and second, we must accept His revelation and believe what He reveals.

The apostle John tells us that "no man hath seen God at any time," but "the only begotten Son which is in the bosom of the Father, he hath declared him." Christ, then, is the revelation of God. We have none of us seen God, and we never can see Him in this present stage of our existence, for we have not the faculties that would make it possible. But He has incarnated Himself in Christ, and we can see Christ, since He was a man like one of us.

A man, who should want to talk with ants, might stand over an anthill and harangue for a whole day, and not one word would reach the ears of the ants. They would run to and fro utterly unconscious of his presence. As far as we know, ants have no faculties by which they can receive human communications. But if a man could incarnate himself in the body of an ant, and could go about among them, living an ant's life and speaking the ants' language, he would make himself intelligible to them at once. Incarnation is always necessary when a higher form of life would communicate with a lower.

Christ revealed God by what He was, by what He did, and by what He said. From the cradle to the grave, every moment of His life was a revelation of God. We must go to Him then for our knowledge of God, and we must refuse to believe anything concerning God that is not revealed to us in Christ. All other revelations are partial, and therefore not wholly true. Only in Christ do we see God as He is; for Christ is declared to be the "express image" of God.

Just what God would have said and done under the circumstances, that Christ said and did. "I do nothing of myself," was His continual assertion. "I say nothing of myself; the Father that dwelleth in me he doeth the works"; "I and my Father are one"; "He that seeth me seeth my Father."

Words could not tell us more plainly than the Bible tells us that in order to know God we have only to look at Christ; we have only to "receive the testimony" of Christ.

Over and over we are assured that God and Christ are one. When the Jews came to Christ, as He was walking in the porch of Solomon's Temple, and asked Him to tell them plainly who He was, He answered, "I and my Father are one." And to His disciples, at His last supper with them, He said, in answer to their questions: "If ye had known me, ye should have known my Father also, and from henceforth ye know him and have seen him." But Philip could not understand this, and said, "Lord, show us the Father, and it sufficeth us." And then Jesus repeated His former statement even more strongly: "Have I been so long time with you, and yet hast thou not known me, Philip? He that hath seen me hath seen the Father; and how sayest thou then, Show us the Father?"

Nothing is more emphatically stated in the New Testament than this fact, that we are to behold the "light of the knowledge of the glory of God in the face of Jesus Christ," and that we can behold it fully nowhere else.

If we would know then the length, and breadth, and height, and depth of what God meant when He gave to Moses that apparently unfinished name of "I am," we shall find it revealed in Christ. He and He alone is the translation of God. He and He alone is the image of the invisible God.

It is evident, therefore, that we must never accept any conception of God that is contrary to what we see in Christ, and most utterly reject any view of His character or of His acts, or any statement of His relations with us as human beings, no matter how strongly upheld, which is at variance with what Christ has revealed.

We are all aware that the Old Testament revelation of God seems sometimes to contradict the revelation in Christ, and the question arises as to which we are to receive as the truest. In view of the fact that God Himself tells us that in these last days He has spoken to us by His Son, who is the "brightness of his glory and the express image of his person," we may not dare reject Christ's testimony, but must look upon the Old Testament revelation, where it differs from the revelation in Christ, as partial and imperfect; and must accept as a true setting forth of God only that which we find in Christ. Christ alone tells us the true and genuine name of God. In His last wonderful prayer He says: "I have manifested thy name unto the men whom thou gavest me out of the world, and they have known that all things whatsoever thou hast given me are of thee, for I have given unto them the words which thou gavest me; and they have received them, and have known surely that I came out from thee, and they have believed that thou didst send me." Could we ask for greater authority than this?

In the whole life of Christ nothing is plainer or more emphatic than the fact that He claimed continually to be a full and complete manifestation of God. "The words that I speak unto you," He says, "I speak not of myself; but the Father that dwelleth in me, he doeth the works." Over and over He asserts that He says only what the Father tells Him to say. "I speak to the world those things which I have heard of him." "I do nothing of myself, but as my Father hath taught me I speak these things."

The apostle declares most emphatically that it "pleased the Father" that in Christ should "dwell all the fullness of the Godhead bodily." And although we may not understand all that this means theologically, we at least cannot fail to see that if we want to know God, we need only to become acquainted with Christ's ways and Christ's character in order to become acquainted with God's ways and God's character. "He that hath seen me," He says, "hath seen the Father." And again He declares that "neither knoweth any man the Father save the Son, and he to whomsoever the Son will reveal him." This settles it beyond the possibility of cavil. We may, and we do, have all sorts of thoughts of God, we may conjecture this or imagine that, but we are wasting our energies in it all. We simply cannot know, no man can, except through the revelation of Christ.

We may know a good many things about Him, but that is very different from knowing Him Himself, as He really is in nature and character. Other witnesses have told us of His visible acts, but from these we get often very wrong impressions of His true character. No other witness but Christ can tell us of the real secrets of God's bosom, for of none other can it be said, as it is of Him, that "the only begotten Son who is in the bosom of the Father, he hath declared him." It will make all the difference between comfort and discomfort in our Christian lives, whether or not we believe this to be a fact. If we do believe it to be a fact, then the stern Judge and hard Taskmaster whom we have feared, even

while we tried to follow Him, and whose service we have
found so irksome and so full of discomfort, will disappear;
and His place will be taken by the God of love who is
revealed to us in "the face of Jesus Christ," the God who
cares for us as He cares for the sparrows, and for the
flowers of the field, and who tells us that He numbers even
the hairs of our head.

No human being could be afraid of a God like this.

If we have been accustomed, therefore, to approach God
with any mistrust of the kindness of His feelings toward us;
if our religion has been poisoned by fear; if unworthy
thoughts of His character and will have filled our hearts
with suspicions of His goodness; if we have pictured Him as
an unjust despot or a self-seeking tyrant; if, in short, we
have imagined Him in any way other than that which has
been revealed to us in "the face of Jesus Christ," we must
go back in all simplicity of heart to the records of that lovely life, lived in human guise among men, and must bring
our conceptions of God into perfect accord with the character and ways of Him who declares that He came to manifest
the name of God to men.

In reply then to the question, "What is His name?" I
have only this one thing to say, Ask Christ. We are told He
was "God manifest in the flesh," and that whoever sees
Him sees the God who sent Him; therefore it is perfectly
plain that, if we want to know the name, we have only to
read the manifestation. And this means simply that we must
study the life, and words, and ways of Christ, and must say
to ourselves, he that seeth Christ seeth God, and what
Christ was on earth that God is in Heaven. All the darkness
that enshrouds the character of God will vanish if we will
but accept the light Christ has shed on the matter, and
believe the "manifestation of His name" that Christ has
given us, and will utterly refuse to believe anything else.

When Nicodemus came to Jesus by night to ask Him how
the things He was saying could possibly be true, Jesus told
him that, whether he understood them or not, they still
were true, and said with greatest emphasis: "Verily, verily,
I say unto thee, we speak that we do know, and testify that
we have seen." No one who believes in Christ at all can
doubt that He knew God; and no one can question whether

or not we ought to receive His testimony. He has assured us over and over again that He knew what He was talking about, and that what He said was to be received as the absolute truth, because He had come down from Heaven, and therefore knew about heavenly things.

We none of us would dare openly to question the truth of this; and yet practically a great many of God's children utterly ignore Christ's testimony, and choose instead to listen to the testimony of their own doubting hearts, which tells them it is impossible that God could be as loving in His care for us, or as tender toward our weakness and foolishness, or as ready to forgive our sins, as Christ has revealed Him to be. And yet I must repeat again and again, at the risk of being accused of useless repetition, what so few people seem to realize, that if there is one thing taught in the Bible more plainly than any other, it is that the name, or, in other words, the character of His Father which Christ gave, must be His real name and character. He declares of Himself over and over that He was a living manifestation of the Father; and in all He said and did He assures us that He was simply saying and doing that which the Father would have said and done had he acted directly out of Heaven, and from off His heavenly throne.

In the face of such unqualified assertions as these out of the lips of our Lord Himself, it becomes, not only our privilege, but our bounden duty to cast out of our conception of God every element that could in any way conflict with the blessed life and character and teaching of Christ. If we would know the real name of God, we must accept the name Christ has revealed to us, and must listen to no other.

Whatever characteristics then we see in Christ, these are the filling out of the "I am" of God. As we look at the life of Christ and listen to His words, we can hear God saying, "I am rest for the weary; I am peace for the storm-tossed; I am strength for the strengthless; I am wisdom for the foolish; I am righteousness for the sinful; I am all that the neediest soul on earth can want; I am exceeding abundantly, beyond all you can ask or think, of blessing, and help, and care."

But here the doubter may say, "Ah yes, this is no doubt all true, but how can I get hold of it? I am such a poor, unworthy creature that I dare not believe such a fullness of grace can belong to me."

How can you get hold of it, you ask. You cannot get hold of it at all, but you can let it get hold of you. It is a piece of magnificent good news declared to you in the Bible; and you only need do with it exactly what you do when any earthly good news is told you by a reliable earthly source. If the speaker is trustworthy, you believe what he says, and act in accordance. And you must do the same here. If Christ is trustworthy when He tells you that He is the manifestation of God, you must believe what He says, and act accordingly.

You must take your stand on His trustworthiness. You must say to yourself, and to your friends if need be, "I am going to believe what Christ says about God. No matter what the seemings may be, nor what my own thoughts and feelings are, nor what anybody else may say, I know that what Christ says about God must be true, for He knew, and nobody else does, and I am going to believe Him right straight through, come what may. He says that He was one with God, so all that He was God is, and I will never be frightened of God any more. I will never again let myself think of Him as a stern Lawgiver who is angry with me because of my sins, nor as a hard Taskmaster who demands from me impossible tasks, nor as a far-off unapproachable Deity, who is wrapped up in His own glory, and is indifferent to my sorrows and my fears. All such ideas of God have become impossible, now that I know that Christ was the true manifestation of God."

If we will take our stand on this one fact, that Christ and God are one, with an intelligent comprehension of what it involves, and will refuse definitely and unwaveringly to cherish any thought of God that is at variance with what Christ has revealed, life will be transformed for us.

We may often have to set our faces like a flint to hold steadfastly here; for our old doubts and fears will be sure to come back and demand admittance; but we must turn our backs on them resolutely, and must declare that now at last we know the name, or in other words, the character of our God, and know that such things would be impossible to Him; and that therefore we simply refuse point-blank to listen for a moment to any such libels on His character or His ways.

It is unthinkable to suppose that when God told Moses His name was "I am," He could have meant to say, "I am a stern Lawgiver," or "I am a hard Taskmaster," or "I am a God who is wrapped up in my own glory, and am indifferent to the sorrows or the fears of my people." If we should try to fill in the blank of His "I am" with such things as these, all the Christians the world over would be horrified. But do not the doubts and fears of some of these very Christians say exactly these things in secret every day of their lives?

May God grant that what we shall learn in our consideration of the names of God may make all such doubts and fears impossible to us from this time forth and forevermore.

Jesus is God! Oh, could I now
But compass land and sea,
To teach and tell this single truth,
How happy I should be!
Oh, had I but an angel's voice,
I would proclaim so loud—
Jesus, the good, the beautiful,
Is the image of our God!

CHAPTER 3
THE GOD OF ALL COMFORT

"Blessed be God, even the Father of our Lord Jesus Christ, the Father of mercies and the God of all comfort; who comforteth us in all our tribulations, that we may be able to comfort them which are in any trouble, by the comfort wherewith we ourselves are comforted of God."

Among all the names that reveal God, this, the "God of all comfort," seems to me one of the loveliest and the most absolutely comforting. The words *all comfort* admit of no limitations and no deductions; and one would suppose that, however full of discomforts the outward life of the followers of such a God might be, their inward religious life must necessarily be always and under all circumstances a comfortable life. But, as a fact, it often seems as if exactly the opposite were the case, and the religious lives of large numbers of the children of God are full, not of comfort, but of the utmost discomfort. This discomfort arises from anxiety as to their relationship to God, and doubts as to His love. They torment themselves with the thought that they are too good-for-nothing to be worthy of His care, and they suspect Him of being indifferent to their trials and of forsaking them in times of need. They are anxious and troubled about everything in their religious life, about their disposition and feelings, their indifference to the Bible, their want of fervency in prayer, their coldness of heart. They are tormented with unavailing regrets over their past, and with devouring anxieties for their future. They feel unworthy to enter God's presence, and dare not believe that they belong to Him. They can be happy and comfortable with their earthly friends, but they cannot be happy or comfortable with God. And although He declares Himself to be the God of all comfort, they continually complain that they cannot find comfort anywhere; and their sorrowful looks and the doleful tones of their voice show that they are speaking the truth.

Such Christians, although they profess to be the followers of the God of all comfort, spread gloom and discomfort around them wherever they go; and it is out of the question for them to hope that they can induce anyone else to believe that this beautiful name, by which He has announced Himself, is anything more than a pious phrase, which in reality means nothing at all. And the manifestly uncomfortable religious lives of so many Christians is, I am very much afraid, responsible for a large part of the unbelief in the world.

The apostle says that we are to be living epistles known and read of all men; and the question as to what men read in us is of far more vital importance to the spread of Christ's kingdom than we half the time realize. It is not what we say that tells, but what we are. It is easy enough to say a great many beautiful things about God being the God of all comfort; but unless we know what it is to be really and truly comforted ourselves, we might as well talk to the winds. People must read in our lives what they hear in our words, or all our preaching is worse than useless. It would be well for us to ask ourselves what they are reading in us. Is it comfort or discomfort that voices itself in our daily walk and life?

But at this point I may be asked what I mean by the comfort God gives. Is it a sort of pious grace, that may perhaps fit us for Heaven, but that is somehow unfit to bear the brunt of our everyday life with its trials and its pains? Or is it an honest and genuine comfort, as we understand comfort, that enfolds life's trials and pains in an all-embracing peace?

With all my heart I believe it is the latter.

Comfort, whether human or divine, is pure and simple comfort, and is nothing else. We none of us care for pious phrases, we want realities; and the reality of being comforted

and comfortable seems to me almost more delightful than
any other thing in life. We all know what it is. When as little
children we have cuddled up into our mother's lap after a
fall or a misfortune, and have felt her dear arms around us,
and her soft kisses on our hair, we have had comfort.
When, as grown-up people, after a hard day's work, we
have put on our slippers and seated ourselves by the fire, in
an easy chair with a book, we have had comfort. When,
after a painful illness, we have begun to recover, and have
been able to stretch our limbs and open oui eyes without
pain, we have had comfort. When someone whom we dearly love has been ill almost unto death, and has been restored
to us in health again, we have had comfort. A thousand
times in our lives probably, have we said, with a sigh of relief, as of toil over or burdens laid down, "Well, this *is*
comfortable," and in that word comfortable there has been
comprised more of rest, and relief, and satisfaction, and
pleasure, than any other word in the English language could
possibly be made to express. We cannot fail, therefore, to
understand the meaning of this name of God, the "God of
all comfort."

But alas, we have failed to believe it. It has seemed to us
too good to be true. The joy and delight of it, if it were really a fact, have been more than our poor suspicious natures
could take in. We may venture to hope sometimes that little
scraps of comfort may be vouchsafed to us; but we have
run away frightened at the thought of the "all comfort"
that is ours in the salvation of the Lord Jesus Christ.

And yet what more could He have said about it than He
has said: "As one whom his mother comforteth, so will I
comfort you; and ye shall be comforted." Notice the *as* and
so in this passage: "*As* one whom his mother comforteth,
so will I comfort you." It is real comforting that is meant
here; the sort of comforting that the child feels when it is
"dandled on its mother's knees, and borne on her sides";
and yet how many of us have really believed that God's
comforting is actually as tender and true as a mother's comforting, or even half or quarter so real. Instead of thinking
of ourselves as being "dandled" on His knees, and hugged
to His heart, as mothers hug, have we not rather been inclined to look upon Him as a stern, unbending Judge, hold-

ing us at a distance, and demanding our respectful homage, and critical of our slightest faults? Is it any wonder that our religion, instead of making us comfortable, has made us thoroughly uncomfortable? Who could help being uncomfortable in the presence of such a Judge?

But I rejoice to say that that the stern Judge is not there. He does not exist. The God who does exist is a God who is like a mother, a God who says to us as plainly as words can say it, "*As* one whom his mother comforteth, *so* will I comfort you."

Over and over again He declares this. "I, even I, am he that comforteth you," He says to the poor, frightened children of Israel. And then He reproaches them with not being comforted. "Why," He says, "should you let anything make you afraid when here is the Lord, your Maker, ready and longing to comfort you. You have feared continually every day the 'fury of the oppressor,' and have forgotten me who have stretched forth the heavens and laid the foundations of the earth? Where is the fury of the oppressor when I am by?"

The God who exists is the God and the Father of our Lord Jesus Christ, the God who so loved the world that He sent His Son, not to judge the world, but to save it. He is the God who "anointed" the Lord Jesus Christ to bind up the brokenhearted, and to proclaim liberty to the captives, and the opening of the prison to them that are bound, and to comfort all that mourn. Please notice that *all*. Not a few select ones only, but all. Every captive of sin, every prisoner in infirmity, every mourning heart throughout the whole world must be included in this "all." It would not be "all" if there should be a single one left out, no matter how insignificant, or unworthy, or even how feeble-minded that one might be. I have always been thankful that the feeble-minded are especially mentioned by Paul in his exhortations to the Thessalonian Christians, when he is urging them to comfort one another. In effect he says, Do not scold the feeble-minded, but comfort them. The very ones who need comfort most are the ones that our God, who is like a mother, wants to comfort — not the strong-minded ones, but the feeble-minded.

For this is the glory of a religion of love. And this is the glory of the religion of the Lord Jesus Christ. He was anointed to comfort "all that mourn." The "God of all comfort" sent His Son to be the comforter of a mourning world. And all through His life on earth He fulfilled His divine mission. When His disciples asked Him to call down fire from Heaven to consume some people who refused to receive Him, He turned and rebuked them, and said: "Ye know not what manner of spirit ye are of. For the Son of man is not come to destroy men's lives but to save them." He received sinners and ate with them. He welcomed Mary Magdalene when all men turned from her. He refused even to condemn the woman who was taken in the very act of sin, but said to the scribes and Pharisees who had brought her before Him, "He that is without sin among you, let him first cast a stone at her"; and when, convicted by their own consciences, they all went out one by one without condemning her, He said to her, "Neither do I condemn thee: go, and sin no more." Always and everywhere He was on the side of sinners. That was what He was for. He came to save sinners. He had no other mission.

Two little girls were talking about God, and one said, "I know God does not love me. He could not care for such a teeny, tiny little girl as I am."

"Dear me, sis," said the other little girl, "don't you know that that is just what God is for — to take care of teeny, tiny little girls who can't take care of themselves, just like us?"

"Is He?" said the first little girl. "I did not know that. Then I don't need to worry any more, do I?"

If any troubled doubting heart, any heart that is fearing continually every day some form or other of evil should read these lines, let me tell you again in trumpet tones that this is just what the Lord Jesus Christ is for — to care for and comfort all who mourn. "All," remember, every single one, even you yourself, for it would not be "all" if you were left out. You may be so cast down that you can hardly lift up your head, but the apostle tells us that He is the "God that comforteth those that are cast down"; and it is just because you are cast down that you can claim the comforting of Christ. All who mourn, all who are cast down — I love to think of such a mission of comfort in a world of mourning like ours; and I long to see every cast down and sorrowing heart comforted with this comforting of God.

And our Comforter is not far off in Heaven where we cannot find Him. He is close at hand. He abides with us. When Christ was going away from this earth, He told His disciples that He would not leave them comfortless, but would send "another Comforter" who would abide with them forever. This Comforter, He said, would teach them all things, and would bring all things to their remembrance. And then He declared, as though it were the necessary result of the coming of this divine Comforter: "Peace I leave with you, my peace I give unto you; not as the world giveth, give I unto you. Let not your heart [therefore] be troubled, neither let it be afraid." Oh, how can we, in the face of these tender and loving words, go about with troubled and frightened hearts?

"Comforter" — what a word of bliss, if we only could realize it. Let us repeat it over and over to ourselves, until its meaning sinks into the very depths of our being. And an "abiding" Comforter, too, not one who comes and goes, and is never on hand when most needed, but one who is always present, and always ready to give us "joy for mourning, and the garment of praise for the spirit of heaviness."

The very words *abiding Comforter* are an amazing revelation. Try to comprehend them. If we can have a human comforter to stay with us for only a few days when we are in trouble, we think ourselves fortunate; but here is a divine Comforter who is always staying with us, and whose power to comfort is infinite. Never, never ought we for a single minute to be without comfort; never for a single minute ought we to be uncomfortable.

I have often wondered whether those early disciples realized at all what this glorious legacy of a Comforter meant. I am very sure the majority of the disciples of Christ now do not. If they did, there could not possibly be so many uncomfortable Christians about.

But you may ask whether this divine Comforter does not sometimes reprove us for our sins, and whether we can get any comfort out of this. In my opinion this is exactly one of the places where the comfort comes in. For what sort of creatures should we be if we had no divine Teacher always at hand to show us our faults and awaken in us a desire to get rid of them?

If I am walking along the street with a very disfiguring hole in the back of my dress, of which I am in ignorance, it is certainly a very great comfort to me to have a kind friend who will tell me of it. And similarly it is indeed a comfort to know that there is always abiding with me a divine, all-seeing Comforter, who will reprove me for all my faults, and will not let me go on in a fatal unconsciousness of them. Emerson says it is far more to a man's interest that he should see his own faults than that anyone else should see them, and a moment's thought will convince us that this is true, and will make us thankful for the Comforter who reveals them to us.

I remember vividly the comfort it used to be to me, when I was young, to have a sister who always knew what was the right and proper thing to do, and who, when we went out together, always kept me in order. I never felt any anxiety or responsibility about myself if she was by, for I knew she would keep a strict watch over me, and nudge me or whisper to me if I was making any mistakes. I was always made comfortable, and not uncomfortable, by her presence. But when it chanced that I went anywhere alone, then I would indeed feel uncomfortable, for then there was no one near to keep me straight.

The declaration is that He "comforts all our waste places"; and He does this by revealing them to us, and at the same time showing us how He can make our "wildernesses like Eden," and our "deserts like the garden of the Lord."

You may object, perhaps, because you are not worthy of His comforts. I do not suppose you are. No one ever is. But you need His comforting, and because you are not worthy you need it all the more. Christ came into the world to save sinners, not good people, and your unworthiness is your greatest claim for His salvation.

In the same passage in Isaiah in which He tells us that He has seen our ways and was "wroth" with us, He assures us that He will heal us and restore comforts to us. It is just because He is wroth with us (wroth in the sense in which love is always wroth with any fault in those it loves), that therefore He "restores comforts" to us. And He does it by revealing our sin, and healing it.

The avenue to the comfortings of the divine Comforter lies through the need of comfort. And this explains to me better than anything else the reason why the Lord so often allows sorrow and trial to be our portion. "Therefore, behold, I will allure her, and bring her into the wilderness, and speak comfortably unto her." We find ourselves, it may be, in a "wilderness" of disappointment and of suffering, and we wonder why the God who loves us should have allowed it. But He knows that it is only in that very wilderness that we can hear and receive the "comfortable words" He has to pour out upon us. We must feel the need of comfort before we can listen to the words of comfort. And God knows that it is infinitely better and happier for us to need His comforts and receive them, than ever it could be not to need them and so be without them. The consolations of God mean the substituting of a far higher and better thing than the things we lose to get them. The things we lose are earthly things, those He substitutes are heavenly. And who of us but would thankfully be "allured" by our God into any earthly wilderness, if only there we might find the unspeakable joys of union with Himself. Paul could say he "counted all things but loss" if he might but "win Christ"; and, if we have even the faintest glimpse of what winning Christ means, we will say so too.

But strangely enough, while it is easy for us when we are happy and do not need comforting, to believe that our God is the "God of all comfort," but as soon as we are in trouble and need it, it seems impossible to believe that there can be any comfort for us anywhere. It would almost seem as if, in our reading of the Bible, we had reversed its meaning, and made it say, not "Blessed are they that mourn, for they shall be comforted," but "Blessed are they that rejoice, for they, and they only, shall be comforted." It is very strange how often in our secret hearts we almost unconsciously alter the Bible words a little, and so make the meaning exactly opposite to what it actually is; or else we put in so many "ifs" and "buts" as to take the whole point out of what is said. Take, for instance, those beautiful words, "God that comforteth those that are cast down," and ask ourselves whether we have never been tempted to make it read in our secret hearts, "God who forsaketh those who are cast down," or,

"God who overlooks those who are cast down," or, "God who will comfort those who are cast down if they show themselves worthy of comfort"; and whether, consequently, instead of being comforted, we have not been plunged into misery and despair.

The psalmist tells us that God will "comfort us on every side," and what an all-embracing bit of comfort this is. "On every side," no aching spot to be left uncomforted. And yet, in times of special trial, how many Christians secretly read this as though it said, "God will comfort us on every side except just the side where our trials lie; on that side there is no comfort anywhere." But God says every side, and it is only unbelief on our part that leads us to make an exception of our special side.

It is with too many, alas, just as it was with Israel of old. On one side God said to Zion: "Sing, O heavens, and be joyful, O earth, and break forth into singing, O mountains; for the Lord hath comforted his people, and will have mercy upon his afflicted"; and on the other side Zion said, "The Lord hath forsaken me, and my Lord hath forgotten me." And then God's answer came in those wonderful words, full forever of comfort enough to meet the needs of all the sorrows of all humanity: "Forget thee! Can a mother forget? Yea, perhaps a mother *may* forget, but I cannot. I have even graven thee upon the palms of my hands, so that it is impossible for me to forget thee! Be comforted, then, and sing for joy."

But you may ask how you are to get hold of this divine comfort. My answer is that you must take it. God's comfort is being continually and abundantly given, but unless you will accept it you cannot have it.

Divine comfort does not come to us in any mysterious or arbitrary way. It comes as the result of a divine method. The indwelling Comforter "brings to our remembrance" comforting things concerning our Lord, and, if we believe them, we are comforted by them. A text is brought to our remembrance, perhaps, or the verse of a hymn, or some thought concerning the love of Christ and His tender care for us. If we receive the suggestion in simple faith, we cannot help being comforted. But if we refuse to listen to the voice of our Comforter, and insist instead on listening to the voice of discouragement or despair, no comfort can by any possibility reach our souls.

It is very possible for even a mother to lavish in vain all her stores of motherly comfort on a weeping child. The child sits up stiff and sullen, and "refuses to be comforted." All her comforting words fall on unbelieving ears. For to be comforted by comforting words it is absolutely necessary for us to believe these words. God has spoken "comforting words" enough, one would think, to comfort a whole universe, and yet we see all around us unhappy Christians, and worried Christians, and gloomy Christians, into whose comfortless hearts not one of these comforting words seems to be allowed to enter. In fact, a great many Christians actually think it is wrong to be comforted. They feel too unworthy. And if any rays of comfort steal into their hearts, they sternly shut them out; and like Rachel, and Jacob, and the psalmist, their souls "refuse to be comforted."

The apostle tells us that whatsoever things are written in the Scriptures are for our learning, in order that we "through patience and comfort of the Scriptures may have hope." But if we are to be comforted by the Scriptures, we must first believe them. Nothing that God has said can possibly comfort a person who does not believe it to be really true. When the captain of a vessel tells us that his vessel is safe, we must first believe him to be telling the truth, before we can feel comfortable on board that vessel. When the conductor on a railway tells us we are on the right train, before we can settle down comfortably in our seats, we must trust his word. This is all so self-evident that it might seem folly to call attention to it. But in religious matters it often happens that the self-evident truths are the very ones most easily overlooked; and I have actually known people who insisted on realizing God's comfort while still doubting His words of comfort; and who even thought they could not believe His comforting words at all, until they had first felt the comfort in their own souls! As well might the passenger on the railway insist on having a feeling of comfortable assurance that he is on the right train, before he could make up his mind to believe the word of the conductor. Always and in everything comfort must follow faith, and can never precede it.

In this matter of comfort it is exactly as it is in every other experience in the religious life. God says, "Believe, and then you can feel." We say, "Feel, and then we can believe." God's order is not arbitrary, it exists in the very nature of things; and in all earthly matters we recognize this, and are never so foolish as to expect to feel we have anything until we first believe that it is in our possession. I could not possibly feel glad that I had a fortune in the bank, unless I knew that it was really there. But in spiritual things we reverse God's order (which is the order of nature as well), and refuse to believe that we possess anything until we first feel as if we had it.

Let me illustrate. We are, let us suppose, overwhelmed with cares and anxieties. It often happens in this world. To comfort us in these circumstances the Lord assures us that we need not be anxious about anything, but may commit all our cares to Him, for He careth for us. We are all familiar with the passages where He tells us to "behold the fowls of the air," and to "consider the lilies of the field," and assures us that we are of much more value than they, and that, if He cares for them, He will much more care for us. One would think there was comfort enough here for every care or sorrow all the wide world over. To have God assume our cares and our burdens, and carry them for us; the Almighty God, the Creator of Heaven and earth, who can control everything, and foresee everything, and consequently can manage everything in the very best possible way, to have Him declare that He will undertake for us; what could possibly be a greater comfort? And yet how few people are really comforted by it. Why is this? Simply and only because they do not believe it. They are waiting to have an inward feeling that His words are true, before they will believe them. They look upon them as beautiful things for Him to say, and they wish they could believe them, but they do not think they can be true in their own special case, unless they can have an inward feeling that they are; and if they should speak out honestly, they would confess that, since they have no such inward feeling, they do not believe His words apply to them; and as a consequence they do not in the least expect Him actually to care for their affairs at all. "Oh, if I could only feel it was all true," we say; and God says, "Oh, if you would only believe it is all true!"

It is pure and simple unbelief that is at the bottom of all our lack of comfort, and absolutely nothing else. God comforts us on every side, but we simply do not believe His words of comfort.

The remedy for this is plain. If we want to be comforted, we must make up our minds to believe every single solitary word of comfort God has ever spoken; and we must refuse utterly to listen to any words of discomfort spoken by our own hearts, or by our circumstances. We must set our faces like a flint to believe, under each and every sorrow and trial, in the divine Comforter, and to accept and rejoice in His all-embracing comfort. I say, "set our faces like a flint," because, when everything around us seems out of sorts, it is not always easy to believe God's words of comfort. We must put our wills into this matter of being comforted, just as we have to put our wills into all other matters in our spiritual life. We must choose to be comforted.

It may seem impossible, when things look all wrong and uncared for, to believe that God really can be caring for us as a mother cares for her children; and, although we know perfectly well that He says He does care for us in just this tender and loving way, yet we say, "Oh, if I could only believe that, of course I should be comforted." Now here is just where our wills must come in. We *must* believe it. We must say to ourselves, "God says it, and it is true, and I am going to believe it, no matter how it looks." And then we must never suffer ourselves to doubt or question it again.

I do not hesitate to say that whosever will adopt this plan will come, sooner or later, into a state of abounding comfort.

The psalmist says, "In the multitude of my thoughts within me thy comforts delight my soul." But I am afraid that among the multitude of our thoughts within us there are far too often many more thoughts of our own discomforts than of God's comforts. We must think of His comforts if we are to be comforted by them. It might be a good exercise of soul for some of us to analyze our thoughts for a few days, and see how many thoughts we actually do give to God's comforts, compared with the number we give to our own discomforts. I think the result would amaze us!

One word I must add in conclusion. If any of my readers are preachers of the Gospel of our Lord Jesus Christ, I would like to ask them what they are commissioned to preach. The true commission in my opinion is to be found in Isaiah 40:1, 2: "Comfort ye, comfort ye my people, saith your God. Speak ye comfortably to Jerusalem, and cry unto her, that her warfare is accomplished, that her iniquity is pardoned; for she hath received of the Lord's hand double for all her sins." "Comfort ye my people" is the divine command; do not scold them. If it is the Gospel you feel called to preach, then see to it that you do really preach Christ's Gospel and not man's. Christ comforts, man scolds. Christ's Gospel is always good news, and never bad news. Man's gospel is generally a mixture of a little good news and a great deal of bad news; and, even where it tries to be good news, it is so hampered with "ifs" and "buts," and with all sorts of man-made conditions, that it utterly fails to bring any lasting joy or comfort.

The only Gospel that, to my thinking, can rightly be called the Gospel is that one proclaimed by the angel to the frightened shepherds, who were in the fields keeping watch over their flocks by night: "Fear not," said the angel, "for behold I bring you good tidings of great joy, which shall be to all people. For unto you is born this day in the city of David, a Saviour which is Christ the Lord."

Never were more comfortable words preached to any congregation. And if only all the preachers in all the pulpits would speak the same comfortable words to the people; and if all the congregations, who hear these words, would believe them, and would take the comfort of them, there would be no more uncomfortable Christians left anywhere. And over the whole land would be fulfilled the apostle's prayer for the Thessalonians: "Now our Lord Jesus Christ himself, and God, even our Father, which hath loved us and hath given us everlasting consolation and good hope through grace, comfort your hearts, and stablish you in every good word and work."

CHAPTER 4

THE LORD OUR SHEPHERD

"The Lord is my shepherd, I shall not want."

Perhaps no aspect in which the Lord reveals Himself to us is fuller of genuine comfort than the aspect set forth in the Twenty-third Psalm, and in its corresponding passage in the tenth chapter of John.

The psalmist tells me that the Lord is my Shepherd, and the Lord Himself declares that He is the *good* Shepherd. Can we conceive of anything more comforting?

It is a very wonderful thing that the highest and grandest truths of the religion of the Lord Jesus Christ are so often shut up in the simplest and commonest texts in the Bible. Those texts with which we have been familiar from our childhood, which we learned in the nursery at our mother's knee, which were used by those who loved us to explain in the simplest possible way the love of our heavenly Father, and the reasons for our trusting Him — these very texts, I have discovered, contain in their simple statements the whole story.

I feel, therefore, that what we all need is just to get back into the nursery again, and take up our childish verses once more, and, while reading them with the intelligence of our grown-up years, to believe them with all our old childish faith.

Let me carry you back then with me, my dear reader, to the children's psalm, that one which is so universally taught

to the little ones in the nursery and in the infant school. Do
we not each one of us remember the Twenty-third Psalm, as
long as we can remember anything, and can we not recall
even now something of the joy and pride of our childish
hearts when first we were able to repeat it without mistake?
Since then we have always known it, and at this moment its
words, perhaps, sound so old and familiar to some of you,
that you cannot see what meaning they can convey.

But in truth they tell us the whole story of our religion in
words of such wondrous depth of meaning that I very much
doubt whether it has ever yet entered into the heart of any
mortal man to conceive of the things they reveal.

Repeat these familiar words over to yourselves afresh:
"The Lord is my shepherd, I shall not want."

Who is it that is your shepherd?

The Lord! Oh, my friends, what a wonderful announcement! The Lord God of Heaven and earth, the Almighty
Creator of all things, He who holds the universe in His
hand as though it were a very little thing, He is your Shepherd, and has charged Himself with the care and keeping of
you, as a shepherd is charged with the care and keeping of
his sheep.

If your hearts will only take in this thought, I can promise you that your religion will from henceforth be full of the
profoundest comfort, and all your old uncomfortable
religion will drop off forever, as the mist disappears in the
blaze of the summer sun.

I had a vivid experience of this at one time in my Christian life. The Twenty-third Psalm had, of course, always
been familiar to me from my nursery days, but it had never
seemed to have any special meaning. Then came a critical
moment in my life when I was sadly in need of comfort, but
coud see none anywhere. I could not at the moment lay my
hands on my Bible, and I cast about in my mind for some
passage of Scripture that would help me. Immediately there
flashed into my mind the words, "The Lord is my shepherd, I shall not want." At first I turned from it almost
with scorn. "Such a common text as that," I said to myself,
"is not likely to do me any good"; and I tried hard to think
of a more *recherche* one, but none would come; and at last
it almost seemed as if there were no other text in the whole

Bible. And finally I was reduced to saying, "Well, if I cannot think of any other text, I must try to get what little good I can out of this one," and I began to repeat to myself over and over, "The Lord is my shepherd, I shall not want." Suddenly, as I did so, the words were divinely illuminated, and there poured out upon me such floods of comfort that I felt as if I could never have a trouble again.

The moment I could get hold of a Bible I turned over its leaves with eagerness to see whether it could possibly be true that such untold treasures of comfort were really and actually mine, and whether I might dare to let out my heart into the full enjoyment of them. And I did what I have often found great profit in doing, I built up a pyramid of declarations and promises concerning the Lord being our Shepherd that, once built, presented an immovable and indestructible front to all the winds and storms of doubt or trial that could assail it. And I became convinced, beyond a shadow of doubt, that the Lord really was my Shepherd, and that in giving Himself this name He assumed the duties belonging to the name, and really would be, what He declares Himself to be, a "good shepherd who giveth his life for his sheep."

He Himself draws the contrast between a good shepherd and a bad shepherd, when He follows up His announcement "I am the good shepherd," with the words, "but he that is an hireling and not the shepherd, whose own the sheep are not, seeth the wolf coming and leaveth the sheep and fleeth; and the wolf catcheth them and scattereth the sheep." And through the mouth of His prophets the Lord pours down a scathing condemnation upon all such faithless shepherds. "And the Lord saith unto me," says the prophet Zechariah, "take unto thee yet the instruments of a foolish shepherd ... Woe to the idle shepherd that leaveth the flock! the sword shall be upon his arm, and upon his right eye; his arm shall be clean dried up, and his right eye shall be utterly darkened."

Again the prophet Ezekiel says: "Thus saith the Lord God unto the shepherds: Woe be to the shepherds of Israel that do feed themselves! Should not the shepherds feed the flocks? ... The diseased have ye not strengthened, neither have ye healed that which was sick, neither have ye bound up that which was broken, neither have ye brought back that which was driven away, neither have ye sought that which was lost; but with force and with cruelty have ye ruled them ... Therefore, O ye shepherds, hear the word of the Lord: Thus saith the Lord God, Behold I am against the shepherds, and I will require my flock at their hand, and cause them to cease from feeding the flock."

Surely one would think that no Christian could ever accuse our divine Shepherd of being as faithless and unkind as those He thus condemns. And yet, if the secrets of some Christian hearts should be revealed, I fear that it would be found that, although they do not put it into words, and perhaps hardly know themselves that such are their feelings about Him, yet at the bottom they do really look upon Him as a faithless Shepherd.

What else can it mean when Christians complain that the Lord has forsaken them; that they cry to Him for spiritual food and He does not hear; that they are beset by enemies on every side and He does not deliver them; that when their souls find themselves in dark places He does not come to their rescue; that when they are weak He does not strengthen them; and when they are spiritually sick He does not heal them?

What are all these doubts and discouragements but secret accusations against our good Shepherd of the very things which He Himself so scathingly condemns?

A dear Christian, who had just discovered what it meant to have the Lord as his Shepherd, said to me, "Of course, I had always known that that was what He was called, but it meant nothing to me; and I believe I read the Twenty-third Psalm as though it was written, 'The Lord is the sheep, and I am the shepherd, and, if I do not keep a tight hold on Him, He will run away.' When dark days came I never for a moment thought that He would stick by me, and when my soul was starving and cried out for food, I never dreamed He would feed me. I see now that I never looked upon Him as a faithful Shepherd at all. But now all is different. I myself am not one bit better or stronger, but I have discovered that I have a good Shepherd, and that is all I need. I see now that it really is true that the Lord is my Shepherd, and that I shall not want."

Dear fellow Christian, I pray you to look this matter fairly in the face. Are you like the Christian I have quoted above? You have said, I know, hundreds of times, "The Lord is my shepherd," but have you ever really believed it to be an actual fact? Have you felt safe and happy and free from care, as sheep must feel when under the care of a good shepherd, or have you felt yourself to be like a poor forlorn sheep without a shepherd, or with an unfaithful, inefficient shepherd, who does not supply your needs, and who leaves you in times of danger and darkness?

I beg of you to answer this question honestly in your own soul. Have you had a comfortable religious life or an uncomfortable one? If the latter has been your condition, how can you reconcile it with the statement that the Lord is your Shepherd, and therefore you shall not want? You say He is your Shepherd, and yet you complain that you do want. Who has made the mistake? You or the Lord?

But here, perhaps, you will meet me with the words, "Oh, no, I do not blame the Lord, but I am so weak and so foolish, and so ignorant, that I am not worthy of His care." But do you not know that sheep are always weak, and helpless, and silly; and that the very reason they are compelled to have a shepherd to care for them is just because they are so unable to take care of themselves? Their welfare and their safety, therefore, do not in the least depend upon their own strength, nor upon their own wisdom, nor upon anything in themselves, but wholly and entirely upon the care of their shepherd. And, if you are a sheep, your welfare also must depend altogether upon your Shepherd, and not at all upon yourself.

Let us imagine two flocks of sheep meeting at the end of the winter to compare their experiences — one flock fat and strong and in good condition, and the other poor and lean and diseased. Will the healthy flock boast of themselves, and say, "See what splendid care we have taken of ourselves, what good, strong, wise sheep we must be?" Surely not. Their boasting would all be about their shepherd. "See what a good shepherd we have had," they would say, "and how he has cared for us. Through all the storms of the winter he has protected us, and has defended us from every wild beast, and has always provided us with the best of food."

Or, on the other hand, would the poor, wretched, diseased sheep blame themselves and say, "Alas, what wicked
sheep we must be, to be in such a poor condition!" No,
they too would speak only of their shepherd, but how different would be their story! "Alas," they would say, "our
shepherd was very different from yours! He fed himself,
but he did not feed us. He did not strengthen us when we
were weak, nor heal us when we were sick, nor bind us up
when we were broken nor look for us when we were lost. It
is true he stayed by us in clear and pleasant weather, when
no enemies were nigh, but in times of danger or of storm,
he forsook us and fled. Oh, that we had had a good shepherd like yours!"

We all understand this responsibility of the shepherd in
the case of sheep; but the moment we transfer the figure to
our religion, we at once shift all the responsibility off the
Shepherd's shoulders, and lay it upon the sheep; and demand of the poor human sheep the wisdom, and care, and
power to provide, that can only belong to the divine Shepherd and be met by Him; and of course the poor human
sheep fail, and their religious lives become thoroughly uncomfortable, and even sometimes most miserable.

I freely confess there is a difference between sheep and
ourselves in this, that they have neither the intelligence nor
the power to withdraw themselves from the care of their
shepherd, while we have. We cannot imagine one of them
saying, "Oh, yes, we have a good shepherd who says he will
take care of us, but then we do not feel worthy of his care,
and therefore we are afraid to trust him. He says he has
provided for us green pastures and a safe and comfortable
fold; but we are such poor good-for-nothing creatures that
we have not dared to enter his fold, nor feed in his pastures.
We have felt it would be presumption; and, in our humility,
we have been trying to do the best we could for ourselves.
The strong, healthy sheep may trust themselves to the shepherd's care, but not such miserable half-starved sheep as we
are. It is true we have had a very hard time of it, and are in a
sad and forlorn condition; but then we are such poor unworthy creatures that we must expect this, and must try to
be resigned to it."

Silly as sheep are, we know well no sheep could be so silly

as to talk in this way. And here comes the difference. We are so much wiser than sheep, in our own estimation, that we think the sort of trust sheep exercise will not do for us; and, in our superior intelligence, we presume to take matters into our own hands, and so shut ourselves out from the Shepherd's care.

Now the fact is simply this, if any sheep in the flock of Christ find themselves in a poor condition, there are only two explanations possible. Either the Lord is not a good Shepherd and does not care for His sheep, or else His sheep have not believed in His care, and have been afraid or ashamed to trust themselves to it. I know not one of you will dare to say, or even to think, that the Lord can be anything but a good Shepherd, if He is a Shepherd at all. The fault, therefore, must lie just here; either you have not believed He was your Shepherd at all, or else, believing it, you have refused to let Him take care of you.

I entreat you to face this matter boldly, and give yourselves a definite answer. For not only your own welfare and comfort are dependent upon your right apprehension of this blessed relationship, but also the glory of your Shepherd is at stake. Have you ever thought of the grief and dishonor this sad condition of yours brings upon Him? The credit of a shepherd depends upon the condition of his flock. He might make a great boast of his qualifications as a shepherd, but it would all go for nothing if the flocks he had charge of were in a diseased condition, with many missing, and many with lean ribs and broken bones.

If an owner of sheep is thinking of employing a shepherd, he requires a reference from the shepherd's last employer, that he may learn from him how his flock fared under this shepherd's care. Now, the Lord makes statements about Himself as a good Shepherd. He is telling the universe, the world, and the Church, "I am the good shepherd"; and if they ask, "Where are Thy sheep, what condition are they in?" can He point to us as being a credit to His care? And is it not grievous if any of us refuse to let the Shepherd take care of us, and so bring discredit upon His name by our forlorn condition? The universe is looking on to see what the Lord Jesus Christ is able to make of us, and what kind of sheep we are, whether we are well fed, and healthy, and happy. Their verdict concerning Him will largely depend upon what they see in us.

When Paul was writing to the Ephesians that he had been called to preach to the Gentiles the unsearchable riches of Christ, and to make all men see what was the fellowship of the mystery which had been hid in God from the beginning of the world, he added the significant words that the object of it all was "to the intent that now unto principalities and powers in heavenly places might be known by the church the manifold wisdom of God, according to the eternal purpose which he purposed in Christ Jesus our Lord."

Well may we be lost in amazement at the thought that God has purposed such a glorious destiny for His sheep as to make known to the universe His "manifold wisdom" by means of what He has done for us! Surely this should make us eager to abandon ourselves to Him in the most generous trust for salvation to the very uttermost, that He may get great glory in the universe, and the whole world may be won to trust Him.

But if we will not let Him save us, if we reject His care, and refuse to feed in His pastures, or to lie down in His fold, then we shall be a starved and shivering flock, sick and wretched, and full of complaints, bringing dishonor upon Him, and, by our forlorn condition, hindering the world from coming to Him.

I do not wonder that unbelievers are not drawn into the church, when I contemplate the condition of believers. I do not wonder that in some churches there are no conversions from one end of the year to the other. If I were a poor sheep, wandering in the wilderness, and I were to see some poor, wretched, sick-looking sheep peeping out of a fold, and calling me to come in, and I were to look into the fold, and should see it hard, bare, and uncomfortable, I do not think I would be much tempted to go into such a fold.

Somebody said once that some churches were too much like well-ordered graveyards: people were brought in and buried, and that was the end of it. Of course you cannot expect living people to want to take up their abodes in graveyards. We must have a fold that shows sheep in good condition if we expect outsiders to come into that fold; and if we want to attract others to the salvation of the Lord Jesus

Christ, we must ourselves be able to show them that it is a satisfying and comfortable salvation. No one wants to add to their earthly discomforts by getting an uncomfortable religion, and it is useless to expect to win outsiders by the sight of our wretchedness.

Surely, if you do not care for yourselves, you cannot fail to care for the dishonor you bring upon your divine Shepherd by your poor and wretched condition. You long to serve Him, and to bring Him glory; and you can do it if you will but show to all the world that He is a Shepherd whom it is safe to trust.

Let me help you to do this. First face the fact of what a Shepherd must necessarily be and do in order to be a good Shepherd, and then face the fact that the Lord is really, and in the very highest sense of the term, a good Shepherd. Then say the words over to yourself with all the will power you can muster, "The Lord is my Shepherd. He is. He is. No matter what I feel, He says He is, and He is. I am going to believe it, come what may." Then repeat the words with a different emphasis each time:

> The *Lord* is my Shepherd.
> The Lord *is* my Shepherd.
> The Lord is *my* Shepherd.
> The Lord is my *Shepherd.*

Realize to yourself what your ideal Shepherd would be, all that you would require from anyone filling such a position of trust and of responsibility, and then know that an ideal far beyond yours, and a conception of the duties of such a position higher than any you ever dreamed of were in the mind of our Lord when He said, "I am the good shepherd." He, better than any other, knew the sheep He had undertaken to save, and He knew the Shepherd's duties. He knew that the Shepherd is responsible for His flock, and that He is bound, at any loss of comfort, or of health, or even of life itself, to care for them and to bring them all home safely to the Master's fold. Therefore, He said: "And this is the Father's will which hath sent me, that of all which he hath given me I should lose nothing, but should raise it up again at the last day.'' And again He said, "The good shepherd giveth his life for the sheep." And still again: "My sheep hear my voice, and I know them and they follow me, and I give unto them eternal life; and they shall never perish, neither shall any man pluck them out of my hand."

Centuries before Jesus came to be the Shepherd, the Father said: "Therefore I will save my flock. And I will set up one shepherd over them, and he shall feed them, even my servant David; he shall feed them, and he shall be their shepherd." And it seems to me, I catch a glimpse of the Father's yearning love as I read these words; and I feel sure He laid help upon One who is mighty; and that none, therefore, who are in this flock need fear any evil.

He has undertaken His duties, knowing perfectly well what the responsibilities are. He knows that He has to do with very silly sheep, who have no strength to protect themselves, no wisdom to guide themselves, and nothing to recommend them but their utter helplessness and weakness. But none of these things baffle Him. His strength and His skill are sufficient to meet every emergency that can possibly arise.

There is absolutely only one thing that can hinder Him, and that is, if the sheep will not trust Him and refuse to let Him take care of them. If they stand off at a distance, and look at the food He has provided, and long for it, and cry for it, but refuse to eat it, He cannot satisfy their hunger. If they linger outside the shelter He has made, and are afraid to go in and enjoy it because they feel too distrustful or too unworthy, He cannot protect them. No sheep is so silly as to act in this way, but we human beings, who are so much wiser than sheep, do it continually.

No sheep, could it talk, would say to the shepherd: "I long for the food you have provided, and for the shelter and peace of your fold, and I wish I might dare to enjoy them; but, alas! I feel too unworthy. I am too weak and foolish; I do not feel grateful enough; I am afraid I do not feel quite hungry enough, or enough in earnest about wanting it. I dare not presume to think you mean all these good things for me."

One can imagine how grieved and wounded a good shepherd would be at such a speech as this. And surely our Lord has given us a glimpse into His tender sorrow over those who would not trust Him, when He beheld Jerusalem and wept over it, saying: "If thou hadst known, even thou, at least in this thy day, the things which belong unto thy peace! But now they are hid from thine eyes."

Ah, dear Christians, have you not sometimes grieved and wounded your divine Shepherd by just such speeches? If you have, let me entreat of you to get over for a few moments on the Shepherd's side of the question, and try to think how He feels, and what His mind concerning you is. If He is your Shepherd, then He wants to care for you in the very best possible way; for He is a good Shepherd, and cares for His sheep. It is no matter what you think about it, or how you feel. You are not the Shepherd, you are only the sheep, and the great point is what He thinks and how He feels. Lose sight of yourself for a moment, and try to put yourself in the Shepherd's place. Consider your condition as He considers it. See Him coming out to seek you in your far-off wandering. See His tender, yearning love, His unutterable longing to save you. Believe His own description of Himself, and take Him at His own sweet word.

> If our faith were but more simple,
>   We would take Him at His word;
> And our lives would be all gladness
>   In the sunshine of our Lord.

Ah, yes, this is the trouble. Our faith is not simple enough to take Him at His word, but we must needs add all sorts of "buts" and "ifs" of our own; and obscure the sunshine of His love with clouds of our own imagining. If we but only knew the things which belong to our peace, how quickly we would throw aside every "if" and "but" of unbelief, and how rapturously we would plunge ourselves headlong into an unquestioning faith in all that He has told us of His almighty and never-failing love and care!

But you may ask me, if all this is true of the Shepherd, what is the part of the sheep?

The part of the sheep is very simple. It is only to trust and to follow. The Shepherd does all the rest. He leads the sheep by the right way. He chooses their paths for them, and sees that those paths are paths where the sheep can walk in safety. When He putteth forth His sheep, He goeth before them. The sheep have none of the planning to do, none of the decisions to make, none of the forethought or wisdom to exercise; they have absolutely nothing to do but to trust themselves entirely to the care of the good Shepherd, and to follow Him whithersoever He leads. It is very simple. There is nothing complicated in trusting, when the One we are called upon to trust is absolutely trustworthy; and nothing complicated in obedience, when we have perfect confidence in the power we are obeying.

Let me entreat you, then, to begin to trust and to follow your Shepherd now and here. Abandon yourself to His care and guidance, as a sheep in the care of a shepherd, and trust Him utterly.

You need not be afraid to follow Him whithersoever He leads, for He always leads His sheep into green pastures and beside still waters. No matter though you may seem to yourself to be in the very midst of a desert, with nothing green about you inwardly or outwardly and you may think you will have to make a long journey before you can get into any green pastures, the good Shepherd will turn the very place where you are into green pastures; for He has the power to make the desert rejoice and blossom as the rose; and He has promised that "instead of the thorn shall come up the fir-tree, and instead of the briar shall come up the myrtle-tree"; and "in the wilderness shall waters break out, and streams in the desert."

Or perhaps you may say, "My life is all a tempest of sorrow or of temptation, and it will be a long while before I can walk beside any still waters." But has not your Shepherd before this said to the raging seas, "Peace! be still. And there was a great calm"? And can He not do it again?

Thousands of the flock of Christ can testify that when they have put themselves absolutely into His hands, He has quieted the raging tempest, and has turned their deserts into blossoming gardens. I do not mean that there will be no more outward trouble, or care, or suffering; but these very places will become green pastures and still waters inwardly to the soul. The Shepherd knows what pastures are best for His sheep, and they must not question or doubt, but must trustingly follow Him. Perhaps He sees that the best pastures for some of us are to be found in the midst of opposition or of earthly trials. If He leads you there, you may be sure they are green pastures for you, and that you will grow to be made strong by feeding in them.

But words fail to tell the half of what the good Shepherd does for the flock that trusts Him. He does indeed, according to His promise, make with them a covenant of peace, and causes the evil beasts to cease out of the land; and they shall dwell safely in the wilderness, and sleep in the woods. And He makes them and the places round about them a blessing; and He causes the shower to come down in its season; and there are showers of blessing. And the tree of the field yields her fruit; and the earth yields her increase; and they are safe in their land, and are no more a prey to the heathen, and none can make them afraid.

And now you will probably ask me how you can get the Lord to be your Shepherd. My answer is that you do not need to get Him to be your Shepherd at all, for He already *is* your Shepherd. All that is needed is for you to recognize that He is, and yield yourself to His control.

When the announcement is made in a family to the children who have been longing for a little sister, that one has just been born to them, they do not go on saying, "Oh, how we wish we had a little sister!" or, "What can we do to get a little sister?" But they begin at once to shout for joy, and to dance about calling out to everybody, "Hurrah! Hurrah! We have a little sister now."

And since likewise the announcement has been made to all of us by the angel of the Lord: "Fear not, for behold I bring you tidings of great joy, which shall be to all people. For unto you is born this day in the city of David, a Saviour which is Christ the Lord," we have no need and no right to go on crying out, "Oh, if I only had a Saviour!" or, "What shall I do to make Christ my Saviour?" He is already *born* our Saviour, and we must begin at once to rejoice that He is, and must give ourselves into His care. There is nothing complicated about it. It is simply to believe it, and act as if it were true. And every soul that will begin from today believing in the good Shepherd and trusting itself to His care will sooner or later find itself feeding in His green pastures, and walking beside His still waters.

What else can the Lord, who is our Shepherd, do with His sheep, but just this? He has no folds that are not good folds, no pastures that are not green pastures, and no waters but still waters. They may not look so outwardly; but we who have tried them can testify that, let the outward seeming be what it may, His fold and His pastures are always places of peace and comfort to the inward life of the soul.

If you seem to have difficulties in understanding all this, and if the life of full trust looks complicated and mysterious, I would advise you not to try to understand it, but simply to begin to live it. Just take our nursery psalm and say, "This is my psalm, and I am going to believe it. I have always known it by heart, but it has never meant much to me. But now I have made up my mind to believe that the Lord really is my Shepherd and that He will care for me as a shepherd cares for his sheep. I will not doubt nor question it again." And then just abandon yourself to His care, as the sheep abandon themselves to the care of their shepherd, trusting Him fully, and following whithersoever He leads.

But we must not forget that while sheep trust unconsciously and by instinct, we shall need to trust intelligently and of purpose, for our instincts, alas, are all against trusting. We shall have to make an effort to trust. We shall have to choose to do it. But we can do this, however weak and ignorant we may be. We may not understand all it means to be a sheep of such a Shepherd, but He knows. And if our faith will but claim Him in this blessed and wondrous relationship, He will care for us according to His love, and His wisdom, and His power, and not according to our poor comprehension of it.

It really seems to me as if we did not need any other passage out of the whole Bible besides this nursery psalm to make our religious lives full of comfort. I confess I do not see where there is any room left for the believer to worry, who actually believes this psalm. With the Lord for our Shepherd, how is it possible for anything to go wrong? With Him for our Shepherd, all that this psalm promises must be ours; and when we have learned thus to know Him, we will be able to say with a triumph of trust: "Surely goodness and mercy shall follow me [pursue, overtake] all the days of my life, and I shall dwell in the house of the Lord forever." Even the future will lose all its terrors for us, and our confidence in our Shepherd will deliver us from all fear of evil tidings.

And I can only say, in conclusion, that if each one of you will just enter into this relationship with Christ, and really be a helpless, docile, trusting sheep, and will believe Him to be your Shepherd, caring for you with all the love, and care, and tenderness that the name involves, and will follow Him withersoever He leads you, you will soon lose all your old spiritual discomfort, and will know the peace of God that passeth all understanding to keep your hearts and minds in Christ Jesus.

CHAPTER 5
HE SPAKE TO THEM OF THE FATHER

"They understood not that he spake to them of the Father."

One of the most illuminating names of God is the one especially revealed by our Lord Jesus Christ, the name of Father. I say especially revealed by Christ, because, while God had been called throughout the ages by many other names, expressing other aspects of His character, Christ alone has revealed Him to us under the all-inclusive name of Father — a name that holds within itself all other names of wisdom and power, and above all of love and goodness, a name that embodies for us a perfect supply for all our needs. Christ, who was the only begotten Son in the bosom of the Father, was the only one who could reveal this name, for He alone knew the Father. "As the Father knoweth me," He said, "even so know I the Father." "Not that any man hath seen the Father save he which is of God, he hath seen the Father."

In the Old Testament God was not revealed as the Father so much as a great warrior fighting for His people, or as a mighty king ruling over them and caring for them. The name of Father is only given to Him a very few times there, six or seven times at the most; while in the New Testament it is given about two or three hundred times. Christ, who knew Him, was the only one who could reveal Him. "No man," He said, "knoweth who the Father is, but the Son, and he to whom the Son will reveal him."

The vital question then that confronts each one of us is whether we individually understand that Christ speaks to us of the Father. We know He uses the word Father continually, but do we in the least understand what the word means? Have we even so much as an inkling of what the Father is?

All the discomfort and unrest of the religious life of so many of God's children come, I feel sure, from this very thing that they do not understand that God is actually and truly their Father. They think of Him as a stern Judge, or a severe Taskmaster, or at the best as an unapproachable dignitary, seated on a far-off throne, dispensing exacting laws for a frightened and trembling world; and in their terror lest they should fail to meet His requirements they hardly know which way to turn. But of a God who is a Father, tender, and loving, and full of compassion, a God who, like a father, will be on their side against the whole universe, they have no conception.

I am not afraid to say that discomfort and unrest are impossible to the souls that come to know that God is their real and actual Father.

But before I go any farther I must make it plain that it is a Father, such as our highest instincts tell us a good father ought to be, of whom I am speaking. Sometimes earthly fathers are unkind, or tyrannical, or selfish, or even cruel, or they are merely indifferent and neglectful; but none of these can by any stretch of charity be called good fathers. But God, who is good, must be a good father or not a father at all. We must all of us have known good fathers in this world, or at least can imagine them. I knew one, and he filled my childhood with sunshine by his most lovely fatherhood. I can remember vividly with what confidence and triumph I walked through my days, absolutely secure in the knowledge that I had a father. And I am very sure that I have learned to know a little about the perfect fatherhood of God, because of my experience with this lovely earthly father.

But God is not only a father. He is a mother as well, and we have all of us known mothers whose love and tenderness have been without bound or limit. And it is very certain that

the God who created them both, and who is Himself father
and mother in one, could never have created earthly fathers
and mothers who were more tender and more loving than
He is Himself. Therefore if we want to know what sort of a
Father He is, we must heap together all the best of all the
fathers and mothers we have ever known or can imagine,
and we must tell ourselves that this is only a faint image of
God, our Father in Heaven.

When our Lord was teaching His disciples how to pray,
the only name by which He taught them to address God
was, "Our Father which are in heaven." And this surely
meant that we were to think of Him only in this light.
Millions upon millions of times during all the centuries
since then has this name been uttered by the children of
God everywhere; and yet how much has it been understood? Had all who used the name known what it meant, it
would have been impossible for the misrepresentations of
His character, and the doubts of His love and care, that
have so desolated the souls of His children throughout all
the ages, to have crept in. Tyranny, unkindness, and neglect
might perhaps be attributed to a God whose name was only
a king, or a judge, or a lawgiver; but of a God, who is before all else a father, and, of necessity, since He is God, a
good father, no such things could possibly be believed.
Moreover, since He is an "everlasting Father," He must in
the very nature of things act, always and under all circumstances, as a good father ought to act, and never in any
other way. It is inconceivable that a good father could forget, or neglect, or be unfair to his children. A savage father
might, or a wicked father; but a good father never! And in
calling our God by the blessed name of Father, we ought to
know that, if He is a father at all, He must be the very best
of fathers, and His fatherhood must be the highest ideal of
fatherhood of which we can conceive. It is, as I have said, a
fatherhood that combines both father and mother in one, in
our highest ideals of both, and comprises all the love, and
all the tenderness, and all the compassion, and all the
yearning, and all the self-sacrifice, that we cannot but
recognize to be the inmost soul of parentage, even though
we may not always see it carried out by all earthly parents.

But you may say what about the other names of God, do

they not convey other and more terrifying ideas? They only
do so because this blessed name of Father is not added to
them. This name must underlie every other name by which
He has ever been known. Has He been called a Judge? Yes,
but He is a Father Judge, one who judges as a loving father
would. Is He a King? Yes, but He is a King who is at the
same time the Father of His subjects, and who rules them
with a father's tenderness. Is He a Lawgiver? Yes, but He is
a Lawgiver who gives laws as a father would, remembering
the weakness and ignorance of his helpless children. "Like
as a father pitieth his children, so the Lord pitieth them that
fear him. For he knoweth our frame; he remembereth that
we are dust." It is not "as a judge judges, so the Lord
judges"; not "as a taskmaster controls, so the Lord controls"; not "as a lawgiver imposes laws, so the Lord imposes laws"; but, "as a father pitieth, so the Lord pitieth."

Never, never must we think of God in any other way than
as "our Father." All other attributes with which we endow
Him in our conceptions must be based upon and limited by
this one of "our Father." What a good father could not do,
God, who is our Father, cannot do either; and what a good
father ought to do, God, who is our Father, is absolutely
sure to do.

In our Lord's last prayer in John 17, He says that He has
declared to us the name of the Father in order that we may
discover the wonderful fact that the Father loves us as He
loved His Son. Now, which one of us really believes this?
We have read this chapter over, I suppose, oftener than
almost any other chapter in the Bible, and yet do we any of
us believe that it is an actual, tangible fact, that God loves
us as much as He loved Christ? If we believed this to be actually the case, could we, by any possibility, ever have an
anxious or rebellious thought again? Would we not be absolutely and utterly sure always under every conceivable circumstance that the divine Father, who loves us just as much
as He loved His only begotten Son, our Lord Jesus Christ,
would of course care for us in the best possible way, and
could not let us want for any good thing? No wonder our
Lord could tell us so emphatically not to be anxious or
troubled about anything, for He knew His Father and knew
that it was safe to trust Him utterly.

It is very striking that He so often said, "Your heavenly Father, not mine only, but yours just as much. Your heavenly Father," He says, "cares for the sparrows and the lilies, and of course, therefore, he will care for you who are of so much more value than many sparrows." How supremely foolish it is then for us to be worried and anxious about things, when Christ has said that our heavenly Father knows that we have need of all these things! For of course, being a good father, He must in the very nature of the case, when He knows our need, supply it.

What can be the matter with us that we do not understand this?

Again, our Lord draws the comparison between earthly fathers and our heavenly Father, in order to show us, not how much less good and tender and willing to bless is our heavenly Father, but how much more. "If ye, being evil," He says, "know how to give good gifts unto your children, how much more shall your Father which is in heaven give good things to them that ask him." Can we conceive of a good earthly father giving a stone or a serpent to a hungry child instead of bread or fish? Would not our whole souls revolt from a father who could so such things? And yet, I fear, there are a great many of God's children who actually think that their heavenly Father does this sort of thing to them, and gives them stones when they ask for bread, or curses when they ask for blessings. And perhaps these very people may belong to the Society for the Prevention of Cruelty to Children, a society which is the nation's protest against such behavior on the part of earthly fathers; and yet they never have thought of the dreadful wickedness of charging their heavenly Father with things which they are banded together to punish in earthly fathers!

But it is not only that our heavenly Father is willing to give us good things. He is far more than willing. Our Lord says, "Fear not, little flock, it is your Father's good pleasure to give you the kingdom." There is no grudging in His giving, it is His "good pleasure" to give; He likes to do it. He wants to give you the kingdom far more than you want to have it. Those of us who are parents know how eager we are to give good things to our children, often far more eager than our children are to have them; and this may help us to understand how it is that it is God's "good pleasure" to give us the kingdom. Why, then, should we ask Him in such fear and trembling, and why should we torment ourselves with anxiety lest He should fail to grant what we need?

There can be only one answer to these questions, and that is, that we do not know the Father.

We are told that we are of the "household of God." Now the principle is announced in the Bible that if any man provides not for his own household, he has "denied the faith and is worse than an infidel." Since then we are of the "household of God," this principle applies to Him, and if He should fail to provide for us, His own words would condemn Him. I say this reverently, but I want to say it emphatically, for so few people seem to have realized it.

It was in my own case a distinct era of immense importance when I first discovered this fact of the responsibility of my Father in Heaven. As it were, in a single moment, the burden of life was lifted off my shoulders and laid on His, and all my fears, and anxieties, and questionings dropped into the abyss of His loving care. I saw that the instinct of humanity, which demands that the parents who bring a child into the world are bound by every law, both human and divine, to care for and protect that child according to their best ability, is a divinely implanted instinct; and that it is meant to teach us the magnificent fact that the Creator, who has made human parents responsible toward their children, is Himself equally responsible toward His children. I could have shouted for joy! And from that glad hour my troubles were over. For when this insight comes to a soul, that soul must, in the very nature of things, enter into rest.

With such a God, who is at the same time a Father, there is no room for anything but rest. And when, ever since that glad day, temptations to doubt or anxiety or fear have come to me, I have not dared in the face of what I then learned to listen to them, because I have seen that to do so would be to cast a doubt on the trustworthiness of my Father in Heaven.

We may have been accustomed to think that our doubts and fears were because of our own unworthiness and arose from humility; and we may even have taken them as a sign of especial piety, and have thought they were in some way

pleasing to God. But if, in their relations with their earthly
parents, children should let in doubts of their love, and
fears lest their care should fail, would these doubts and
fears be evidences of filial piety on the children's part, and
would they be at all pleasing to their parents?

If God is our Father, the only thing we can do with
doubts, and fears, and anxious thoughts is to cast them
behind our backs forever, and have nothing more to do
with them ever again. We *can* do this. We can give up our
doubts just as we would urge a drunkard to give up his
drink. We can pledge against doubting. And if once we see
that our doubts are an actual sin against God, and imply a
question of His trustworthiness, we will be eager to do it.
We may have cherished our doubts heretofore because perhaps we have thought they were a part of our religion, and a
becoming attitude of soul in one so unworthy; but if we
now see that God is in very truth our Father, we will reject
every doubt with horror, as being a libel on our Father's
love and our Father's care.

What more can any soul want than to have a God whose
name is "our Father," and whose character and ways must
necessarily come up to the highest possibilities of His
name? As Phililp said, so we find it to be, "Show us the
Father and it sufficeth us." It does indeed suffice, beyond
what words can express!

A friend of mine went one day to see a poor negro woman
living in one of the poorest parts of Philadelphia, whose case
had been reported to her as being one of great need. She
found things even worse than she had feared. The poor
woman was old, crippled with rheumatism, and lived alone
in a poor little room with only the help of a kind neighbor
now and then to do things for her; and yet she was bright
and cheerful, and full of thanksgiving for her many mercies.
My friend marveled that cheerfulness or thankfulness could
be possible under such circumstances, and said, "But do you
never get frightened at the thought of what may happen to
you, all alone here, and so lame as you are?"

The old negro saint looked at her with surprise, and said
in a tone of utmost amazement, "Frightened! Why, honey,
doesn't you know I have got a Father, and doesn't you
know He takes care of me the whole endurin' time?" And

then, as my friend looked perplexed, she added in a tone of wondering reproof, "Why, honey, sholy my Father is your Father too, and you knows about Him, and you knows He always takes care of His chilluns." It was a lesson my friend never forgot.

"Behold," says the apostle John, "what manner of love the Father hath bestowed upon us, that we should be called the sons of God." The "manner of love" bestowed upon us is the love of a father for his son, a tender protecting love, that knows our weakness and our need, and cares for us accordingly. He treats us as sons, and all He asks in return is that we shall treat Him as a Father, whom we can trust without anxiety. We must take the son's place of dependence and trust, and must let Him keep the father's place of care and responsibility. Because we are the children and He is the Father, we must let Him do the father's part. Too often we take upon our own shoulders the father's part, and try to take care of and provide for ourselves. But no good earthly father would want his children to take upon their young shoulders the burden of his duties, and surely much less would our heavenly Father want to lay upon us the burden of His.

No wonder we are told to cast all our care upon Him, for He careth for us. He careth for us; of course He does. It is His business, as a Father, to do so. He would not be a good Father if He did not. All He asks of us is to let Him know when we need anything, and then leave the supplying of that need to Him; and He assures us that if we do this the "peace of God that passeth all understanding shall keep our hearts and minds." The children of a good, human father are at peace because they trust in their father's care; but the children of the heavenly Father too often have no peace because they are afraid to trust in His care. They make their requests known to Him perhaps, but that is all they do. It is a sort of religious form they feel it necessary to go through. But as to supposing that He really will care for them, no such idea seems to cross their minds; and they go on carrying their cares and burdens on their own shoulders, exactly as if they had no Father in Heaven, and had never asked Him to care for them.

What utter folly it all is! For if ever an earthly father was worthy of the confidence of his children, surely much more is our heavenly Father worthy of our confidence. And why it is that so few of His children trust Him can only be because they have not yet found out that He is really their Father; or else that, calling Him Father every day in their prayers, they still have never seen that He is the sort of Father a good and true human father is, a Father who is loving, and tender, and pitiful, and full of kindness toward the helpless beings whom He has brought into existence, and whom He is therefore bound to protect. This sort of Father no one could help trusting; but the strange and far-off Creator, whose fatherhood stops at our creation, and has no care for our fate after once we are launched into the universe, no one could be expected to trust.

The remedy, therefore, for your discomfort and unrest is to be found in becoming acquainted with the Father.

"For," says the apostle, "ye have not received the spirit of bondage again to fear; but ye have received the spirit of adoption, whereby we cry, Abba, Father." Is it this "spirit of adoption" that reigns in your hearts, my readers, or is it the "spirit of bondage"? Your whole comfort in the religious life depends upon which spirit it is; and no amount of wrestling, or agonizing, no prayers, and no efforts will be able to bring you to comfort, while the "spirit of adoption" is lacking in your heart.

But you may ask how you are to get this "spirit of adoption." I can only say that it is not a thing to be gotten. It comes; and it comes as the necessary result of the discovery that God is in very truth a real Father. When we have made this discovery, we cannot help feeling and acting like a child; and this is what the "spirit of adoption" means. It is nothing mystical nor mysterious; it is the simple natural result of having found a Father where you thought there was only a Judge.

The great need for every soul, therefore, is to make this supreme discovery. And to do this we have only to see what Christ tells us about the Father, and then believe it. "Verily, verily," He declares, "I say unto thee, We speak that we do know, and testify that we have seen," but, He adds sadly, "ye receive not our witness." In order to come to the knowledge of the Father, we must receive the testimony of

Christ, who declares: "The words that I speak unto you I speak not of myself; but the Father that dwelleth in me, he doeth the works." Over and over He repeated this, and in John, after grieving over the fact that so few received His testimony, He adds these memorable words: "He that hath received his testimony hath set to his seal that God is true."

The whole authority of Christ stands or falls with this. If we receive His testimony, we set to our seal that God is true. If we reject that testimony, we make Him a liar.

"If ye had known me," says Christ, "ye should have known my Father also; and from henceforth ye know him, and have seen him." The thing for us to do then is to make up our minds that from henceforth we will receive His testimony, and will "know the Father." Let other people worship whatever sort of a God they may, for us there must be henceforth "but one God, even the Father."

"For though there be that are called gods, whether in heaven or in earth (as there be gods many, and lords many), but to us there is but one God, the Father, of whom are all things, and we in him; and one Lord Jesus Christ, by whom are all things, and we by him."

CHAPTER 6
JEHOVAH

"That men may know that thou, whose name alone is
JEHOVAH, *art the most High over all the earth."*

Among all the names of God perhaps the most compre-
hensive is the name Jehovah. Cruden describes this name as
the incommunicable name of God. The word Jehovah
means the self-existing One, the "I am"; and it is generally
used as a direct revelation of what God is. In several places
an explanatory word is added, revealing some one of His
special characteristics; and it is to these that I want particularly to call attention. They are as follows:

Jehovah-jireh, i.e., The Lord will see, or the Lord will
    provide.
Jehovah-nissi, i.e., The Lord my Banner.
Jehovah-shalom, i.e., The Lord our Peace.
Jehovah-tsidkenu, i.e., The Lord our Righteousness.
Jehovah-shammah, i.e., The Lord is there.

These names were discovered by God's people in times of
sore need; that is, the characteristics they describe were discovered, and the names were the natural expression of these
characteristics.

When Abraham was about to sacrifice his son, and saw
no way of escape, the Lord provided a lamb for the sacri-

fice and delivered Isaac; and Abraham made the grand discovery that it was one of the characteristics of Jehovah to
see and provide for the needs of His people. Therefore he
called Him Jehovah-jireh — the Lord will see, or the Lord
will provide.

The counterparts to this in the New Testament are very
numerous. Over and over our Lord urges us to take no care,
because God careth for us. "Your heavenly Father knoweth," He says, "that ye have need of all these things." If
the Lord sees and knows our need, it will be a matter of
course with Him to provide for it. Being our Father, He
could not do anything else. As soon as a good mother sees
that her child needs anything, at once she sets about supplying that need. She does not even wait for the child to ask,
the sight of the need is asking enough. Being a good
mother, she could not do otherwise.

When God, therefore, says to us, "I am he that seeth thy
need," He in reality says also, "I am he that provideth,"
for He cannot see, and fail to provide.

"Why do I not have everything I want, then?" you may
ask. Only because God sees that what you want is not really
the thing you need, but probably exactly the opposite.
Often, in order to give us what we need, the Lord is obliged
to keep from us what we want. Your heavenly Father knoweth what things ye have need of, you do not know; and were
all your wants gratified, it might well be that all your needs
would be left unsupplied. It surely ought to suffice us that
our God is indeed Jehovah-jireh, the Lord who will see, and
who will therefore provide.

But I am afraid a great many Christians of the present
day have never made Abraham's discovery, and do not
know that the Lord is really Jehovah-jireh. They are trusting Him, it may be, to save their souls in the future, but
they never dream He wants to carry their cares for them
now and here. They are like a man I have heard of, with a
heavy load on his back, who was given a lift by a friend,
and who thankfully availed himself of it. Climbing into the
conveyance, but still keeping his burden on his back, he sat
there bowed down under the weight of it. "Why do you not
put your burden down on the bottom of the carriage?" asked his friend.

"Oh," replied the man, "it is a great deal to ask you to carry me myself, and I could not ask you to carry my burden also." You wonder that anyone could be so foolish, and yet are you not doing the same? Are you not trusting the Lord to take care of yourself, but are still going on carrying your burdens on your own shoulders? Which is the silliest —that man or you?

Jehovah-nissi, i.e., "The Lord my banner," was a discovery made by Moses when Amalek came to fight with Israel in Rephidim, and the Lord gave the Israelites a glorious victory. Moses realized that the Lord was fighting for them, and he built an altar to Jehovah-nissi, "The Lord my banner." The Bible is full of developments of this name. "The Lord is a man of war"; "The Lord your God, he it is that fighteth for you"; "The Lord shall fight for you, and ye shall hold your peace"; "Be not afraid nor dismayed, by reason of this great multitude, for the battle is not yours, but God's"; "God himself is with us for our captain."

Nothing is more abundantly proved in the Bible than this, that the Lord will fight for us if we will but let Him. He knows that we have no strength nor might against our spiritual enemies; and, like a tender mother when her helpless children are attacked by an enemy, He fights for us; and all He asks of us is to be still and let Him. This is the only sort of spiritual conflict that is ever successful. But we are very slow to learn this, and when temptations come, instead of handing the battle over to the Lord, we summon all our forces to fight them ourselves. We believe, perhaps, that the Lord is somewhere near, and, if the worst comes to the worst, will step in to help us; but for the most part we feel that we ourselves, and we only, must do all the fighting. Our method of fighting consists generally in a series of repentings, and making resolutions and promises, and weary struggles for victory, and then failing again; and again repentance, and resolutions, and promises, and renewed struggles, and all this over, and over, and over again, each time telling ourselves that now at last we certainly will have the victory, and each time failing even worse than before. And this may go on for weeks, or months, or even years, and no real or permanent deliverance ever comes.

But you may ask, "Are we not to do any fighting ourselves?'' Of course we are to fight, but not in this fashion. We are to fight the "good fight of faith," as Paul exhorted Timothy; and the fight of faith is not a fight of effort or of struggle, but it is a fight of trusting. It is the kind of fight that Hezekiah fought when he and his army marched out to meet their enemy, singing songs of victory as they went, and finding their enemy all dead men. Our part in this fight is to hand the battle over to the Lord, and to trust Him for the victory.

And we are to put on His armor, not our own. The apostle tells us what it is. It is the girdle of truth, and the breastplate of righteousness, and the preparation of the gospel of peace on our feet, and the helmet of salvation, and the sword of the Spirit which is the Word of God; but above all, he says, we are to take the shield of faith wherewith we shall be able to quench all the fiery darts of the wicked.

There is nothing here about promises or resolutions; nothing about hours and days of agonizing struggles, and of bitter remorse. "Above all things taking the shield of faith." Above all things, faith. Faith is the one essential thing, without which all else is useless. And it means that we must not only hand the battle over to the Lord, but we must leave it with Him, and must have absolute faith that He will conquer. It is here where the fight comes in. It seems so unsafe to sit still, and do nothing but trust the Lord; and the temptation to take the battle back into our own hands is often tremendous. To keep hands off in spiritual matters is as hard for us as it is for the drowning man to keep hands off the one who is trying to rescue him. We all know how impossible it is to rescue a drowning man who tries to help his rescuer, and it is equally impossible for the Lord to fight our battles for us when we insist upon trying to fight them ourselves. It is not that He will not, but He cannot. Our interference hinders His working. Spiritual forces cannot work while earthly forces are active.

Our Lord tells us that without Him we can do nothing, and we have read and repeated His words hundreds of times; but does anyone really believe they are actually true? If we should drag out into the light our secret thoughts on the subject, should we not find them to be something like this: "When Christ said those words He meant of course to say that we cannot of ourselves do much, or at any rate no great things. But nothing; ah, no, that is impossible. We are not babies, and we are certainly meant to use all the strength we have in fighting our enemies; and, when our own strength gives out, we can then call upon the Lord to help us." In spite of all our failures, we cannot help thinking that, if only we should try harder and be more persistent, we should be equal to any encounter. But we entirely overlook the vital fact that our natural powers are of no avail in spiritual regions or with spiritual enemies. The grub of the dragonfly, that lives at the bottom of the pond, may be a finely developed and vigorous grub; but, when it becomes a dragonfly, the powers of its grub life, that availed for creeping about in the mud, would be useless for winging its flight in the free air.

And just as our skill in walking on the earth would avail us nothing if we had to fly in the air, so our natural powers are of no avail in spiritual warfare. They are, in fact, if we try to depend on them, real hindrances, just as trying to walk would hinder us, if we sought to float or to fly. We can easily see, therefore, that the result of trusting in ourselves, when dealing with our spiritual enemies, must inevitably be very serious. It not only causes failure, but in the end it causes rebellion; and a great deal of what is called "spiritual conflict" might far better be named "spiritual rebellion." God has told us to cease from our own efforts, and to hand our battles over to Him, and we point blank refuse to obey Him. We fight, it is true, but it is not a fight of faith, but a fight of unbelief. Our spiritual "wrestling," of which we are often so proud, is really a wrestling, not for God against His enemies, but against Him on the side of His enemies. We allow ourselves to indulge in doubts and fears, and as a consequence we are plunged into darkness, and turmoil, and wrestlings of spirit. And then we call this "spiritual conflict," and look upon ourselves as an interesting and "peculiar case." The single word that explains our "peculiar case" is the word *unbelief,* and the simple remedy is to be found in the word *faith.*

But you may ask, what about "wrestling Jacob"? Did he not gain his victory by wrestling? To this I reply, that on the contrary he gained his victory by being made so weak that he could not wrestle any longer. It was not Jacob who wrestled with the angel, but the angel who wrestled with Jacob. Jacob was the one to be overcome; and when the angel found that Jacob's resistance was so great that he could not "prevail against him," he was obliged to make him lame by putting his thigh out of joint, and then the victory was won. As soon as Jacob was too weak to resist any longer, he prevailed with God. He gained power when he lost it. He conquered when he could no longer fight.

Jacob's experience is ours. The Lord wrestles with us in order to bring us to a place of entire dependence on Him. We resist as long as we have any strength; until at last He is forced to bring us to a place of helplessness, where we are obliged to yield; and then we conquer by this very yielding. Our victory is always the victory of weakness. Paul knew this victory when he said: "And the Lord said unto me, My grace is sufficient for thee; for my strength is made perfect in weakness. Most gladly therefore will I rather glory in my infirmities, that the power of Christ may rest upon me. Therefore I take pleasure in infirmities, in reproaches, in necessities, in persecutions, in distresses for Christ's sake; for when I am weak, then am I strong."

Who would ask for a more magnificent victory than this!

And this victory will be ours, if we take the Lord to be our Banner, and commit all our battles to Him.

The name of Jehovah-shalom, or "The Lord our peace," was discovered by Gideon when the Lord had called him to a work for which he felt himself to be utterly unfitted. "Oh, my Lord," he had said, "wherewith shall I save Israel? Behold, my family is poor in Manasseh, and I am the least of my father's house." And the Lord answered him, saying: "Surely I will be with thee, and thou shalt smite the Midianites as one man ... And the Lord said unto him, Peace be unto thee: fear not; for thou shalt not die." Then Gideon believed the Lord; and, although the battle had not yet been fought, and no victories had been won, with the eye of faith he saw peace already secured, and he built an altar unto the Lord, and called it Jehovah-shalom, i.e., "The Lord our peace."

Of all the needs of the human heart none is greater than the need for peace; and none is more abundantly promised in the Gospel. "Peace I leave with you," says our Lord, "my peace I give unto you. Let not your heart be troubled, neither let it be afraid." And again He says: "These things have I spoken unto you, that in me ye might have peace. In the world ye shall have tribulation: but be of good cheer, I have overcome the world."

Our idea of peace is that it must be outward before it can be inward, that all enemies must be driven away, and all troubles cease. But the Lord's idea was of an interior peace that could exist in the midst of turmoil, and could be triumphant over it. And the ground of this sort of peace is found in the fact, not that we have overcome the world, or that we ever can, but that Christ has overcome it. Only the conqueror can proclaim peace, and the people, whose battles He has fought, can do nothing but enter into it. They can neither make nor unmake it. But, if they choose, they can refuse to believe in it, and so can fail to let it reign in their hearts. You may be afraid to believe that Christ has made peace for you, and so may live on in a weary state of warfare; but nevertheless, He has done it, and all your continued warfare is worse than useless.

The Bible tells us that Christ is our peace, and consequently, whether I feel as if I had peace or not, peace is really mine in Christ, and I must take possession of it by faith. Faith is simply to believe and assert the thing that God says. If He says there is peace, faith asserts that there is, and enters into the enjoyment of it. If He has proclaimed peace in the Bible, I must proclaim it in my own heart, let the seemings be what they may. "The kingdom of God is righteousness, peace, and joy, in the Holy Ghost," and the soul that has not taken possession of peace has not yet fully entered into this kingdom.

Practically I believe we can always enter into peace by a simple obedience to Philippians 4:6, 7: "Be careful for nothing; but in everything by prayer and supplication with thanksgiving let your requests be made known unto God. And the peace of God, which passeth all understanding, shall keep your hearts and minds through Christ Jesus." The steps here are very plain, and they are only two. First, give up all anxiety; and second, hand over your cares to God; and then stand steadfastly here; peace must come. It simply must, for there is no room for anything else.

The name Jehovah-tsidkenu, "The Lord our righteousness," was revealed by the Lord Himself through the mouth of the prophet Jeremiah, when he was announcing the coming of Christ. "Behold, the day is come, saith the Lord, that I will raise unto David a righteous Branch, and a King shall reign and prosper, and shall execute judgment and justice in the earth. In his days Judah shall be saved, and Israel shall dwell safely, and this is the name whereby he shall be called, Jehovah-tsidkenu, The Lord our righteousness."

Greater than any other need is our need for righteousness. Most of the struggles and conflicts of our Christian life come from our fights with sin, and our efforts after righteousness. And I need not say how great are our failures. As long as we try to conquer sin or attain to righteousness by our own efforts, we are bound to fail. But if we discover that the Lord is our righteousness, we shall have the secret of victory. In the Lord Jesus Christ we have a fuller revelation of this wonderful name of God. The apostle Paul in his character as the "ambassador for Christ" declares that God hath made Christ to be sin for us, that we might be made the righteousness of God in Him. And again he says that Christ is made unto us wisdom, and righteousness, and sanctification, and redemption. I am afraid that very few Christians really understand what this means. We repeat the words as belonging to our religious vocabulary, and in a vague sort of way think of them as being somehow a part of the salvation of Christ, but what part or of what practical use we have very little real idea.

To me this name of God, the Lord our righteousness, seems of such tremendously practical use that I want if possible to make it plain to others. But it is difficult; and I cannot possibly explain it theologically. But experimentally it seems to me like this: We are not to try to have a stock of righteousness laid up in ourselves, from which to draw a supply when needed, but we are to draw continual fresh supplies as we need them from the righteousness that is laid up for us in Christ. I mean, that if we need righteousness of any sort, such as patience, or humility, or love, it is useless for us to look within, hoping to find a supply there, for we never will find it; but we must simply take it by faith, as a possession that is stored up for us in Christ, who is our righteousness. If I cannot tell theologically how this is done, I know experimentally that it can be done, and that the results are triumphant. I have seen sweetness and gentleness poured like a flood of sunshine into dark and bitter spirits, when the hand of faith has been reached out to grasp them as a present possession, stored up for all who need in Christ. I have seen sharp tongues made tender, anxious hearts made calm, and fretful spirits made quiet by the simple step of taking by faith the righteousness that is ours in Christ.

The apostle, after proving to us in the third chapter of Romans the absolute impossibility of any satisfying righteousness coming to us by the law (that is, by our own efforts) goes on to say: "But now the righteousness of God without the law is manifested, being witnessed by the law and the prophets, even the righteousness of God which is by faith of Jesus Christ unto all and upon all them that believe; for there is no difference."

It is faith and faith only that can appropriate this righteousness that is ours in Christ. Just as we appropriate by faith the forgiveness that is ours in Christ, so must we appropriate by faith the patience that is ours in Him, or the gentleness, or the meekness, or the long-suffering, or any other virtue we may need. Our own efforts will not procure righteousness for us, any more than they will procure forgiveness. And yet how many Christians try! Paul describes them when he says: "For I bear them record that they have a zeal of God, but not according to knowledge. For they being ignorant of God's righteousness, and going about to establish their own righteousness, have not submitted themselves unto the righteousness of God. For Christ is the end of the law for righteousness to every one that believeth."

Would that all such zealous souls could discover this wonderful name of God, "The Lord of our righteousness," and would give up at once and forever seeking to establish their own righteousness, and would submit themselves to the righteousness of God. The prophet tells us that our own righteousness, even if we could attain to any, is nothing but filthy rags; and Paul prays that he may be found in Christ, not having his own righteousness, which is of the law, but

that which is through the faith of Christ, the righteousness
which is of God by faith.

Do we at all comprehend the meaning of this prayer?
And are we prepared to join in it with our whole hearts? If
so, our struggle after righteousness will be over. Jehovah-
tsidkenu will supply all our needs.

The name Jehovah-shammah, or "The Lord is there,"
was revealed to the prophet Ezekiel when he was shown by
a vision, in the twenty-fifth year of their captivity, what was
to be the future home of the children of Israel. He described
the land and the city of Jerusalem, and ended his description by saying: "And the name of that city shall be called
Jehovah-shammah, or the Lord is there."

To me this name includes all the others. Wherever the
Lord is, all must go right for His children. Where the good
mother is, all goes right, up to the measure of her ability,
for her children. And how much more God. His presence is
enough. We can all remember how the simple presence of
our mothers was enough for us when we were children. All
that we needed of comfort, rest, and deliverance was in-
sured to us by the mere fact of our mother, as she sat in her
accustomed chair with her work, or her book, or her
writing, and we had burst in upon her with our doleful
budget of childish woes. If we could but see that the
presence of God is the same assurance of comfort, and rest,
and deliverance, only infinitely more so, a wellspring of joy
would be opened up in our religious lives that would drive
out every vestige of discomfort and distress.

All through the Old Testament the Lord's one universal
answer to all the fears and anxieties of the children of Israel
was the simple words, "I will be with thee." He did not
need to say anything more. His presence was to them a
perfect guarantee that all their needs would be supplied;
and the moment they were assured of it, they were no
longer afraid to face the fiercest foe.

You may say, "Ah, yes, if the Lord would only say the
same thing to me, I should not be afraid either." Well, He
has said it, and has said it in unmistakable terms. When the
"angel of the Lord" announced to Joseph the coming birth
of Christ, he said: "They shall call his name Emmanuel:
which being interpreted is, God with us." In this short sen-

tence is revealed to us the grandest fact the world can ever know — that God, the Almighty God, the Creator of Heaven and earth, is not a far-off God, dwelling in a Heaven of unapproachable glory, but has come down in Christ to dwell with us right here in this world, in the midst of our poor, ignorant, helpless lives, as close to us as we are to ourselves. If we believe in Christ at all, we are shut up to believing this, for this is His name, "God with us."

Both these names then, *JEHOVAH-SHAMMAH* and *EMMANUEL,* mean the same thing. They mean that God is everywhere present in His universe, surrounding everything, and sustaining everything, and holding all of us in His safe and blessed keeping. They mean that we can find no place in all His universe of which it cannot be said, "The Lord is there." The psalmist says: "Whither shall I go from thy spirit? And whither shall I flee from thy presence? If I ascend up into heaven, thou art there; if I make my bed in hell, behold, thou art there. If I take the wings of the morning, and dwell in the uttermost parts of the sea, even there shall thy hand lead me, and thy right hand shall hold me."

We cannot drift from the love and care of an ever-present God. And those Christians who think He has forsaken them, and who cry out for His presence, are crying out in ignorance of the fact that He is always and everywhere present with them. In truth they cannot get out of His presence, even should they try. Oh, that they knew this wonderful and satisfying name of God!

Speak to Him, thou, for He hears; and spirit with spirit
    may meet;
Closer is He than breathing, and nearer than hands and
    feet.

Let us sum up, once more, the teaching of these five names of God. What is it they say to us?

Jehovah-jireh, i.e., "I am he who sees thy need, and therefore provides for it."

Jehovah-nissi, i.e., "I am thy captain, and thy banner, and he who will fight thy battles for thee."

Jehovah-shalom, i.e., "I am thy peace. I have made peace for thee, and my peace I give unto thee."

Jehovah-tsidkenu, i.e., "I am thy righteousness. In me thou wilt find all thou needest of wisdom, and righteousness, and sanctification, and redemption."

Jehovah-shammah, i.e., "I am with thee. I am thy ever-present, all-environing God and Saviour. I will never leave thee nor forsake thee. Whereever thou goest, there I am, and there shall my hand hold thee, and my right hand lead thee."

All this is true, whether we know it and recognize it or not. We may never have dreamed that God was such a God as this, and we may have gone through our lives thus far starved, and weary, and wretched. But all the time we have been starving in the midst of plenty. The fullness of God's salvation has awaited our faith; and "abundance of grace and of the gift of righteousness" have awaited our receiving.

Would that I could believe that for some of my readers all this was ended, and that henceforth they would see that these all-embracing names of God leave no tiny corner of their need unsupplied. Then would they be able to testify with the prophet to all around them: "Behold, God is my salvation: for the Lord Jehovah is my strength and my song; he also is become my salvation. Therefore with joy shall we draw water out of the wells of salvation."

CHAPTER 7
"THE LORD IS GOOD"

"O taste and see that the Lord is good; blessed is the man that trusteth in him."

Have you ever asked yourself what you honestly think of God down at the bottom of your heart, whether you believe Him to be a good God or a bad God? I dare say the question will shock you, and you will be horrified at the suggestion that you could by any possibility think that God is a bad God. But before you have finished this chapter, I suspect some of you will be forced to acknowledge that, unconsciously perhaps, but nonetheless truly, you have, by your doubts and your upbraidings, attributed to Him a character that you would be horrified to have attributed to yourself.

I shall never forget the hour when I first discovered that God was really good. I had, of course, always known that the Bible said He was good, but I had thought it only meant He was religiously good; and it had never dawned on me that it meant He was actually and practically good, with the same kind of goodness He has commanded us to have. The expression, "The goodness of God," had seemed to me nothing more than a sort of heavenly statement, which I could not be expected to understand. And then one day I came in my reading of the Bible across the words, "O taste and see that the Lord is good," and suddenly they meant something. The Lord is good, I repeated to myself. What does it mean to be good? What but this, the living up to the best and highest that one knows. To be good is exactly the opposite of being bad. To be bad is to know the right and not to do it, but to be good is to do the best we know. And I saw that, since God is omniscient, He must know what is the best and highest good of all, and that therefore His goodness must necessarily be beyond question. I can never express what this meant to me. I had such a view of the real actual goodness of God that I saw nothing could possibly go wrong under His care, and it seemed to me that no one could ever be anxious again. And over and over, when appearances have been against Him, and when I have been tempted to question whether He had not been unkind, or neglectful, or indifferent, I have been brought up short by the words, "The Lord is good"; and I have seen that it was simply unthinkable that a God who was good could have done the bad things I had imagined.

You shrink with horror, perhaps, from the suggestion that you could under any circumstances, even in the secret depths of your heart, attribute to God what was bad. And yet you do not hesitate to accuse Him of doing things, which, if one of your friends should do them, you would look upon as most dishonorable and unkind. For instance, Christians get into trouble; all looks dark, and they have no sense of the Lord's presence. They begin to question whether the Lord has not forsaken them, and sometimes even accuse Him of indifference and neglect. And they never realize that these accusations are tantamount to saying that the Lord does not keep His promises, and does not treat them as kindly and honorably as they expect all their human friends to treat them. If one of our human friends should forsake us because we were in trouble, we would consider such a friend as very far from being good. How is it, then, that we can even for one moment accuse our Lord of such actions? No, dear friend, if the Lord is good, not pious only, but really good, it must be because He always under every circumstance acts up to the highest ideal of that which He Himself has taught us is goodness. Goodness in Him must mean, just as it does with us, the living up to the best and highest He knows.

Practically, then, it means that He will not neglect any of

His duties toward us, and that He will always treat us in the best possible way. This may sound like a platitude, and you may exclaim, "Why tell us this, for it is what we all believe?" But do you? If you did, would it be possible for you ever to think He was neglectful, or indifferent, or unkind, or self-absorbed, or inconsiderate? Do not put on a righteous air, and say, "Oh, but I never do accuse Him of any such things. I would not dare to." Do you not? Have you never laid to His charge things you would scorn to do yourselves? How was it when that last grievous disappointment came? Did you not feel as if the Lord had been unkind in permitting such a thing to come upon you, when you were trying so hard to serve Him? Do you never look upon His will as a tyrannical and arbitrary will, that must be submitted to, of course, but that could not by any possibility be loved? Does it never seem to you a hard thing to say, "Thy will be done"? But could it seem hard if you really believed that the Lord is good, and that He always does that which is good?

The Lord Jesus took great care to tell us that He was a good Shepherd, because He knew how often appearances would be against Him, and how tempted we should be to question His goodness. "I am a good Shepherd," He says in effect, "not a bad one. Bad shepherds neglect and forsake their sheep, but I am a good Shepherd, and never neglect nor forsake My sheep. I give My life for the sheep." His ideal of goodness in a shepherd was that the shepherd must protect the sheep entrusted to his care, even at the cost of his own life; and He came up to His own ideal. Now, can we not see that if we really believe that He is good, not in some mysterious, religious way, but in this common-sense, human way, we shall be brought out into a large place of peace and comfort at once. If I am a sheep, and the Lord is a good Shepherd, in the ordinary common-sense definition of *good,* how utterly secure I am! How sure I may be of the best of care in every respect! How safe I am for time and for eternity!

Let us be honest with ourselves. Have we never in our secret hearts accused the Lord of the very characteristics that He has told us in Ezekiel are the marks of a bad shepherd? Have we not thought that He cared for His own comfort or glory more than He cared for ours? Have we not complained that He has not strengthened us when we were weak, or bound up our broken hearts, or sought for us when we were lost? Have we not even actually looked upon our diseased, and helpless, and lost condition, as a reason why He would not any longer have anything to do with us? In what does this differ from if we should say out plump and plain, the Lord is a bad shepherd, and does not fulfill His duties to His sheep. You shrink in horror, perhaps, at this translation of your inward murmurings and complainings, but what else, I ask you, can they in all honesty mean? It is of vital importance now and then to drag out our secret thoughts and feelings about the Lord into the full light of the Holy Spirit, that we may see what our attitude about Him really is. It is fatally easy to get into a habit of wrong thoughts about God, thoughts which will insensibly separate us from Him by a wide gulf of doubt and unbelief. More than anything else, more even than sin, wrong thoughts about God sap the foundations of our spiritual life, and grieve His heart of love. We can understand this from ourselves. Nothing grieves us so much as to have our friends misjudge and misunderstand us, and attribute to us motives we scorn. And nothing, I believe, so grieves the Lord. It is, in fact, idolatry. For what is idolatry but creating and worshiping a false God, and what are we doing but this very thing, when we allow ourselves to misjudge Him, and attribute to Him actions and feelings that are unkind and untrustworthy.

It is called in the Bible a speaking against God. "Yea, they spake against God; they said, Can God furnish a table in the wilderness?" This seemed a very innocent question to ask. But God had promised to supply all their needs in the wilderness; and to ask this question implied a secret want of confidence in His ability to do as He had promised; and it was therefore, in spite of its innocent appearance, a real "speaking against" Him. A good God could not have led His people into the wilderness, and then have failed to "furnish a table" for them; and to question whether He was able to do it was to imply that He was not good. In the same way we are sometimes sorely tempted to ask a similar question. Circumstances often seem to make it so impossible for God to supply our needs, that we find ourselves tempted over and over to "speak against" Him by asking if He can. Often as He has done it before, we seem unable to believe He can do it again, and in our hearts we "limit" Him, because we do not believe His Word or trust in His goodness.

If our faith were what it ought to be, no circumstances, however untoward, could make us "limit" the power of God to supply our needs. The God who can make circumstances can surely control circumstances, and can, even in the wilderness, "furnish a table" for all who trust in Him.

There are many similar questions to be found in the Bible, each one throwing doubts upon the goodness of God, and each one, I am afraid, is a duplicate of questions asked by God's children now.

"Is God among us or not?"

"Hath God forgotten to be gracious?"

"Is God's mercy clean gone forever?"

"Hath God in anger shut up his tender mercies?"

"Do God's promises fail forevermore?"

"O God, why hast thou cast us off forever?"

"Why hast thou made me thus?"

Let us consider these questions for a little, and see whether we can find any counterparts to them in our own secret questionings.

"Is God among us or not?"

He has declared to us in unmistakable terms, as He did to the children of Israel, that He is always with us, and will never leave nor forsake us; and yet when trouble comes, we begin, as they did, to doubt His Word and to question whether He really can be there. Moses called this, when the Israelites did it, "tempting the Lord," and it deserves the same condemnation when we do it. No one can ask such a question without casting a doubt upon the truthfulness and trustworthiness of the the Lord; and to ask it is, if we only knew it, to insult Him, and to libel His character. I know that it is, alas! a common question even among God's own children, and I know also that many of them think it is only true humility to ask it, and that, for such unworthy creatures as they feel themselves to be, it would be the height of presumption to be sure of His presence with them. But what about His own Word in the matter? He has declared to us in every possible way that He is with us, and will never leave us nor forsake us, and dare we "make him a liar" by questioning the truth of His Word? A good God cannot lie, and we must give up forever asking such a question as this. The Lord is with us as truly as we are with ourselves, and we have simply just got to believe that He is, no matter what the seemings may be.

"Hath God forgotten to be gracious?"

To ask this question is to "speak against" Him as grievously as it would be to ask a good mother if she had forgotten her child. And yet the Lord Himself says: "Can a woman forget her sucking child? Yea, they may forget, yet will I not forget thee?" Those of us who are mothers know very well how grieved and insulted we should feel if anyone should suggest the possibility of our forgetting our children; and we mothers at least, if no one else does, should be able to understand how such questioning must grieve the Lord.

"Is God's mercy clean gone forever?" "Hath God in anger shut up his tender mercies?"

To ask these two questions of a good God is to insult Him. It would be as impossible for His tender mercies to be shut up toward us, or for His mercy to go from us forever, as it would be for the tender mercies of a mother to come to an end. The psalmist says: "The Lord is good to all, and his tender mercies are over all his works." In the very nature of things this must be, because He is a good God, and cannot do otherwise.

"Do God's promises fail forevermore?"

There come times in every Christian's life when we are tempted to ask this question. Everything seems to be going wrong, and all God's promises seem to have failed. But if we remember that the Lord is good, we shall see that He would cease to be good if such a thing could be. A man who breaks his promises is looked upon as a dishonorable and untrustworthy man; and a God who could break His, if one could imagine such a thing, would be dishonorable and untrustworthy also. And to ask such a question is to cast a stigma on His goodness, that may well be characterized as "speaking against God." No matter how affairs may look, we may be sure of this that because God is good no promise of His has ever failed, or can ever fail. Heaven and earth may pass away, but His Word never.

"O God, why has thou cast us off forever?"

It will be as impossible for a good God to cast us off as it would be for a good mother to cast off her child. We may be in trouble and darkness, and may feel as if we were cast off and forsaken, but our feelings have nothing to do with the facts, and the fact is that God is good, and could not do it. The good Shepherd does not cast off the sheep that is lost, and take no further care of it, but He goes out to seek for it, and He seeks until He finds it. To suspect Him of casting us off forever is to wound and grieve His faithful love, just as it would wound a good mother's heart if she should be supposed capable of casting off her child, let that child have wandered as far as it may. The thing is impossible in either case, but far more impossible in the case of God than even in the case of the best mother that ever lived.

"Why has thou made me thus?"

This is a question we are very apt to ask. There is, I imagine, hardly one of us who has not been tempted at one time or another to "reply against God" in reference to the matter of our own personal make-up. We do not like our peculiar temperaments or our especial characteristics, and we long to be like someone else who has, we think, greater gifts of appearance or of talent. We are discontented with our make-up, both inward and outward, and we feel sure that all our failures are because of our unfortunate temperaments; and we are inclined to blame our Creator for having "made us thus."

I remember vividly a time in my life when I was tempted to be very rebellious about my own make-up. I was a plain-spoken, energetic sort of an individual, trying to be a good Christian, but with no especial air of piety about me. But I had a sister who was so saintly in her looks, and had such a pious manner, that she seemed to be the embodiment of piety; and I felt sure I could be a great deal better Christian if only I could get her saintly looks and manner. But all my struggles to get them were useless. My natural temperament was far too energetic and outspoken for any appearance of saintliness, and many a time I said upbraidingly in my heart to God, "Why hast thou made me thus?" But one day I came across a sentence in an old mystic book that seemed to open my eyes. It was as follows: "Be content to be what thy God has made thee"; and it flashed on me that it really was a fact that God had made me, and that He must know the sort of creature He wanted me to be; and that, if He had made me a potato vine, I must be satisfied to grow potatoes, and must not want to be a rosebush and grow roses; and if He had fashioned me for humble tasks, I must be content to let others do the grander work. We are "God's workmanship," and God is good, therefore His workmanship must be good also; and we may securely trust that before He is done with us, He will make out of us something that will be to His glory, no matter how unlike this we may as yet feel ourselves to be.

The psalmist seemed to delight in repeating over and over again this blessed refrain, "for the Lord is good." It would be worth while for you to take your concordances and see how often he says it. And he exhorted everyone to join him in saying it. "Let the redeemed of the Lord say so," was his earnest cry. We must join our voices to his — The Lord is good — The Lord is good. But we must not say it with our lips only, and then by our actions give the lie to our words. We must "say" it with our whole being, with thought, word, and action, so that people will see we really mean it, and will be convinced that it is a tremendous fact.

A great many things in God's divine providences do not look like goodness to the eye of sense, and in reading the Psalms we wonder perhaps how the psalmist could say, after some of the things he records, "for his mercy endureth forever." But faith sits down before mysteries such as these, and says, "The Lord is good, therefore all that He does must be good, no matter how bad it looks, and I can wait for His explanations."

A housekeeping illustration has often helped me here. If I have a friend whom I know to be a good housekeeper, I do not trouble over the fact that at housecleaning time things in her house may seem to be more or less upset, carpets up, and furniture shrouded in coverings, and even perhaps painting and decorating making some rooms uninhabitable. I say to myself, "My friend is a good housekeeper, and although things look so uncomfortable now, all this upset is only because she means in the end to make it far more comfortable than ever it was before." This world is God's housekeeping; and although things at present look grievously upset, yet, since we know that He is good, and therefore must be a good Housekeeper, we may be perfectly sure that all this present upset is only to bring about in the end a far better state of things than could have been without it. I dare say we have all felt at times as though we could have done God's housekeeping better than He does it Himself, but, when we realize that God is good, we can feel this no longer. And it comforts me enormously, when the world seems to me to be going all wrong, just to say to myself, "It is not my housekeeping, but it is the Lord's; and the Lord is good, therefore His housekeeping must be good too; and it is foolish for me to trouble."

A deeply taught Christian was asked by a despairing child of God, "Does not the world look to you like a wreck?"

"Yes," was the reply, in a tone of cheerful confidence, "yes, like the wreck of a bursting seed." Any of us who have watched the first sproutings of an oak tree from the heart of a decaying acorn will understand what this means. Before the acorn can bring forth the oak, it must become itself a wreck. No plant ever came from any but a wrecked seed.

Our Lord uses this fact to teach us the meaning of His processes with us. "Verily, verily, I say unto you, Except a corn of wheat fall into the ground and die, it abideth alone: but, if it die, it bringeth forth much fruit."

The whole explanation of the apparent wreckage of the world at large, or of our own personal lives in particular, is here set forth. And, looked at in this light, we can understand how it is that the Lord can be good, and yet can permit the existence of sorrow and wrong in the world He has created, and in the lives of the human beings He loves.

It is His very goodness that compels Him to permit it. For He knows that, only through such apparent wreckage, can the fruition of His glorious purposes for us be brought to pass. And we whose hearts also long for that fruition will, if we understand His ways, be able to praise Him for all His goodness, even when things seem hardest and most mysterious.

The apostle tells us that the will of God is "good and acceptable, and perfect." The will of a good God cannot help being "good" — in fact, it must be perfect; and, when we come to know this, we always find it "acceptable"; that is we come to love it. I am convinced that all trouble about submitting to the will of God would disappear, if once we could see clearly that His will is good. We struggle and struggle in vain to submit to a will that we do not believe to be good, but when we see that it is really good, we submit to it with delight. We want it to be accomplished. Our hearts spring out to meet it.

> I worship thee, sweet Will of God!
>   And all thy ways adore;
> And, every day I live, I seem
>   To love thee more and more.
> I love to kiss each print where thou
>   Has set thine unseen feet:
> I cannot fear thee, blessed Will!
>   Thine empire is so sweet.

Space fails me to tell all that I might of the infinite goodness of the Lord. Each one must "taste and see" for himself. And if he will but do it honestly and faithfully, the words of the psalmist will become true of him: "They shall abundantly utter the memory of thy great goodness, and shall sing of thy righteousness."

CHAPTER 8

THE LORD OUR DWELLING PLACE

"Lord, thou has been our dwelling place in all generations."

The comfort or discomfort of our outward lives depends more largely upon the dwelling place of our bodies than upon almost any other material thing; and the comfort or discomfort of our inward life depends similarly upon the dwelling place of our souls.

Our dwelling place is the place where we live, and not the place we merely visit. It is our home. All the interests of our earthly lives are bound up in our home; and we do all we can to make them attractive and comfortable. But our souls need a comfortable dwelling place even more than our bodies; inward comfort, as we all know, is of far greater importance than outward; and, where the soul is full of peace and joy, outward surroundings are of comparatively little account.

It is of vital importance, then, that we should find out definitely where our souls are living. The Lord declares that He has been our dwelling place in all generations, but the question is, Are we living in our dwelling place? The psalmist says of the children of Israel that "they wandered in the wilderness, in a solitary way; they found no city to dwell in. Hungry and thirsty, their soul fainted in them." And I am afraid there are many wandering souls in the church of Christ, whom this description of the wandering Israelites would exactly fit. All their Christian lives they have been wandering in a spiritual wilderness, and have found no city to dwell in, and, hungry and thirsty, their souls have fainted in them. And yet all the while the dwelling place of God has been standing wide open, inviting them to come in and take up their abode there forever. Our Lord Himself urges this invitation upon us. "Abide in me," He says, "and I in you"; and He goes on to tell us what are the blessed results of this abiding, and what are the sad consequences of not abiding.

The truth is, our souls are made for God. He is our natural home, and we can never be at rest anywhere else. "My soul longeth, yea, even fainteth for the courts of the Lord; my heart and my flesh crieth out for the living God." We always shall hunger and faint for the courts of the Lord, as long as we fail to take up our abode there.

> God only is the creature's home;
>   Though rough and straight the road,
> Yet nothing else can satisfy
>   The soul that longs for God.

How shall we describe this divine dwelling place? David describes it when he says: "The Lord is my rock, and my fortress, and my deliverer; the God of my rock; in him will I trust; he is my shield, and the horn of my salvation, my high tower, and my refuge, my Saviour; thou savest me from violence."

So we see that our dwelling place is also our fortress, and our high tower, and our rock, and our refuge. We all know what a fortress is. It is a place of safety, where everything that is weak and helpless can be hidden from the enemy and kept in security. And when we are told that God, who is our dwelling place, is also our fortress, it can mean only one thing, and that is, that if we will but live in our dwelling place, we shall be perfectly safe and secure from every assault of every possible enemy that can attack us. "For in the time of trouble he shall hide me in his pavilion; in the secret of his tabernacle shall he hide me; he shall set me up upon a rock." "He that dwelleth in the secret place of the most High, shall abide under the shadow of the Almighty."

"Thou shalt hide them in the secret of thy presence from the pride of man; thou shalt keep them secretly in a pavilion from the strife of tongues."

In the "secret of God's tabernacle" no enemy can find us, and no troubles can reach us. The "pride of man" and the "strife of tongues" find no entrance into the "pavilion" of God. The "secret of his presence" is a more secure refuge than a thousand Gibraltars. I do not mean that no trials will come. They may come in abundance, but they cannot penetrate into the sanctuary of the soul, and we may dwell in perfect peace even in the midst of life's fiercest storms.

But alas! how few of us know this. We use David's language, it may be, but to us it is only a figure of speech that has no reality in it. We say the things he said, in the conventional, pious tone that is considered proper when speaking of religious matters. "Oh, yes, the Lord is my dwelling place I know, and I have committed myself and all my interests to His keeping, as of course every Christian ought to do. But" — and here one's natural tones are resumed — "but then I cannot forget that I am a poor good-for-nothing sort of person, and have no strength to conquer my temptations; and I can hardly expect that I can be kept in the perfect security David speaks of." And here will follow a story of all sorts of fears, and anxieties, exactly as if the dwelling place of God had never been heard of, and as if the soul was wandering alone and unprotected in a world of trouble and danger.

There is a psalm that I call the "Dwelling Place of God." It is the Ninety-first Psalm, and it gives us a wonderful description of what this dwelling place is. "He that dwelleth in the secret place of the most High shall abide under the shadow of the Almighty. I will say of the Lord, he is my refuge and my fortress; my God; in him will I trust." Our idea of a fortress is generally of a hard, granite building, where one would be safe, perhaps, but also at the same time sadly uncomfortable. But there are other sorts of fortresses that are soft, and tender, and full of comfort; and this psalm describes them. "He shall cover thee with his feathers," just as the mother hen covers her little helpless chickens in the fortress of her warm, brooding wings. The fortress of a mother's heart, whether it be of a human mother, or a hen mother, or a tiger mother, is the most impregnable fortress the world knows, and yet the tenderest. And it is this sort of a fortress that the Lord is. "Under his wings shalt thou trust"; "he shall carry them in his bosom"; "underneath are the everlasting arms."

Wings, bosom, arms! What blessed fortresses are these! And how safe is everything enfolded by them. Nature is full of such fortresses. Listen to what a late writer says of the tiger mother. "When her children are born, some power teaches the tiger to be gentle. A spirit she cannot resist, for it is the spirit of her Creator, enters her savage heart. It is a tiger's impulse to resent an injury. Pluck her by the hair, smite her on the flank, she will leap upon and rend you. But to resent an injury is not her strongest impulse. Watch those impotent kitten creatures playing with her. They are so weak, a careless movement of her giant paw will destroy them; but she makes no careless movement. They have caused her a hundredfold the pain your blow produced; yet she does not render evil for evil. These puny mites of helpless impotence she strokes with love's light in her eyes; she licks the shapeless forms of her tormentors, and, as they plunge at her, love transforms each groan of her anguish into a whinny of delight. She moves her massive head in a way which shows that He who bade you turn the other cheek created her. When strong enough to rise, the terrible creature goes forth to sacrifice herself for her own. She will starve that they may thrive. She is terrible for her little ones, as God is terrible for His."

We have all seen these mother fortresses hundreds of times, and have called them Godlike. And one would think that the sight would have made us fly to our refuge in the dwelling place of God, and leave outside all fear! But the trouble is, we point-blank refuse to believe that the Bible means any such good news. Not in words, perhaps, but in effect, we say, "The Lord's arms are not so dependable as the strong, loving arms of the weakest earthly mother; the Lord's bosom is not as tender as the tiger's bosom; the Lord's wings are not as brooding as the wings of the little mother hen. We know that all these beautiful earthly fortresses are made and fashioned by Him, but we cannot believe that He Himself is equal to them. To have Him for

our fortress does not really mean to us anything half so safe
or half so tender as to have a mother for our fortress." And
so mothers are trusted, and God is not!

And yet how safe the psalmist declares this divine dwelling place to be! Notice how he says, that we who are in this
dwelling place shall be afraid of nothing; not for the terror
by night, nor the arrow by day, nor for the pestilence that
walketh in darkness, nor for the destruction that wasteth at
noonday; thousands shall fall beside us and around us, but
no evil shall befall the soul that is hidden in this divine
dwelling place; no plague shall come nigh those who have
made God their "habitation."

All the terrors and all the plagues that have made our
religious lives so uncomfortable, and even so wretched, are
provided for here and from all of them we shall be
delivered, if we make the Lord our habitation. This does
not mean that we shall have no outward trials. Plagues in
abundance may attack your body and your goods, but your
body and your goods are not yourself; and nothing can
come nigh you, the real interior you, while you are dwelling
in God.

A large part of the pain of life comes from the haunting
"fear of evil" which so often besets us. Our lives are full of
supposes. Suppose this should happen, or suppose that
should happen; what could we do; how could we bear it?
But, if we are living in the "high tower" of the dwelling
place of God, all these supposes will drop out of our lives.
We shall be "quiet from fear of evil," for no threatenings
of evil can penetrate into the "high tower" of God. Even
when walking through the valley of the shadow of death,
the psalmist could say, "I fear no evil"; and, if we are
dwelling in God, we can say so too.

But you may ask here how you are to get into this divine
dwelling place. To this I answer that you must simply move
in. If a house should be taken for us by a friend, and we
were told it was ready, and that the lease and all the necessary papers were duly attested and signed, we should not
ask how we could get into it — we should just pack up and
move in. And we must do the same here. God says that He
is our dwelling place, and the Bible contains all the necessary papers, duly attested and signed. And our Lord invites

us, nay more, commands us to enter in and abide there. In effect He says, "God is your dwelling place, and you must see to it that you take up your abode there. You must move in." But how, you ask, how can I move in? You must do it by faith. God has said that He is your dwelling place, and now you must say it too. "I will say of the Lord, he is my refuge and my fortress: my God; in him will I trust." Faith takes up the Word of God, and asserts it to be true. Christ says, "Abide," and we must say, "I will abide." Thus we "make him our habitation" by faith. He is our habitation already, as to His side of it, but we must make Him so, as to our side of it, by believing that He is, and by continually asserting it. Coleridge says:

> Faith is an affirmation and an act,
> That bids eternal truth be present fact.

And we must make the eternal truth that the Lord is our dwelling place become present fact by the affirmation of our faith, and by putting on the thoughts and actions that would naturally result from having moved into the tabernacle of God.

And one of the first things we would have to do would be to give up forever all worry and anxiety. It is unthinkable that worry and anxiety could enter into the dwelling place of God; and when we enter there, we must leave them behind.

We talk about obeying the commands of the Lord, and make a great point of outward observances and outward duties, and all the while neglect and ignore the commands as to the inward life, which are a thousandfold more important. "Let not your heart be troubled, neither let it be afraid," is one of our Lord's commands that is almost universally disobeyed; and yet I question whether our disobedience of any other command is so grievous to His heart. I am very sure for myself, that I would be far more grieved if my child should mistrust me, and should feel her interests were unsafe in my care, than if in a moment of temptation she should disobey me. And I am convinced that none of us have appreciated how deeply it wounds the loving heart of our Lord, when He finds that His people do not feel safe in His care.

We can know this by ourselves. Suppose one of our friends should commit something to our keeping, receiving from us every assurance that we would keep it safe, and then should go away and worry over it, as we worry over the things we commit to God, and should express to others the anxieties about it that we allow ourselves to express about the things we have put into God's care. How, I would like to know, would we feel about it? Would we not be deeply hurt and wounded; and would we not finally be inclined to hand the thing back into our friend's own care, and to say, "Since it is very plain that you do not trust me, had you not better take care of your things yourself?" It is amazing that God's own children can dare to be anxious, after once they have committed a matter to Him; it is such a libel on His trustworthiness. And of course outsiders judge it in this way, and think to themselves that to have the Lord for your dwelling place does not evidently amount to much after all, or those who profess to be living there could not be so troubled.

He who cares for the sparrows, and numbers the hairs of our head, cannot possibly fail us. He is an impregnable fortress into which no evil can enter and no enemy penetrate. I hold it, therefore, as a self-evident truth that the moment I have really committed anything into this divine dwelling place, that moment all fear and anxiety should cease. While I keep anything in my own care, I may well fear and tremble, for it is indeed to the last degree unsafe; but in God's care, no security could be more absolute.

The psalmist says: "The name of the Lord is a strong tower: the righteous runneth into it, and is safe." The only point, therefore, is to "run into" this strong tower and stay there forever. It would be the height of folly, when the enemy was surrounding us on every side to stand outside of a fortress and cry out for safety. If I want to be safe, I must go in.

"O Jerusalem, Jerusalem!" said our Lord, "thou that killest the prophets, and stonest them which are sent unto thee, how often would I have gathered thy children together, even as a hen gathereth her chickens under her wings, and ye would not." If the little chicken wants to be safe, it must "run into" the fortress of its mother's wings.

A great many people stay outside of God's dwelling place, because they feel themselves too unworthy and too weak to dare to go in. What would we think of the little chicken that would see the hawk coming, would hear the mother calling, and see her outspread wings, but would stand outside trembling with fright, saying, "Oh, I am such a poor, weak, foolish, helpless little chicken that I am afraid I am not worthy to go under my mother's wings"? If the mother hen could speak, I am sure she would say, "You poor, foolish little thing, it is just because you are weak, and helpless, and good for nothing, that I want you under my wings. If you were a great, big, strong rooster, able to take care of yourself, I would not want you at all." Need I make the application?

But we must not only "run into" our dwelling place. The psalmist says: "I will abide in thy tabernacle forever: I will trust in the covert of thy wings"; and we must do the same. This "abiding in his tabernacle forever" is, I am free to confess, sometimes very hard. It is comparatively easy to take a step of faith, but it is a far more difficult thing to abide steadfastly in the place into which we have stepped. A great many people "run into" God's fortress on Sunday, and come out of it again as soon as Monday morning dawns. Some even run into it when they kneel down to say their prayers at night, and come out of it five minutes afterward when they get into bed. Of course, this is the height of folly. One cannot imagine any sensible refugee running into a fortress one day, and the next day running out among the enemy again. We should think such a person had suddenly lost all his senses. But is it not even more foolish when it comes to the soul? Are our enemies any less active on Mondays than they are on Sundays, or are we any better able to cope with them when we are in bed than when we were kneeling at our prayers?

The question is, Do we want to pay visits only to the dwelling place of God, or do we want to live there? Do we want to "trust in the covert of his wings" today, and tomorrow be exposed to the buffetings of our enemies outside? No one would deliberately choose the latter, but far too many drift into it. Our abiding in Christ is altogether a matter of faith, but we fail to realize this. We think our earnest wrestlings or our strenuous efforts are a large part of the matter; and, when these slacken, our faith weakens. But if there is one thing more certain than another, it is that the whole Christian life is to be lived by faith. Without faith it is impossible to please God; and it is perfect folly to fancy that any amount of fervency or earnestness or anything whatever of our own doing can take its place; and it is manifestly useless to waste our time and energy over things that amount to nothing.

What we must do is to put all our will power and all our energy into our faith. We must "set our faces like a flint" to move into the dwelling place of God, and to abide there steadfastly, let the temptations to doubt or discouragement be what they may.

"He that dwelleth in the secret place of the most High shall abide under the shadow of the Almighty." *Abiding* and *trusting* are synonymous words, and mean exactly the same thing. While I trust the Lord, I am abiding in Him. If I trust Him steadfastly, I am abiding in Him steadfastly; if I trust Him intermittently, I am running into Him and running out again. I used to think there was some mystery about abiding in Christ, but I see now that it only means trusting Him fully. When once you understand this, it becomes really the simplest matter in the world. We sometimes say, speaking of two human beings, that they "live in each other's hearts," and we simply mean that perfect love and confidence exists between them, and that doubts of one another are impossible. If my trust in the fortress of the Lord is absolute, I am abiding in that fortress; and this is the whole story.

The practical thing to do, therefore, in the face of the fact that God is declared to be our fortress and our high tower, is, by a definite act of surrender and faith, to put ourselves and all our interests of every kind into this divine dwelling place, and then dismiss all care or anxiety about them from our minds. Since the Lord is our dwelling place, nothing can possibly come to any harm that is committed to His care. As long as we believe this, our affairs remain in His care; the moment we begin to doubt, we take our affairs into our own hands, and they are no longer in the divine fortress. Things cannot be in two places at once. If they are in our own care, they cannot be in God's care; and if they are in God's care, they cannot be in our own. This is as clear as daylight, and yet, for the want of a little common sense, people often get mixed up over it. They put their affairs into God's fortress, and at the same time put them into their own fortress as well, and then wonder why they are not taken care of. This is all folly. Either trust the Lord out and out, or else trust yourself out and out; but do not try to mix the two trusts, for they will not mix.

It will help you practically if you will put your trust into words. Say definitely, "God is my dwelling place, and I am going to abide in Him forever. It is all settled; I am in this divine habitation, and I am safe here, and I am not going to move out again." You must meet all assaults of doubt and discouragement with the simple assertion that you are there, and that you know you will not be confounded, for no one ever yet trusted in the Lord and was confounded; let other people do as they may, but you must declare that you at any rate are going to abide in your divine dwelling place forever. And then, having taken this stand, you must utterly refuse to reconsider the matter. It is all settled; and there is nothing more to be said about it.

In all this I do not, of course, mean that we are to lie in bed and let things go. I am talking about the inward aspect of our affairs, not the outward. Outwardly we may have to be full of active carefulness, but it must all be from the inward basis of a soul that has hidden itself and all its interests in the dwelling place of God, and that is therefore "careful for nothing" in the beautiful Bible sense of having no anxious thoughts. To be thus without care inwardly is the surest foundation for successful outward care; and the soul that is hidden in the dwelling place of God is the soul that will be able to bear triumphantly earth's greatest trials, and to conquer its strongest foes.

There is one point I must not fail to mention. When we move into a new house, we not only move in ourselves, but we take with us all our belongings of every sort or description, and above all we take our family. No one would be so foolish as to leave anything he cared for or anyone he loved outside. But I am afraid there are some of God's children, who are so abandoned. We would be horrified at a father who, in a time of danger, should flee into a fortress for safety, but should leave his children outside; and yet hundreds of Christians do this very thing. Every anxious thought in which we indulge about our children proves that we have not really taken them with us into the dwelling place of God.

What I mean is this, that if we trust for ourselves, we must trust for our loved ones also, and especially for our children. God is more their Father than their earthly fathers are and if they are dear to us, they are far dearer to Him. We cannot, therefore, do anything better for them than to trust them to His care, and hardly anything worse than to try to keep them in our own. I knew a Christian mother who trusted peacefully for her own salvation, but was racked with anxiety about her sons, who seemed entirely indifferent to all religious subjects. One evening she heard about the possibility of putting those we love into the fortress of God by faith and leaving them there; and, like a flash of heavenly light, she saw the inconsistency of hiding herself in God's fortress and leaving her beloved sons outside. At once her faith took them into the fortress with her, and she abandoned them to the care of God. So fully and completely did she do this that all her anxiety vanished, and perfect peace dawned upon her soul. She told me she felt somehow that her sons were God's sons now — no longer hers — and that He loved them far better than she could, and would care for them far more wisely and effectually. She held herself in readiness to do for them whatever the Lord might suggest; but she felt that He was the One who would know what was best, and she was content to leave the matter in His hands.

She went home from that meeting and called her sons into her room, telling them what had happened; she said, "You know, my dear boys, how anxious and troubled I have been about you, and how continually I have preached to you, and I am afraid have often worried you. But now I have learned to trust, and I have put you by faith into the fortress of God, and have left you in His care. I am sure that He will care for you far better than your poor mother ever could, and will save you in His own way. My anxieties are over."

I did not see her again for a year, but when I did, she came up to me with a beaming face; and with tears of joy filling her eyes, she said, "Rejoice with me, dear friend, that I learned how to put my boys into the fortress of God. They have been safe there ever since, and all of them are good Christian boys today."

The conclusion of the whole matter, then, is simply this, that we must make up our minds to move into our dwelling place in God and to take there with us all our possessions, above all, those we love. We must hide ourselves in Him away from ourselves, away from all others, and we must lose sight of everything that is outside of Him except as we see it through His eyes. God's eyes are the windows of God's house, and the only windows there are; and seen through His eyes, all things will put on a new aspect. We shall see our trials as blessings, and our enemies as disguised friends. We shall be calm and at rest in the face of all the frets and worries of life, untouched by any of them. "For he that dwelleth in God dwelleth in a peaceable habitation and in a quiet resting place."

CHAPTER 9
MUCH MORE VERSUS MUCH LESS

"But where sin abounded grace did much more abound.

In our preceding chapters we have been trying to learn something about the Lord and His great salvation; and now the vital point is, what view do we take of it all? A very great deal of the comfort or discomfort of our religious lives depends on the view we take of things. I do not mean of course that our view of things affects their reality in any way, but what I do mean is that our view makes all the difference in our apprehension of this reality; and while our safety comes from what things really are, our comfort comes from what we suppose them to be.

There is an expression used over and over again in the Bible to describe the salvation of the Lord Jesus Christ, which gives a view of that salvation, so amazing and so perfectly satisfying, that I cannot help wondering whether any of us have ever yet grasped its full meaning. One thing is certain, that no one who grasps it could ever be uncomfortable or miserable again. It is the expression, "much more," and it is used to tell us, if only we would believe it, that there is no need which any human being can ever know that cannot be much more than met by the glorious salvation that is provided. But we are continually tempted to think that *much less* would be a truer term; and that, so far from this salvation being much more than our needs, it turns out in actual experience to be much less. And this "much less' view, if I may so express it, is in danger of making our whole spiritual lives a misery to us.

If all we have been learning in our preceding chapters of the fullness of God's salvation is indeed true, it would seem as if nothing but the language of "much more" could ever be used by any child of God. But since there are some Christians, who seem by their thoughts and their actions to declare that they consider the language of "much less" to be the only prudent language for poor sinners, I want us carefully to consider the matter in the light of what the Bible tells us, and discover whether we are really justified in saying much more.

It is, I believe, a far more vital question for each one of us than may appear at first sight. For if God declares that the salvation He has provided is much more than enough to meet our needs, and if we insist on declaring in our secret thoughts that it is much less, we are casting discredit on His trustworthiness, and are storing up for ourselves untold discomfort and misery.

"Much less" is the language of the seen thing, "much more" is the language of the unseen thing. "Much less" seems on the surface to be far more reasonable than "much more," because every seen thing confirms it. Our weakness and foolishness are visible; God's strength and wisdom are invisible. Our need is patent before our very eyes; God's supply is hidden in the secret of His presence, and can only be realized by faith.

It seems a paradox to tell us that we must see unseen things. How can it be possible? But there are other things to see than those which appear on the surfaces, and other eyes to look through than those we generally use. An ox and a scientist may both *look* at the same field, but they will see very different things there. To see unseen things requires us to have that interior eye opened in our souls which is able to see below surfaces, and which can pierce through the outer appearance of things into their inner realities. This interior eye looks not at the seen things, which are temporal, but at the things that are not seen, which are eternal; and the vital question for each of us is, whether that interior eye has been opened in us yet, and whether we can see the things that are

eternal, or whether our vision is limited to the things that
are temporal only.

Can and do we say of the salvation of the Lord Jesus Christ
that it is much more than our need, or that it is much less?

There is a wonderful instance in the history of the children of Israel, when they saw the unseen things with such
clearness of vision, that the "much less" of their enemy,
and of the seen things around them, was powerless to disturb them. The story is told in II Chronicles 32:1-15. An
enemy had come up against Judah, and had threatened to
overwhelm them. This enemy had been so universally successful hitherto in all his wars with the nations round about
that he had no doubt he would be able to conquer the
Israelites also. But Hezekiah, the king of Israel, looked not
at the seen enemy, but at the unseen God, and he saw that
God was the strongest; and he spake comfortably to the
people, and said: "Be strong and courageous, be not afraid
nor dismayed for the king of Assyria, nor for all the multitude that is with him; for there be more with us than with
him. With him is an arm of flesh; but with us is the Lord
our God, to help us, and to fight our battles." What a tremendous contrast: on one side an arm of flesh; on the
other, the Lord our God! No wonder the people "rested
themselves" upon a declaration such as this.

And yet, I cannot help questioning whether if we had
been there, we would have had faith enough to have so
rested ourselves?

When Sennacherib saw their faith, he was enraged, and
upbraided them with their folly in being persuaded by
Hezekiah to expose themselves to the risk of death by thirst
and famine in the vain hope that the Lord would deliver
them. And then comes the taunt of the "much less":
"Know you not," he said, "what I and my father have
done unto all the people of other lands? Were the gods of
the nations of those lands in any way able to deliver their
lands out of mine hand? Who was there among all the gods
of those nations that could deliver his people out of mine
hand, that your God shall be able to deliver you out of mine
hand? Now therefore let not Hezekiah deceive you, nor persuade you on this manner, neither yet believe him; for no
god of any nation or kingdom was able to deliver his people

out of mine hand, how much less shall your God deliver you out of mine hand.''

"How much less" — what a temptation to unbelief was contained in those words! All the seen things were on that side; and it did look impossible, in the face of the fact that all the nations round about had been defeated, that the nation of Israel, no stronger, and no better equipped than the others, should find deliverance. But Hezekiah kept his eyes and the eyes of the people fixed on the unseen things, and their faith stood firm; and the Lord in whom they trusted did not fail them, but sent them a grand deliverance. The "much less" of the enemy was turned for the Israelites into a "much more" of victory. The man who had promised them defeat and death was himself defeated; he was obliged to return to his own land with "shame of face," and was there slain by his disappointed relatives.

Is there nothing analogous to this story in our own personal history? Have we never been taunted with the discouraging thought that God is "much less" able to deliver us than His promises would lead us to expect? And when we have looked at the formidable *seen* things of our need has it not sometimes seemed to us as if it would be equivalent to giving ourselves over to "die by famine and thirst," if we were brought to the point of having absolutely nothing else to trust to but the Lord alone? I remember hearing of a Christian who was in great trouble, and who had tried every way for deliverance, but in vain, who said finally to another in a tone of the utmost despair, "Well, there is nothing left for me now but to trust the Lord."

"Alas!" exclaimed the friend in the greatest consternation, "is it possible it has come to *that?*"

We may shrink with horror from the thought of using such an expression, but, if we are honest with ourselves, I believe we shall be obliged to confess that sometimes, in the very bottom of our hearts, we have indulged in just this feeling. To come to the point of having nothing left to trust in but the Lord has, I am afraid, seemed to us at times a desperate condition of things. And yet, if our Lord is to be believed, His "much mores" of grace are abundantly equal to the worst emergency that can befall us. The apostle tells us that God is able to do "exceeding abundantly above all that we can ask or think"; and this describes what His "much mores" mean. We can think of very wonderful things in the way of salvation — spiritual blessings that would transform life for us, and make the whole universe resplendent with joy and triumph — and we can ask for them. But do we really believe that God is able and willing to do for us "exceeding abundantly" above all that we can ask or think? Is the language of our hearts "much more" or "much less"?

In another place we are told that "eye hath not seen, nor ear heard, neither have entered into the heart of man, the things which God hath prepared for them that love him." If God has prepared more for us than it has ever entered into our hearts to conceive, surely we can have no question about obtaining that which has entered into our hearts, and "much more" beside. What can it be then but downright unbelief that leads any of us to harbor a thought of God's salvation being "much less" than the things it has entered into our hearts to long for.

Let us settle it then that the language of our souls must henceforth be not the "much less" of unbelief, but the "much more" of faith. And I feel sure we shall find that God's "much mores" will be enough to cover the whole range of our needs, both temporal and spiritual.

"For if through the offense of one many be dead, much more the grace of God and the gift by grace which is by one man, Jesus Christ, hath abounded unto many." This is a "much more" that really reaches, if only we could understand it, into the deepest depth of human need. There is no question in our minds as to the fact that "many be dead," but how is it with the "much more" of grace that is to abound unto many? Are we as sure of the grace as we are of the death? Do we really believe that the remedy is "much more" than the disease? Does the salvation seem to us "much more" than the need? Or do we believe in our hearts that it is "much less"? Which does God declare?

One of the deepest needs of our souls is the need for being saved. Is there a "much more" to meet this need? What does the apostle say? "But God commendeth his love toward us, in that, while we were yet sinners, Christ died for us. Much more then, being now justified by his blood, we shall be saved from wrath through him. For if, when we were enemies, we were reconciled to God by the death of his Son, much more, being reconciled, we shall be saved by his life.'' The question of salvation seems to me to be absolutely settled by these ''much mores.'' Since Christ has died for us, and has thereby reconciled us to God (not God to us, He did not need reconciling), of course ''much more,'' if only we will let Him, will He now save us. There can be no question as to whether He will or will not, for the greater must necessarily include the lesser, and, having done the greater, ''much more'' will He do the lesser. We none of us doubt that He did the greater, and, in the face of these ''much mores,'' we dare not doubt He will do the lesser.

Now the practical point for us in all this is, Do we really believe it? Have we got rid of all doubts as to our salvation? Can we speak with assurance of forgiveness and of eternal life? Do we say with timidity of unbelief, ''I *hope* I am a child of God''; or do we lift up our heads, with joyous confidence in God as our Father, and say with John, ''Now *are* we the sons of God''? Is it in this respect ''much more'' with us, or ''much less''?

We long and pray for the gift of the Holy Spirit, but it seems all in vain. We feel that our prayers are not answered. But our Lord gives faith a wonderful ''much more'' to lay hold of for this. ''If ye then, being evil, know how to give good gifts unto your children, how much more shall your heavenly Father give the Holy Spirit to them that ask him?'' There is not one of us who does not know how thankful and eager good parents are to give good gifts to their children — how they thrust them on the children often before the child is ready to receive, or even knows that it has a need. And yet, who of us really believes that God is actually ''much more'' eager to give the Holy Spirit to them that ask Him? Is it not rather that many feel secretly that He is ''much less'' willing, and that we will have to beg, and entreat, and wrestle, and wait, for this sorely needed gift? If we could only believe this ''much more,'' how full of faith our asking would be in regard to it. We should then truly be able to believe that we actually did receive that for which we had asked, and should find that we were in actual possession of the Holy Spirit as our present and personal Comforter and Guide; and all our

weary struggles and agonizing prayers for this promised gift
would be over.

Sorer, perhaps, than any other need is our need of victory
over sin and over circumstances. Like Juggernaut cars they
roll over us with irresistible power, and crush us into the
dust. And the language of "much less" seems the only
language that our souls dare utter. But God has given us for
this a most triumphant "much more." "For, if by one
man's offense, death reigned by one, much more they
which receive abundance of grace, and of the gift of righteousness, shall reign in life by one, Jesus Christ."

We have known the reigning of that spiritual death which
comes by sin, and have groaned under its power. But how
much do we know of that "much more" reigning in life
by Jesus Christ of which the apostle speaks? That is, have
we now greater victories than we used to have defeats? Do
we reign over things "much more" than they once reigned
over us?

I mean this, that in the Gospel it is promised that we shall
be "more than conquerors" over the very things that once
conquered us, and the question is whether we really are. We
have been reigned over by thousands of things, by the fear
of man, by our peculiar temperaments, by our outward circumstances, by our irritable tempers, even by bad weather,
by our environment of every kind. We have been slaves
where we ought to have been kings. We have found our
reigning to be "much less" rather than "much more." Why
is this? Simply because we have not "received" enough of
the abundance of grace that is ours in Christ. We have let
unbelief cheat us out of our rightful possessions. We are
called to be kings and are "made to have dominion," but
here God declares that it shall be "much more" of a dominion than it was formerly a bondage; have we so found it? If
not, why not? The lack cannot possibly be on God's side.
He has not failed to provide the "much more" of victory. It
must be that we have in some way failed to avail ourselves
of it. And I cannot but believe that our failure arises from
the fact that we have substituted our "much less" for God's
"much more"; and in our heart of hearts have not believed
there really is a sufficiency in the gift of righteousness in
Christ to enable us to reign. We have failed through our un-

belief to "receive the abundance of grace" that is necessary for reigning.

What then is our remedy? Only this — to abandon forever our "much less" of unbelief, and to accept as true God's declaration of "much more," and to claim at once the promised victory. And according to our faith it must and will be unto us.

But these assurances of the "much mores" of God's salvation are not for our spiritual needs only, but for our temporal needs as well. Do not be anxious, He says, about earthly things, for "if God so clothe the grass of the field, which today is, and tomorrow is cast into the oven, shall he not much more clothe you, O ye of little faith?"

I know that to many Christians this passage and others like it are so familiar that they have almost lost all meaning. But they do mean something, and something almost too wonderful for belief. They tell us that God cares for us human beings "much more" than He cares for the universe around us, and that He will watch over and provide for us much more than He will even for it.

Incredible, yet true! How often we have marveled at the orderly working of the universe, and have admired the great creative Power that made it and now controls it! But none of us, I suppose, has ever felt it necessary to take the burden of the universe upon our own shoulders. We have trusted the Creator to manage it all without our help. Although I must confess, from the way some people find fault with the Creator's management of things, and the advice they seem to feel it necessary to give Him in their prayers, one would think the whole burden was resting upon them!

But even where we have fully recognized that the universe is altogether in God's care, we have failed to see that we also are there, and have never dreamed that it could be true that "much more" than He cares for the universe will He care for us. We have looked at the seen things of our circumstances and our surroundings, and at the greatness of our need and our own helplessness, and have been anxious and afraid. We have burdened ourselves with the care of ourselves, feeling in our unbelief that, instead of being of "much more" value than the fowls of the air, or the lilies of the field, we are in reality of infinitely "much less"; and it seems to us that the God who cares for them is not at all likely to care for us. We say with the psalmist: "When I consider thy heavens, the work of thy fingers, the moon and the stars, which thou hast ordained; what is man, that thou art mindful of him? and the son of man that thou visitest him?" Man so puny, so insignificant, of so little account when compared with the great, wide universe, what is he, we ask, that God should care for him? And yet God declares that He does care for him, and that He even cares for him much more than He cares for the universe. Much more, remember, not much less. So that every thought of anxiety about ourselves must be immediately crushed with the common-sense reflection that, since we are not so foolish as to be anxious about the universe, we must not be so much more foolish as to be anxious about ourselves.

In the Sermon on the Mount, our Lord gives us the crowning "much more" of all. "Or what man is there of you, whom if his son ask bread, will he give him a stone? Or if he ask a fish, will he give him a serpent? If ye then, being evil, know how to give good gifts unto your children, how much more shall your Father which is in heaven give good things to them that ask him?"

In this "much more" we have a warrant for the supply of every need. Whatever our Father sees to be good for us is here abundantly promised. And the illustration used to convince us is one of universal application. In all ranks and conditions of life, among all nations, and even in the hearts of birds and beasts the mother instinct never fails to provide for its offspring the best it can compass. Under no conditions of life will a mother, unless she is wicked beyond compare, give a stone when asked for bread, or a serpent when asked for fish. And could our God, who created the mother heart, be worse than a mother? No, no, a thousand times no! What He will do is "much more," oh, so much more than even the tenderest mother could do. And if mothers "know how," as surely they do, to give good things to their children, "how much more" does He. But do we really believe this "much more"? Our hours of anxious tossing on our beds must answer. If God is actually much more willing and able to give good things to us than parents are to give good things to their children, then all possibility of doubt or anxiety as to our prayers being answered must vanish forever. All "good things" must be given to us when we ask, as inevitably as the mother who is able feeds her child when it asks her for bread. As inevitably, do I say? Ah, dear friends, far more inevitably. For it is "how much more" shall your Father which is in Heaven. Which of us has fathomed the meaning of this "how much more"? But at least this it must mean, that all human readiness to hear and answer the cry of need can only be a faint picture of God's readiness, and that, therefore, we can never dare to doubt again. And if parents would not give a stone for bread, neither would He; so that when we ask, we must be absolutely sure that we do receive the "good thing" for which we asked, whether what we receive looks like it or not.

The mother of St. Augustine, in her longing for the conversion of her son, prayed that he might not go to Rome, as she feared its dissipations. God answered her by sending him to Rome to be converted there. Things we call good are often God's evil things, and our evil is His good. But, however things may look, we always know that God must give the best because He is God and could do no other.

"He that spared not his own Son, but delivered him up for us all, how shall he not with him also freely give us all things." Since He has done the supreme thing of having given us Christ, "much more" will He do the less by giving us all things with Him. And yet we continually hear God's own children lamenting their spiritual poverty, and their state of spiritual starvation, and even, it seems sometimes, thinking it rather a pious thing to do and a mark of true humility. But what is this but glorying in the "much less" of their unbelief, instead of in the "much more" of God.

"Oh, I am such a poor creature," I heard a child of God say once with actual complacency when urged to some victory of faith; "I am such a poor creature that I cannot expect to attain to the heights you grand Christians reach." "Poor creature," indeed; of course you are, and so are we all! But God is not poor, and it is His part to supply your needs, not your part to supply His. He is able, no matter what unbelief may say, to "make all grace abound toward you, that ye always having all sufficiency in all things may abound to every good work." "All," "always," "every" — what all-embracing words these are! They include our needs to their utmost limit, and leave us no room for any question. How can we, how dare we, in the face of such declarations, ever doubt or question again?

We have only touched upon the wonders of grace hidden in these "much mores" of God. We can never exhaust their meaning in this life. But let us at least resolve henceforth to lay aside every "much less" of unbelief on all the lines of salvation, and out of the depths of our utter weakness, sinfulness, and need assert with a conquering faith always and everywhere the mighty "much more" of the grace of God!

CHAPTER 10
SELF-EXAMINATION

"Examine yourselves, whether ye be in the faith."

Probably no subject connected with the religious life has been the cause of more discomfort and suffering to tender consciences that has this subject of self-examination; and none has led more frequently to the language of "much less," which we found in our last chapter to be so great an obstacle to all spiritual growth. And yet it has been so constantly impressed upon us that it is our duty to examine ourselves, that the eyes of most of us are continually turned inward, and our gaze is fixed on our own interior states and feelings to such an extent that self, and not Christ, has come at last to fill the whole horizon.

By *self* I mean here all that centers around this great big "me" of ours. Its vocabulary rings out the changes on "I," "me," "my." It is a vocabulary with which we are all very familiar. The questions we ask ourselves in our times of self-examination are proof of this. Am I earnest enough? Have I repented enough? Have I the right sort of feelings? Do I realize religious truth as I ought? Are my prayers fervent enough? Is my interest in religious things as great as it ought to be? Do I love God with enough fervor? Is the Bible as much of a delight to me as it is to others? All these, and a hundred more questions about ourselves and our experiences fill up all our thoughts, and sometimes our little self-examination books as well; and day and night we ring the changes on the personal pronoun "I," "me," "my," to the utter exclusion of any thought concerning Christ, or any word concerning "He," "His," "Him."

The misery of this, many of us know only too well. But the idea that the Bible is full of commands to self-examination is so prevalent that it seems one of the most truly pious things we can do; and, miserable as it makes us, we still feel it is our duty to go on with it in spite of an ever-increasing sense of hopelessness and despair.

In view of this idea many will be surprised to find that there are only two texts in the whole Bible that speak of self-examination, and that neither of these can at all be made to countenance the morbid self-analysis that results from what we call self-examination.

One of these passages I have quoted at the head of this chapter: "Examine yourselves, whether ye be in the faith." This is simply an exhortation to the Corinthians, who were in a sadly backsliding condition, to settle definitely whether they were still believers or not. "Examine yourselves, whether ye be in the *faith.*" It does not say examine whether you are sufficiently earnest, or whether you have the right feelings, or whether your motives are pure, but simply and only, whether you are "in the faith." In short, do you believe in Christ or do you not? A simple question that required only a simple, straightforward answer, Yes or No. This is what it meant for the Corinthians then, and it is what it means for us now.

The other passage reads: "Wherefore, whosoever shall eat this bread and drink this cup of the Lord unworthily, shall be guilty of the body and blood of the Lord. But let a man examine himself, and so let him eat of that bread and drink of that cup." Paul was here writing of the abuses of greediness and drunkenness which had crept in at the celebration of the Lord's Supper; and, in this exhortation to examine themselves, he was simply urging them to see to it that they did none of these things, but partook of this religious feast in a decent and orderly manner.

In neither of these passages is there any hint of that morbid searching out of one's emotions and experiences that is called self-examination in the present day. And it is amazing that out of two such simple passages should have been evolved a teaching fraught with so much misery to earnest, conscientious souls.

The truth is there is no Scripture authority whatever for this disease of modern times; and those who are afflicted with it are the victims of mistaken ideas of God's ways with His children.

Some of my readers, however, are probably asking themselves whether I have not overlooked a large class of passages that tell us to "watch"; and whether these passages do not mean watching ourselves, or, in other words, self-examination. I will quote one of these passages as a sample, that we may see what their meaning really is. "But of that day and that hour knoweth no man, no not the angels which are in heaven, neither the Son, but the Father. Take ye heed, watch and pray; for ye know not when the time is. For the Son of man is as a man taking a far journey, who left his home, and gave authority to his servants, and to every man his work, and commanded the porter to watch. Watch ye therefore, for ye know not when the master of the house cometh, at even, or at midnight, or at the cock-crowing, or in the morning: lest coming suddenly he find you sleeping. And what I say unto you, I say unto all, Watch."

I think if we carefully examine this passage and others like it, we shall see that instead of teaching self-examination, they teach something that is exactly the opposite. They tell us to "watch," it is true, but they do not tell us to watch ourselves. They are plainly commands to forget ourselves in watching for Another. The return of the Lord is the thing we are to watch for. His coming footsteps, and not our own past footsteps, are to be the object of our gazing. We are to watch as a porter watches for the return of the master of the house, and are to be ready as a good watchman should be to receive and welcome Him at any moment that He may appear.

"Blessed are those servants whom the Lord when he cometh shall find watching." Watching what? Themselves? No, watching for Him, of course. If we can imagine a porter, instead of watching for the return of his master, spending his time morbidly analyzing his own past conduct, trying to discover whether he had been faithful enough, and becoming so absorbed in self-examination as to let the master's call go unheeded and the master's return unnoted, we shall have a picture of what goes on in the experience of the soul that is given up to the mistaken habit of watching and looking at self instead of watching and looking for Christ.

These passages, therefore, instead of teaching self-examination, teach exactly the opposite. God says, "Look unto me, and ye shall be saved"; but the self-analyzing soul says, "I must look into myself, if I am to have any hope of being saved. It must be by getting myself right that salvation is to come." And yet the phrase, "Looking unto Jesus," is generally acknowledged to be one of the watchwords of the Christian religion; and all Christians everywhere will unhesitatingly declare that, of course, this is the one thing we all ought to do. But, after saying this, they will go on in their old way of self-introspection, trying to find some salvation in their own inward feelings, or in their own works of righteousness, and being continually plunged into despair because they never find it.

It is a fact that we see what we look at, and cannot see what we look away from; and we cannot look unto Jesus while we are looking at ourselves. The power for victory and the power for endurance are to come from looking unto Jesus and considering Him, not from looking unto or considering ourselves, or our circumstances, or our sins, or our temptations. Looking at ourselves causes weakness and defeat. The reason for this is that when we look at ourselves, we see nothing but ourselves, and our own weakness, and poverty, and sin; we do not and cannot see the remedy and the supply for these, and as a matter of course we are defeated. The remedy and the supply are there all the time, but they are not to be found in the place where we are looking, for they are not in self but in Christ; and we cannot be looking at ourselves and looking at Christ at the same time. Again I repeat that it is in the inexorable nature of things that what we look at that we shall see, and that, if we want to see the Lord, we must look at the Lord and not at self. It is a simple question of choice for us, whether it shall be I or Christ; whether we shall turn our backs on Christ and look at ourselves, or whether we shall turn our backs on self and look at Christ.

I was very much helped many years ago by the following

sentence in a book by Adelaide Proctor: "For one look at self take ten looks at Christ." It was entirely contrary to all I had previously thought right; but it carried conviction to my soul, and delivered me from a habit of morbid self-examination and introspection that had made my life miserable for years. It was an unspeakable deliverance. And my experience since leads me to believe that even a better motto would be, "Take no look at self at all, but look only and always at Christ."

The Bible law in regard to the self-life is not that the self-life must be watched and made better, but that it must be "put off." The apostle, when urging the Ephesian Christians to walk worthy of the vocation wherewith they had been called, tells them that they must "put off" the old man which is corrupt according to the deceitful lusts. The "old man" is, of course, the self-life, and this self-life (which we know only too well is indeed corrupt according to deceitful lusts) is not to be improved, but to be "put off." It is to be crucified. Paul says that our old man is crucified, put to death, with Christ; and he declares of the Colossians that they could no longer lie, seeing that they had "put off the old man with his deeds." Some people's idea of crucifying the "old man" is to set him up on a pinnacle, and then walk around him and stick nagging pins into him to make him miserable, but keeping him alive all the time. But, if I understand language, crucifixion means death, not making miserable; and to crucify the old man means to kill him outright, and to put him off as a snake puts off its dead and useless skin.

It is of no use, then, for us to examine self and to tinker with it in the hope of improving it, for the thing the Lord wants us to do with it is to get rid of it. Fenelon, in his *Spiritual Letters,* says that the only way to treat self is to refuse to have anything to do with it. He says we must turn our backs on this great big "I" of ours, and to say to it, "I do not know you, and am not interested in you, and I refuse to pay any attention to you whatever." But self is always determinted to secure attention, and would rather be thought badly of than not to be thought of at all. And self-examination with all its miseries often gives a sort of morbid satisfaction to the self-life in us, and even deludes self into thinking it a very humble and pious sort of self after all.

The only safe and scriptural way is to have nothing to do with self at all, either with good self or with bad self, but simply to ignore self altogether; and to fix our eyes, and our thoughts, and our expectations on the Lord and on Him alone. We must substitute for the personal pronouns "I," "me," "my," the pronouns "He," "Him," "His"; and must ask ourselves, not "am I good?" but "is He good?"

The psalmist says: "Mine eyes are ever toward the Lord, for he shall pluck my feet out of the net." As long as our eyes are toward our own feet, and toward the net in which they are entangled, we only get into worse tangles. But when we keep our eyes toward the Lord, He plucks our feet out of the net. This is a point in practical experience that I have tested hundreds of times, and I know it is a fact. No matter what sort of a snarl I may have been in, whether inward or outward, I have always found that while I kept my eyes on the snarl and tried to unravel it, it grew worse and worse; but when I turned my eyes away from the snarl and kept them fixed on the Lord, He always sooner or later unraveled it and delivered me.

Have you ever watched a farmer plowing a field? If you have, you will have noticed that in order to make straight furrows he is obliged to fix his eyes on a tree, or a post in the fence, or some object at the farther end of the field, and to guide his plow unwaveringly toward that object. If he begins to look back at the furrow behind him in order to see whether he has made a straight furrow, his plow begins to jerk from side to side, and the furrow he is making becomes a zigzag. If we would make straight paths for our feet we must do what the apostle says he did. We must forget the things that are behind, and, reaching forth to those which are before, we must press toward the mark for the prize of the high calling of God in Christ Jesus.

To forget the things that are behind is an essential part of the pressing forward toward the prize of our high calling; and I am convinced this prize can never be reached unless we will consent to this forgetting. When we do consent to it, we come near to putting an end to all our self-examination; for, if we may not look back over our past misdoings, we shall find but little food for self-reflective acts.

We complain of spiritual hunger, and torment ourselves to know why our hunger is not satisfied. The psalmist says: "The eyes of all wait upon thee, and thou givest them their meat in due season." Having our eyes upon ourselves and on our own hunger will never bring a supply of spiritual meat. When a man's larder is empty and he is starving, his eyes are not occupied with looking at the emptiness of his larder, but are turned toward the source from which he hopes or expects to get a supply of food. To examine self is to be like a man who should spend his time in examining his empty larder instead of going to the market for a supply to fill it. No wonder such Christians seem to be starving to death in the midst of all the fullness there is for them in Christ. They never see that fullness, for they never look at it; and again I repeat that the thing we look at is the thing we see.

I feel as if I could not repeat this evident truism too often, for somehow people seem to lay aside their common sense when they come to the subject of religion, and seem to expect to see things upon which they have deliberately kept their backs turned. They cry out, "O Lord, reveal thyself"; but instead of looking at Him they look at themselves, and keep their gaze steadily fixed on their own inward feelings, and then wonder at the "mysterious dealings" of God in hiding His face from their fervent prayers. But how can they see what they do not look at?

It is never God who hides His face from us, but it is always we who hide our face from Him, by "turning to him the back and not the face." The prophet reproaches the children of Israel with this, and adds that they "set up their abominations in the house which is called by God's name." When Christians spend their time examining their own condition, raking up all their sins, and bemoaning their shortcomings, what is this but to set up the "abomination" of their own sinful self upon the chief pedestal in their hearts, and to make it the center of their whole religious life, and of all their care and efforts. They gaze at this great, big, miserable self until it fills their whole horizon, and they "turn their back" on the Lord, until He is lost sight of altogether.

I will venture to say that there are many Christians who, for one look at the Lord, will give a thousand looks at self, and who, for one hour spent in rejoicing in Him, will spend hundreds of hours bemoaning themselves.

We are never anywhere commanded to behold our emotions, nor our experiences, nor even our sins, but we are commanded to turn our backs upon these, and to behold the Lamb of God who taketh away our sins. One look at Christ is worth more for salvation than a million looks at self. Yet so mistaken are our ideas, we seem unable to avoid thinking that the mortification which results from self-examination must have in it some saving power, because it makes us so miserable. For we have to travel a long way on our heavenly journey before we fully learn that there is no saving power in misery, and that a cheerful, confident faith is the only successful attitude for the aspiring soul.

In Isaiah we see God's people complaining because they fasted, and He did not see; afflicted their souls, and He took no knowledge; and God gave them this significant answer: "Is it such a fast that I have chosen, a day for a man to afflict his soul? Is it to bow down his head as a bulrush, and to spread sackcloth and ashes under him? Wilt thou call this a fast, and an acceptable day to the Lord?" Whoever else is pleased with the miseries of our self-examination, it is very certain that God is not. He does not want us to bow down our heads as a bulrush, any more than He wanted His people of old to do it; and He calls upon us, as He did upon them, to forget our own miserable selves, and to go to work to lessen the miseries of others. "Is not this the fast that I have chosen," He says, "to loose the bands of wickedness, to undo the heavy burdens, and to let the oppressed go free, and that ye break every yoke? Is it not to deal thy bread to the hungry, and that thou bring the poor that are cast out to thy house; when thou seest the naked, that thou cover him?"

This service for others is of infinitely greater value to the Lord than the longest seasons of self-examination and self-abasement. And I am convinced that He has shown us here what is the surest way of deliverance out of the slough of misery into which our habits of self-examination have plunged us. He declares emphatically that if we will only keep the sort of "fast" He approves of, by giving up our own "fast" of afflicting our souls and bowing down our heads as a bulrush, and will instead "draw out our souls to the hungry," and will try to bear the burdens and relieve the miseries of others, then shall our light rise in obscurity, and our darkness be as the noonday; and the Lord shall guide us continually, satisfying our souls in drought, and making fat our bones; we shall be like a watered garden, and like a spring of water whose waters fail not.

All this is exactly what we have been striving for, but our strivings have been in our own way, not in God's. The fast we have chosen has been to afflict our souls, to bow down our heads as bulrushes, and to sit in sackcloth and ashes; and, as a consequence, instead of our bones being made fat, and our souls refreshed like a watered garden, we have found only leanness, and thirst, and misery. Our own fasts, no matter how fervently they may be carried on, nor how many groans and tears may accompany them can never bring us anything else.

Now let us try God's fast. Let us lay aside all care for ourselves, and care instead for our needy brothers and sisters. Let us stop trying to do something for our own poor miserable self-life, and begin to try to do something to help the spiritual lives of others. Let us give up our hopeless efforts to find something in ourselves to delight in, and delight ourselves only in the Lord and in His service. And if we will but do this, all the days of our misery will be ended.

But some may ask whether it is not necessary to examine ourselves in order to find out what is wrong and what needs mending. This would, of course, be necessary if we were our own workmanship, but since we are God's workmanship and not our own, He is the One to examine us, for He is the only One who can tell what is wrong. The man who makes watches is the one to examine a watch when it is out of order, and to set it straight. We have too much good sense to meddle with our watches; why is it that we have not enough good sense to give up meddling with ourselves? Surely we must see that the examining of the Lord is the only kind of examination that is of any use. His examination is like that of a physician who examines in order to cure; while our self-examination is like that of the patient who only becomes more of a hypochondriac the more he examines the symptoms of his disease.

But the question may be asked whether, when there has been actual sin, there ought not to be self-examination and self-reproach at least for a time. This is a fallacy which deceives a great many. It seems too much to believe that we can be forgiven without first going through a season of self-reproach. But what is the Bible teaching? John tells us that if we confess our sins (not bewail them, nor yet try to excuse them), but simply confess them, He is faithful and just to forgive us our sins, and to cleanse us from all unrighteousness. All that God wants is that we should turn to Him at once, acknowledge our sin, and believe in His forgiveness; and every minute that we delay doing this, in order to spend the time in self-examination and self-reproach, is only adding further sin to that which we have already committed. If ever we need to look away from self, and to have our eyes turned to the Lord, it is just when we become conscious of having sinned against Him. The great the multitude of our enemies, the greater and more immediate our need of God.

All through the Bible we are taught this lesson of death to self and life in Christ alone. "Not I, but Christ," was not intended to be a unique experience of Paul's, but was simply a declaration of what ought to be the experience of every Christian. We sing sometimes, "Thou O Christ, art all I want," but as a fact, we really want a great many other things. We want good feelings, we want fervor and earnestness, we want realizations, we want satisfying experiences; and we continually examine ourselves to try to find out why we do not have these things. We think if we could only discover our points of failure, we should be able to set them straight. But there is no healing or transforming power in gazing at our failures. The only road to Christlikeness is to behold, not our own hatefulness, but His goodness and beauty. We grow like what we look at, and if we spend our lives looking at our hateful selves, we shall become more and more hateful. Do we not find as a fact that self-examination, instead of making us better, always seems to make us worse? Beholding self, we are more and more changed into the image of self. While on the contrary if we spend our time beholding the glory of the Lord, that is, letting our minds dwell upon His goodness and His love, and trying to drink in His spirit, the inevitable result will be that we shall be, slowly perhaps, but surely, changed into the image of the Lord upom whom we are gazing.

Fenelon says that we should never indulge in any self-reflective acts, either of mortification at our failures, or of congratulation at our successes; but that we should continually consign self and all self's doings to oblivion, and should keep our interior eyes upon the Lord only. It is very hard in self-examination not to try to find excuses for our faults; and our self-reflective acts are often in danger of being turned into self-glorying ones. The only way is to ignore self altogether and to forget there is any such being in existence.

No one who does not understand this can possibly appreciate the comfort and relief it is to be done with self and all self-reflective acts. I have known Christian workers whose lives have been one long torment because of these self-reflective acts; and I am convinced that the "Blue Mondays," of which so many clergymen complain, are nothing but the result of an indulgence in self-reflective acts concerning their services in the church the day before.

The only way to treat all forms of self-reflective acts, of whatever kind, is simply to give them up. They always do harm and never good. They are bound to result in one of two things; either they fill us full of self-praise and self-satisfaction, or they plunge us into the depths of discouragement and despair; and whichever it may be, the soul is in this way inevitably shut out from any sight of God and of His salvation.

One of the most effectual ways of conquering the habit is to make a rule that, whenever we are tempted to examine ourselves, we will always at once begin to examine the Lord instead, and will let thoughts of His love and His all-sufficiency sweep out all thoughts of our own unworthiness or our own helplessness.

I have been trying in this book to set the Lord before our eyes in all the beauty of His character and His ways in the hope that the sight will be so ravishing as to take our eyes off everything else. But no revelation of God will be of any use if we will not look at it, but will persist in turning our backs on what has been revealed, and in gazing instead at our own inward experiences. For again I must repeat that we cannot see self and see the Lord at the same time, and that while we are examining self we cannot be looking at Him.

Fenelon says concerning self-examination: "There is something very hidden and very deceptive in the suffering it causes; for while you seem to yourself to be wholly occupied with the glory of God, in your inmost soul it is self alone that occasions all your trouble. You are indeed desirous that God should be glorified, but you wish it should take place by means of your perfection, and you thus cherish the sentiments of self-love. It is simply a refined pretext for dwelling in self ... It is a sort of infidelity to simple faith when we desire to be continually assured that we are doing well. It is, in fact, a desire to know what we are doing, which we shall never know, and of which it is the will of God we should be ignorant. It is trifling by the way, in order to reason about the way. The safest and shortest course is to renounce, forget, and abandon self, and, through faithfulness to God, to think no more of it. This is the whole of religion — to get out of self and self-love in order to get into God."

What we must do, therefore, is to shut the door definitely and resolutely at once and forever upon self, and all of self's experiences, whether they be good or bad; and to say with the psalmist: "I have set the Lord [not self] always before me; because he is at my right hand, I shall not be moved. Therefore my heart is glad, and my glory rejoiceth: my flesh also shall rest in hope."

CHAPTER 11
THINGS THAT CANNOT BE SHAKEN

*"And this word, Yet once more, signifies the remov-
ing of those things that are shaken, as of things that
are made, that those things which cannot be shaken
may remain."*

After all we have been considering of the unfathomable
love and care of God, it might seem to those, who do not
understand the deepest ways of love, that no trials or hardness could ever come into the lives of His children. But if we
look deeply into the matter, we shall see that often love itself must needs bring the hardness. "Whom the Lord loveth
he chasteneth, and scourgeth every son whom he receiveth.
If ye endure chastening, God dealeth with you as with sons;
for what son is he whom the father chasteneth not? But if
ye be without chastisement, whereof all are partakers, then
are ye bastards, and not sons."

If love sees those it loves going wrong, it must, because of
its very love, do what it can to save them; and the love that
fails to do this is only selfishness. Therefore, just because of
His unfathomable love, the God of love, when He sees His
children resting their souls on things that can be shaken,
must necessarily remove those things from their lives in
order that they may be driven to rest only on the things that
cannot be shaken; and this process of removing is sometimes very hard.

We will all acknowledge, I think, that if our souls are to rest in peace and comfort, it can only be on unshakable foundations. It is no more possible for the soul to be comfortable when it is trying to rest on "things that can be shaken," than it is for the body. No one can rest comfortably in a shaking bed, or sit in comfort on a rickety chair.

Foundations to be reliable must always be unshakable. The house of the foolish man, which is built on the sand, may present a very fine appearance in clear and sunshiny weather; but when storms arise, and the winds blow, and floods come that house will fall, and great will be the fall of it. The wise man's house, on the contrary, which is built on the rock, is able to withstand all the stress of the storm, and remains unshaken through winds and floods, for it is "founded on the rock."

It is very possible in the Christian life to build one's spiritual house on such insecure foundations, that when storms beat upon it, the ruin of that house is great. Many a religious experience that has seemed fair enough when all was going well in life has tottered and fallen when trials have come, because its foundations have been insecure. It is therefore of vital importance to each one of us to see to it that our religious life is built upon "things that cannot be shaken."

Of course the immediate thought that will come to every mind is that it must be "built upon the rock Christ Jesus." This is true; but the great point is what is meant by that expression. It is one of those religious phrases that is often used conventionally with no definite or real meaning attached to it. Conventionally we believe that Christ is the only Rock upon which to build, but practically, though perhaps unconsciously, we believe that in order to have a rock upon which it will be really safe to build, many other things must be added to Christ. We think, for instance, that the right frames and feelings must be added, or the right doctrines or dogmas, or whatever else may seem to each one of us to constitute the necessary degree of security. And if we were only perfectly honest with ourselves, I suspect we should often find that our dependence was almost wholly upon these additions of our own; and that Christ Himself, as our rock of dependence, was of altogether secondary importance.

What we ought to mean when we talk of building upon the Rock Christ Jesus is what I am trying all through this book to make plain, and that is that the Lord is enough for our salvation, just the Lord only without any additions of our own, the Lord Himself, as He is in His own intrinsic character, our Creator and Redeemer, and our all-sufficient portion.

The "foundation of God standeth sure," and it is the only foundation that does. Therefore, we need to be "shaken" from off every other foundation in order that we may be forced to rest on the foundation of God alone. And this explains the necessity for those "shakings" through which so many Christians seem called to pass. The Lord sees that they are building their spiritual houses on flimsy foundations, which will not be able to withstand the "vehement beating" of the storms of life; and not in anger but in tenderest love, He shakes our earth and our heaven until all that "can be shaken" is removed, and only those "things which cannot be shaken" are left behind.

The apostle tells us that the things that are shaken are the "things that are made"; that is, the things that are manufactured by our own efforts, feelings that we get up, doctrines that we elaborate, good works that we perform. It is not that these things are bad things in themselves. It is only when the soul begins to rest on them instead of upon the Lord that He is compelled to "shake" us from off them. And this shaking applies, we are told, "not to the earth only, but also to Heaven." This means, I am sure, that it is possible to have "things that are made" even in religious matters.

How much of the so-called religiousness of many Christians consists of these "things that are made," I cannot say; but I sometimes think the great overturnings and tossings in matters of faith, which so distress Christians in these times, may be only the necessary shaking of the "things that are made," in order that only that which "cannot be shaken" may remain.

There are times, it may be, in our religious lives, when our experience seems to us as settled and immovable as the roots of the everlasting mountains. But there comes an upheaval, and all our foundations are shaken and thrown down, and we are ready to despair and to question whether we can be Christians at all. Sometimes it is an upheaval in our outward circumstances, and sometimes it is in our inward experience. If people have rested on their good works and their faithful service, the Lord is often obliged to take away all power for work or else all opportunity in order that the soul may be driven from its false resting place and forced to rest in the Lord alone. Sometimes the dependence is upon good feelings or pious emotions, and the soul has to be deprived of these before it can learn to depend only upon God. Sometimes it is upon "sound doctrine" that the dependence is placed, and the man feels himself to be occupying an invulnerable position, because his views are so correct, and his doctrines are so orthodox; and then the Lord is obliged to shake his doctrines, and to plunge him, it may be, into confusion and darkness as to his views.

It was at just such a moment as this that my own soul caught its first real sight of God; and what had seemed certain spiritual ruin and defeat was turned into the most triumphant victory.

Or it may be that the upheaval comes in our outward circumstances. Everything has seemed so firmly established in prosperity that no dream of disaster disturbs us. Our reputation is assured, our work has prospered, our efforts have all been successful beyond our hopes, and our soul is at ease; and the need for God is in danger of becoming far off and vague. And then the Lord is obliged to put an end to it all, and our prosperity crumbles around us like a house built on the sands, and we are tempted to think He is angry with us. But in very truth it is not anger, but tenderest love. His very love it is that compels Him to take away the outward prosperity that is keeping our souls from entering into the interior spiritual kingdom for which we long. When the fig tree ceases to blossom, and there is no fruit in the vines; when the labor of the olive shall fail, and the fields shall yield no meat; when the flock shall be cut off from the fold, and there shall be no herd in the stalls, then, and often not until then, will our souls learn to rejoice in the Lord only, and to joy in the God of our salvation.

Paul declared that he counted all things but loss that he might win Christ; and when we learn to say the same, the peace and joy that the Gospel promises become our permanent possession.

"What iniquity," asks the Lord of the children of Israel, "have your fathers found in me that they are gone far from me and have walked after vanity? For my people have committed two evils; they have forsaken me, the fountain of living waters, and hewed them out cisterns, broken cisterns that can hold no water." Like the Israelites, we too forsake the fountain of living waters, and try to hew out for ourselves cisterns of our own devising. We seek to slake our thirst with our own experiences or our own activities, and then wonder that we still thirst. And it is to save us from perishing for want of water that the Lord finds it necessary to destroy our broken cisterns; since only so can we be forced to drink from the fountain of living waters.

We are told that if we "trust in vanity," vanity shall be our recompense; and many a time have we found this to be true. Have you ever crossed a dangerous swamp abounding in quicksands, where every step was a risk, and where firm-looking hillocks continually deceived you into a false dependence, causing you to sink in the mire and water concealed beneath their deceptive appearances? If you have, you will be able to understand what it means to "trust in vanity," and you will appreciate the blessedness of any dispensation that shall discover to you the rottenness of your false dependences, and shall drive you to trust in that which is safe and permanent. When our feet are walking on "miry clay," we can have nothing but welcome for the divine Guide who shall bring us out from the clay, and shall "set our feet upon a rock," and "establish our goings," even though the ways in which He calls us to walk may seem narrow and hard.

The prophet Jeremiah, when lamenting the sins of his people, says: "We have made lies our refuge, and under falsehoods have we hid ourselves," and he adds that the Lord had declared He would sweep away the refuge of lies, and would cause the waters to overflow the hiding place. It might look, as far as the outward seeming goes, as though it was God's wrath that did this, and many a frightened Christian thinks it is; but His wrath is only against the refuge of lies, not against us, and love could do no less than destroy these refuges in order that we may be delivered.

A dear old friend of mine, who was very much interested

in my spiritual welfare, gave me a little book called, *The Seventeen False Rests of the Soul,* evidently feeling that I was in danger of settling down upon one or another of these false rests. The book set forth in quaint old language the idea that the soul was continually tempted to sit down upon some falsity, as though it were a final resting place, and that God was continually obliged to "unbottom" all such false resting places, as though one should unbottom a chair and let the sitter fall through. All these seventeen false rests were described, and it was shown how the soul, being "unbottomed" off each one successively, settled down at last upon the only true rest in God. This "unbottoming" is only another word for the "shakings" and "emptyings" of which I have been writing. It is always a painful process, and often a most discouraging one. Everything seems unstable, and rest seems utterly unattainable. No sooner do we find an experience or a doctrine in which we think we may surely rest, than a great "shaking" comes, and we are forced out again. And this process must continue until all that can be shaken is removed, and only "those things which cannot be shaken" remain.

Often the answer to our most fervent prayers for deliverance comes in such a form that it seems as if the "very foundations of the hills moved and were shaken"; and we do not always see at first that it is by means of this very shaking that the deliverance for which we have prayed is to be accomplished, and we are to be brought forth into the "large place" for which we long.

The old mystics used to teach what they called "detachment"; meaning the cutting loose of the soul from all that could hold it back from God. This need for "detachment" is the secret of many of our "shakings." We cannot follow the Lord fully so long as we are tied fast to anything else, any more than a boat can sail out into the boundless ocean so long as it is tied fast to the shore.

If we could reach the "city which hath sure and steadfast foundations," we must go out like Abraham from all other cities, and must be detached from every earthly tie. Everything in Abraham's life that could be shaken was shaken. He was, as it were, emptied from vessel to vessel, here today and gone tomorrow; all his resting places were disturbed, and no settlement or comfort anywhere. We, like Abraham, are looking for a city which hath foundations, whose builder and maker is God, and therefore we too shall need to be emptied from vessel to vessel. But we do not realize this, and when the overturnings and shakings come, we are in despair and think we shall never reach the city that hath foundations at all. But it is these very shakings that make it possible for us to reach it. The psalmist had learned this, and after all the shakings and emptyings of his eventful life, he cried: "My soul, wait thou only upon God; for my expectation is from him. He only is my rock and my salvation: he is my defense; I shall not be moved. In God is my salvation and my gloyr: the rock of my strength and my refuge is in God."

At last God was everything to him; and then he found that God was enough.

And it is the same with us. When everything in our lives and experience is shaken that can be shaken, and only that which cannot be shaken remains, we are brought to see that God only is our rock and our foundation, and we learn to have our expectation from Him alone.

"Therefore will not we fear though the earth be removed, and though the mountains be carried into the midst of the sea; though the waters thereof roar and be troubled, though the mountains shake with the swelling thereof ... God is in the midst of her, she shall not be moved. God shall help her, and that right early." "Shall not be moved" — what an inspiring declaration! Can it be possible that we, who are so easily moved by the things of earth, can arrive at a place where nothing can upset our temper or disturb our calm? Yes, it is possible; and the apostle Paul knew it. WHen he was on his way to Jerusalem, where he foresaw that "bonds and afflictions" awaited him, he could say triumphantly, "But none of these things move me." Everything in Paul's life and experience that could be shaken had been shaken, and he no longer counted his life, or any of life's possessions, dear unto him. And we, if we will but let God have His way with us, may come to the same place so that neither the fret and tear of the little things of life, nor its great and heavy trials, can have power to move us from the peace that passeth all understanding, which is declared to be the portion of those who have learned to rest only on God.

In that wonderful Revelation made to John in the "Isle that is called Patmos," where the Spirit tells to the churches what awaits those who overcome, we have a statement that expresses in striking terms just what I mean. "Him that overcometh will I make a pillar in the temple of my God; and he shall go no more out." To be as immovable as a pillar in the house of our God is an end for which one would gladly endure all the "shakings" and "unbottomings" that may be necessary to bring us there!

"Wherefore we receiving a kingdom that cannot be moved, let us have grace whereby we may serve God acceptably with reverence and godly fear; for our God is a consuming fire." A great many people are afraid of the consuming fire of God, but that is only because they do not understand what it is. It is the fire of God's love, that must in the very nature of things consume everything that can harm His people; and if our hearts are set on being what the love of God would have us be, His fire is something we shall not be afraid of, but shall warmly welcome.

> Implacable is love.
> Foes may be bought or teased
> From their malign intent;
> But he goes unappeased,
> Who is on kindness bent.

Let us thank God, then, that He is "on kindness bent" toward us, and that the consuming fire of His love will not cease to burn until it has refined us as silver is refined. For the promise is that He shall sit as a refiner and purifier of silver, and He shall purge us as gold and silver are purged in order that we may offer unto Him an offering in righteousness; and He gives us this inspiring assurance, that if we will but submit to this purifying process, we shall become "pleasant unto the Lord," and all nations shall call us blessed, "for ye shall be a delightsome land, saith the Lord of Hosts."

To be "pleasant" and "delightsome" to the Lord may seem to us impossible, when we look at our shortcomings and our unworthiness. But when we think of this lovely, consuming fire of God's love, we can be of good heart and take courage, for He will not fail nor be discouraged until all our dross and reprobate silver is burned up, and we ourselves come forth in His likeness and are conformed to His image.

Our souls long for the "kingdom which cannot be moved," and He "who is on kindness bent," will, if we will let Him, shake everything in our lives that can be shaken, and will unbottom us off every false rest, until only that which cannot be shaken shall remain.

One of the most impressive sermons I ever heard was preached by a sweet-faced old Quaker lady, who rose in the stillness and said, "Yesterday Sister Tabitha broke all to pieces my best china teapot, but the Lord, whom I trust, kept my soul in perfect peace, and enabled me not to utter a single word of reproach." That was all; the sermon was ended; but into every heart there entered a sense of what it would mean to be kept in the immovable kingdom of the love of God.

And this kingdom may be our home, if we will but submit to the shakings of God, and will learn to rest only and always on Him.

May He hasten the day for each one of us!

CHAPTER 12

A WORD TO THE WAVERING ONES

"But let him ask in faith, nothing wavering. For he that wavereth is like a wave of the sea driven with the wind and tossed. For let not that man think that he shall receive anything of the Lord."

It would be difficult to find any one thing that produces more discomfort in the religious life than does a wavering faith. The figure given us by the apostle James exactly describes it — "a wave of the sea driven by the wind and tossed." And just as it is impossible for a traveler to reach his destination by advancing one day, and retracing his steps the next, so is it equally impossible for the wavering soul, while it wavers, to reach any place of settled peace.

In our last chapter we considered the shakings of God; and it might be thought that our waverings would be akin to His shakings. But God's shakings are caused by His love, and are for our blessing, and always lead to rest and peace; while our waverings are caused by our want of faith, and always lead to discomfort and turmoil.

A wavering Christian is a Christian who trusts in the love of God one day and doubts it the next, and who is alternately happy or miserable accordingly. He mounts to the hilltop of joy at one time, only to descend at another time into the valley of despair. He is driven to and fro by every wind of doctrine, is always striving and never attaining, and is a prey to each changing influence, caused by his state of health, or by the influences around him, or even by the state of the weather.

You would suppose that even the most ignorant child of God would know without telling that this sort of experience is all wrong, and that to waver in one's faith after such a fashion is one of the things most dishonoring to the Lord, whose truth and faithfulness it so impugns. But as a fact, there are many Christians whose eyes are so blinded in the matter, that they actually think this tendency to waver is a tribute to the humility of their spirits, and who exalt every fresh attack of doubt into a secret and most pious virtue. A wavering Christian will say complacently, "Oh, but I know myself to be so unworthy, that I am sure it is right for me to doubt," and they will imply by their tone of superiority, that their hearer, if truly humble, would doubt also.

In fact, I knew one really devoted Christian, whose religious life was one long torment of doubt, who said to me once in solemn earnestness, after I had been urging him to have more faith, "My dear friend, if once I should be so presumptuous as to feel sure that God loved me, I should be certain I was on the direct road to Hell." He thought, no doubt, that such an assurance could only arise from a feeling that he was good enough to be worthy of God's love, and that to feel this would be presumption. And in this he would have been right, for to think ourselves good enough to be worthy of God's love would be presumption indeed. But the ground for our assurance is not to come from our own goodness, but from the goodness of God; and while we never can be and never ought to be satisfied with the first, there cannot possibly be any question to one who believes the Bible as to the all-sufficiency of the last.

To see the absurdity, not to call it by any harsher name, of the position of doubt taken up by this dear Christian, it is only necessary to consider how it would work with any of our human relations in life. Try to imagine what it would be in the marriage relation, or in the relation of children to a parent, both of which relations are used by the Lord as figures of our relation to Himself. Suppose either wife or husband should have a wavering experience of confidence in the other, one day trusting, and the next day doubting;

would this be considered a sign of true humility on the doubter's part, and therefore a thing to be cherished as a virtue? Or, similarly, if children should waver in their confidence toward their earthly parents, as Christians seem to feel at liberty to do with their heavenly Parent, what name could be found severe enough by which to call such unfilial conduct? Of course in earthly relations such wavering might come from the fact that one of the parties concerned was unworthy of confidence, and in this case it could be excused. But in the case of God there could not possibly be any such excuse; although the wavering faith of some of His children may, I am afraid, sometimes lead outsiders to conclude that He cannot be worthy of much confidence, or their faith would be more steadfast.

We would shrink in horror from being the cause of any such imputation on the character of God; but I think, if we are honest with ourselves, we will be forced to acknowledge that our wavering faith is calculated to convey just such an impression; and that it really is, therefore, in its essence disloyalty to a trustworthy God, and should be mourned over as a grievous sin. The truth is, although we may not know it, our wavering comes, not from humility, but from a subtle and often unconscious form of pride. True humility accepts the love that is bestowed upon it, and the gifts of that love, with a meek and happy thankfulness, while pride shrinks from accepting gifts and kindnesses, and is afraid to believe in the disinterested goodness of the one who bestows them. Were we truly humble, we would accept God's love with thankful meekness, and, while acknowledging our own unworthiness, would only think of it as enhancing His grace and goodness in choosing us as the recipients of such blessings.

A wavering faith is not only disloyal to God, but it is a source of untold misery to ourselves, and cannot in any way advance our spiritual interests, but must always under all circumstances hinder and upset them. The apostle tells us that we are made partakers of Christ if we "hold the beginning of our confidence steadfast unto the end." To be steadfast is the exact contrary of wavering, and to expect the results of steadfastness as the outcome of wavering is as foolish as it would be to expect to reach the top of a mountain by alternately climbing two steps and sliding back three.

And yet many people expect this very thing. They make a "beginning of confidence," and for a little time, while the freshness of it lasts, are full of joy and triumph. Then trials come, and temptations; and doubts begin to intrude; and instead of treating these doubts as enemies to be resisted and driven away, they receive them as friends, and give them entertainment; and sooner or later they begin to waver in their faith and in their allegiance, and from that moment all settled peace is gone. When skies are bright and all goes well with them, their faith revives, and they are happy; but when skies are dark and things go wrong doubts triumph, and they waver again.

I was having a conversation with a very eminent clergyman on the possibility of a religious life of abiding peace and rest, and he told me frankly that he did not believe it was possible, and that he thought most Christian experience was like his own. "Now I," he said, "when I want to write my sermons, get up on the mountaintop by prayer and by climbing. I put my foot first on one promise and then on another, and so, by hard climbing and much praying, I reach the summit, and can begin my sermon. All goes swimmingly for a little while, and then suddenly an interruption comes, some trouble with my children, or some domestic upset in the house, or some quarrel with a neighbor, and down I tumble from the mountaintop, and can only get back again by another wearisome climb. Sometimes," he said, "I stay on the summit for two or three days, and once in a great while, even for two or three weeks. But as to there being any possibility of being seated in heavenly places in Christ, and abiding there continually, I cannot believe it."

I am sure this will describe the experience of many of God's children, who are hungering and thirsting for the peace and rest Christ has promised them, but who seem unable to attain to it for more than a few moments at a time. They may get now and then a faint glimmer of faith, and peace seems to be coming, and then all the old doubts spring up again with tenfold power. "Look at your heart," they say: "see how cold it is, how indifferent. How can you for a moment believe that God can love such a poor, unworthy creature as you are?" And it all sounds so reasonable that they are plunged into darkness again.

The whole trouble arises from a want of faith. It seems commonplace to say it, for I have to say it so often, but in the spiritual life it is to us always, *always,* ALWAYS according to our faith. This is a spiritual law that can neither be neglected nor evaded. It is not an arbitrary law which we might hope could be repealed in our own especial case, but it is inherent in the very nature of things, and is therefore unalterable. And equally inherent in the nature of things is its converse, that if it is to be to us according to our faith, so will it also be to us according to our doubts.

The whole root and cause then of our wavering experience is not, as we may have thought, our sins, but is simply and only our doubts. Doubts create and impassable gulf between our souls and the Lord, just as inevitably as they do between us and our earthly friends; and no amount of fervor or earnestness can bridge this gulf in one case any more than in the other. "Let not that man that wavereth think that he shall receive anything of the Lord." This is not because God is angry, and visits His displeasure in this way on the man who doubts, but it is because of that inherent nature of things that makes it impossible for doubt and confidence to exist together, whether in earthly relations or heavenly, and which neither God nor man can alter. "To whom sware he that they should not enter into his rest but to them that believed not. So we see they could not enter in because of unbelief." It was not that God would not allow them to enter in as a punishment for their unbelief, but they simply could not. It was an impossibility. Faith is the only door into the kingdom of Heaven, and there is no other. If we will not go in by that door, we cannot get in at all, for there is no other way.

God's salvation is not a purchase to be made, nor wages to be earned, nor a summit to be climbed, nor a task to be accomplished; but it is simply and only a gift to be accepted, and can only be accepted by faith. Faith is a necessary element in the acceptance of any gift, whether earthly or heavenly. My friends may put their gifts upon my table, or even place them in my lap, but unless I believe in their friendliness and honesty of purpose enough to accept these gifts, they can never become really mine.

It is plain, therefore, that the Bible is simply announcing, as it always does, the nature of things, when it declares that "according to your faith" it shall be unto you. And the sooner we settle down to this the better. All our wavering comes from the fact that we do not believe in this law. We acknowledge, of course, that it is in the Bible, but we think it cannot really mean what it says, and that there must be some additions made to it; for instance, as "according to our fervency it shall be unto us," or "according to our importunity," or "according to our worthiness." And, if the whole truth were told, we are inclined to think that these additions of ours are, if anything, by far the most important part of the whole matter. As a consequence of this, our attention is mostly directed to getting these matters settled, and we watch our own frames and feelings, and search into our own worthiness or unworthiness with so much assiduity that we overlook almost altogether the one fundamental principle of faith, without which nothing whatever can be done. Moreover, as our disposition and feelings are the most variable things in the universe, and our sense of worthiness or unworthiness changes with our changing feelings, our experience cannot but waver; and the possibility of a steadfast faith recedes farther and farther into the background. We in short make the faithfulness of God, and the truth of His Word, depend upon the state of our feelings.

I am very certain that if any of our friends should treat us in this doubting fashion, we would be wounded and indignant beyond measure; and no feeling of unworthiness on their part could excuse them in our eyes for such a wavering of their confidence in us. In fact, we would far rather our friends should even sin against us than doubt us. No form of sinfulness ever hindered the Lord Jesus while on earth from doing His mighty works. The only thing that hindered Him was unbelief. In His own town, and among His own neighbors and friends, where naturally He would have liked to have performed some of His miracles, we are told that, "He did not many mighty works there because of their unbelief." It was not that He would not, but simply that He could not. And He cannot in our case, any more than in theirs.

But I am afraid some of you may think I am making a mistake, and that, in spite of what God has said, the man whose faith wavers can after all, if he is only fervent and earnest enough, receive something from the Lord. That means that you do not believe that God understands the laws of His kingdom as well as you yourself do, and that it is safer to follow your own ideas rather than His Word. And yet you must know that hitherto your doubts have brought you nothing but darkness and misery. Recall the days, and weeks, and even perhaps months and years of a halting, stumbling, uncomfortable, religious life, and ask yourself honestly whether the cause of it all has not been your wavering faith. If you believe one day that God loves you and is favorable to you, and the next day doubt His love, and fear He is angry with you, does it not stand to reason that you must waver in your experience from joy to misery; and that only a steadfast faith in His love and care could give you an unwavering experience?

The one question, therefore, for all whose faith wavers is how to put an end at once and forever to their wavering. And here I am thankful to say that I know of a perfect remedy. The only thing you have to do is to *give it up.* Your wavering is caused by your doubting, and by nothing else. Give up your doubting, and your wavering will stop. Keep on with your doubting, and your wavering will continue. The whole matter is as simple as daylight; and the choice is in your own hands.

Perhaps you may think this is an extreme statement, for it has probably never entered your heads that you could give up doubting altogether. But I assert that you can. You can simply refuse to doubt. You can shut the door against every suggestion of doubt that comes, and can by faith declare exactly the opposite. Your doubt says, "God does not forgive my sins." Your faith must say, "He does forgive me; He says He does, and I choose to believe Him. I am His forgiven child." And you must assert this steadfastly, until all your doubts vanish. You have no more right to say that you are of such a doubting nature that you cannot help doubting, than to say you are of such a thieving nature that you cannot help thieving. One is as easily controlled as the other. You must give up your doubting just as you would give up your thieving. You must treat the temptation to doubt exactly as a drunkard must treat the temptation to drink; you must take a pledge against it.

The process I believe to be the most effectual is to lay our doubts, just as we lay our other sins, upon God's altar, and make a total surrender of them. We must give up all liberty to doubt, and must consecrate our power of believing to Him, and must trust Him to keep us trusting. We must make our faith in His Word as inevitable and necessary a thing as is our obedience to His will. We must be as loyal to our heavenly Friend as we are to our earthly friends, and must refuse to recognize the possibility of such a thing as any questioning or doubting of His love or His faithfulness, or of any wavering in our absolute faith in His Word.

Of course temptations to waver will come, and it will sometimes look to us impossible that the Lord can love such disagreeable, unworthy beings as we feel ourselves to be. But we must turn as deaf an ear to these insinuations against the love of God as we would to any insinuations against the love of our dearest friend. The fight to do this may sometimes be very severe, and may even at times seem almost unendurable. But our unchanging declaration must continually be, "Though he slay me, yet will I trust in him." Our steadfast faith will unfailingly bring us, sooner or later, a glorious victory.

Probably it will often seem to us as if it would be a righteous thing, in view of our many shortcomings, and only what a truly humbled soul would do, to waver in our faith and to question whether the salvation of the Lord Jesus can be meant for us. But if we at all understand what the salvation of the Lord Jesus Christ is, we cannot fail to recognize that all this is only temptation; and that what we must do is to lift up the shield of faith persistently against it; for the shield of faith always does and always will quench every fiery dart of the enemy.

The Spirit of God never under any circumstances could suggest a doubt of the love of God. Wherever doubts come from, one thing is certain, they do not come from Heaven. All doubts are from an evil source, and they must always be treated as the suggestions of an enemy. We cannot, it is true, prevent the suggestions of doubt making themselves heard in our hearts, any more than we can prevent our ears from hearing the oaths of wicked men in the streets. But just as we can refuse to approve of or join in the oaths of these men, so can we refuse to pay any attention to these suggestions of doubt. The cases are exactly similar. But while in the case of the oaths, we know without any question that it would be wicked to join in with them, in the case of the doubts we have a lurking feeling that, after all, doubts may have something pious in them, and ought to be encouraged. But I believe one is as displeasing to God as the other.

Again I would repeat that the only way to treat the doubts that make you waver is to give them up. An absolute surrender is the only remedy. It is like the drunkard with his drink, half measures are of no manner of use. Total abstinence is the only hope.

The most practical way of doing this is not only to make the interior surrender, but to meet, as I have said, each doubt with a flat denial; and to carry the war into the enemy's country, as it were, by an emphatic assertion of faith in direct opposition to the doubt. For instance, if the doubt arises as to whether God can love anyone so sinful and unfaithful as you feel yourself to be, you must at once assert in definite words in your own heart, and if possible aloud to someone, that God does love you; that He says He does, and that His Word is a million times more trustworthy than any of your feelings, no matter how well founded they may seem to you to be. If you cannot find anyone to whom to say this, then write it in a letter, or else say it aloud to yourself and to God. Be very definite about it.

If in anything you have had a "beginning of confidence," if you have ever laid hold of any promise or declaration of the Lord's, hold on steadfastly to that promise or declaration without wavering, let come what may. There can be no middle ground. If it was true once, it is true still, for God is unchangeable. The only thing that can deprive you of it is your unbelief. While you believe, you have it. "Whatsoever things ye desire when ye pray, believe that ye receive them and ye shall have them."

Let nothing shake your faith. Should even sin unhappily overtake you, you must not let it make you doubt. At once, on the discovery of any sin, take I John 1:9 and act on it. "If we confess our sins, he is faithful and just to forgive us our sins, and to cleanse us from all unrighteousness." Confess your sin, therefore, immediately upon the discovery of it, and believe at once that God does forgive it, as He declares, and does again cleanse you from all unrighteousness. No sin, however grievous, can separate us from God for one moment, after it has been treated in this fashion. To allow sin to cause your faith to waver is only to add a new sin to the one already committed. Return at once to God in the way the Bible teaches, and let your faith hold steadfastly to His Word. Believe it, not because you feel it, or see it, but because He says it. Believe it, even when it seems to you that you are believing a lie. Believe it actively and steadfastly, through dark and through light, through ups and through downs, through times of comfort and through times of despair, and I can promise you, without a fear, that your wavering experience will be ended.

"Therefore, beloved brethren, be ye steadfast, immovable, always abounding in the work of the Lord, forasmuch as ye know that your labor is not in vain in the Lord." To be "immovable" in one's religious life is the exact opposite of wavering. In the Forty-sixth Psalm we can see what it is. The earth may be removed, and the mountains may be carried into the midst of the sea, our whole universe may seem to be in ruins, but while we trust in the Lord we "shall not be moved."

The man who wavers in his faith is upset by the smallest trifles; the man who is steadfast in his faith can look on calmly at the ruin of all his universe.

To be thus immovable in one's religious life is a boon most ardently to be desired, and it may be ours if we will only hold the beginning of our confidence steadfast to the end.

Faith is sweetest of worships to him who so loves
His unbearable splendors in darkness to hide;
And to trust in Thy Word, dearest Lord, is true love,
For those prayers are most granted which seem most denied.
And faith throws her arms around all Thou hast told her,
And able to hold as much more, can but grieve;
She could hold Thy grand self, Lord! if Thou wouldst
    reveal it.
And love makes her long to have more to believe.

CHAPTER 13
DISCOURAGEMENT

*"The soul of the people was much discouraged
because of the way."*

The church of Christ abounds with people who are "discouraged because of the way." Either inwardly or outwardly, and oftentimes both, things look all wrong, and there seems no hope of escape. Their souls faint in them, and their religious lives are full of discomfort and misery. There is nothing that so paralyzes effort as discouragement, and nothing that more continually and successfully invites defeat. The secret of failure or success in any matter lies far more in the soul's interior attitude than in any other cause or causes. It is a law of our being, which is only now beginning to be discovered, that the inward man counts for far more in every conflict than anything the outward man may do or may possess.

And nowhere is this truer than in the spiritual life. Again I must repeat what I find it necessary to say so continually, that the Bible declares from beginning to end that faith is the law of the spiritual life, and that according to our faith it always shall be and always will be unto us. Then, since faith and discouragement cannot, in the very nature of things, exist together, it is perfectly manifest that discouragement must be an absolute barrier to faith. And that where discouragement rules, the converse to the law of faith must rule also, and it shall be to us, not according to our faith, but according to our discouragement.

In fact, just as courage is faith in good, so discouragement is faith in evil; and, while courage opens the door to good, discouragement opens it to evil.

An allegory that I heard very early in my Christian life has always remained in my memory as one of those warnings to motorists that we often see at the top of hills on country roads, "This hill is dangerous"; and it has many a time warned me away from the dangerous descent of discouragement.

The allegory declared that once upon a time Satan, who desired to entrap a devoted Christian worker, called a council of his helpers to decide on the best way of doing it, and to ask for volunteers. After the case had been explained, an imp offered himself to do the work.

"How will you do it?" asked Satan.

"Oh," replied the imp, "I will paint to him the delights and pleasures of a life of sin in such glowing colors that he will be eager to enter upon it."

"That will not do," said Satan, shaking his head. "The man has tried sin, and he knows better. He knows it leads to misery and ruin, and he will not listen to you."

Then another imp offered himself, and again Satan asked, "What will you do to win the man over?"

"I will picture to him the trials and the self-denials of a righteous life, and will make him eager to escape from them."

"Ah, that will not do either," said Satan, "for he has tried righteousness, and he knows that its paths are paths of peace and happiness."

Then a third imp started up and declared that he was sure he could bring the man over.

"Why, what will you do," asked Satan, "that you are so sure?"

"I will discourage his soul," replied the imp triumphantly.

"That will do, that will do," exclaimed Satan, "you will be successful. Go and bring back your victim."

An old Quaker has this saying, "All discouragement is from the Devil"; and I believe he stated a far deeper and more universal truth than we have yet fully understood. Discouragement cannot have its source in God. The religion of the Lord Jesus Christ is a religion of faith, of good cheer, of courage, of hope that maketh not ashamed. "Be discouraged," says our lower nature, "for the world is a place of temptation and sin." "Be of good cheer," says Christ, "for I have overcome the world." There cannot possibly be any room for discouragement in a world which Christ has overcome.

We must settle it then, once for all, that discouragement comes from an evil source, only and always. I know this is not the general idea, at least in the spiritual region of things. In temporal things, perhaps, we have more or less learned that discouragement is foolish, and even wrong; but, when it comes to spiritual things, we are apt to reverse the order, and make that commendable in one case, which is reprehensible in the other; and we even succeed in persuading ourselves that to be discouraged is a very pious state of mind, and an evidence of true humility.

The causes for our discouragement seem so legitimate, that to be discouraged seems to our short-sightedness the only right and proper state of mind to cultivate. The first and perhaps the most common of these causes is the fact of our own incapacity. It is right for us to be cast down, we think, because we know ourselves to be such poor, miserable, good-for-nothing creatures. It would be presumption, in the face of such incapacity, to be anything but discouraged.

Moses is an illustration of this. The Lord had called him to lead the children of Israel out of the land of Egypt; and Moses, looking at his own natural infirmities and weaknesses, was discouraged, and tried to excuse himself: "I am not eloquent, but I am slow of speech and of a slow tongue. They will not believe me nor hearken unto my voice." Naturally, one would think that Moses had plenty of cause for discouragement, and for discouragement very similar to that which is likely to assail us, when, because of our distrust in our own eloquence, or our own power to convince those to whom we are to be sent, we shrink from the work to which the Lord may be calling us. But notice how the Lord answered Moses, for in the same way I am convinced does He answer us. He did not do, what no doubt Moses would have liked best, try to convince him that he really was eloquent, or that his tongue was not slow of speech. He passed all this by as being of no account whatever, and simply called attention to the fact that, since He had made man's mouth and would Himself be with the mouth He had made, there could not possibly be any cause for discouragement, even if Moses did have all the infirmities of speech of which he had complained. "And the Lord said unto him, Who hath made man's mouth? or who maketh the dumb, or deaf, or the seeing, or the blind? Have not I, the Lord? Now therefore go, and I will be with thy mouth, and teach thee what thou shalt say."

When the word of the Lord came to Jeremiah telling him that He had ordained him to be a prophet to the nations, Jeremiah felt himself to be entirely unequal to such a work, and said: "Ah, Lord God, behold, I cannot speak, for I am a child." But the Lord answered: "Say not, I am a child; for thou shalt go to all that I shall send thee, and whatever I command the, thou shalt speak. Be not afraid of their faces, for I am with thee to deliver thee, saith the Lord."

Gideon is another illustration. The Lord had called him to undertake the deliverance of His people from the oppression of the Midianites, and had said to him: "Go in this thy might, and thou shalt save Israel from the hands of the Midianites: have I not sent thee?" This ought to have been enough for Gideon, but he was a poor unknown man, of no family or position, and no apparent fitness for such a great mission; and, looking at himself and his own deficiencies, he naturally became discouraged, and said: "Wherewith shall I save Israel? Behold, my family is poor in Manasseh, and I am the least in my father's house." Other men, he felt, who had power and influence, might perhaps accomplish this great work, but not one so poor and insignificant as himself. How familir this sort of talk must sound to the victims of discouragement among my readers, and how sensible and reasonable it seems! But what did the Lord think of it? "And the Lord said unto him, Surely I will be with thee, and thou shalt smite the Midianites as one man" — simply and only the promise, "Surely I will be with thee." Not one word of encouragement did He give Gideon, nor does He give us as to our own capacities or fitness for the work required, but merely the bare statement of the fact of being sufficient for all possible needs, "I will be with thee." To all words of discouragement in the Bible this is the invariable answer, "I will be with thee"; and it is an answer that precludes all possibility of argument or of any further discouragement. I thy Creator and Redeemer, I thy strength and thy wisdom, I thy omnipresent and omniscient God, I will be with thee, and will protect thee through everything; no enemy shall hurt thee, no strife of tongues shall disturb thee; My presence shall be thy safety and thy sure defense.

One would think that in the face of such assertions as these not even the most fainthearted among us could find any loophole for discouragement. But discouragement comes in many subtle forms, and our spiritual enemies attack us in many disguises. Our own especial make-up or temperament is one of the most common and insidious of our enemies. Other people, who are made differently, can be cheerful and courageous, we think, but it is right that we should be discouraged when we see the sort of people we are, how foolish, how helpless, how unfit to grapple with any enemies! And there would indeed be ample cause for discouragement if we were to be called upon to fight our battles ourselves. We would be right in thinking we could not do it. But if the Lord is to fight them for us, it puts an entirely different complexion on the matter, and our want of ability to fight becomes an advantage instead of a disadvantage. We can only be strong in Him when we are weak in ourselves, and our weakness, therefore, is in reality our greatest strength.

The children of Israel can give us a warning lesson here. After the Lord had delivered them out of Egypt, and had brought them to the borders of the promised land, Moses urged them to go up and possess it. "Behold," he said, "the Lord thy God hath set the land before thee; go up and possess it, as the Lord God of thy fathers hath said unto thee; fear not, neither be discouraged." But the circumstances were so discouraging, and they felt themselves to be so helpless, that they could not believe God would really do all He had said; and they murmured in their tents, and declared that it must be because the Lord hated them that He had brought them out of Egypt in order to deliver them into the hands of their enemies. "And they said, Whither shall we go up? Our brethren have discouraged our heart, saying, The people is greater and taller than we; the cities are great and walled up to heaven; and moreover we have seen the sons of the Anakims there.''

When we read the report of the spies we cannot be surprised at their discouragement; and we can even believe they would have felt that courage under such circumstances would be only foolhardiness. ''The land through which we have gone to search it,'' the spies declared, ''is a land that eateth up the inhabitants thereof: and all the men that we saw in it are men of a great stature. And there we saw the giants, the sons of Anak, which come of the giants: and we were in our own sight as grasshoppers, and so we were in their sight.'' Nothing could have seemed humbler than for them to look upon themselves as poor, good-for-nothing grasshoppers; and true humility would have seemed to teach that it would be the height of presumption for grasshoppers to try to conquer giants. We also often feel ourselves to be but grasshoppers in the face of the giants of temptation and trouble that assail us, and we think ourselves justified in being discouraged. But the question is not, whether we are grasshoppers, but whether God is; for it is not we who have to fight these giants, but God.

In vain Moses reminded the Israelites of this. In vain he assured them that they had no need to be afraid of even the sons of the Anakims, for the Lord their God would fight for them. He even reminded them of past deliverances, and asked them if they did not remember how that ''in the wilderness the Lord thy God bear thee as a man doth bear his son in all the way that ye went''; but they were still too discouraged to believe. And the result was that not one of that ''evil generation'' was allowed to see the Promised Land, except only Caleb and Joshua, who had steadfastly believed that God could and would lead them in.

Such are the fruits of giving way to discouragement, and such is the reward of a steadfast faith.

The apostle in commenting on this story in Hebrews says: ''And to whom sware he that they should not enter into his rest, but to them that believed not? So we see that they could not enter in because of unbelief.''

Is there no parallel in all this to our case? Do we not look at our weakness instead of looking at the Lord's strength; and have we not sometimes become so discouraged as to sink into such "anguish of spirit," that we cannot even hearken to the Lord's own declarations that He will fight for us and will give us the victory? Our souls long to enter into the rest the Lord has promised; but giants and cities great and walled up to Heaven seem to stand in our pathway, and we are afraid to believe. So we too, like the Israelites, cannot enter in because of unbelief.

How different it would be if we only had faith enough to say with the psalmist: "Though an host should encamp against me, my heart shall not fear; though war should rise against me, in this will I be confident ... For in the time of trouble he shall hide me in his pavilion: in the secret of his tabernacle he shall hide me. He shall set me up upon a rock." How joyfully and triumphantly would we be able to enter into rest, if this were our language!

Another very subtle cause for discouragement is to be found in what is called the fear of man. There seems to exist in this world a company of beings called "they" who lord it over life with an iron hand of control. What will "they" say? What will "they" think? are among the most frequent questions that assail the timid soul when it seeks to work for the Lord. At every turn this omnipotent and ubiquitous "they" stands in our way to discourage us and make us afraid. This form of discouragement is apt to come under the subtle disguise of a due consideration for the opinion of others; but it is especially dangerous, because it exalts this "they" into the place of God, and esteems "their" opinions above His promises. The only remedy here, as in all other forms of discouragement, is simply the reiteration of the fact that God is with us. "Be not afraid of their faces; for I am with thee to deliver thee, saith the Lord." "For he hath said, I will never leave thee nor forsake thee. So that we may boldly say, The Lord is my helper, and I will not fear what man shall do unto me." How can any heart, however timid, dare to indulge in discouragement in the face of such assertions as these?

There is, however, one sort of discouragement that is very common, and that seems as if it must be right, even though in all other cases it may be wrong, and that is the discouragement that arises from our own failures. It was from this sort of discouragement that the children of Israel suffered after their defeat at Ai. They had "committed a trespass in the accursed thing," and "therefore they could not stand before their enemies"; and so great was their discouragement that it is said, "wherefore the hearts of the people melted and became as water," and "Joshua rent his clothes, and fell to the earth upon his face before the ark of the Lord, until the eventide, he and all the elders of Israel, and put dust upon their heads." When God's own people "turn their backs before their enemies" one might well think they ought indeed to "lie on their faces," and "put dust on their heads," because of the dishonor they have brought upon His great name. Discouragement and despair would seem the only proper and safe condition after such failures. But evidently the Lord thought otherwise, for He said to Joshua, "Get thee up; wherefore liest thou upon thy face?" The proper thing to do after a failure is not to abandon ourselves to utter discouragement, humble as this may appear; but at once to face the evil, and get rid of it, and afresh and immediately to consecrate ourselves again to the Lord. "Up, sanctify yourselves," is always God's command. "Lie down and be discouraged" is always our temptation.

But you may ask whether a sense of sin produced by the convictions of the Holy Spirit ought not to cause discouragement. If I see myself to be a sinner, how can I help being discouraged? To this I answer that the Holy Spirit does not convict us of sin in order to discourage us, but to encourage us. His work is to show us our sin, not that we may lie down in despair under its power, but that we may get rid of it. A good mother points out the faults of her children for the purpose of helping them correct those faults; and the convictions of the Holy Spirit are in truth one of our greatest privileges, if we only had the sense to see it; for they mean, not that we are to give up in discouragement, but that we are to be encouraged to believe that deliverance is coming.

The good housewife discovers the stains on her table linen, not in order that she may have it thrown aside as no longer fit for use, but in order that she may have it cleansed for future use; and, if she has a good laundress, she will not be discouraged by the worst of stains. Surely then when God says to us, "Though your sins be as scarlet, they shall be white as snow," it is pure unbelief on our part to allow ourselves to be discouraged at even the worst of our failures, for God's "washing of regeneration" must be at least as effectual as the washing of any human laundress could possibly be.

Fenelon says concerning this: "It is of great importance to guard against discouragement on account of our faults. Discouragement is not a fruit of humility, but of pride, and nothing can be worse. It springs for a secret love of our own excellence. We are hut at feeling what we are. If we become discouraged we are the more enfeebled, and from our reflections on our own imperfections, a chagrin arises that is often worse than the imperfection itself. Poor nature longs from self-love to behold itself perfect; it is vexed that it is not so, it is impatient, haughty, and out of temper with itself and with everybody else. Sad state; as though the work of God could be accomplished by our ill-humor. As though the peace of God could be attained by our interior restlessness."

Discouragement, from whatever source it may come, produces many sad results. One of its very worst is that it leads people to "murmur," and to "speak against God." When the children of Israel were "discouraged because of the way," we are told that they "spake against God," and asked all sorts of God-dishonoring questions. And I believe, if we could examine the causes of the rebelling and murmuring thoughts that sometimes beset us, we could find that they always begin in discouragement. The truth is that discouragement is really, in its essense, a "speaking against God," for it necessarily implies some sort of a failure on His part to come up to that which His promises have led us to expect of Him. The psalmist recognizes this, and says concerning the discouraging questions His people asked in the days of their wilderness wandering, "Yes, they 'spake against God'; they said, 'Can God furnish a table in the wilderness?'" It appears, therefore, that even our questions as to God's power or willingness to help us, which perhaps seem to us so reasonable and even so humble, are really a "speaking against God," and are displeasing to Him, because they reveal the sad fact that we "believe not in him, and trust not in his salvation."

Another grievous quality in discouragement is its contagiousness. Nothing is more catching than discouragement.

When the spies sent out by Moses brought up, as we have seen, an "evil report of the promised land," and told of the giants there, they so "discouraged the hearts of their brethren," that the people "lifted up their voices and cried," and utterly refused to go into the very land which the Lord had given them, and which they had started out to possess.

The "evil report" that so many Christians bring of their failures and their disappointments in the Christian life is one of the most discouraging things in our intercourse with one another. The hearts of many young Christians are, I believe, far too often thus discouraged by their older brethren, who have but little idea of the harm they are doing by their doleful accounts of the trials of the way.

I can never look back without shame to a time in my own life when I "discouraged the heart" of a young Christian friend, by the "evil report" I gave her of the "giants" of doubt and difficulty I had met with in my Christian pathway. And afterward, when a stronger faith in God had delivered me from all fear of these giants, I found that my former evil report had so effectually "discouraged her heart" that it was a long time before I could induce her to hearken to the good report I had then to bring.

So important did the Lord feel it to be that no one should discourage the heart of another than when Moses was giving to the Israelites God's laws concerning their methods of warfare, he said: "And the officers shall speak further unto the people, and they shall say, What man is there that is fearful and fainthearted? let him go and return unto his house, lest his brethren's heart faint as well as his heart."

Discouraged people, if they must be discouraged, ought at least to keep their discouragements to themselves, hidden away in the privacy of their own bosoms lest they should discourage the hearts of their brethren. We know from experience that courage is contagious, and that one really brave soul in moments of danger can save a crowd from a panic. But we too often fail to remember that the converse of this is true, and that one fainthearted man or woman can infect a whole crowd with fear. We consequently think nothing of expressing with the utmost freedom the foolish and wicked discouragements that are paralyzing all our own courage. We even sometimes, strange to say, sing our discouragements in our hymns at church or in prayer meeting.

> Where is the blessedness I knew
> When first I saw the Lord?
> Where is that soul-refreshing view
>   Of Jesus and His Word?
> What peaceful hours I then enjoyed,
>   How sweet their memory still;
> But now I find an aching void,
>   The world can never fill.

Or this:

> And shall we then forever live
>   At this poor dying rate,
> Our love so faint, so cold to Thee,
>   And Thine to us so great?
> In vain we tune our formal songs,
>   In vain we strive to rise;
> Hosannas languish on our tongues,
>   And our devotion dies.

To sing such hymns seems to me the greatest travesty on the worship of God that could well be conceived of. If there are "aching voids" in our experience, if our "love is cold and faint," and if we are living at a "poor, dying rate," at least let us keep it to ourselves. Because "hosannas languish on our tongues" is no reason why complainings and murmurings should be exalted into their place. Surely we cannot think it can be pleasing to God to hear them. What would we think of wives who should meet together to sing such things about their relation to their husbands? I do not believe they would be tolerated in society a single day.

If the church of Christ would only expurgate all the hymns of discouragement from its hymn books, and would allow none but hymns of courage and good cheer to be sung by its members, I believe the faith of Christians would go up with a mighty bound. "Be of good cheer" is the command of the Lord for His disciples, always and under all circumstances; and He founded this command on the tremendous fact that He had overcome the world, and that therefore there was nothing left for us to be discouraged about. As I have said before, if we only understood what it means that Christ has overcome the world, I believe we would be aghast at the very idea of any one of His followers ever being discouraged again.

If you had been an Israelite in those days, which would you rather have been, dear reader, the spies who brought an evil report of the land, and so discouraged the hearts of their brethren as to bring upon them the dreary forty years of wilderness wandering, or Caleb and Joshua, who "stilled the people before Moses, and said, Let us go up at once and possess the land; for we are well able to overcome it"?

Which will you be now?

In the divine review of this episode, Moses spoke of Caleb as one who had "wholly followed" the Lord; and this "wholly following" consisted simply and only in the fact that Caleb had given his brethren a good report of the land, and, when his colleagues had made the heart of the people to melt by their evil report, had encouraged them to go up and possess it.

I hardly think that this is the general interpretation of what "wholly following" means; and I fear that many otherwise really devoted Christians fail in this essential point and seem to make it almost the principal mission of their lives to discourage the hearts of their brethren by the doleful and despairing reports they bring of the difficulties and dangers of the way.

How different it would be if discouragement were looked upon in its true light as a "speaking against God," and only encouraging words were permitted among Christians and encouraging reports heard! How many times would the children of Israel have failed in conquering their enemies had there been no men of faith among them to encourage and cheer them? And, on the other hand, who can tell how many spiritual defeats and disasters your discouragements, dear reader, may have brought about in your own life, and in the lives of those around you?

In one of Isaiah's prophecies which begins with, "Comfort ye, comfort ye my people, saith your God," he gives us a wonderful description of God as the ground of comfort, and then sets forth what His people ought to be; and says in the course of the latter: "They helped everyone his neighbor, and everyone said to his brother, Be of good courage. So the carpenter encouraged the goldsmith, and he that smootheth with the hammer him that smote the anvil."

Shall we follow their example, and from henceforth encourage one another instead of discouraging?

If I am asked how we are to get rid of discouragements, I can only say, as I have had to say of so many other wrong spiritual habits, we must give them up. It is never worth while to argue against discouragement. There is only one argument that can meet it, and that is the argument of God. When David was in the midst of what were perhaps the most discouraging moments of his life, when he had found his city burned, and his wives stolen, and he and the men with him had wept until they had no more power to weep; and when his men, exasperated at their misfortunes, spake of stoning him, then we are told, "But David encouraged himself in the Lord his God"; and the result was a magnificent victory, in which all that they had lost was more than restored to them. This always will be, and always must be the result of a courageous faith, because faith lays hold of the omnipotence of God.

Over and over the psalmist asks himself this question: "Why art thou cast down, O my soul, and why art thou disquieted within me?" And each time he answers himself with the argument of God: "Hope thou in God; for I shall yet praise him, who is the health of my countenance, and my God." He does not analyze his disquietude, or try to argue it away, but he turns at once to the Lord and by faith begins to praise Him.

It is the only way. Discouragement flies where faith appears; and, vice versa, faith flies when discouragement appears. We must choose between them, for they will not mix.

CHAPTER 14
THE SHOUT OF FAITH

"And when ye hear the sound of the trumpet, all the people shall shout with a great shout; and the wall of the city shall fall down flat, and the people shall ascend up, every man straight before him."

The shout of a steadfast faith is an experience that is in direct contrast to the moans of a wavering faith, and to the wails of discouraged hearts, both of which we have been considering in our last two chapters. In the history of the children of Israel there were many occasions when they indulged in these moanings and wailings and always to their sad undoing; but on one occasion at least they gave a magnificent shout of steadfast faith that brought them a glorious victory. And among the many "secrets of the Lord" that are discovered by the soul in its onward progress, I do not know of any that is more practically valuable than the secret of this shout of faith.

The occasion when it took place was at the time when the Israelites had just crossed the River Jordan, and were about to take possession of the Promised Land. God had said to Joshua, just before they crossed: "Now therefore arise, go over this Jordan, thou, and all this people, unto the land which I do give to them, even to the children of Israel. Every place that the sole of your foot shall treat upon, that have I given unto you, as I said unto Moses."

With this warrant they had crossed the river and entered into the land, no doubt expecting to get immediate possession. But at once upon their entrance they were brought face to face with one of those "cities great and walled up to heaven" that had so discouraged the heart of the spies forty years before. Well might they be appalled at the sight of it. To the eye of sense there seemed no possibility that they could ever conquer Jericho. They had no engines of warfare with which to attack it; and one can easily imagine the despair that must have seized upon them when they found themselves confronted with the walls and fortresses of such a city.

But the Lord had said to Joshua: "See, I have given into thine hand Jericho, and the king thereof, and the mighty men of valor." He had not said, "I will give," but, "I have given." It belonged to them already; but now they were called upon to take possession of it. It was as if a king should bestow an estate upon a courtier who was away in a foreign land, and this courtier should come back to take possession of it.

But the great question was, How? It looked impossible. But the Lord declared His plan; and after a few directions as to the order of their march, and the blowing of their trumpets, He closed with these strange words: "And it shall come to pass, that when they make a long blast with the ram's horn, and when ye hear the sound of the trumpet, all the people shall shout with a great shout; and the wall of the city shall fall down flat, and the people shall ascend up, every man straight before him" (Joshua 6:5).

Strange words but true, for it came to pass just as the Lord had said. On the seventh day, when the priests blew with the trumpets, Joshua said to the people, "Shout, for the Lord hath given you the city." "And it came to pass, when the people heard the sound of the trumpet, and the people shouted with a great shout, that the walls fell down flat, so that the people went up into the city, every man straight before him, and they took the city."

Now, no one can suppose for a moment that this shout caused the walls to fall. And yet the secret of their victory lay in just this shout. For it was the shout of a faith which dared, on the authority of God's Word alone, to claim a promised victory while as yet there were no signs of this victory being accomplished. And according to their faith God did unto them; so that, when they shouted, He made the walls to fall.

God had declared that He had given them the city, and faith reckoned this to be true. Unbelief might well have said, "It would be better not to shout until the walls do actually fall, for, should there be any failure about it, the men of Jericho will triumph, and we shall bring dishonor on the name of our God." But faith laughed at all such prudential considerations, and, confidently resting on God's Word, gave a shout of victory while yet to the eye of sense that victory seemed impossible. And long centuries afterward the Holy Ghost thus records this triumph of faith in Hebrews: "By faith the walls of Jericho fell down, after they were compassed about seven days."

> Faith, mighty faith, the promise sees
> And looks at that alone;
> Laughs at impossibilities,
> And cries, It shall be done.

Jehoshaphat is another example of this shout of faith. He was told that a great multitude was coming up against him from beyond the sea, and he realized that he and his people had "no might" against them, and he could not tell "what to do." He did not waste his time and his energies in trying to prepare engines of warfare or in arranging plans for a battle, but he at once "set himself to seek the Lord." He stood in the congregation of the people, and said: "O Lord God of our fathers, art not thou God in heaven? and rulest not thou over all the kingdoms of the heathen? And in thine hand is there not power and might, so that none is able to withstand thee? Art not thou our God, who didst drive out the inhabitants of this land before thy people Israel, and gavest it to the seed of Abraham, thy friend, forever? ... And now behold, the children of Ammon and Moab and Mount Seir ... come to cast us out of thy possession, which thou hast given us to inherit. O our God, wilt thou not judge them? For we have no might against this great company that cometh against us; neither know we what do do:

but our eyes are upon thee."

To this appeal the Lord answered through the mouth of His prophet in the following words: "Thus saith the Lord unto you, Be not afraid nor dismayed by reason of this great multitude, for the battle is not yours but God's ... Ye shall not need to fight in this battle; set yourselves, stand ye still, and see the salvation of the Lord with you. O Judah and Jerusalem, fear not, nor be dismayed; tomorrow go out against them; for the Lord will be with you."

Without a thought of doubt Jehoshaphat and the children of Israel believed the Word of the Lord and began at once to praise Him beforehand for the victory that they were sure was coming. The next morning they rose early and went out to meet their enemy; and Jehoshaphat, instead of exhorting them as an ordinary general would have done to look to their arms and to be brave in battle, simply called upon them to have a courageous faith. "Hear me, O Judah, and ye inhabitants of Jerusalem," he said, "believe in the Lord your God, so shall ye be established; believe his prophets, so shall ye prosper."

Jehoshaphat then consulted with the people; and as their faith proved equal to his own, they appointed singers to go out before the army to sing praises as they went forward to meet the enemy. And it came to pass that when they began to sing and to praise, the Lord began to set ambushments against the enemy, so that they smote one another; and when the children of Israel came to a watchtower in the wilderness, from which they could see the great multitude that had come up against them, "behold, they were dead bodies fallen to the earth, and none escaped."

By this wonderful method of warfare they were made even "more than conquerors"; for they were "three days in gathering the spoil, it was so much."

David's fight with Goliath is another example of this method of victory. To the eye of sense David had no chance whatever of conquering the mighty giant, who had been defying the armies of Israel. But David, looking with the eye of faith, could see the unseen divine forces that were fighting on his side, and when Saul said to him: "Thou art not able to go against this Philistine to fight with him, for thou art but a youth, and he a man of war from his youth,"

David stood firm in his faith; and, after recounting some of his past deliverances, said calmly: "The Lord that delivered me out of the paw of the lion, and out of the paw of the bear, he will deliver me out of the hand of this Philistine." Saul, partly convinced by this strong faith, said, "Go, and the Lord be with thee." He could not, however, quite give up all his trust in his own accustomed armor, and he armed David with a helmet of brass, and a coat of mail, and his own powerful sword, and David "assayed to go." But David soon found that he would not be able to fight in this sort of armor, and he put it off, and took instead the simple weapons that the Lord had blessed before — his staff, and his sling, and five smooth stones out of the brook; and thus equipped, he drew near to the giant.

When the giant saw the stripling who had come to fight him, he disdained him, and said contemptuously: "Come to me, and I will give thy flesh to the fowls of the air and the beasts of the field." And truly to the eye of sense it looked as though this must necessarily be the end of such an apparently unequal battle. But David's faith triumphed, and he shouted a shout of victory before even the battle had begun. "Thou comest to me," he said, "with a sword, and with a spear, and with a shield; but I come to thee in the name of the Lord of hosts, the God of the armies of Israel, whom thou defiest. This day will the Lord deliver thee into mine hand, and I will smite thee, and take thy head from thee ... that all the earth may know that there is a God in Israel. And all this assembly shall know that the Lord saveth not with sword and spear; for the battle is the Lord's, and he will give you into our hands."

In the face of such faith as this, what could even a giant do? Every word of that triumphant shout of victory was fulfilled; and the mighty enemy was delivered into the hands of the stripling he had disdained.

And so it will always be. Nothing can withstand the triumphant faith that links itself to omnipotence. For "this is the victory that overcometh the world, even our faith."

The secret of all successful warfare lies in this shout of faith. It is a secret incomprehensible to those who know nothing of the unseen divine power that waits on the demands of faith; a secret that must always seem, to those who do not understand it, the height of folly and imprudence.

We are all called to be "good soldiers of Jesus Christ," and to fight the "good fight of faith" against worse enemies than those which attacked the Israelites. Our enemies are interior, and the giant that defies us is the strength of our temptations and the powerlessness of our own strength to resist. It is a hard, and often a very discouraging fight, and many of God's children are weighed down under a dreary sense of apparently hopeless failure. They have sinned, and repented, and prayed, and resolved, and then sinned and repented again, so often, that they can see no hope of victory, and are ready to despair. They hate sin, and they love righteousness, and they long for victory, but the good that they would they do not, and the evil that they would not that they do. In the language of the apostle they find a law in their members warring against the law of their mind, and bringing them into captivity to the law of sin that is in their members. They know they ought to conquer, but they do not know how. And it is for these that this chapter is written. If they can but discover the secret of this shout of faith they will know how, for it is absolutely certain that it never fails to bring victory.

In John 16:33 our Lord reveals the ground of this triumphant shout of faith. "Be of good cheer," He says, "for I have overcome the world." Not "I will overcome," but "I have overcome." It is already done; and nothing remains but for us to enter into the power of it. Joshua did not say to the people, "Shout, for the Lord will give you the city," but "Shout, for he hath given it." It has always seemed to me that it must have drained all Joshua's will power to his lips to render it possible for him to make such a statement, in face of the fact that the walls of the city were at that very minute standing up as massive and as impregnable as ever. But God was a reality to Joshua, and he was not afraid to proclaim the victory that had been promised, even before it was accomplished.

There is a great difference between saying, "The Lord will give," and "The Lord hath given." A victory promised in the future may be hindered or prevented by a thousand contingencies, but a victory already accomplished cannot be gainsaid. And when our Lord assures us, not that He will overcome the world, but that He has already done so, He gives an assured foundation for a shout of the most triumphant victory. Henceforward the forces of sin are a defeated and demoralized foe; and, if we believe the words of Christ, we can meet them without fear, since we have been made more than conquerors through Him who loves us.

It is a well-known fact that as long as a defeated army can keep its defeat a secret, it can still make some show of resistance. But the moment it finds out that its defeat is known, it loses all heart and becomes utterly demoralized, and has no resource left but to retreat.

The secret then lies in this that we must meet sin, not as a foe that has yet to be conquered, but as one that has already been conquered. When Rahab helped the spies who had been sent by Joshua to escape from the king of Jericho, she made this confession: "I know that the Lord hath given you the land, and that your terror is fallen upon us, and that all the inhabitants of the land faint because of you." If we were gifted with eyes that could see the unseen kingdom of evil, I believe we also should find that a terror and faintness has fallen upon all the forces of that unknown region, and that they see in every man and woman of faith a sure and triumphant conqueror.

It is because we do not know this secret that we meet our spiritual enemies with such fear and trembling, and suffer such disastrous defeats.

A Christian I know, who had been fearfully beset by temptation against which she had seemed to struggle in vain, was told this secret by one who had discovered it. It brought conviction at once, and she went forth to a fresh battle with the assurance of an already accomplished victory. It is needless to say that she was victorious; and she said afterward that it seemed to her as if she could almost hear the voice of the tempter saying as he slunk away, "Alas! it is all up with me now. She has found out the secret. She knows that I am an already conquered foe, and I am afraid I shall never be able to overcome her again!"

We are told that "for this purpose the Son of God was manifested, that he might destroy the works of the devil"; and again: "Ye know that he was manifested to take away our sins; and in him is no sin"; and again: "Now once in the end of the world hath he appeared to put away sin by the sacrifice of himself." We must accept it as a fact, therefore, that sin is for us a conquered foe. And if our faith will only lay hold of this fact, reckoning sin to be dead to us, and ourselves to be dead to sin; and will dare, when we come in sight of temptation, to raise the shout of victory, we shall surely find as the Israelites did that every wall will fall down flat, and that a pathway will be opened straight before us to take the city!

Our enemies are giants now just as truly as they were in Israel's day; and cities as great as Jericho, with walls as high, confront us in our heavenly pathway. Like the Israelites of old, we have no human weapons with which to conquer them. Our armor, like theirs, must be the "armor of God." Our shield is the same invisible shield of faith that protected them; and our sword must be, as theirs was, the sword of the Spirit which is the Word, that is, the promises and declarations of God. When our faith puts on this "armor of God," and lays hold of this "sword of the Spirit," and we confront our enemy with a shout of undaunted faith, we cannot fail to conquer the mightiest giant, or to take the strongest city.

But alas! how different is the usual method of our Christian warfare. Instead of a triumphant shout of victory, we meet our temptations with feeble resolutions, or with futile arguments, or with halfhearted self-upbraiding, or, failing all else, with despairing prayers, "O Lord, save me!" we cry; "O Lord, deliver me!" And when no deliverance has come, and the temptation has swept aside all our arguments and all our resolutions, and we have been grievously defeated, then we have cried out in our despair that God has failed us, and that there is for us no truth in the apostle's declaration that with every temptation there is a way of escape that we may be able to bear it. This is the usual and the unsuccessful way of meeting temptation, as many of us know to our cost. But what we ought to do is very different. We must recognize it as a fact that sin is a conquered foe, and must meet it, therefore, with a shout of victory instead of with a cry for help. Where we prayed before that the Lord would save us, we must make now the assertion that He does save us, and that he saves us now. We must add the little letter *s* to the word *save,* and make it the present instead of the future tense.

The walls may look as high and as immovable as ever; and prudence may say it is not safe to shout until the victory is actually won. But the faith that can shout in the midst of the sorest stress of temptation, "Jesus saves me; He saves me now!" such a faith will be sure to win a glorious and a speedy victory. Many of God's children have tried this plan, and have found it to work far beyond even their expectations. Temptations have come in upon them like a flood — temptations to irritability, or to wicked thoughts, or to bitterness of spirit, or to a thousand other things, and they have seen their danger; and their fears and their feelings have declared that there was no hope of escape. But their faith has laid hold of this grand fact that Christ has conquered; and they have fixed their gaze on the unseen power of God's salvation, and have given their shout of victory, "The Lord saves! He saves me now! I am more than conqueror through Him that loves me!" And the result is always a glorious victory.

It may sometimes seem so impossible that the Lord can or does save that the words will not say themselves inside, but have to be said aloud, forcing one's lips to utter them over and over, shutting one's eyes and closing one's ears against every suggestion of doubt no matter how plausible it may seem. These declarations of faith often seem untrue at first, so apparently real are the seen reasons for doubt and discouragement. But the unseen facts are truer than the seen, and if the faith that lays hold of them is steadfastly persisted in, they never fail in the end to prove themselves to be the very truth of God. "According to our faith" it always must be unto us, sooner or later, and when we shout the shout of faith, the Lord invariably gives the victory of faith.

I knew a Christian man who had entered upon this life of faith. He had naturally a violent temper and when about his daily work among his ungodly companions was sorely beset with temptations to give way to it. He knew it was wrong, and he struggled valiantly against it, but all in vain. Finally, one morning on his way to work he called in despair at the house of his Christian teacher and told him his difficulties. After explaining the suddenness of the temptations that came upon him, and the lack of time even to pray for help before he was overcome, he said, "Now can you tell me of any short road to victory; something that I can lay hold of just at the needed moment?''

"Yes," replied the minister; "when the temptation comes, at once lift up your heart to the Lord, and by faith claim the promised victory. Shout the shout of faith, and the temptation will flee before you."

After a little explanation of the glorious fact that sin is an already conquered foe, the man seemed to understand and went on his way to take his place in the ranks with his fellow men at the station where they were engaged in hauling freight. As usual he was met by taunts and sneers; and in addition he found that they had jostled him out of his rightful place in the ranks. The temptation to anger was almost overwhelming, but, folding his arms, he said inwardly over and over, "Jesus saves me; He saves me now!" At once his heart was filled with peace, and the victory was complete. Again he was tried; a heavy box was so rolled as to fall on his foot badly injuring him, and again he folded his arms and repeated his shout of victory, and at once all was calm. And so the day passed on. Trials and temptations abounded, but his triumphant shout carried him safely through them all, and the fiery darts of the enemy were all quenched by the shield of faith which he continually lifted up. Nighttime found him more than conqueror through Him who loved him; and even his fellow carmen were forced to own the reality and the beauty of a religion that could so triumph over their aggravating assaults.

The psalmist, after telling of the enemies who were daily trying to swallow him up, declared triumphantly: "When I cry unto thee, then shall mine enemies turn back: this I know; for God is for me."

Dear reader, do you know what the psalmist knew? Do you know that God is for you, and that He will cause your enemies to turn back? If you do, then go out to meet your temptations, singing a song of triumph as you go. Meet your very next temptation in this way. At its first approach being to give thanks for the victory. Claim continually that you are more than conqueror through Him that loves you, and refuse to be daunted by any foe. Shout the shout of faith with Joshua, and Jehoshaphat, and David, and Paul; and I can assure you that when you shout, the Lord will "set ambushments," and all your enemies shall fall down dead before you.

CHAPTER 15

THANKSGIVING VERSUS COMPLAINING

*"In everything give thanks, for this is the will of God
in Christ Jesus concerning you."*

Thanksgiving or complaining — these words express two contrastive attitudes of the souls of God's children in regard to His dealings with them; and they are more powerful than we are inclined to believe in furthering or frustrating His purposes of comfort and peace toward us. The soul that gives thanks can find comfort in everything; the soul that complains can find comfort in nothing.

God's command is, "In everything give thanks"; and the command is emphasized by the declaration, "for this is the will of God in Christ Jesus concerning you." It is an actual and positive command; and if we want to obey God, we have simply got to give thanks in everything. There is no getting around it.

But a great many Christians have never realized this; and although they may be familiar with the command, they have always looked upon it as a sort of counsel of perfection to which mere flesh and blood could never be expected to attain. And they, unconsciously to themselves perhaps, change the wording of the passage to make it say "be resigned" instead of "give thanks," and "in a few things" instead of "in everything," and they leave out altogether the words, "for this is the will of God in Christ Jesus concerning you."

If brought face to face with the actual wording of the command, such Christians will say, "Oh, but it is an impossible command. If everything came directly from God, one might do it perhaps, but most things come through human sources, and often are the result of sin, and it would not be possible to give thanks for these." To this I answer that it is true we cannot always give thanks for the things themselves, but we can always give thanks for God's love and care in the things. He may not have ordered them, but He is in them somewhere, and He is in them to compel, even the most grievous, to work together for our good.

The "second causes" of the wrong may be full of malice and wickedness, but faith never sees second causes. It sees only the hand of God behind the second causes. They are all under His control, and not one of them can touch us except with His knowledge and permission. The thing itself that happens cannot perhaps be said to be the will of God, but by the time its effects reach us they have become God's will for us, and must be accepted as from His hands.

The story of Joseph is an illustration of this. Nothing could have seemed more entirely an act of sin, or more utterly contrary to the will of God than his being sold to the Ishmaelites by his wicked brethren; and it would not have seemed possible for Joseph, when he was being carried off into slavery in Egypt, to give thanks. And yet, if he had known the end from the beginning, he would have been filled with thanksgiving. The fact of his having been sold into slavery was the direct doorway to the greatest triumphs and blessings of his life. And, at the end, Joseph himself could say to his wicked brethren: "As for you, ye thought evil against me, but God meant it unto good." To the eye of sense it was Joseph's wicked brethren who had sent him into Egypt, but Joseph, looking at it with the eye of faith, said, "God did send me."

We can all remember, I think, similar instances in our own lives when God has made the wrath of man to praise Him, and has caused even the hardest trials to work together for our greatest good. I recollect once in my own life when a trial was brought upon me by another person, at which I was filled with bitter rebellion and could not see in it from beginning to end anything to be thankful for. But, as it was in the case of Joseph, that very trial worked out for me the richest blessings and the greatest triumphs of my whole life; and in the end I was filled with thanksgiving for the very things that had caused me such bitter rebellion before. If only I had had faith enough to give thanks at first, how much sorrow would have been spared me.

But I am afraid that the greatest heights to which most Christians in their shortsightedness seem able to rise is to strive after resignation to things they cannot alter, and to seek for patience to endure them. And the result is that thanksgiving is almost an unknown exercise among the children of God; and, instead of giving thanks in everything, many of them hardly give thanks in anything. If the truth were told, Christians as a body must be acknowledged to be but a thankless set. It is considered in the world a very discourteous thing for one man to receive benefits from another man and fail to thank him, and I cannot see why it is not just as discourteous a thing not to thank God. And yet we find people who would not for the world omit an immediate note of thanks upon the reception of any gift, however trifling, from a human friend, but who have never given God real thanks for any one of the innumerable benefits He has been showering upon them all their long lives.

Moreover, I am afraid a great many not only fail to give thanks, but they do exactly the opposite, and allow themselves instead to complain and murmur about God's dealings with them. Instead of looking out for His goodness, they seem to delight in picking out His shortcomings, and think they show a spirit of discernment in criticizing His laws and His ways. We are told that "when the people complained, it displeased the Lord"; but we are tempted to think that our special complaining, because it is spiritual complaining, cannot displease Him since it is a pious sort of complaining, and is a sign of greater zeal on our part, and of deeper spiritual insight than is possessed by the ordinary Christian.

But complaining is always alike, whether it is on the temporal or the spiritual plane. It always has in it the element of fault-finding. Webster says to complain means to make a charge or an accusation. It is not merely disliking the thing we have to bear, but it contains the element of finding fault with the agency that lies behind it. And if we will carefully examine the true inwardness of our complainings, I think we shall generally find they are founded on a subtle fault-finding with God. We secretly feel as if He were to blame somehow; and, almost unconsciously to ourselves, we make mental charges against Him.

On the other hand, thanksgiving always involves praise of the giver. Have you ever noticed how much we are urged in the Bible to "praise the Lord"? It seemed to be almost the principal part of the worship of the Israelites. "Praise ye the Lord, for the Lord is good: sing praises to his name, for it is pleasant." This is the continual refrain of everything all through the Bible. I believe, if we should count up, we would find that there are more commands given and more examples set for the giving of thanks "always for all things" than for the doing or the leaving undone of anything else.

It is very evident from the whole teaching of Scripture that the Lord loves to be thanked and praised just as much as we like it. I am sure that it gives Him real downright pleasure, just as it does us; and that our failure to thank Him for His "good and perfect gifts" wounds His loving heart, just as our hearts are wounded when our loved ones fail to appreciate the benefits we have so enjoyed bestowing upon them. What a joy it is to us to receive from our friends an acknowledgement of their thanksgiving for our gifts, and is it not likely that it is a joy to the Lord also?

When the apostle is exhorting the Ephesian Christians to be "followers of God as dear children," one of the exhortations he gives in connection with being filled with the Spirit is this: "Giving thanks always for all things unto God and the Father, in the name of our Lord Jesus Christ." "Always for all things" is a very sweeping expression, and it is impossible to suppose it can be whittled down to mean only the few and scanty thanks, which seem all that many Christians manage to give. It must mean, I am sure, that there can be nothing in our lives which has not in it somewhere a cause for thanksgiving, and that, no matter who or what may be the channel to convey it, everything contains for us a hidden blessing from God.

The apostle tells us that "every creature of God is good,

and nothing to be refused, if it be received with thanksgiving." But it is very hard for us to believe things are good when they do not look so. Often the things God sends into our lives look like curses instead of blessings; and those who have no eyes that can see below surfaces judge by the outward seemings only and never see the blessed realities beneath.

How many "good and perfect gifts" we must have had during our lives, which we have looked upon only as curses, and for which we have never returned one thought of thanks! And for how many gifts also, which we have even acknowledged to be good, have we thanked ourselves, or our friends, or our circumstances, without once looking behind the earthly givers to thank the heavenly Giver, from whom in reality they all come! It is as if we should thank the messengers who bring us our friends' gifts, but should never send any word of thanks to our friends themselves.

But, even when we realize that things come directly from God, we find it very hard to give thanks for what hurts us. Do we not, however, all know what it is to thank a skillful physician for his treatment of our diseases, even though that treatment may have been very severe. And surely we should no less give thanks to our divine Physician, when He is obliged to give us bitter medicine to cure our spiritual diseases, or to perform a painful operation to rid us of something that harms.

But instead of thanking Him we complain against Him; although we generally direct our complaints, not against the divine Physician himself who has ordered our medicine, but against the "bottle" in which He has sent it. This "bottle" is usually some human being, whose unkindness or carelessness, or neglect, or cruelty has caused our suffering; but who has been after all only the instrumentality or "second cause" that God has used for our healing.

Good common sense tells us that it would be folly to rail against the bottles in which the medicines, prescribed by our earthly physicians, come to us; and it is equal folly to rail against the "second causes" that are meant to teach us the lessons our souls need to learn.

When the children of Israel found themselves wandering in the wilderness, they "murmured against Moses and Aaron," and complained that they had brought them forth into the wilderness to kill them with hunger. But in reality their complaining was against God, for it was really He who had brought them there, and not Moses and Aaron, who were only the "second causes." And the psalmist in recounting the story afterward called this murmuring against Moses and Aaron a "speaking against God." Divine history takes no account of second causes, but goes directly to the real cause behind them.

We may settle it, therefore, that all complaining is at the bottom "speaking against God," whether we are conscious of it or not. We may think, as the Israelites did, that our discomforts and deprivations have come from human hands only, and may therefore feel at liberty to "murmur against" the second causes which have, we may think, brought about our trials. But God is the great Cause behind all second causes. The second causes are only the instrumentalities that He uses; and when we murmur against these, we are really murmuring, not against the instrumentalities, but against God Himself. Second causes are powerless to act, except by God's permission; and what He permits becomes really His arranging. The psalmist tells us that when the Lord heard the complainings of His people "He was wroth," and His anger came up against them "because they believed not in God, and trusted not in his salvation." And, at the bottom, all complainings mean just this, that we do not believe in God, and do not trust in His salvation.

The psalmist says: "I will praise the name of God with a song, and magnify him with thanksgiving. This also shall please the Lord better than an ox or bullock that hath horns and hoofs." A great many people seem quite ready and willing to offer up an "ox or a bullock," or some great sacrifice to the Lord, but never seem to have realized that a little genuine praise and thanksgiving offered to Him now and then would "please him better" than all their great sacrifices made in His cause.

As I said before, the Bible is full of this thought from beginning to end. Over and over it is called a "sacrifice of thanksgiving," showing that it is as really an act of religious worship, as is any other religious act. In fact, the "sacrifice of thanksgiving" was one of the regular sacrifices ordained by God in the Book of Leviticus. "Oh that men would praise the Lord for his goodness, and for his wonderful works to the children of men! And let them sacrifice the sacrifices of thanksgiving, and declare his works with rejoicing." By Him, therefore, let us offer the sacrifice of praise to God continually, that is, the fruit of our lips, giving thanks to His name.

It is such an easy thing to offer the "sacrifice of thanksgiving," that one would suppose everybody would be keen to do it. But somehow the contrary seems to be the case; and if the prayers of Christians were all to be noted down for any one single day, I fear it would be found that with them, as it was with the ten lepers who had been cleansed, nine out of every ten had offered no genuine thanks at all. Our Lord Himself was gireved at these ungrateful lepers, and said: "Were there not ten cleansed? But where are the nine? There are not found that returned to give glory to God, save this stranger." Will He have to ask the same question regarding any of us? We have often, it may be, wondered at the ingratitude of those nine cleansed lepers, but what about our own ingratitude? Do we not continually pass by blessings innumerable without notice, and instead fix our eyes on what we feel to be our trials and our losses, and think and talk about these, until our whole horizon is filled with them, and we almost begin to think we have no blessings at all?

We can judge of how this must grieve the Lord by our own feelings. A child who complains about the provision the parent has made wounds that parent's heart often beyond words. Some people are always complaining, nothing ever pleases them, and no kindness seems ever to be appreciated. We know how uncomfortable the society of such people makes us; and we know, on the contrary, how life is brightened by the presence of one who never complains, but who finds something to be pleased with in all that comes. I believe far more misery than we imagine is caused in human hearts by the grumblings of those they love; and I believe also that woundings, we never dream of, are given to the heart of our Father in Heaven by the continual murmuring of His children.

How often is it despairingly said of fretful, complaining spirits upon whom every care and attention has been lavished, "Will nothing ever satisfy them?" And how often must God turn away, grieved by our complainings, when His love has been lavished upon us in untold blessings. I have sometimes thought that if we could but realize this, we would check our inordinate grief over even the trials that come from the death of those we love, and would try, for His dear sake, to be cheerful and content even in our lonely and bereft condition.

I remember hearing of a dear girl who was obliged to undergo a serious and very painful treatment for some disease, and the doctors had dreaded the thought of her groans and outcries. But to their amazement not even a moan escaped her lips, and all the time she smiled at her father who was present, and uttered only words of love and tenderness. The doctors could not understand it, and when the worst was over one of them asked how it could have been. "Ah," she said, "I knew how much my father loved me, and I knew how he would suffer if he saw that I suffered, so I tried to hide my suffering; and I smiled to make him think I did not mind."

Can any of us do this for our heavenly Father?

Job was a great complainer; and we may perhaps think, as we read his story, that if ever anyone had good cause for complaining, he had. His circumstances seemed to be full of hopeless misery. "My soul is weary of my life; I will leave my complaint upon myself; I will speak in the bitterness of my soul. I will say unto God, Do not condemn me; show me wherefore thou contendest with me. Is it good unto thee that thou shouldest oppress, that thou shouldest despise the work of thine hands?"

We can hardly wonder at Job's complaint. And yet could he but have seen the divine side of all his troubles, he would have known that they were permitted in the tenderest love, and were to bring him a revelation of God such as he could have had by no other means. Could he have seen that this was to be the outcome he would not have uttered a single complaint, but would have given triumphant thanks for the trials which were to bring him such a glorious fruition. And could we but see, in our heaviest trials, the end from the beginning, I am sure that thanksgiving would take the place of complaining in every case.

The children of Israel were always complaining about something. They complained because they had no water; and when water was supplied they complained that it was bitter to their taste. And we likewise complain because the spiritual water we have to drink seems bitter to our taste. Our souls are athirst, and we do not like the supply that seems to be provided. Our experiences do not quench our thirst, our religious exercises seem dull and unsatisfying; we feel ourselves to be in a dry and thirsty land where no water is. We have turned from the "Fountain of living waters," and then we complain because the cisterns we have hewed out for ourselves hold no water.

The Israelites complained about their food. They had so little confidence in God that they were afraid they would die of starvation; and then when the heavenly manna was provided they complained again because they "loathed such light food." And we also complain about our spiritual food. Like the Israelites, we have so little confidence in God that we are always afraid we shall die of spiritual starvation. We complain because our preacher does not feed us, or because our religious privileges are very scanty, or because we are not supplied with the same spiritual fare as others are, who seem to us more highly favored; and we covet their circumstances or their experiences. We have asked God to feed us, and then our souls "loathe" the food He gives, and we think it is too "light" to sustain or strengthen us. We have asked for bread, and we complain that He has given a stone.

But, if we only knew it, the provision our divine Master has made of spiritual drink and spiritual food is just that which is best for us, and is that for which we would be the most thankful if we knew. The amazing thing is that we cannot believe now, without waiting for the end, that the Shepherd knows what pasture is best for His sheep. Surely if we did, our hearts would be filled with thanksgiving and our mouths with praise even in the wilderness.

Jonah was a wonderful illustration of this. His prayer of thanksgiving out of the "belly of hell" is a tremendous lesson. "I have cried by reason of mine affliction unto the Lord, and he heard me; out of the belly of hell cried I, and thou heardest my voice. For thou hadst cast me into the deep, in the midst of the sea: and the floods compassed me about; all thy billows and thy waves passed over me ... But I will sacrifice unto thee with a voice of thanksgiving; I will pay that I have vowed. Salvation is of the Lord.''

No depth of misery, not even the ''belly of hell,'' is too great for the sacrifice of thanksgiving. We cannot, it is true, give thanks for the misery, but we can give thanks to the Lord in the misery, just as Jonah did. No matter what our trouble, the Lord is in it somewhere; and, of course, being there, He is there to help and bless us. Therefore, when our ''souls faint within us'' because of our troubles, we have only to remember this, and to thank Him for His presence and His love.

It is not because things are good that we are to thank the Lord, but because He is good. We are not wise enough to judge as to things, whether they are really, in their essence, joys or sorrows. But we always know that the Lord is good, and that His goodness makes it absolutely certain that everything He provides or permits must be good; and must therefore be something for which we would be heartily thankful, if only we could see it with His eyes.

In a little tract called ''Mrs. Pickett's Missionary Box,'' a poor woman, who had never done anything but complain all her life long, and who, consequently, had got to thinking that she had no benefits for which to give thanks, received a missionary box with the words written on it: ''What shall I render unto the Lord for all His benefits toward me?'' And she was asked by her niece, who believed in being thankful, to put a penny into the box for every benefit she could discover in her life. I will let her tell her own story.

'''Great benefits I have!' says I, standing with my arms akimbo, an' lookin' that box all over. 'Guess the heathen won't get much out of me at that rate.' An' I jest made up my mind I would keep count, jest to show myself how little I did have. 'Them few pennies won't break me,' I thought, and I really seemed to kinder enjoy thinkin' over the hard times I had.

''Well, the box sot there all that week, an' I used to say it must be kinder lonesome with nothin' in it; for not a penny went into it until next missionary meetin' day. I was sittin' on the back steps gettin' a breath of fresh air, when Mary came home, an' sat down alongside o' me an' began to tell me about the meetin', an' it was all about Injy an' the widders there, poor creturs, an' they bein' abused, an' starved, an' not let to think for themselves — you know all about it better'n I do! — an' before I thought I up an' said —

"'Well, if I be a widder, I'm thankful I'm where I kin earn my own livin', an' no thanks to nobody, an' no one to interfere!'

"Then Mary, she laughed an' said there was my fust benefit. Well, that sorter tickled me, for I thought a woman must be pretty hard up for benefits when she had to go clear off to Injy to find them, an' I dropped in one penny, an' it rattled round a few days without any company. I used to shake it every time I passed the shelf, an' the thought of them poor things in Injy kep' a comin' up before me, an' I really was glad when I got a new boarder for me best room, an' felt as if I'd oughter put in another. An' next meetin', Mary she told me about China, an' I thought about that till I put in another because I warn't a Chinese. An' all the while I felt kinder proud of how little there was in that box. Then one day, when I got a chance to turn a little penny sellin' eggs, which I warn't in the habit of, Mary brought the box in, where I was countin' of my money, an' says —

"'A penny for your benefit, Aunt Mirandy.'

"An' I says, 'This ain't the Lord's benefit.'

"An' she answered, 'If 'tain't His, whose is it?' An' she begun to hum over somethin' out of one of the poetry books that she was always a readin' of —

> 'God's grace is the only grace,
> And all grace is the grace of God.'

"Well, I dropped in my penny, an' them words kep' ringin' in my ears, till I couldn't help puttin' more to it, on account of some other things I never thought of callin' the Lord's benefits before. An' by that time, what with Mary's tellin' me about them meetin's, an' me most always findin' somethin' to put in a penny for, to be thankful that I warn't it, an' what with gettin' interested about it all, and sorter searchin' round a little now and then to think of somethin' or other to put a penny in for, there really come to be quite a few pennies in the box, an' it didn't rattle near so much when I shook it.''

There is a psalm which I call our Benefit Psalm. It is Psalm 103, and it recounts some of the benefits the Lord has bestowed upon us, and urges us not to forget them. "Bless the Lord, O my soul, and forget not all his benefits.'' Our dear sister's Benefit Box had taught her something of the meaning of this psalm. All her life she had been forgetting the benefits the Lord had bestowed upon her, but now she was beginning to remember them.

Have we begun to remember ours?

If during the past year we had kept count of those benefits for which we had actually given thanks, how many pennies, I wonder, would our boxes have contained?

We sometimes sing at mission meetings a hymn of thanksgiving, with the chorus, "Count your many blessings, name them one by one, and it will surprise you what the Lord has done.'' And sometimes I have wondered whether any of us who were singing it so heartily had ever kept the slightest record of our blessings, or even in fact knew that we had any.

For the trouble is that very often God's gifts come to us wrapped up in such rough coverings that we are tempted to reject them as worthless; or the messengers who bring them come in the guise of enemies, and we want to shut the door against them, and not give them entrance. But we lose far more than we know when we reject even the most unlikely.

> Evil is only the slave of good,
>   And sorrow the servant of joy:
> And the soul is mad that refuses food
>   From the meanest in God's employ.

We are commanded to enter into His gates with thanksgiving, and into His courts with praise, and I am convinced that the giving of thanks is the key that opens these gates more quickly than anything else. Try it, dear reader. The next time you feel dead, cold, and low-spirited begin to praise and thank the Lord. Enumerate to yourself the benefits He has bestowed upon you, thank Him heartily for each one, and see if your spirits do not begin to rise, and your heart get warmed up.

Sometimes it may be that you feel too disheartened to pray; then try giving thanks instead; and, before you know it, you will find yourself "glad" in the multitude of His loving-kindnesses and His tender mercies.

One of my friends told me that her little boy one night flatly refused to say his prayers. He said there was not a single thing in all the world he wanted, and he did not see what was the good of asking for things that he did not want. A happy thought came to his mother as she said, "Well, Charlie, suppose then we give thanks for all the things you have got." The idea pleased the child, and he very willingly knelt down and began to give thanks. He thanked God for his marbles, and for a new top that had just been given him, and for his strong legs that could run so fast, and that he was not blind like a little boy he knew, and for his kind father and mother, and for his nice bed, and for one after another of his blessings, until the list grew so long that at last he said he believed he would never get done. And when finally they rose from their knees, he said to his mother, with his face shining with happiness, "Oh, Mother, I never knew before how perfectly splended God is!" And I believe, if we sometimes followed the example of this little boy, we too would find out, as never before, the goodness of our God.

It is very striking to notice how much thanksgiving had to do with the building of the Temple. When they had collected the treasures for the Temple, David gave thanks to the Lord for enabling them to do it. When the Temple was finished, they gave thanks again. And then a wonderful thing happened, for it came to pass as the trumpeters and singers were as one to make one sound to be heard in praising and thanking the Lord ... that then the house was filled with a cloud, even the house of the Lord, so that the priests could not stand to minister by reason of the cloud; for the glory of the Lord had filled the house of God. When the people praised and gave thanks, then the house was filled with the glory of the Lord. And we may be sure that the reason our hearts are not oftener filled with the "glory of the Lord" is because we do not often enough make our voices to be heard in praising and thanking Him.

If the giving of thanks is the way to open the gates of the

Lord, complaining on the other hand closes these gates.
Jude quotes a prophecy of Enoch's concerning murmurers:
"The Lord cometh," he says, "to execute judgment upon
all, and to convince all that are ungodly among them ... of
all their hard speeches which ungodly sinners have spoken
against him. These are murmurers, complainers, walking
after their own lusts."

People who are "murmurers" and "complainers" make in
their complainings more "hard speeches" against the Lord
than they would like to own, or than they will care at the last
day to face. And it is not to be wondered that the judgment of
God, instead of the "glory of God," is the result.

I wish I had room to quote all the passages in the Bible
about giving thanks and praises to the Lord. It is safe to say
that there are hundreds and hundreds of them; and it is an
amazing thing how they can have been so persistently ignored. I beg of you to read the last seven psalms, and see
what you think. They are simply full to overflowing with a
list of the things for which the psalmist calls upon us to give
thanks; all of them are things relating to the character and
the ways of God, which we dare not dispute. They are not
for the most part private blessings of our own, but are the
common blessings that belong to all humanity, and that
contain within themselves every private blessing we can
possibly need. But they are blessings which we continually
forget, because we take them for granted, hardly noticing
their existence, and never give thanks for them.

But the psalmist knew how to count his many blessings
and name them one by one, and he would have us to do
likewise. Try it, dear reader, and you will indeed be surprised to see what the Lord has done. Go over these psalms
verse by verse, and blessing by blessing, and see if, like the
little boy of our story, you are not made to confess that you
never knew before "how perfectly splendid God is."

The last verse of the Book of Psalms, taken in connection
with the vision of John in the Book of Revelation, is very
significant. The psalmist says, "Let everything that hath
breath praise the Lord." And in the Book of Revelation,
John, who declares himself to be our brother and our com-
panion in tribulation, tells us that he heard this being done.
"And every creature which is in heaven, and on the earth,

and under the earth, and such as are in the sea, and all that are in them, heard I saying, Blessing, and honor, and glory, and power, be unto him that sitteth upon the throne, and unto the Lamb, forever and ever."

The time for universal praise is sure to come some day. Let us begin to do our part now.

I heard once of a discontented, complaining man who, to the great surprise of his friends, became bright, and happy, and full of thanksgiving. After watching him for a little while, and being convinced that the change was permanent, they asked him what had happened. "Oh," he replied, "I have changed my residence. I used to live in Grumbling Lane, but now I have moved into Thanksgiving Square, and I find that I am so rich in blessings that I am always happy."

Shall we each one make this move now?

CHAPTER 16

CONFORMED TO THE IMAGE OF CHRIST

"For whom he did foreknow, he also did predestinate to be conformed to the image of his Son, that he might be the firstborn among many brethren."

God's ultimate purpose in our creation was that we should finally be "conformed to the image of Christ." Christ was to be the firstborn among many brethren, and His brethren were to be like Him. All the discipline and training of our lives is with this end in view; and God has implanted in every human heart a longing, however unformed and unexpressed, after the best and highest it knows.

Christ is the pattern of what each one of us is to be when finished. We are "predestinated" to be conformed to His image, in order that He might be the firstborn among many brethren. We are to be "partakers of the divine nature" with Christ; we are to be filled with the spirit of Christ; we are to share His resurrection life, and to walk as He walked. We are to be one with Him, as He is one with the Father; and the glory God gave to Him, He is to give to us. And when all this is brought to pass, then, and not until then, will God's purpose in our creation be fully accomplished, and we stand forth "in his image and after his likeness."

Our likeness to His image is an accomplished fact in the mind of God, but we are, so to speak, in the manufactory as yet, and the great master Workman is at work upon us. "It doth not yet appear what we shall be: but we know that, when he shall appear, we shall be like him; for we shall see him as he is."

And so it is written: "The first man Adam was made a living soul; the last Adam was made a quickening spirit. Howbeit that was not first which is spiritual, but that which is natural; and afterward that which is spiritual. The first man is of the earth, earthy; the second man is the Lord from heaven. As is the earthy, such are they also that are earthy; and as is the heavenly, such are they also that are heavenly. And as we have borne the image of the earthy, we shall also bear the image of the heavenly."

It is deeply interesting to see that this process, which was begun in Genesis, is declared to be completed in Revelation, where the "one like unto the Son of man" gave to John this significant message to the overcomers: "Him that overcometh will I make a pillar in the temple of my God; and he shall go no more out: and I will write upon him the name of my God, and the name of the city of my God which is new Jerusalem, which cometh down out of heaven from my God: and I will write upon him my new name." Since *name* always means character in the Bible, this message can only mean that at last God's purpose is accomplished, and the spiritual evolution of man is completed — he has been made, what God intended from the first, so truly into His likeness and image, as to merit having written upon him the name of God!

Words fail before such a glorious destiny as this! But our Lord foreshadows it in His wonderful prayer when He asks for His brethren that "they all may be one; as thou, Father, art in me, and I in thee, that they also may be one in us: that the world may believe that thou hast sent me. And the glory which thou gavest me I have given them: that they may be one even as we are one. I in them, and thou in me, that they may be made perfect in one." Could oneness be closer or more complete?

Paul also foreshadows this glorious consummation when he declares that if we suffer with Christ we shall also be glorified together with Him, and when he asserts that the "sufferings of this present time are not worthy to be compared with the glory that shall be revealed in us." The whole Creation awaits for the revealing of this glory, for Paul goes on to say that the "earnest expectation of the creature waiteth for the manifestation of the sons of God." And he adds finally: "And not only they, but ourselves also, which have the first fruits of the Spirit, even we ourselves groan within ourselves, waiting for the adoption, to wit, the redemption of our body."

In view of such a glorious destiny, at which I dare not do more than hint, shall we not cheerfully welcome the processes, however painful they may be, by which we are to reach it? And shall we not strive eagerly and earnestly to be "laborers together with God" in helping to bring it about? He is the great master Builder, but He wants our co-operation in building up the fabric of our characters, and He exhorts us to take heed how we build. We are all of us at every moment of our lives engaged in this building. Sometimes we build with gold, and silver, and precious stones, and sometimes we build with wood, and hay, and stubble. And we are solemnly warned that every man's work is to be made manifest, "for the day shall declare it, because it shall be revealed by fire." There is no escaping this. We cannot hope, when that day comes, to conceal our wood, and hay, and stubble, however successflly we may have managed to do so beforehand.

To my mind there is no more solemn passage in the whole Bible than the one in Galatians which says: "Be not deceived: God is not mocked: for whatsoever a man soweth, that shall he also reap. For he that soweth to the flesh shall of the flesh reap corruption; but he that soweth to the Spirit, shall of the Spirit reap life everlasting." It is the awful inevitableness of this that is so awe-inspiring. It is far worse than any arbitrary punishment; for punishment can sometimes be averted, but there is no possibility of altering the working of a natural law such as this.

In a Catechism I saw were the following questions and answers:

Q. What is the reward for generosity?
A. More generosity.
Q. What is the punishment for meanness?
A. More meanness.

No Catechism ever spoke more truly. We all of us know it for ourselves. In the parable of the talents our Lord illustrates this inevitable law. The condemnation on the unfaithful servant may have sometimes seemed to us unfair, but it was only the reaping of what the servant had sowed. "Take therefore the talent from him and give it unto him which hath ten talents. For unto every one that hath shall be given, and he shall have abundance: but from him that hath not, shall be taken away even that which he hath." This is no arbitrary pronouncement, but is simply a revelation of the inherent nature of things from which none of us can escape.

But in order to be laborers together with God, we must not only build with His materials but also by His processes, and of these we are often very ignorant. Our idea of building is of hard laborious work done in the sweat of our brow; but God's idea is far different. Paul tells us what it is. "We all," he says, "with open face beholding as in a glass the glory of the Lord, are changed into the same image from glory to glory, even as by the Spirit of the Lord." Our work is to "behold," and as we behold the Lord effects the marvelous transformation, and we are "changed into the same image by the Spirit of the Lord." This means, of course, to behold not in our earthly sense of merely looking at a thing, but in the divine sense of really seeing the thing. We are to behold with our spiritual eyes the glory of the Lord, and are to continue beholding it. The glory of the Lord does not mean, however, a great shine or halo. The real glory of the Lord is the glory of what He is and of what He does — the glory of character. And it is this we are to behold.

Let me give an illustration. Someone offends me, and I am tempted to get angry and retaliate. But I look at Christ and think of what He would have done, and dwell upon the thought of His gentleness and meekness and His love for the offending one; and, as I look, I begin to want to be like Him, and I ask in faith that I may be made a "partaker of his nature," and anger and revenge die out of my heart, and I love my enemy and long to serve him.

It is by this sort of beholding Christ that we are to be changed into His image; and the nearer we keep to Him the more rapid the change will be.

I have heard of a wonderful mirror known to science, which is called the parabolic mirror. It is a hollow cone lined with a mirror all over its inside surface. It possesses the power of focusing rays of light in different degrees of intensity in proportion to the increasing nearness to its meeting point at the top end of the cone, the power being more and more intense as the terminal point is approached. It has been discovered by science that at a certain stage in this advance toward the interior point where all the sides of the mirror meet in absolute oneness, the power of the focus concentrates all the light-giving properties of the sun's rays into such an intense brilliancy, as to make visible things never before discerned by the human eye, rendering even flesh transparent, and enabling us to see through the outer covering of our bodies to the inner operations beneath.

Advancing a little farther into the interior of our mirror, the heat properties of the sun's rays are so concentrated as to generate a heat sufficient to melt iron in sixteen seconds, and to dissipate in fourteen seconds the alloy of gold, leaving only the solid globule of the pure metal.

Advancing farther still, the photographing properties of the sunlight are so concentrated as to impress an ineffaceable image of the mirror upon anything that is passed for only one second through the focus.

Advancing still farther, nearly to the point of oneness, the magnetizing powers of light are so concentrated that anything exposed to it for a single instant becomes a powerful magnet, drawing afterward all things to itself.

Whether all this is scientifically correct or not, I am not enough of a scientist to know, but at least it will serve as an allegory to show the progress of the soul as it is changed from glory to glory in its evolution "into his image."

First, as we behold as in a mirror the glory of the Lord, we come to the light focus, which reveals our sinfulness and our need. "Then spake Jesus again unto them, saying, I am the light of the world; he that followeth me shall not walk in darkness, but shall have the light of life."

Second, as we draw closer, we reach the heat focus, where all our dross and reprobate silver is burned up. For He is like a refiner's fire, and like fuller's soap: and "he shall sit as a refiner and purifier of silver; and he shall purify the sons of Levi, and purge them as gold and silver, that they may offer unto the Lord an offering in righteousness.''

Third, as we draw closer still, we come to the photographing focus, where the image of Christ is indelibly impressed upon our souls, and we are made like Him because we see Him as He is. ''We know that when he shall appear, we shall be like him, for we shall see him as he is.''

Fourth and finally, as we come to the point of oneness, we reach the magnetic focus, where our character is so conformed to Christ, that men seeing it will be irresistibly drawn to glorify our Father which is in Heaven.

If we would be conformed to the image of Christ, then we must live closer and ever closer to Him. We must become better and better acquainted with His character and His ways; we must look at things through His eyes, and judge all things by His standards.

It is not by effort or by wrestling that this conformity is to be accomplished; it is by assimilation. According to a natural law, we grow like those with whom we associate, and the stronger character always exercises the controlling influence. And, as divine law is all one with natural law, only working in a higher sphere and with more unhindered power, it need not seem mysterious to us that we should become like Christ by a spiritual union with Him.

But again I must repeat that this union with Christ cannot come by our own efforts, no matter how strenuous they may be. Christ is to ''dwell in our hearts by faith,'' and He can dwell there in no other way. Paul, when he tells us that he was crucified with Christ, says: ''Nevertheless I live: yet not I but Christ liveth in me: and the life that I now live, I live by the faith of the Son of God who loved me, and gave himself for me.''

''Christ liveth in my,'' this is the transforming secret. If Christ liveth in me, His life must, in the very nature of things, be manifested in my mortal flesh, and I cannot fail to be changed from glory to glory into His image.

Our Lord's teaching about this is very emphatic. ''Abide in me,'' He says, ''and I in you. As the branch cannot bear fruit of itself except it abide in the vine; no more can ye, except ye abide in me. I am the vine, ye are the branches. He that abideth in me, and I in him, the same bringeth forth much fruit; for without me ye can do nothing.''

This is literally true. If we abide in Him, and He in us, we can no more help bring forth much fruit than can the branches of a flourishing vine. In the very nature of things the fruit must come.

But we cannot take the "old man" into Christ. We must put off the old man with his deeds before we can "put on the Lord Jesus Christ." And the apostle, in writing to the Colossians, bases his exhortations to holiness of life on the fact that they had done this. "Lie not one to another," he says, "seeing that ye have put off the old man with his deeds, and have put on the new man, which is renewed in knowledge after the image of him that created him."

Sin must disappear at the incoming of Christ; and no soul that is not prepared to surrender all that is contrary to His will can hope to welcome Him. The "old man" must be put off if the new man is to reign. But both the putting off and the putting on must be done by faith. There is no other way. As I have tried to explain elsewhere, we must move our personality, our ego, our will out of self and into Christ. We must reckon ourselves to be dead to self, and alive only to God. "Reckon ye also yourselves to be dead indeed to sin, but alive unto God through Jesus Christ our Lord." "Neither yield ye your members as instruments of unrighteousness unto sin; but yield yourselves unto God as those that are alive from the dead, and your members as instruments of righteousness unto God."

The same kind of reckoning of faith, which brings the forgiveness of sins within our grasp, brings also this union with Christ. To those who do not understand the law of faith, this will no doubt be as great a mystery as the secrets of gravitation were before the law of gravitation was discovered; but, to those who understand it, the law of faith works as unerringly and as definitely as the law of gravitation, and produces its results as certainly. No one can read the seventh chapter of Hebrews and fail to see that faith is an all-conquering force. I believe myself it is the creative force of the universe. It is the higher law that controls all the lower laws beneath it; and what looks like a miracle is simply the working of this higher controlling law.

Faith is, as I say, the law of Creation. "Through faith we understand that the worlds were framed by the word of God, so that things which are seen were not made of things which do appear." We are told that "God spake and it was done, he commanded and it stood fast." And our Lord tells us that if we have faith we can do the same. "And Jesus answering saith unto them, Have faith in God. For verily I say unto you, That whosoever shall say unto this mountain, Be thou removed, and be thou cast into the sea, and shall not doubt in his heart, but shall believe that those things which he saith shall come to pass, he shall have whatsoever he saith. Therefore I say unto you, What things soever ye desire when ye pray, believe that ye receive them, and ye shall have them."

Faith, we are told, calls those things which be not as though they were; and, in so calling them, brings them into being. Therefore, although we cannot see any tangible sign of change when by faith we put off the old man, which is corrupt according to the deceitful lusts, and by faith put on the new man which after God is created in righteousness and true holiness, yet nevertheless, it has really been done, and faith has accomplished it. I cannot explain this theologically, but I can fearlessly assert that it is a tremendous practical reality; and that those souls who abandon the self-life, and give themselves up to the Lord to be fully possessed by Him, do find that He takes possession of the inner springs of their being, and works there to will and to do of His good pleasure.

Paul prayed for the Ephesians that "Christ might dwell in their hearts by faith," and this is the whole secret of being conformed to His image. If Christ is dwelling in my heart I must necessarily be Christlike. I cannot be unkind, or irritable, or self-seeking, or dishonest; but His gentleness, and sweetness, and tender compassion, and loving submission to the will of His Father must be manifested in my daily walk and conversation.

We shall not be fully changed into the image of Christ until He shall appear, and we shall "see him as he is." But meanwhile, according to our measure, the life of Jesus is to be made "manifest in our mortal flesh." Is it made manifest in ours? Are we so "conformed to the image" of Christ that men in seeing us see a glimpse of Him also?

A Methodist minister's wife told me that at one time, when they had moved to a new place, her little boy came in after the first afternoon of play, and exclaimed joyfully, "Oh, Mother, I have found such a lovely, good little girl to play with here, that I never want to go away again."

"I am very glad, darling," said the loving mother, happy over her child's happiness. "What is the little girl's name?"

"Oh," replied the child, with a sudden solemnity, "I think her name is Jesus."

"Why, Frank!" exclaimed the horrified mother, "what do you mean?"

"Well, Mother," he said deprecatingly, "she was so lovely that I did not know what she could be called but Jesus."

Are our lives so Christlike that anyone could have such a thought of us? Is it patent to all around us that we have been with Jesus? Is it not, alas, often just the contrary? Are not some of us so cross and uncomfortable in our living that exactly the opposite thing would have to be said about us?

Paul says we are to be "epistles of Christ," known and read of all men, "written, not with ink, but with the Spirit of the living God, not in tables of stone, but in fleshy tables of the heart." I firmly believe that if every child of God, all the world over, would begin from this day onward to be an "epistle of Christ," living a truly Christlike life at home and abroad, it would not be a month before the churches would all be crowded with inquirers, coming in to see what was the religion that could so transform human nature into something divine.

The world is full of unbelievers in the reality of the Christian religion, and nothing will convince them but facts which they cannot disprove. We must meet them with transformed lives. If they see that whereas once we were cross, now we are sweet; once we were proud, now we are humble; once we were fretful, now we are patient and calm; and if we are able to testify that it is the religion of Christ that has wrought this change, they cannot help but be impressed.

A Christian man who, on account of his earnest work, had gained a great reputation for piety, had unfortunately gained an equally great reputation for a bad temper and a sharp tongue. But at last, for some reason which no one could understand, a change seemed to come over him, and his temper and his tongue became as sweet and as gentle as they had before been violent and sharp. His friends watched and wondered, and at last one of them approached him on the subject, and asked him if he had changed his religion. "No," replied the man, "I have not changed my religion, but I have at last let my religion change me."

How much has our religion changed us?

It is very easy to have a church religion, or a prayer-meeting religion, or a Christian-work religion; but it is altogether a different thing to have an everyday religion. To "show piety at home" is one of the most vital parts of Christianity, but it is also one far too rare; and it is not at all an uncommon thing to find Christians who "do their righteousness" before outsiders "to be seen of men," but who fail lamentably in showing their piety at home. I knew a father of a family who was so powerful in prayer at the weekly prayer meeting, and so impressive in exhortation that the whole church was much edified by his piety; but who, when he went home after the meetings, was so cross and ugly that his wife and family were afraid to say a word in his presence.

"And when thou prayest, thou shalt not be as the hypocrites are; for they love to pray standing in the synagoges and in the corners of the streets, that they may be seen of men. Verily I say unto you, They have their reward." These words, "They have their reward," seem to me among the most solemn in the Bible. What we do to be seen of men is seen of men, and that is all there is to it. There is no conformity to the image of Christ in this sort of righteousness. The righteousness that is Christlike, is the righteousness that bears everyday trials cheerfully, and is patient under home provocations; that returns good for evil, and meets all the homely friction of daily life with sweetness and gentleness; that suffereth long and is kind; that envieth not; that vaunteth not itself; that is not puffed up; that seeketh not its own; is not easily provoked, and thinketh no evil; that beareth all things, believeth all things, hopeth all things, endureth all things. This is what it means to be conformed to the image of Christ! Do we know anything of such righteousness as this?

We sometimes talk about performing what we call our "religious duties," meaning by this expression our church services, or our stated seasons of devotion, or our Christian work of one sort or another; and we never dream that it is far more our "religious duty" to be Christlike in our daily walk and conversation than to be faithful even in these other things, desirable as they may be in themselves.

The righteousness of the scribes and Pharisees was a righteousness of words and phrases and of ceremonial observances, and this is often very impressive to outsiders. But, because it was nothing more, our Lord condemns it in unmeasured terms: "Woe unto you, scribes and Pharisees, hypocrites! for ye pay tithe of mint and anise, and cummin, and have omitted the weightier matters of the law, judgment, mercy, and faith: these ought ye to have done, and not to leave the other undone. Woe unto you, scribes and Pharisees, hypocrites! for ye are like unto whited sepulchres, which indeed appear beautiful outward, but are within full of dead men's bones, and of all uncleanliness." And He adds: "Even so ye also outwardly appear righteous unto men, but within ye are full of hypocrisy and iniquity."

It is very easy to say beautiful things about the religious life, but to *be* what we say is an altogether different matter. I know a Sunday school teacher who had been teaching her scholars a great deal about casting all your cares on the Lord, and trusting Him in times of trial; and they had been very much impressed. But at last a trouble came into the life of this teacher, and some of her scholars saw her in her own home while it lasted. To their amazement and distress they saw her fretting, and chafing, and worrying, and complaining, acting, in short, just as if there was no God to trust, or as if His ways were not ways of love and goodness. It was an "object lesson" to those children that undid all the good which that teacher's previous teaching had seemed likely to accomplish; and one of them, who was very observant, said to me triumphantly, "I thought it could not be true while Miss _____ was telling us about how we might trust the Lord for everything; and now I see it was only goody talk, for she doesn't do it herself."

Across Christian, or an anxious one, a discouraged gloomy

Christian, a doubting Christian, a complaining Christian, an exacting Christian, a selfish, cruel, hard-hearted Christian, a self-indulgent Christian, a Christian with a sharp tongue or a bitter spirit; a Christian, in short, who is not Christlike may preach to the winds with as much hope of success, as to preach to his own family or friends, who see him as he is. There is no escape from this inevitable law of things, and we may as well recognize it at once. If we want our loved ones to trust the Lord, volumes of talk about it will not be one-thousandth part as convincing to them as the sight of a little real trust on our own part in the time of need. The longest prayer and the loudest preaching are of no avail in any family circle, however, they may do it in the pulpit, unless there is on the part of the preacher a living out of the things preached.

Some Christians seem to thing that the fruits which the Bible calls for are some form of outward religious work, such as holding meetings, visiting the poor, conducting charitable institutions, and so forth. Whereas the fact is that the Bible scarcely mentions these at all as fruits of the Spirit, but declares that the fruit of the Spirit is love, joy, peace, longsuffering, gentleness, goodness, faith, meekness, temperance. A Christlike character must necessarily be the fruit of Christ's indwelling. Other things will no doubt be the outcome of this character; but first and foremost comes the character, or all the rest is but a hollow sham. A late writer has said: "A man can never be more than his character makes him. A man can never do more nor better than deliver or embody that which is his character. Nothing valuable can come out of a man that is not first in the man. Character must stand behind and back up everything — the sermon, the poem, the picture, the book. None of them is worth a straw without it."

In order to become conformed to the image of Christ, we must of necessity be made "partakers of the divine nature." And, where this is the case, that divine nature must necessarily manifest itself. Our tastes, our wishes, our purposes will become like Christ's tastes, and wishes, and purposes; we shall change eyes with Him, and see things as He sees them. This is inevitable; for where the divine nature is, its fruits cannot fail to be manifest; and, where they are not manifest, we are forced to conclude that that individual, no matter how loud his professions, has not yet been made a partaker of the divine nature.

I can hear someone asking, But do you really mean to say that, in order to be made partakers of the divine nature, we must cease from our own efforts entirely, and must simply by faith put on Christ, and must let Him live in us and work in us to will and to do of His good pleasure? And do you believe He will then actually do it?

To this I answer most emphatically, Yes, I mean just that. I mean that if we abandon ourselves entirely to Him, He comes to abide in us, and is Himself our life. We must commit our whole lives to Him, our thoughts, our words, our daily walk, our downsittings, our uprisings. By faith we must abandon ourselves, and, as it were, move over into Christ, and abide in Him. By faith we must put off the old man, and by faith we must put on the new man. By faith we must reckon ourselves dead unto sin, and alive unto God; as truly dead as alive. By faith we must realize that our daily life is Christ living in us; and, ceasing from our own works, we must suffer Him to work in us to will and to do of His good pleasure. It is no longer truth about Him that must fill our hearts, but it is Himself — the living, loving, glorious Christ — who will, if we let Him, in very deed make us His dwelling place, and who will reign and rule within us, and "subdue all things unto himself." "Therefore if any man be in Christ, he is a new creature; old things are passed away; behold, all things are become new."

It was no mere figure of speech when our Lord in that wonderful Sermon on the Mount said to His disciples: "Be ye therefore perfect even as your Father in heaven is perfect." He meant, of course, according to our measure, but He meant that reality of being conformed to His image to which we have been predestined. And in the Epistle to the Hebrews we are shown how it is to be brought about. "Now the God of peace, that brought again from the dead our Lord Jesus, that great Shepherd of the sheep, through the blood of the everlasting covenant, make you perfect in every good work to do his will; working in you that which is well pleasing in His sight, through Jesus Christ: to whom be glory forever and ever. Amen."

It is to be by His working in us, and not by our working in ourselves, that this purpose of God in our creation is to be accomplished; and if it should look as regards some of us that we are too far removed from any conformity to the image of Christ for such a transformation ever to be wrought, we must remember that our Maker is not finished making us yet. The day will come, if we do not hinder, when the work begun in Genesis shall be finished in Revelation, and the whole Creation, as well as ourselves, shall be delivered from the bondage of corruption into the glorious liberty of the children of God.

"For we know that the whole creation groaneth and travaileth in pain together until now. And not only they, but ourselves also, which have the first fruits of the Spirit, even we ourselves groan within ourselves, waiting for the adoption, to wit the redemption of our body."

'Tis, shall Thy will be done for me? or mine,
And I be made a thing, not after Thine;
My own, and full of paltriest pretense?
Shall I be born of God, or of mere man?
Be made like Christ, or on some other plan?
What though Thy work in me transcends my sense,
Too fine, too high for me to understand.
I trust entirely. On, Lord, with Thy labor grand!
I have not knowledge, wisdom, insight, thought,
Nor understanding fit to justify
Thee in Thy work, O Perfect. Thou hast brought
Me up to this, and lo! what thou hast wrought
I cannot call it good. But I can cry
"O enemy, the Maker hath not done;
One day thou shalt behold, and from the sight wilt run."

CHAPTER 17

GOD IS ENOUGH

"My soul wait thou only upon God, for my expectation is from him. He only is my rock and my salvation; he is my defense; I shall not be moved. In God is my salvation, and my glory: the rock of my strength and my refuge is in God."

The last and greatest lesson that the soul has to learn is the fact that God, and God alone, is enough for all its needs. This is the lesson that all His dealings with us are meant to teach; and this is the crowning discovery of our whole Christian life. *God is enough!*

We have been considering in this book some aspects of the character and the ways of God as revealed to us in the Lord Jesus Christ; and also some of the mistakes which prevent us from appropriating the fullness that is ours in Him. And now in conclusion I want to tell, as best I can, what seems to me the outcome of the whole matter.

If God is what He would seem to be from the revealings we have been considering; if He is indeed the "God of all comfort," as we have seen; if He is our Shepherd; if He is really and truly our Father; if, in short, all the many aspects we have been studying of His character and His ways are actually true, then we must, it seems to me, come to the positive conviction that He is, in Himself alone, enough for all our possible needs, and that we may safely rest in Him absolutely and forever.

Most Christians have, I suppose, sung more often than they could count, these words in one of our most familiar hymns:

> Thou, O Christ, art all I want,
> More than all in Thee I find.

But I doubt whether all of us could honestly say that the words have expressed any reality in our own experience. Christ has not been all we want. We have wanted a great many things besides Him. We have wanted fervent feelings about Him, or realizations of His presence with us, or an interior revelation of His love; or else we have demanded satisfactory schemes of doctrine, or successful Christian work, or something of one sort or another, besides Himself, that will constitute a personal claim upon Him. Just Christ Himself, Christ alone, without the addition of any of our experiences concerning Him, has not been enough for us in spite of all our singing; and we do not even see how it is possible that He could be enough.

The psalmist said in those old days: "My soul, wait thou only upon God: for my expectation is from him." But now the Christian says, "My soul, wait thou upon my sound doctrines, for my expectation is from them"; or, "My soul, wait thou on my good disposition and feelings, or upon my righteous works, or upon my fervent prayers, or upon my earnest striving, for my expectation is from these." To wait upon God only seems one of the unsafest things they can do, and to have their expectation from Him alone is like building on the sand. They reach out on every side for something to depend on, and, not until everything else fails, will they put their trust in God alone. George Macdonald says: "We look upon God as our last and feeblest resource. We only go to Him when we have nowhere else to go. And then we learn that the storms of life have driven us, not upon the rocks, but into the desired haven."

No soul can be really at rest until it has given up all dependence on everything else and has been forced to depend on the Lord alone. As long as our expectation is from other things, nothing but disappointment awaits us. Feelings may change, and will change with our changing circumstances; doctrines and dogmas may be upset; Christian work may come to nought; prayers may seem to lose their fervency; promises may seem to fail; everything that we have believed in or depended upon may seem to be swept away, and only God is left, just God, the bare God, if I may be allowed the expression; simply and only God.

We say sometimes, "If I could only find a promise to fit my case, I could then be at rest." But promises may be misunderstood or misapplied, and, at the moment when we are leaning all our weight upon them, they may seem utterly to fail us. But the Promiser, who is behind His promises, and is infinitely more than His promises, can never fail nor change. The little child does not need to have any promises from its mother to make it content; it has its mother herself, and she is enough. Its mother is better than a thousand promises. In our highest ideal of love or friendship, promises do not enter. One party may love to make promises, just as our Lord does, but the other party does not need them; the personality of lover or friend is better than all their promises. And should every promise be wiped out of the Bible, we would still have God left, and God would be enough. Again I repeat it, only God, He Himself, just as He is, without the addition of anything on our part, whether it be disposition or feelings, or experiences, or good works, or sound doctrines, or any other thing either outward or inward. "God only is my rock and my salvation; he is my defense: I shall not be moved."

I do not mean by this that we are not to have feelings, or experiences, or revelations, or good works, or sound doctrines. We may have all of these, but they must be the result of salvation, and never the procuring cause; and they can never be depended upon as being any indication of our spiritual condition. They are all things that come and go, and are dependent often upon the state of our health, or the condition of our surroundings, or even sometimes upon the quarter of the wind. Some people, for instance, can never believe that God loves them when the wind is in the East. And if we rely upon any of these things in the slightest degree as the groundwork for our confidence or our joy, we are sure to come to grief. What I do mean is that we are to hold ourselves absolutely independent of them all, resting in only the grand, magnificent fact that God is, and that He is our Saviour; our inner life prospers just as well and is just as triumphant without these personal experiences or personal doings as it is with them. We are to find God, the fact of God, sufficient for all our spiritual needs, whether we feel ourselves to be in a desert or in a fertile valley. We are to say with the prophet: "Although the fig-tree shall not blossom, neither shall fruit be in the vines; the labor of the olive shall fail, and the field shall yield no meat, the flock shall be cut off from the fold, and there shall be no herd in the stall; yet I will rejoice in the Lord, I will joy in the God of my salvation."

The soul is made for this, and can never find rest short of it. All God's dealings with us, therefore, are shaped to this end; and He is often obliged to deprive us of all joy in everything else in order that He may force us to find our joy only and altogether in Himself. It is all very well, perhaps, to rejoice in His promises, or to rejoice in the revelations He may have granted us, or in the experiences we may have realized; but to rejoice in the Promiser Himself — Himself alone — without promises, or experiences, or revelations, this is the crowning point of Christian life; and this is the only place where we can know the peace which passes all understanding, and which nothing can disturb.

It is difficult to explain just what I mean. We have so accustomed ourselves to consider all these accompaniments of the spiritual life as being the spiritual life itself that it is hard to detach ourselves from them. We cannot think that the Lord can be anything to us unless we find in ourselves something to assure us of His love and His care. And when we talk about finding our all in Him, we generally mean that we find it in our feelings or our views about Him. If, for instance, we feel a glow of love toward Him, then we can say heartily that He is enough; but when this glow fails, as sooner or later it is almost sure to do, then we no longer feel that we have found our all in Him. The truth is that what satisfies us is not the Lord, but our own feelings about the Lord. But we are not conscious of this; and consequently when our feelings fail we think it is the Lord who has failed, and we are plunged into darkness.

Of course, all this is very foolish, but it is such a common experience that very few can see how foolish it is. Perhaps an illustration may help us to clearer vision. Let us think of a man accused of a crime, standing before a judge. Which would be the thing of moment for that man: his own feelings toward the judge, or the judge's feelings toward him? Would he spend his time watching his own emotions, and trying to see whether he felt that the judge was favorable to him, or would he watch the judge and try to discover from his looks or his words whether or not to expect a favorable judgment? Of course we will say at once that the man's own feelings are not of the slightest account in the matter, and that only the opinions and feelings of the judge are worth a moment's thought. The man might have all the "glows" and all the "experiences" conceivable, but these would avail absolutely nothing. Upon the judge only would everything depend.

This is what we would call a self-evident fact.

In the same way, if we will only bring our common sense to bear upon the subject, we cannot help seeing that the only really vital thing in our relations with the Lord is, not what are our feelings toward Him, but what are His feelings toward us. The man who is being tried must find in the judge all he needs, if he is to find it at all. His sufficiency cannot possibly be of himself, but it must be of the one upon whom his fate depends. And our sufficiency, the apostle says, is not of ourselves but of God.

This, then, is what I mean by God being enough. It is that we find in Him, in the fact of His existence, and of His character, all that we can possibly want for everything. *God is,* must be our answer to every question and every cry of need. If there is any lack in the One who has undertaken to save us, nothing supplementary we can do will avail to make it up; and if there is no lack in Him, then He, of Himself and in Himself, is enough.

I wish it were possible to make my meaning plain, for I believe it is the secret of permanent deliverance from all the discomfort and unrest of every Christian life. Your discomfort and unrest arise from your strenuous but useless efforts to get up some satisfactory basis of confidence within yourselves; such, for instance, as what you consider to be the proper feelings, or the right amount of fervor or earnestness, or at least, if nothing else, a sufficient degree of interest in spiritual matters. And because none of these things are ever satisfactory (and, I may tell you, never will be), it is impossible for your religious life to be anything but uncomfortable.

But if we see that all our salvation from beginning to end depends on the Lord alone; and if we have learned that He is able and willing to do for us "exceeding abundantly above all we can ask or think," then peace and comfort cannot fail to reign supreme. Everything depends upon whether the Lord, in and of Himself, is enough for our salvation, or whether other things must be added on our part to make Him sufficient.

The thing that helped me personally more than anything else to come to a conviction that God was really enough for me was an experience I had some years ago. It was at a time in my religious life when I was passing through a great deal of questioning and perplexity, and I felt that no Christian had ever had such peculiar difficulties as mine before. There happened to be staying near me just then for a few weeks a lady who was considered to be a deeply spiritual Christian, and to whom I had been advised to apply for spiritual help. I summoned up my courage, therefore, one afternoon and went to see her, pouring out my troubles; I expected of course that she would take a deep interest in my, and would be at great pains to do all she could to help me.

She listened patiently enough, and did not interrupt me; but when I had finished my story, and had paused, expecting sympathy and consideration, she simply said, "Yes, all you say may be very true, but then, in spite of it all, there is God." I waited a few minutes for something more, but nothing came, and my friend and teacher had the air of having said all that was necessary.

"But," I continued, "surely you did not understand how very serious and perplexing my difficulties are."

"Oh, yes, I did," replied my friend, "but then, as I tell you, there is God." And I could not induce her to make any other answer. It seemed to me most disappointing and unsatisfactory. I felt that my peculiar and really harrowing experiences could not be met by anything so simple as merely the statement, "Yes, but there is God." I knew God was there, of course, but I felt I needed something more than just God; and I came to the conclusion that my friend, for all her great reputation as a spiritual teacher, was at any rate not able to grapple with a peculiar case such as mine.

However, my need was so great that I did not give up with my first trial, but went to her again and again, always with the hope that she would sometime begin to understand the importance of my difficulties and would give me adequate help. It was of no aval. I was never able to draw forth any other answer. Always to everything would come the simple reply, with an air of entirely dismissing the subject, "Yes, I know; but there is God." And at last by dint of her continual repetition I became convinced that my friend really and truly believed that the mere fact of the existence of God, as the Creator and Redeemer of mankind, and of me as a member of the race, was an all-sufficient answer to every possible need of His creatures. And at last, because she said it so often and seemed so sure, I began dimly to wonder whether after all God might not be enough, even for my need, overwhelming and peculiar as I felt it to be. From wondering I came gradually to believing, that, being my Creator and Redeemer, He must be enough; and at last a conviction burst upon me that He really was enough, and my eyes were opened to the fact of the absolute and utter all-sufficiency of God.

My troubles disappeared like magic, and I did nothing but wonder how I could ever have been such an idiot as to be troubled by them, when all the while there was God, the Almighty and all-seeing God, the God who had created me, and was therefore on my side, and eager to care for me and help me. I had found out that God was enough, and my soul was at rest.

The all-sufficiency of God ought to be as complete to the child of God as the all-sufficiency of a good mother is to the child of that mother. We all know the utter rest of the little child in the mother's presence and the mother's love. That its mother is there is enough to make all fears and all troubles disappear. It does not need the mother to make any promises; she herself, just as she is, without promises and without explanations, is all that the child needs.

My own experience as a chid taught me this, beyond any

possibility of question. My mother was the remedy for all my own ills, and, I fully believed, for the ills of the whole world, if only they could be brought to her. And when any-one expressed doubts as to her capacity to remedy every-thing, I remembered with what fine scorn I used to annihi-late them, by saying, "Ah! but you don't know my mother."

And now, when any tempest-tossed soul fails to see that God is enough, I feel like saying, not with scorn, but with infinite pity, "Ah, dear friend, you do not know God! Did you know Him, you could not help seeing that He is the remedy for every need of your soul, and that He is an all-sufficient remedy. God is enough, even though no promise may seem to fit your case, nor any inward assurance give you confidence. The Promiser is more than His promises; and His existence is a surer ground of confidence than the most fervent inward feelings."

> Oh, utter but the name of God
> Down in your heart of hearts,
> And see how from the soul at once
> All anxious fear departs.

But someone may say, "All this is no doubt true, and I could easily believe it, if I could only be sure it applied to me. But I am so good-for-nothing and so full of sin, that I do not feel as if I had any claim to such riches of grace."

All the more, if you are good-for-nothing and full of sin, have you a claim on the all-sufficiency of God. Your very good-for-nothingness and sinfulness are your loudest claims. As someone has said, it is only the sinner that wants salvation who stands in the Saviour's path. And the Bible declares that Christ Jesus came into the world to save sin-ners; not to save the righteous, not to save the fervent, not to save the earnest workers, but simply and only to save sin-ners. Why then should we spend our time and energies in trying to create a claim, which after all is no claim, but only a hindrance?

As long as our attention is turned upon ourselves and our own experiences, just so long is it turned away from the Lord. This is plain common sense. As I have said elsewhere, we can only see the thing we look at, and while we are looking at ourselves, we simply cannot "behold God." It is not that He hides Himself; He is always there in full view of all who look unto Him; but if we are looking in another direction, we cannot expect to see Him.

Heretofore, it may be, our eyes have been so exclusively fixed upon ourselves that all our interior questioning has been simply and only as regarded our own condition. Is my love for God warm enough? Am I enough in earnest? Are my feelings toward Him what they ought to be? Have I enough zeal? Do I feel my need as I ought? And we have been miserable because we have never been able to answer these questions satisfactorily. Although we do not know it, it has been a mercy we never could answer them satisfactorily, for if we had, the self in us would have been exalted, and we should have been filled with self-congratulation and pride.

If we want to see God, our interior questioning must be, not about ourselves, but about Him. How does God feel toward me? Is His love for me warm enough? Has He enough zeal? Does He feel my need deeply enough? Is He sufficiently in earnest? Although these questions may seem irreverent to some, they simply embody the doubts and fears of a great many doubting hearts, and they only need to be asked in order to prove the fact that these doubts and fears are in themselves the real irreverence. We all know what would be the triumphant answers to such questions. No doubts could withstand their testimony; and the soul that asks and answers thelm honestly will be shut up to a profound and absolute conviction that God is and must be enough.

"All things are yours," declares the apostle, "whether Paul, or Apollos, or Cephas, or the world, or life, or death, or things present, or things to come; all are yours; and ye are Christ's; and Christ is God's." It would be impossible for any statement to be more all-embracing. And all things are yours because you belong to Christ, not because you are so good and so worthy, but simply and only because you belong to Christ. All things we need are part of our inheritance in Him, and they only await our claiming. Let our needs and difficulties be as great as they may, there is in these "all things" a supply exceeding abundantly above all we can ask or think.

Because He is, all must go right for us. Because the mother is, all must go right, up to the measure of her ability, for her children; and infinitely more must this be true of the Lord. To the child there is, behind all that changes and can change, the one unchangeable fact of the mother's existence. While the mother lives, the child must be cared for; and, while God lives, His children must be cared for as well. What else could He do, being what He is? Neglect, indifference, forgetfulness, ignorance are all impossible to Him. He knows everything, He cares about everything, He can manage everything, and He loves us. What more could we ask?

God's saints in all ages have known this, and have realized that God was enough for them. Job said out of the depths of sorrows and trials, which few can equal, "Though he slay me, yet will I trust him." David could say in the moment of his keenest anguish, "Yea, though I walk through the valley of the shadow of death," yet "I will fear no evil, for thou art with me." And again he could say: "God is our refuge and strength, a very present help in trouble. Therefore will not we fear though the earth be removed, and though the mountains be carried into the midst of the sea; though the waters thereof roar and be troubled; though the mountains shake with the swelling thereof ... God is in the midst of her; she shall not be moved; God shall help her, and that right early."

Paul could say triumphantly in the midst of many and grievous trials: "For I am persuaded that neither death, nor life, nor angels, nor principalities, nor powers, nor things present, nor things to come, nor height, nor depth, nor any other creature, shall be able to separate us from the love of God, which is in Christ Jesus our Lord."

Therefore, O doubting and sorrowful Christian hearts, in the face of all we have learned concerning the God of all comfort, cannot you realize with Job, and David, and Paul, and the saints of all ages that nothing else is needed to quiet all your fears, but just this, that *God is*. His simple existence is all the warrant your need requires for its certain relieving. Nothing can separate you from His love, absolutely nothing, neither death nor life, nor angels, nor principalities, nor powers, nor things present, nor things to come, nor height, nor depth, nor any other creature. Every possible contingency is provided for here; and not one of them can separate you from the love of God which is in Christ Jesus our Lord.

After such a declaration as this, how can any of us dare to question or doubt God's love? And, since He loves us, He cannot exist and fail to help us. Do we not know by our own experience what an imperative necessity it is for love to pour itself out in blessing on the ones it loves; and can we not understand that God, who is love, who is, if I may say so, made out of love, simply cannot help blessing us? We do not need to beg Him to bless us, He simply cannot help it.

Therefore God is enough! God is enough for time, God is enough for eternity. *God is enough!*

> Only to sit and think of God,
>   Oh, what a joy it is!
> To think the thought, to breathe the name
>   Earth has no higher bliss.

Hannah Whitall Smith

The Unselfishness of God

CONTENTS

Introduction

On the fly leaf of my Bible I find the following words, taken from I know not where: "This generation has rediscovered the unselfishness of God."

If I were called upon to state in one sentence the sum and substance of my religious experience, it is this sentence I would choose. And no words could express my thankfulness for having been born into a generation where this discovery has been comparatively easy.

If I am not mistaken, the generation before mine knew very little of the unselfishness of God; and, even of my own generation, there are I fear many good and earnest Christians who do not know it yet. Without putting it into such words as to shock themselves or others, many Christians still at bottom look upon God as one of the most selfish, self-absorbed Beings in the universe, far more selfish than they could think it right to be themselves, intent only upon His own honor and glory, looking out continually that His own rights are never trampled on, and so absorbed in thoughts of Himself and of His own righteousness as to have no love or pity to spare for the poor sinners who have offended Him.

I grew up believing God was like this. I have discovered that He is exactly the opposite. And it is of this discovery I want to tell.

After more than seventy years of life I have come to the profound conviction that every need of the soul is to be met by the discovery I have made. In that wonderful prayer of our Lord's in John 17, He says, "And this is life eternal, that they might know Thee the only true God, and Jesus Christ whom Thou has sent." This used to seem to me a mystical saying, that might perhaps have a pious esoteric meaning, but certainly could have no practical application. But every year of my religious life I have discovered in it a deeper and more vital meaning; until now at last I see, that, rightly understood, it contains the gist of the whole matter. To know God, as He really is, in His essential nature and character, is to have reached the absolute, and unchangeable, and utterly satisfying foundation, upon which, and upon which only, can be reared the whole superstructure of our religious life.

To discover that He is not the selfish Being we are so often apt to think Him, but is instead really and fundamentally unselfish, caring not at all for Himself, but only and always for us and for our welfare, is to have found the answer to every human question, and the cure for every human ill.

But how to make this discovery is the crucial question. In our present stage of existence we have not the faculties developed that would make it possible for us to see God as He is in His essential and incomprehensible Being. We need an Interpreter. We must have an Incarnation. If I should want to make a colony of ants know me as I am in the essential essence of my being, I would need to incarnate myself in the body of an ant, and speak to them in their own language, as one ant to another. As a human being I might stand over an ant-hill and harangue for a lifetime, and not one word would reach the ears of the ants. They would run to and fro unconscious of my speech.

To know God, therefore, as He really is, we must go to His incarnation in the Lord Jesus Christ. The Bible tells us that no man hath seen God at any time, but that the only begotten Son of the Father, He hath revealed Him. When one of the disciples said to Christ, "Show us the Father, and it sufficeth us," Christ answered—"Have I been so long time with you, and yet hast thou not known me, Philip? He that hath seen Me hath seen the Father, and how sayest thou then, Show us the Father? Believest thou not that I am in the Father, and the Father in Me? The words I speak unto you I speak not of Myself: but the Father that dwelleth in Me, He doeth the works."

Here then is our opportunity. We cannot see God, but we can see Christ. Christ was not only the Son of God, but He was the Son of man as well, and, as a man to men, He can reveal His Father. Whatever Christ was, that God is. All the unselfishness, all the tenderness, all the kindness, all the justice, all the goodness, that we see in Christ is simply a revelation of the unselfishness, the tenderness, the kindness, the justice, the goodness, of God.

Some one has said lately, in words that seem to me inspired, "Christ is the human form of God." And this is the explanation of the Incarnation.

I do not mean, however, to say that no one can have any revelation of God to their souls except those who believe the Bible, and who know Christ as He is there revealed. I believe reverently and thankfully that "God is no respecter of persons: but in every nation, he that feareth Him and worketh righteousness is accepted with Him." God has "not left Himself without a witness" at any age of the world. But what I do believe is exactly what is declared in the opening words of the Epistle to the Hebrews, that God, who "at sundry times and in divers manners spake in times past to the Fathers by the Prophets, hath in these last days spoken unto us by His Son," who is the "brightness of His glory, and the express image of His person;"

and that, therefore, although we may find many partial revelations elsewhere, if we would know Him as He really is, we can only see Him fully revealed in His "express image," the Lord Jesus Christ.

It was a long time before I found this out, and, until I did, I was, as my story will show, as really ignorant of Him as the most benighted savage, notwithstanding the fact that I lived in a Christian community, and was brought up in a Christian Church, and had the open Bible in my hand. God was a terror to me, until I began to see Him in the face of Jesus Christ, when He became an unmixed joy. And I believe many weary souls are in similar case, who, if they could once be made to see that God is like Christ, would experience an unspeakable relief.

A friend of mine told me that her childhood was passed in a perfect terror of God. Her idea of Him was that He was a cruel giant with an awful "Eye" which could see everything, no matter how it might be hidden, and that He was always spying upon her, and watching for chances to punish her, and to snatch away all her joys. She said she would creep into bed at night with dreadful feeling that even in the dark the "Eye of God" was upon her ; and she would pull the bed covers over her head in the vain hope, which all the while she knew was vain, of hiding herself from this terrifying Eye, and would lie there in a tremble of fright, saying to herself in an agonized whisper, "What shall I do? Oh, what shall I do? Even my mother cannot save me from God!"

With a child's strange reticence she never told anyone of her terror; but one night mother, coming into the room unexpectedly, heard the poor little despairing cry, and, with a sudden comprehension of what it meant, sat down beside the bed, and, taking the cold little hand in hers, told her God was not a dreadful tyrant to be afraid of, but was just like Jesus; and that she knew how good and kind Jesus was, and how He loved little children, and took them in His arms and blessed them. My friend said she had always loved the stories about Jesus, and when she heard that God was like Him, it was a perfect revelation to her, and took away her fear of God forever. She went about all that day saying to herself over and over, "Oh, I am so glad I have found out that God is like Jesus, for Jesus is so nice. Now I need never be afraid of God any more." And when she went to bed that night she fairly laughed out loud at the thought that such a dear kind Eye was watching over her and taking care of her.

This little child had got a sight of God "in the face of Jesus Christ," and it brought rest to her soul.

By the discovery of God, therefore, I do not mean anything mysterious, or mystical, or unattainable. I simply mean becoming acquainted with Him as one becomes acquainted with a human friend; that is, finding out what is His nature, and His character, and coming to understand His ways. I mean in short discovering what sort of Being He really is—whether good or bad, whether kind or unkind, whether selfish or unselfish, whether strong or weak, whether wise or foolish, whether just or unjust.

It is of course evident that everything in one's religious life depends upon the sort of God one worships. The character of the worshiper must necessarily be molded by the character of the object worshiped. If it is a cruel and revengeful God, or a selfish and unjust God, the worshiper will be cruel, and revengeful, and selfish, and unjust, also. If it is a loving, tender, forgiving, unselfish God, the worshiper will be loving, and tender, and forgiving, and unselfish, as well. Also the peace and happiness of the worshiper must necessarily be absolutely bound up in the character of the God worshiped; for everything depends upon whether He is a good God or a bad God. If He is good, all is well, of course, and one's peace can flow like a river; while, if he is bad, nothing can be well, no matter how earnest or devoted the worshiper may be, and no peace is possible.

This was brought very vividly to my mind by hearing once in a meeting an educated Negro, belonging to one of the savage tribes of Africa, giving an account of their tribal religion.

He said that they had two gods, a good god and a bad god; that they did not trouble themselves about the good god, because, as he was good, he would do right anyhow, whether they sacrificed to him or not; but the bad god they had to try and propitiate by all sorts of prayers, and sacrifices, and offerings, and religious ceremonies, in order, if possible, to get him into a good humor, so that he might treat them well. To my thinking, there was a profound truth in this. The poorer and more imperfect is one's conception of God, the more fervent and intense will be one's efforts to propitiate Him, and to put Him into a good humor; whereas on the other hand, the higher and truer is the knowledge of the goodness and unselfishness of God, the less anxiety, and fuss, and wrestling, and agonizing, will there be in one's worship. A good and unselfish God will be sure to do right anyhow, whether we try to propitiate Him or not, and we can safely trust Him to carry on His affairs with very little advice from us. As to wrestling or agonizing with Him to fulfill what are really only the duties of His position, it could never be necessary; for, of course a good person always does his duty.

I have discovered therefore that the statement of the fact that "God is good," is really, if we only understand it, a sufficient and entirely satisfactory assurance that our interests will be safe in His hands. Since He is good, He cannot fail to do His duty by us, and, since He is unselfish, He must necessarily consider our interests before His own. When once we are assured of this, there can be nothing left to fear.

Who is there on earth who could see and know the goodness, and the kindness, and the justice, and the loving unselfishness, of our God, as He is revealed to us in the face of Jesus Christ, and fail to be irresistibly drawn to adore Him? Who could have anything but peace in coming to know that the God who has created us, and to whom we belong forever, is a God of Love? Who of us can have any more fears, after once we have found out that He cares for us as for the apple of His eye? And what else is there that can bring an unwavering peace? Acquaintance with doctrines or dogmas may give peace for a time, or blissful experience may, or success in service; but the peace from these can never be trusted to abide. Doctrines may become obscure, experiences may be dulled or may change, we may be cut off by providential circumstances from our work, all things and all people may seem to fail us; and unless our peace is founded upon something more stable than any of these, it will waver as the waves of the sea. The only place therefore of permanent and abiding peace is to be found in an acquaintance with the goodness and the unselfishness of God.

It is difficult to explain just what I mean by this acquaintance with God. We are so accustomed to think that knowing things *about* Him is sufficient—what He has done, what He has said, what His plans are, and what are the doctrines concerning Him,—that we stop short of that knowledge of what He really is in nature and character, which is the only satisfactory knowledge.

In human relations we may know a great deal about a person without at all necessarily coming into any actual acquaintance with that person; and it is the same in our relations with God. We may blunder on for years thinking we know a great deal about Him, but never quite sure of what sort of Being He actually is, and consequently never finding any permanent rest or satisfaction. And then, perhaps suddenly, we catch a sight of Him as He is revealed in the face of Jesus Christ, and we discover the real God, as He is, behind, and beneath, and within, all the other conceptions of Him which may have heretofore puzzled us; and from that moment our peace flows like a river, and in everything and through everything, when perhaps we can rejoice in nothing else, we can always and everywhere "rejoice in God, and joy in the God of our Salvation." We no longer need His promises; we have found Himself, and He is enough for every need.

My own experience has been something like this. My knowledge of God, beginning on a very low plane, and in the midst of the greatest darkness and ignorance, advanced slowly through many stages, and with a vast amount of useless conflict and wrestling, to the place where I learned at last that Christ was the "express image" of God, and where I became therefore in a measure acquainted with Him, and discovered to my amazement and delight His utter unselfishness, and saw that it was safe to trust Him. And from this time all my doubts and questionings have been slowly but surely disappearing in the blaze of this magnificent knowledge.

It is of the processes leading to this discovery by my own soul that I want to tell. But in order to do this I must begin with the earliest influences of my life, for I am convinced that my knowledge of my Heavenly Father began first of all in my knowledge of my earthly father and mother, who were, I feel sure, the most delightful father and mother any child ever had. Having known them and their goodness, it was only reasonable for me to believe that my Heavenly Father, who had made them, must be at least as good as the earthly father and mother He had made; and no story of my soul would be complete without beginning with them.

Chapter 1

MY PARENTS

I was born in Philadelphia, Pennsylvania, in the year 1832. My parents were strict Quakers, and until my marriage at nineteen, I knew nothing of any other religion. I had an absolutely happy childhood and girlhood. I think so now, as I look back upon it, and my diary, kept from the time I was sixteen years old, shows that I thought so then. One of my first entries made in 1848 was as follows:—

"Sixteen years of my life have passed; and, as I look back at the bright happy days of my childhood, and at the quieter but more earnest enjoyments of my youth, my heart feels almost bursting with gratitude to my kind and gracious Creator who has filled my cup of joy almost to overflowing. Truly my life has been one fairy scene of sunshine and of flowers."

This may seem a very roseate view to take of one's life, and might be set down to the enthusiasm and glamor of youth. But on looking back now at seventy years of age, I can still say the same.

Under date of 10th mo., 7th, 1849, when I was seventeen years old I wrote:—

"I cannot understand it. I have thought that unless trials and afflictions come to wean me from the joys of this life, I shall never seek the higher and holier joys of Heaven. But instead of afflictions, every day my blessings increase. All around me conduces to my happiness; the world is very beautiful, my friends are the loveliest and kindest that any one ever had; and scarcely a trial or vexation comes to cast a cloud over my pathway. And this happiness, this Fate of happiness, I might almost call it, extends even to the smallest circumstances. Whatever I leave to God to decide for me He always decides just as I want Him to ... There is a continual clapping of hands and shouting of joyful voices in my heart, and every breath feels almost as if it must terminate in a smile of happiness. Mother says I laugh too much, but the laugh is in me."

The same year under date of 12th mo., 29th, I wrote:—

"What a happy, happy home is ours. I could not but think of it today as the merry jokes and tones of heartfelt pleasure echoed around our family board. And this evening, too, as we gathered together in our simple but comfortable parlor, it came over me with a perfect throb of joy. Father was sitting on one end of a sofa leaning his head on one hand, with the other hand resting on mother's lap; she sat next, and my head was in her lap, and I occupied the rest of the sofa, I have no doubt, gracefully and well. Sallie was sitting in a chair at the end of the sofa leaning her head on father's shoulder, and Lop-no-Nose (my sister Mary) was seated at all our feet, leaning first on one and then on another. All of us were talking as hard as we could, and feeling as if there was nothing wanting, but our absent, dearly loved brother Jim, to make our happiness complete. Many perhaps would smile at such quiet, unobtrusive pleasures, but for my part they are the kind of pleasures I enjoy most heartily and entirely. We can never weary of them, nor feel that their first beauty has gone, but each succeeding day makes them deeper and more earnest. Perhaps I am weak and foolish to take so much enjoyment in things which so many laugh at as unworthy of thought. I know I am but a child, and pleased, as children are, with very little things. And yet to me they are not little. A few of my father's pleasant jokes, spoken when I am brushing his hat or coat in the morning, will fill my heart with sunshine for a whole day. And I am happy if I may read aloud to my mother some book which I love, or even if I may sit quite still and think. Oh, I do love my home better than any other place I know of! I wonder if I love it too much. Sometimes I fear I do, for even if I leave it for one night I am more homesick than I would like any one to know, except those for whom I long. Even when I simply take a walk I often almost feel as if I could cry to go home again. It is very foolish, but I cannot help it. I should die if I had no one to love, no home!

"But for one thing, and I would be *perfectly* happy,—a father and mother, dearer, nobler far, that I can express, a brother and sisters, uncles and aunts, and cousins, and friends, all to love me, and, better far, all for me to love—with these priceless blessings I could not but be happy. One thing I say, prevents it, but it prevents it only a very little. It is the knowledge that I am not prepared for eternity, and the small prospect I have that I ever shall be. I wish it would give me more uneasiness, and that I might feel the urgent necessity there is for me to act. But I cannot compel myself to feel it, and so I go on as careless and indifferent as though I had not the eternal salvation of my soul resting upon me. I know it is very dangerous, but I really can do nothing towards rousing myself; and so, in spite of it, I am happy—happy in myself, happy in my home—my own dear home, happy in my parents, my brother and sisters, and my friends, happy in this beautiful world in which I am placed—in short, happy everywhere and in everything,—thank God!"

In 1850, when I was eighteen, under date 4th mo., 25th 1850, I write:—

"I have been thinking today of my present life, and I could hardly find words to express its happiness. Relatives, friends,

circumstances, all are nearly perfect. Outwardly I have
scarcely anything to wish for, unless it is for plenty of money
to give away, and to buy flowers with. I am crowned with
blessings every day and all the day long. Oh, there never was
any one so blessed! . . . Everything is so beautiful, and
everybody is so lovely, and I can enjoy it, and do enjoy it all to
the very full. Sometimes I have such heart gushes, as I call
them, that I can scarcely contain myself. I love them dearly,
and yet after all perhaps they are a little foolish. They are
caused by such slight things—a blade of grass, a leaf waving
in the wind, a bright happy golden dandelion, even an old
barrel, or a heap of stones, or the creaking of a shoe, often the
rattling of a cart, or some equally common sound, give me for
the moment a sense of most exquisite happiness. Why, I cannot
tell. It is not the beauty of the sight nor the harmony of the
sound, but only a something, I know not what, that causes my
heart to gush up joyfully, and my very soul to expand. I
sometimes think it must be association; but with what? I do not
love creaking shoes or rattling carts, and yet often when
walking along the street I fairly laugh from inward pleasure at
the something in that creaking or rattling. It is not so always.
A hundred shoes may creak, and a hundred carts may rattle,
and a hundred barrels or heaps of stones may be around me, and
jar painfully on ear and eye; but once in a while comes *the one*,
and then comes the heart gush. Today a drop of rain fell on my
forehead, and I could have laughed aloud. But it was very silly;
and I am a foolish child altogether, and fear I always shall be
. . . . Yesterday we went with mother to the Shelter (a home for
little colored orphans). It was very interesting there, but
nothing pleased me so much as when the little Blackies
repeated, 'Sparkle, sparkle, water pure, dirty hands I can't
endure.' That gave me a right earnest heart-gush. I seemed

almost to see myself in short frocks and panties, a little white apron, and one of the (as we thought) inimitable nets with a beautiful bow on the side, which mother used to think was almost too gay, enclosing my frisky hair, sitting on the highest bench of all in the school, and feeling, and no doubt looking, as proud as a queen."

Again under date 7th mo., 9th, 1850 (after describing the pleasure of a little trip away from home):—

"And yet the pleasantest of all was to get home again last night. Home is home, and there is no place like unto it. Every day I enjoy it more and more, and every day I am happier. Last night I felt too happy almost. I fairly wanted to turn heels over head in my exuberance, and I did scream with delight. And all for no particular reason; only the influences around me were so beautiful, and it seemed just then so glorious to live—to live, and suffer patiently, and work earnestly and nobly, and trust cheerfully, for years and years, until the glorious end shall come and bring the reward of peace and everlasting happiness."

Later in the same year I write under date of 7th mo., 16th:—

"In two weeks we start for a journey through the New England States and to Newport. It is grand, this plan of going to Newport—just the very place I had set my heart on visiting this summer, though I did not at all expect it. But somehow, I can scarcely tell how, whenever I set my heart on anything I am nearly always gratified. From a child it has been so. I can scarcely remember being ever much disappointed, and I am sure every step of my life hitherto has been through sunshine and flowers. But I do not wonder, with such kind and good parents it could not be otherwise. They really could not do more than they do to make us happy, and they succeed beautifully. . . . I believe I do not know any children who have so many enjoyments clustered in their home, although I know many whose parents are far richer."

I might multiply these extracts almost indefinitely, for my diaries up to the age of nineteen are, with the exception of my religious struggles, which seemed very tragic, but did not really affect my spirits much, one long jubilant song of happiness. At nineteen I married, and a new life began for me, which had its own more mature joys; but girlhood was over, and its simple girlish "Fate of happiness," as I called it, was exchanged for the woman's life of sober responsibilities, and weighty, although delightful, cares.

In looking back now I can see that this "Fate of happiness" was created by two causes,—my health and my parents. As to health, I never knew, through all the first eighteen years of my life, except once when I had an attack of bilious fever, what it was to be ever ailing. I never had a headache, I did not know I had a back, I never got tired, I had a perfect digestion, and nothing ever caused me the loss of a single hour's sleep. Moreover I was blessed with what people nowadays call "*la joie de vivre,*" and simply to live seemed often happiness enough for me.

But the chiefest charm of my life was that I possessed the most delightful father and mother that ever lived. In the narrow Quaker circle into which I was born, very few of the opportunities for amusement or excitement that come to young people nowadays, were open to us, and all the fun we could extract from life was of the most simple and innocent kind. But with such a father and mother as ours, no outside pleasures were needed. They were so sympathetic and loving, and so entirely on our side under all circumstances, that we looked upon them, not as uncomfortable criticizing "grownups," but almost as children like ourselves, with the same tastes and interests as our own. We considered them far better comrades than any others we knew, and no fun the world ever had to offer was half so attractive to us as a quiet talk with our mother, or a good game of romps with our fun-loving father.

They often used to say that they wanted their children to have a happy childhood "tucked under their jackets"; for they were sure it would make us better men and women, and they took care that we should have this priceless boon. In looking back it seems to me that there were absolutely no clouds over my childhood's sky. One of the much amused young people of the present day said to me once, with rather an accent of pity, "It seems to me you did not have many amusements when you were young." "We did not need to," was my prompt reply. "We had our father and mother, and they were all the amusements we needed. They made our lives all sunshine."

I wish I could give to others the vivid picture I have of their inexpressible delightfulness. We knew, down to the very bottom of our hearts, that they were on our side against the whole world, and would be our champions in every time of need. No one could oppress us, neither playmates, nor friends, nor enemies, not even our teachers (those paid oppressors of children, as we felt all teachers to be), nor any one the whole world over, without having to reckon with those dear champions at home; and the certain conviction of this surrounded us with such a panoply of defense, that nothing had power to trouble us overmuch. "We will tell father," or "We will tell mother," was our unfailing resource and consolation in every sorrow. In fact, so sure was I of their championship, that, when any of my friends or school fellows were in trouble, I used to say, "Oh well, never mind, come home with me and let us tell my father and mother;" feeling sure that that dear father and mother could set the whole world straight, if the chance were only given them. And when the answer would come, as it often did, "Oh, that would be of no use, for your father and mother cannot do everything," I would say, with a profound pity for their ignorance, "Ah, you do not know my father and mother!"

One of my sisters remembered to her dying day, with a deep sense of gratitude, a deliverance our father gave her from an oppressively long lesson before she was six years old. Kindergartens were not invented then, and all children were required to study abstract lessons in a way that would be considered almost inhuman in these days. My sister was toiling over a sum with a hopeless sense of incapacity, and with tears trickling over her cheeks, when my father entered the room and said: "Ho, Liney, what is going wrong?" She told him as well as she could, and she says she could never forget his tone of absolute comprehension and sympathy as he said, "why, of course it is too hard for my little Sally Dimple; but never mind, put it away, and I will make it all right with thy teacher." And my sister says so strong a conviction came to her at that moment of her father's championship, that she went through all the rest of her school life with an absolute sense of protection that made it impossible for any "hard lessons" ever to trouble her again.

It was not that our father or mother encouraged us to shirk any duty that they felt we were capable of performing. But they had so much sympathy with us, and such a sense of real justice in their dealings with us, that they seemed always able to discriminate between the possible and the impossible, and to protect us from the latter, while cheerily stimulating our efforts after the former. They never took it for granted, as so many "grown-ups" do, that, because we were children, we must necessarily be in the wrong; but they judged the case on its own merits. I believe it was this certainty of their justice that was more of a steady comfort to us than almost anything; and I am very sure it has helped me to understand the perfect justice of my Heavenly Father in a way I could not otherwise have done.

As I say, they always stimulated us to all right effort, but this was never by commands or by harsh scolding, but always by sympathy and encouragement. They recognized our individuality, and respected it, giving us principles for our guidance rather than many burdensome rules. As far as possible they threw the responsibility of our conduct upon ourselves. This degree of personal liberty was a necessity to my freedom loving nature. Under any other *régime* I should have wilted and withered; or else, which I think is more likely, should have openly rebelled. But as it was, no matter how averse I might be to any task, or how discouraged at any difficulty, my father's cheery voice repeating one of his homely proverbs, "Come, come, Han, stand up to the rack, fodder or no fodder," would always drive away all my reluctance; and discouragements melted like snow before the sun, in the face of his courage-giving assertion, "What man has done, man can do, and" (he would slyly add) "consequently woman." No child could have withstood such inspiring courage.

My father's own life had been a living illustration of the courage that he so continually tried to instill into us. When a boy of sixteen, his father lost a large part of his fortune in some West Indian transactions, and his sons were obliged to do what they could for their own support. My father, with his adventurous spirit, chose the sea, and, beginning in the lowest place, he so rapidly worked his way upward, that, at the early age of twenty-four, he was made captain of an East Indiaman, at that time the largest ship in the port of Philadelphia; and his voyages in this ship were remarkably successful. He always attributed his success to the care and guidance of his Heavenly Father, upon whom he relied in all his affairs, and whose special help he always asked and believed he always received, in every time of need. At the age of twenty-nine he gave up the sea, and went into business in Philadelphia, and here the same energy and the same reliance upon Divine help so prospered him, that he was able to make a comfortable competence for his declining years.

I well remember when I was a little girl often wondering what sort of a boy my father had been, and deciding, as I watched the roguish twinkles in the corners of his clear grey eyes, and the curves of fun around his genial mouth, that he must have been a perfectly splendid boy, and just the kind I would have liked for a playmate. For, getting on towards middle age as he was when we were young, we found him the best playmate we children ever had. Some of his old friends, who remembered him as a boy, used to tell us that he was at once the most provoking and the best beloved boy in all their circle. No one could keep their anger against him for more than a moment. Let his tricks be as vexatious as they might,—and he was, they say, full and brimming over with mischief all the day long,—no anger could withstand his genuine and openly expressed sorrow at any trouble he may have caused, and the hearty and generous restitution he was always ready to offer, nor the merry rebound of fun that would burst out the moment his apologies had been accepted. He was always the first to help in every case of need; and every one, whether friend or foe, knew they could rely on him for any service he was capable of performing. All his friends loved and admired him, even while they scolded him, and they generally found them-selves laughing at the very moment when they meant to be the most severe and frowning. From childhood to old age this power of winning love approval continued with him; and the fun of his boyhood, developing into the genial merriment of the chastened Christian heart, gave his mature character a name-less charm.

In fact I do not believe there ever was a more contagiously cheerful being than our father. No one could help feeling happier because of his presence. His very handshake was an uplift, and seemed somehow to make the world brighter than it was before, and to put you in a better humor with yourself and with every one around you. Many of my friends have told me that they would rather have had a handshake from him than receive a valuable gift from another man, because somehow, in the handshake, his heart seem to go right to their hearts, with power to cheer and help. I remember well how, when my childhood's sky would be all darkened by some heavy childish affliction, a cheery "Well, Broadie," in his hearty voice, or some little passing joke spoken with a roguish twinkle of his loving grey eyes, would clear my sky in a moment, and make life all sunshine again. And, even when I was older, his power to cheer grew no less, and it was quite my habit, whenever I found myself down in the depths, to put myself somewhere in his way, with the certainty that even a moment's peep at his strong cheery face would lift me out. I can even remember that, in his absence, the sight and feel of his dear old overcoat would somehow brighten everything, and send me off encouraged to be braver and stronger. To make life happier for every one with whom he came in contact seemed to be his aim and his mission, and rarely has any one succeeded so well. Some one said to me, many years after his death, that "John M. Whithall was the best loved man in Philadelphia"; and in certain circles I am sure this was true.

Our mother also was equally well beloved. She was a most delightful mother, not so full of fun perhaps as our father, but always ready to champion her children's cause everywhere and at all times, and an unfailing rock of refuge to us in every emergency. Sweetness and goodness, purity and truth, seemed to emanate from her gracious presence; and, for every one who came in contact with her, she was an inspiration to all that was noble and good.

People talk in these days of an atmosphere surrounding each one of us, something like the nimbus that is always painted about the heads of saints. They say it seems to envelop the whole figure, and that it influences for good or evil all who come near it. It is called the "aura," and is the outcome of each one's character and inmost personality. Some auras, we are told, are dark and gloomy, and exert a depressing or even a wicked influence, while others are rose color, or gold, or opal, or sky blue and full of light, and their influence is cheering and uplifting; and all this without perhaps a word being said in either case. If this theory is true I feel sure that my father and mother possessed "auras" full of heaven's own sunshine, and, without knowing the reason, their children lived in perpetual cheer.

That a childhood so lived could not fail to have an enormous influence on the after history of any soul, seems to me incontrovertible; and I attribute my final satisfying discovery of my Heavenly Father largely to what I had known of the goodness of my earthly parents. They never said much about religion, for the Quaker fear of meddling between a soul and its Maker had created a habit of reserve that could not easily be broken through, but they showed plainly that their lives were lived in the region of profound faith in an ever present God. We could not but see that He was to them a reality beyond all other realities. Of religious teaching we had but little, but of religious example and influence we had a never-failing supply. Not by talking, but by daily living, were impressions made on our childish hearts.

I remember once however when my father did speak out of the fullness of his heart, and when what he said made a profound and lasting impression upon me. I was a very imaginative child, and consequently very frightened of the dark, which I peopled with all sorts of terrible monsters, lurking under beds or behind doors, ready to rush out and devour me at any moment. Of course, with the profound reticence of childhood, I never spoke of this; but somehow my father at last found out that I was afraid of the dark, and instead of ridiculing my fears or scolding me, as I felt in my poor foolish little heart I deserved for making such a row, he took me lovingly on his knee, and, putting his dear strong arm around me, he said, in tones of the most profound conviction, "Why, Han, did thee not know there is never anything to be afraid of? Did thee not know that thy Heavenly Father is always with thee?" And as I still trembled and shivered, he added, as though surprised that there could be any one in the world who did not know this, "I thought of course thee knew this, child." I never shall forget the profound impression this made upon me, nor the immediate and permanent relief from fear it gave me; and I have always been sure that this one statement of a fact, which was to my father the most tremendous reality of his life, has had more than anything else to do with the satisfying sense of God's presence which has for so long been my portion. It was not a religious dogma my father stated on this, to me, memorable occasion, but it was a simple, incontrovertible fact which he was surprised I did not know; and, as being the statement of a fact, it was far more comforting than any amount of preaching or arguing could possibly have been. God was with me—and that was enough; for of course, being with me, He would naturally take care of me. I remember that when my father lifted me down from his lap and told me cheerily to run along and not to be frightened any more, I walked off in a stately sort of way, feeling as if somehow I was safe inside an invisible fortress where I could laugh to scorn all the lurking monsters of the dark, and could hear their angry rustles unmoved.

I dare say the rarity of any direct religious teaching from our parents helped to make the few occasions when they did speak more impressive; but, however this may be, I can truly say that, though often obscured for a time, the convictions of that occasion have always been with me at bottom, and thousands of times in my life since, my father's words then, have brought me help.

Chapter 2

MY QUAKER CHILDHOOD

Next to the influence of my parents upon my young life, was the influence of the religious Society of which I was a birthright member. I do not think it would be possible for me to express in words how strong and all pervading this influence was. Every word and thought and action of our lives was steeped in Quakerism. Never for a single moment did we escape from it. Not that we wanted to, for we knew nothing different; but, as my narrative will show, every atom of our consciousness was infused and possessed with it. Daily I thank God that it was such a righteous and ennobling influence.

But, though so all powerful in our lives, the Quakerism of my day did not achieve its influence by much outward teaching. One of its most profound beliefs was in regard to the direct inward teaching of the Holy Spirit to each individual soul; and this discouraged much teaching by human lips. The Quakers accepted as literally true the declarations of the Apostle John that there is a "true Light which lighteth every man that cometh into the world"; and their fundamental teaching was that this "Light," if faithfully looked for and obeyed, would lead every man into all truth. They felt therefore that it would be an interference between the soul and its Divine Guide and Teacher to intrude with any mere teaching of man. They taught us to listen for and obey the voice of God in our soul, and they believed if we did this up to our best knowledge, our Divine Guide would teach us all it was necessary for us to know of doctrines or dogmas.

There was something grand in this recognition of human individuality. It left each soul in an absolute independence before its Creator, ready to be taught directly by Him, without the interference of any human being, except as that human being might be inspired by Himself. And although in my youthful days I did not consciously formulate this, yet the atmosphere it created, and the individual dignity with which it endowed every human soul, whether wise or simple, rich or poor, learned or unlearned, old or young, made each of us feel from our earliest days a royal interior independence that nobody, not even our parents, could touch.

When the Bible was read to us, which was frequently done, especially on "First Day" afternoons, very little explanation was ever attempted, but instead a few moments of profound silence were always observed at the close of the reading, in order that the "Inward Light" might, if it should be the Divine Will, reveal to us the meaning of what had been read. I am afraid however that personally I was still too unawakened for much ever to be revealed to me. But so strong was this feeling among the Quakers in my day, that direct religious teaching from the lips of human beings, except in inspired preaching, always seemed to me to be of the world, worldly, and I felt it was good only for the "world's people," who, because of their ignorance regarding the inward light, were necessarily obliged to look outward for their teaching. In fact all Bible expositions, except such as might be directly inspired, were felt to be worldly; and Bible classes and Sunday-schools were considered to be places of worldly amusement, which no true Quaker ought to attend. Our teaching was to come to us, not from the lips of human teachers, but from the inward voice of the Divine Teacher Himself.

In this the early Friends only believed what Saint Augustine taught when he said: "It is the inward Master that teacheth, it is the inspiration that teacheth; where the inspiration and unction are wanting, it is vain that words from without are beaten in."

Their preaching therefore was mostly composed of exhortations to listen for this "inward voice," and to obey it, when heard; and never once, during all my young days, do I remember hearing any other sort of preaching.

Not that there might not have been, however, doctrinal preaching as well, had I had the ears to hear it; but as a fact no religious questions of any sort except the one overpowering conviction that somehow or other I must manage to be good, occupied my mind up to the age of sixteen. I lived only in that strange mysterious world of childhood, so far removed from the "grown-up world" around it, where everything outside seemed only a mere passing show. In my world all was plain and simple, with no need for any questionings. The grown-up people around me seemed to have their ridiculous interests and their foolish bothers, but these were nothing to me in my enchanted sphere. Sometimes, when one of these silly grown-ups would suggest that a time would come when I would be grown up, a pang would come over me at the dreadful thought, and I would resolve to put off the evil day as long as possible, by refusing to have my hair done up in a knot behind, or to have my dresses come below my knees. I had an idea that grown up people wanted to live children's lives, and play children's plays, and have children's fun, just as much as children did, but that there was a law which forbade it. And when people talked in my presence about the necessity of "taking up the cross" as you grew older, I thought they meant that you would have to stop climbing trees or rolling hoops, or running races, or walking on the tops of fences, although all the while you would want to do these things as much as ever; and my childish heart was often with a profound pity for the poor unfortunate grown-ups around me.

I was a wild harum-scarum sort of being, and up to the age of sixteen was nothing but a light-hearted, irresponsible child, determined to get all the fun I could out of life, and with none of the morbid self-consciousness that is so often such a torment to young people.

The fact was, as far as I can recollect, I scarcely ever thought of myself, as myself, at all. My old friends tell me now that I was considered a very pretty girl, but I never knew it. The question as to my looks never occurred to me. The only question that really interested me was as to my fun; and how I looked, or what people thought of me were things that did not seem in the least to concern me.

I remember distinctly the first time such questions intruded themselves, and the indignant way in which I rejected them. I think I must have been about eleven years old. My mother had sent for me to go into the drawing-room to see some of her friends who had asked for me. Without a fear I left my lessons, and went towards the drawing-room; when suddenly, just as I was about to enter, I was utterly surprised and taken aback by an attack of shyness. I had never had the feeling before, and I found it most disagreeable. And as I turned the door-knob I said to myself, "This is ridiculous. Why should I be afraid of those people in there? I am sure they won't shoot me, and I do not believe they will think anything about me; and, even if they do, it can't hurt, and I simply *will not* be frightened." And as I said this, I deliberately threw my shyness behind my back, and walked fearlessly into the room, leaving it all outside the door. I had made the discovery, although I did not know enough then to formulate it, that shyness was simply thinking about oneself, and that to forget oneself was a certain cure; and I do not remember ever really suffering from shyness again. If it ever came, I just threw it behind me as I had done the first time, and literally refused to pay any attention to it.

As far as I can remember therefore my life, up to the age of sixteen, when my religious awakening came, was an absolutely thoughtless child's life. Self-introversion and self-examination were things of which I knew nothing, and religious questions were not so much as dreamed of by me. I look back with wonder that so thoughtless a being could have been so preserved from outbreaking sins as I was, but I recognize that for this I must thank the grand all-enveloping Quaker atmosphere of goodness and righteousness, in which I lived, and which made any such outbreaks almost an impossibility.

I have spoken of the Church into which I was born as a religious society. It was always called in my young days, "The religious Society of Friends," and was never by any chance spoken of, as it often is now, as "The Quaker Church." The early Quakers had a strong testimony against calling themselves a Church in any exclusive or inclusive sense of that word. The Church, according to their view, was the invisible body of all believers, belonging to every creed and every nation, and they as "Friends" were only a "Society" within this great universal invisible Church. They took their name from our Lord's words in John 15:14, 15: "Ye are My friends if ye do whatsoever I command you. Henceforth I call you not servants; for the servant knoweth not what his Lord doeth; but I have called you friends, for all things that I have heard of My Father I have made known unto you." Their one aim in life was to do whatsoever the Lord commanded, and they believed therefore that they had been admitted into this sacred circle of the Divine friendship. They had at first no idea of forming a separate sect, but their association was to their minds only a society of friends (with neither a capital s nor a capital f), who met together to share as friends, one with another, the Divine revelations that were made to each, and to encourage one another to strive after the righteousness that the Divine friendship demanded. That this "society for friends" gradually assumed a definite article and capital letters to itself, and became "The Religious Society of Friends," and developed into a separate sect, was I suppose, the necessary outcome of all such movements, but it has always seemed to me a falling away from the simplicity and universality of the original idea.

The name of Quaker had been bestowed upon them in their early days from the fact that, when preaching in their Meetings, they were seen to quake or tremble under what they believed to be the power of the Holy Ghost. I myself, even in the quieter times when I was a child, would often see the preachers in our meetings trembling and quaking from head to foot, and I confess I always felt that messages delivered under this condition had a special inspiration and unction of their own, far beyond all others. In fact, unless a preacher had at least enough of this "quaking" to make their hearts palpitate and their legs tremble, they were not considered by many to have the real "call" to the ministry at all; and one cannot therefore be surprised that the name "Quaker" had fastened itself on the society.

But the name chosen by themselves was a far happier one, and far more descriptive of what they really were. The "quaking" was after all only an incident in their religion, but friendliness was its very essence. Because they believed themselves to be the friends of God, they realized that they must be in the truest sense the friends of all the creatures He had created. They believed it was literally true that He had made all the nations of men of one blood, and that all were therefore their brethren. One could not fail to realize this sense of universal friendship through all the worship and the work of the society; and personally, so deeply was it impressed upon my young life, that to this day to be a member of the Society of Friends means to me to be everybody's friend; and whenever there is any oppression or suffering anywhere in the world, I instinctively feel sure that among the first to hasten to the rescue will be a committee of the Society of Friends. They have in fact a standing Committee which meets regularly to consider cases of wrong and of need, and it is called significantly "The Meeting for Sufferings." The society is and always has been the friend of all who are oppressed.

Therefore, while the outside world generally calls them "Quakers," I am glad that they themselves have held steadfastly to the endearing name of "Friends."

Chapter 3

QUAKERISM

Before entering upon the subject of the influence of Quakerism on my young life, I want it to be thoroughly understood that I am not trying in any sense to give a true transcript of Quakerism, as my elders understood it and lived it, but only as it influenced an undeveloped eager girl, who had a decidedly religious side to her nature, but who was too full of life and spirits to be very seriously interested in any abstract questions outside of her every-day duties and fun.

I cannot trace back my notions to any definite teaching, and at the time I did not formulate them, but the impressions I retain of those days seem to me now to have had their rise in the general atmosphere that surrounded me. It is very likely that my adult relatives and friends had no idea of creating such an atmosphere, and, if they were alive now, would be very much surprised at some of my interpretations. But the fact remains that the Quakerism of my young life has left the strong impressions I record, and I want to give them as truthfully as I can, as part of my own personal history, and not at all as an authoritative exposition of Quaker view.

In tracing back the line of our ancestors, we find that they came over from England during the seventeenth century, in company with a great body of Quakers who, unable to find in their own land that spirit of religious liberty which was a fundamental article of their faith, sought an asylum in the new Western world, hoping there to found a state where their children might enjoy that freedom to worship God according to the dictates of their own consciences, which had been denied to themselves in the old world. These Quakers had settled largely in the colonies founded by William Penn in and around Philadelphia, on both sides of the Delaware river, and had become, by the time I was born, a most influential and respected body.

A good deal of their early freshness and fervor had however passed away, and it was a very sober, quiet sort of religion that remained, which allowed of but little expression, and was far more entirely interior than seems to me now to have been wise. There had been left from earlier days a firm belief in what was always spoken of as the "perceptible guidance of the Holy Spirit," meaning the distinct and conscious voice of God in the heart; and a loyal devotion to what were called "Friends' testimonies," which testimonies were the outward expression of the convictions of truth that had, they believed, been directly revealed by the "inward light" to George Fox, the founder of the society, and to his early followers.

Many of these convictions were opposed to the usual ideas of people around us, and their observance therefore made the Quakers of my day very peculiar. But we were taught that it was a great honor to be God's "peculiar people," and I for one fully believed that we Quakers were meant where it says in Deuteronomy, "The Lord hath chosen thee to be a peculiar people unto Himself above all the nations that are upon the earth." In the face of such honor, the things in which we were "peculiar," which often, I acknowledge, caused us considerable embarrassment and even trial, seemed to be a sort of "hallmark" of special Divine favor; and, instead of being mortified over their peculiarities, the Quakers of my day were secretly proud of them, and of the singularity they caused. We Quaker children imbibed somewhat of this feeling, and when we walked along the streets in our quaint Quaker garb, and the street gamins called after us, as they often did "Quaker, Quaker, mash potato" we felt a sustaining sense of superiority, that took some of the sting out of the intended insult, and enabled us to call back with a fine scorn, as having far the best of the matter, "Dutchy, Dutchy, Mashy-pay-touchy!" If we were Quakers, they were perhaps the descendants of the early German, or, as they were called, "Dutch Redemptioners" who were the servants of the first colonists; and at any rate we were determined they should know we thought they were. I remember that after my sisters and I had discovered this effective retort, we were able to silence most of our persecutors.

But it was sometimes very hard for us Quaker children to be obliged to take our share of persecution for "conscience sake," since it was the consciences of our elders and not our own; and, combined with our pride in being God's peculiar people, we also often had a sense of ostracism that I feel on looking back, we ought not to have been asked to endure. Still I have no doubt it imparted to our characters a sort of sturdy independence that was of real value to us in our after life, and I for one have always been thankful for the deliverance from the fear of man, and the indifference to criticism, that was, I am convinced, engendered in my spirit by these early persecutions for "conscience sake."

There was, as I have said, very little direct religious teaching to the young Quakers in my time. We were sometimes preached to in our meetings, when a Friend in the gallery would exhort the "dear young people" to be faithful to their Divine Guide; but no doctrines or dogmas were ever taught us; and, unless one was especially awakened in some way, none of the questions that exercise the minds of young people in the present day were even so much as dreamed of by the young people of my circle, at least so far as I knew; and a creature more utterly ignorant of all so-called religious truth than I was up to the age of sixteen, when my awakening came, could hardly be conceived of in these modern times. The whole religious question for me was simply as to whether I was good enough to go to heaven, or so naughty as to deserve hell. As to there being a "plan of salvation," or any such thing as "justification by faith," it was never heard of among us. The one vital point in our ideas of religion was as to whether or not we looked for and obeyed that "perceptible guidance" of the Holy Spirit, to which we were constantly directed; and the only definite teaching we received as to our religious life was comprised in "Friends' testimonies," and in the "queries" read and answered every month in the "monthly meetings for business" which were regularly held by every congregation of Quakers.

We had no Sunday-school nor Bible classes; in fact, as I have said, these were considered to be a form of "creaturely activity" only to be excused in the "world's people" (by which we meant everybody who was not a Quaker), because they were in ignorance, as we believed, of the far higher teachings of the Holy Spirit which were our special inheritance. Neither did our Society teach us any regular prayers, for Friends believed they could only pray acceptably when moved by the Spirit to pray. As little children our parents had taught us a childish prayer, which we repeated every night after we were tucked up in bed before the last farewell kisses were given. But as we grew older, and our parents recognized more and more our individual independence, these nightly childish prayers were omitted, and the Quaker atmosphere as regards to prayer gradually gained the ascendancy; and in time I, at least, came to feel as if, because of my light-hearted carelessness and indifference, it was almost wrong for me to try to pray.

What this Quaker teaching about prayer was may be gathered from the following extract from the writings of Isaac Pennington. He says, "Prayer is a gift. A man cannot pray when he will; but he is to watch and to wait, when the Father will kindle in him living breathings towards Himself." In consequence we knew no formal prayers, and were not even taught the Lord's prayer, and until I was a woman I actually did not know it by heart, and even to this day I am often puzzled for a moment when I try to repeat it. The real truth is that as a child I got the impression somehow that the Lord's prayer was "gay," and that only "gay" people were expected to use it. By "gay" we meant anything that was not Quakerly. Quakers were "plain" and all the rest of the world, and even of the Church were "gay."

It even seemed to me that it was distinctly "gay" to kneel in prayer. We Friends always stood when prayer was offered in our meetings, and if we ever prayed on retiring at night, it was done after we got into bed. And when, as sometimes happened, one of our little circle ventured to kneel beside her bed for her evening devotions, we always felt that it was a lamentable yielding to a worldly spirit, and was to be mourned over as a backsliding from the true faith.

As a fact all Church or Chapel services seemed to us very gay and worldly, and to join in them seemed almost to amount to sinning; and until I was married I had actually never entered any place of worship other than Friends' Meeting houses. I should have felt it a distinct "falling from grace" to have done so.

I cannot remember that we were distinctly taught any of these things, or that any one ever said to me in so many words that Quakers were the "peculiar people" spoken of in the Bible as being especially dear to God; but the sort of preaching to which we listened, and only of course half understood, in regard to the privileges and the blessings of our peculiarities, made the impression upon my young ignorance that in some way, because of our "peculiarities," we were the objects of special Divine favor; and I can remember very well having the distinct feeling that we were the true Israelites of whom the Bible spoke, and that all who were not Quakers belonged to the "outside Gentiles." To tell the whole truth I had as a child a confused idea in my mind that we Quakers had a different and a far higher God than others, and that God other Christians worshiped was one of the "Gods of the Gentiles" whom the Bible condemned.

That I was not singular in these feelings will be shown in the following extracts from the lately published reminiscences of an American Friend, who is an able educationalist of the present day.[1] He says:

"I am quite sure no Israelite in the days of Israel's prosperity ever had a more certain conviction that he belonged to a peculiar people whom the Lord had chosen for His own, than I did. There was for me and absolute break between 'us' and anybody else. This phariseeism was never taught me, nor encouraged directly by anybody, but I none the less had it. If I had anything in the world to glory over it was that I was a Quaker. Others about me had a good deal more that was tangible than I had. Their life was easier, and they did not have as hard a struggle to get the things they wanted as we did. But they were not 'chosen,' and we were! As far back as I can travel in my memory I find this sense of superiority—a sort of birthright into Divine grace and favor. I think it came partly from impressions I got from 'travelling friends,' whose visits had an indescribable influence upon me. It will of course seem

1. "A Boy's Religion," by Rufus M. Jones.

to have been a very narrow view, and so it was, but its influence was decidedly important upon me. It gave somewhat of a dignity to my little life to feel that I belonged to God's own people; that, out of all the world, *we* had been selected to be His, and that His wonders had been worked for *us*, and *we* were objects of His special love and care.

"Everybody at home, as well as many of our visitors, believed implicitly in immediate divine guidance. Those who went out from our meeting to do extended religious service, and there were many such visits undertaken, always seemed as directly selected for these momentous missions, as were the prophets of old. As far back as I can remember I can see Friends sitting talking with my grandmother of some 'concern' which was 'heavy upon them,' and the whole matter seemed as important as though they had been called by an earthly king to carry on the affairs of an empire. It was partly these cases of divine selection, and the constant impression that God was using these persons, whom I knew, to be His messengers, that made me so sure of the fact that we were His chosen people. At any rate I grew up with this idea firmly fixed."

I believe every young "Friend," in the circle to which I belonged, would have owned to the same feelings. We were God's "chosen people," and, as such, belonged to a religious aristocracy as real as any earthly aristocracy could be; and I do not believe any earl or duke was ever prouder of his earthly aristocratic position than we were of our heavenly one.

Chapter 4

QUAKER "TRUTH," AND QUAKER "MINISTRY"

So certain were the "Friends" that theirs was the true faith set forth in the Bible and preached by the Apostles, that in speaking of it they always in my day called it the "Truth," with a capital "T," and spoke of the religious work of the society as the "service of Truth." And I remember that my father's horses and carriages were called "Truth's horses and carriages," because they were so continually in requisition to convey preachers from one meeting to another, or to do errands for the Elders or Overseers. With the unquestioning faith of childhood I fully believed all this, and grew up with a distinct idea that we "Friends" had practically a monopoly of "The Truth," with a strong emphasis on the definite article, which differentiated it entirely from the holding of one truth among many. Ours was the whole truth, and nothing but the truth, and could not be improved upon. Such was my idea in the days of my youth.

That "Friends" did, however, hold a great deal of truth (without any definite article) cannot be denied. Nearly every view of divine things that I have since discovered, and every reform I have since advocated, had, I now realize, their germs in the views of the Society; and over and over again, when some new discovery or conviction has dawned upon me, I have caught myself saying, "Why, *that* was what the early Friends meant, although I never understood it before."

Many of their great moral and religious principles have

been gradually adopted and taught by other Christians—namely the spiritual interpretation of the Bible instead of the literal, the use of the Sabbath for man, and not man for the Sabbath, the subordination of the symbol to the spiritual belief symbolized, the comparative unimportance of creeds and dogmas, or of rites and ceremonies, the abhorrence of slavery, the vital importance of temperance, the direct access of the soul to God without human intermediary. But in the day when the Quakers first declared these things, they seemed like hard sayings which only a few could bear. And even those of us who were brought up with them from our very cradles, needed many years of spiritual growth and enlightenment before we could fully comprehend them.

One of the truths they had got hold of far ahead of their time was in regard to the equality in the sight of God between men and women. They gave to their "women Friends" an equal place with "men Friends" in the work of the Society. There were women Preachers, and women Elders, and women Overseers, who sat in equal state with the men Preachers, and Elders, and Overseers, on the raised benches in solemn rows, facing the body of the meeting, the men on one side of the middle aisle, and the women on the other. The preachers, (or Ministers, as we called them), sat at the head of these solemn rows, the oldest and weightiest nearest the top, and gradually tapering down to the younger neophytes, whose gifts had only lately been "acknowledged."

The system of the ministry among Friends was very different from that of any other church. They believed profoundly that only God could make a Minister, and that no preaching was right except such preaching as was directly and immediately inspired by Him. They accepted, as the only true equipment for the work of the ministry, the declaration contained in Matthew 10: 18-20, and they believed its promises would be literally fulfilled to every faithful soul, whether man or woman, young or old, learned or unlearned. "And ye shall be brought before governors and kings for My sake for a testimony against them and the Gentiles. But when they deliver you up take no thought how or what ye shall speak; for it shall be given you in that same hour what ye shall speak, for it is not ye that speak but the spirit of your Father which speaketh in you." This promise contained for them the Quaker "Call" and the Quaker "Ordination"; and to "study for the ministry" in colleges or out of books, or to be ordained by the laying on of human hands, seemed to them the rejection of the only Divine call and ordination, and to result in what they termed a "man made ministry." In their view Ministers could be made only by God, and the power to preach was a direct "gift" bestowed by Him alone. All that could be done was for the Elders and Overseers of the meeting to watch the development of this gift; and, when it seemed to them that the speaking bore unmistakable signs of a Divine "unction," they would meet together and decide whether or no to record on their meeting-books that they "acknowledged" so and so to be a Minister. This act of "recording" or "acknowledging" did not make the speakers Ministers; it was only the recognition and acknowledgment of the fact that God had already made them such. When this had been done, they were called "acknowledged Ministers," and were felt by us young people to have been admitted into the hierarchy of heaven itself.

Moreover, since God had made them Ministers, their payment or remuneration must come from Him alone. No stipends or salaries were ever given them, but their ministry, freely bestowed from above, was freely handed forth to their fellow-members, without money and without price. Consequently all

Quaker Ministers continued in their usual occupations while "exercising their gifts," living on their own incomes, or carrying on their usual trades or businesses. It often left them but little time for study or preparation; but, as no study or preparation was permitted, this was no drawback.

For not only was there to be no special training for the ministry, but it was not thought right to make preparation for any particular service or meeting. "Friends" were supposed to go to their meetings with their minds a blank, ready to receive any message that the Holy Spirit might see it fit to impart. None of them could tell beforehand whether the inspiration would or would not come to them; and the promise was clear that, should it come, it would be given them in that same hour what they should speak. All preparation for preaching therefore was felt to be a disloyalty to the Holy Spirit, and was called "creaturely activity," meaning that it was the creature in the individual, and not the Spirit of God, that had taken control. And no such preaching was ever felt to have that "unction of the Spirit" which was the Quaker test of all ministry. I have found in an old book of selections from Isaac Penington's writings the following concerning ministers, which clearly expressed the Quaker view.

"It is not preaching things that are true which makes a true minister, but the receiving of his ministry from the Lord. The gospel is the Lord's which is to be preached, and it is to be preached in His power; and the ministers who preach it are to be endued with His power, and to be sent by Him. . . . He that will be a true Minister must receive both his gift, his ministry, and the exercise of both, from the Lord, and must be sure in his ministering to keep in the power. . . . He must wait in his several exercises, to be endued with matter and power from on high, before he opens his mouth in a testimony for the Lord."

With this view of preaching it can easily be understood that to "appear in the ministry," as it was quaintly expressed, would be felt by all to be, not only a very solemn step, but also a truly awful one. In my young days it was always referred to as "taking up the cross," and was looked upon as the supreme sacrifice a soul could make. It has always been hard for me to understand this feeling, as in my own personal experience preaching has been far more of a pleasure than a sacrifice. But probably this may have been because I have let in more or less of what the early Friends would call the "creature" into my ministry, and have not attributed quite such a high origin to my utterances. An old letter of my mother's concerning the "appearance in the ministry" of her brother, my Uncle John Tatum, will illustrate the state of feeling I have described. She is writing to her father and mother about a visit to this uncle, and says:

"Have you heard of the sacrifice that dear brother John has lately made in yielding to what I believe has been a long-felt impression of duty, by giving up to appear in public testimony and supplication in their meetings. It is since we were there; but we were both particularly struck with the marks of exercise and humble devotedness that appeared in his daily walk and conversation. I hope we shall all be willing to yield him the strength of our tenderest sympathy, and to pray that he may be led, and guided, and kept in the right way. He does, I believe, feel often much alone. He said to me, 'Ah, my dear sister, it has been an awful time with me lately, in which I have had to seek the fields and woods alone, and pray mightily for strength and preservation.'"

I cannot but think that it was a false view of Christian service that led the Friends to go through such conflicts over what nowadays is embraced as a glorious privilege. But all Quakerism in my day was more or less tinged with this ascetic spirit of sacrifice, and it was so entirely the customary way of regarding the matter that each new recruit to the ministry unconsciously fell into it. That some of them had now and then a glimpse into the privilege of service, is shown by an incident that occurred with this very Uncle John some years later. He was speaking with my brother about a "religious visit" he had lately paid to some neighboring Meetings, and, as they separated, he said in a very solemn and mournful tone, "So thou wilt see, dear James, what a heavy cross has been laid upon me." My brother expressed his sympathy, and they parted, going different ways. But in a moment or two my uncle walked hastily back, and touching my brother on the arm said, "I am afraid, dear James, that I conveyed a false impression in what I said about my ministry being a cross. Truth compels me to confess to thee that it is not a cross at all, but a very blessed and delightful privilege. I am afraid we preachers talk as we do about the cross in preaching, more from habit than from any reality."

Everything conspired however to make Quaker ministry a most mysterious and solemn affair to us young people. There was something indescribably enticing in the idea of the direct and immediate inspiration of our preachers. We seemed to be living, as it were, on the very verge of the spiritual world, where at any moment the veil might be lifted, and we might have some mystical revelation from the other side; and the eager longing yet solemn awe with which we watched and waited for these revelations could not, I feel sure, be comprehended by the present generation of young people, even though they should themselves be Quakers. An awe and mystery surrounded for us every "ministering Friend" whether man or woman, rich or poor, wise or simple; and this wholly apart from the personality of the Minister. It was due only and entirely to the fact that we believed Ministers to be the divinely chosen oracles to declare the mind of God, and that every word they might say was directly inspired, and was almost as infallible as the Bible itself. Consequently what any one of them might be "led" to say to oneself was a matter of the most vital importance, and the most profound belief. One of the greatest excitements of my young life therefore was the possibility of being at any moment personally preached to or prophesied about by some "ministering Friend."

Chapter 5

Quaker "Opportunities"

Friends in my days had a way of having what were called "Opportunities." What this word really meant, I suppose now, was that they had an opportunity to "relieve their minds" of some "message" that was burdening it. But in those days no such ordinary explanation of the word every occurred to me, but an "Opportunity" seemed a most mysterious divinely appointed function, that was akin to a council in the courts of Heaven itself; and the one longing yet fear of my young life was for some preacher to have an "Opportunity" with me. On such occasions the preacher was supposed to be divinely enabled to see into your most secret thoughts, and to uncover with an unsparing hand the secret sins which you had fondly hoped were known to yourself alone. They were also supposed to be endowed with the power of reading the future, and might be expected to foretell any great blessings or dire misfortunes that were in store for you. The excitement, therefore, when a "traveling Friend" came to the house and asked for an "Opportunity" was intense. Whether fear or hope as to the revelations that might be made, predominated, it would be hard to say; but, no matter what our feelings might be, no member of the family, not even the smallest servant, might dare to be absent. In fact, when now and then circumstances appeared to make it desirable that some one should stay away, the preacher often seemed to have a sense of it, and would ask solemnly if there was no one else, and would decline to go on with the "Opportunity" until the absent one was summoned.

In these "Opportunities" the preacher was expected to "speak to the condition" of special ones present, and the great excitement was as to whether one's own condition would be spoken to. With what eager hope and fear I always waited to see if the preacher would speak to *my* condition, no words can describe; but never once in my recollection was this supreme favor conferred upon me. No preacher ever vouch-safed to notice me in any special manner, nor seemed aware of the presence of an eager hungry soul reaching blindly out after the Light, to whom a few words "direct from God" would have come as an unspeakable boon. To tell the truth I was always expecting some wonderful prophecy to be made concerning me—that I was to be a great preacher, and was to do some great work for God; and though I dreaded the revelations of my unrighteous condition that might be made, I felt that the glory of the hoped-for prophecies would more than make up for them. I remember well how I used to hang about any "travelling Friends" who might come to the house, in the hope that at some unexpected moment the Divine afflatus would come upon them, and the "message" I longed for might be delivered to me.

For it must be understood that these "Opportunities" were never by any manner of means arranged for. They were always ushered in by a solemn hush falling suddenly upon the company, and this hush might come at any moment, even the most inconveniently; but nothing was allowed to hinder. I remember once assisting at one when I was waiting on a preaching aunt on a visit to a Friend's house in Burlington, New Jersey. We had packed our trunks, and they were piled on the carriage at the door ready to take us to the train, when suddenly, as we were standing up bidding our hosts farewell, a silence fell, and an "Opportunity" came upon my aunt, and, while I stood, holding her shawl, in a fever of impatience to be gone, she had to stop and deliver her message, regardless of all considerations of time and trains. I was a woman by this time, and had lost a little of my faith in the divine origin of these "Opportunities," and I remember that I could not help upbraiding her a little, when at last we got off to our train, for the inopportune moment she had chosen. But her reply silenced me when she said with the most guileless faith, "But, my dear, I could not disobey my Guide, and thee sees He has brought us to the train in time after all."

No one but those who had experienced them could possibly understand the profound impression these "Opportunities" made upon the Quaker life of my childhood. And even to this day when, as sometimes happens, a silence for a moment suddenly falls upon a company, my first instinctive terror is lest it should be an "Opportunity," and somebody should have to preach.

The awe-inspiring effect of these "Opportunities," and the absolute confidence that was placed in the messages so delivered, cannot be better illustrated than by what happened during a visit of some "English Friends" to our meetings in Philadelphia, when I was about seventeen. I should say here that it was the custom among the "Friends" for preachers in different places to have what they called "religious concerns" to visit other Meetings and neighborhoods, in, as they quaintly expressed it, "the service of Truth." These visits were always occasions of great interest to us young people, even though the preacher might not have come from any great distance; but when they came from England, which was to us an unknown land of grandeur and of mystery, our awe and reverence knew no bounds. "English Friends" seemed to us almost like visitants from an angelic sphere; and to be noticed or spoken to by one of them made the fortunate recipients feel as though Heaven itself had come down to them.

The English Friends I speak of were entertained, during their stay in Philadelphia, by Marmaduke and Sarah Cope, who lived in Filbert Street opposite to our house. Their daughter Madgie, was an intimate friend of mine, and one morning she came to me in a great state of excitement over a remarkable "Opportunity," which she said one of the "English Friends" had had the evening before with a young man we both knew. She said some Friends had dropped in to see the English Friends, and during the course of the evening, an "Opportunity" had come upon them, and one of the travelling Friends had begun to preach. After a short exhortation, he had singled out this young man, and had addressed him in a most remarkable manner, telling him that he had received a direct call from God to enter into the ministry, and prophesying that he was to become a great preacher, and was to visit far distant lands in the "service of Truth."

I can remember vividly to this day the profound impression made upon me by this occurrence. The preacher who had delivered the message to this young man was one upon whom I had placed all my hopes for a direct message, and had been disappointed; and now he had prophesied about a young man, who in my opinion was no more deserving than myself, the very things that I was always wanting some preacher to prophesy about me. I confess I felt deep pangs of jealousy that the "Divine favor" should have overlooked me, and been bestowed upon one who really seemed to me no more worthy. However, it was all a part of the great romance of our lives, and there was always the possibility that it might still, at some blessed "Opportunity," be bestowed upon me, and I went about for days full of the subject.

A day or two after it occurred I was out driving with a very special friend, the one who, as will appear in another part of my story, had been the means of my awakening at sixteen. I was at this time nearly seventeen, and my friend was perhaps nine or ten years older. I had for her a very adoring friendship, and always poured out into her sympathizing ears everything that interested me. Being this day full of the subject, I of course detailed the whole story to her, investing it with all the importance it had assumed in my own eyes. My friend seemed deeply interested, and asked a great many questions as to the details of the "message" and how it had affected the young man. Not many weeks afterwards she told me she was engaged to be married to this very young man, and confessed that she had been largely influenced in her decision by what I had told her, as she was sure the prophecy made in that "Opportunity" would be fulfilled, and she felt it would be a great privilege to be united to one whose future was to be so full of work in the "service of Truth."

I have always watched the career of that young man with the deepest interest, because I could not help feeling at the time that he had received a message which by rights ought to have come to me; and I must confess that the prophecies which made me so jealous have never been fulfilled in his case; and, now that we are both old people, I cannot but see that my life has come far nearer their fulfillment than his. He has been a most upright, conscientious man, and truly religious in a quiet way, but he has never become a preacher, nor done any public Christian work. While I, without any "message" or any "call," such as I was always longing for, and supposed to be necessary, did become a preacher and have tried to proclaim in many countries the "good news of the gospel of the Lord Jesus

Christ."

In this case, therefore, the "message" seemed to fail to find entrance. But on so many occasions similar messages were so marvelously fulfilled, and the accounts of these cases were so constantly retailed to us as strengtheners to our faith, that it is no wonder we grew up with a profound belief in their infallibility. I have many times known a Quaker preacher in a "Meeting" or an "Opportunity" make a revelation to an individual present of something known only to that individual, or prophesy something for the future of an individual or of a community, of which there was no present indication, but which came true just as it had been declared it would.

I knew one woman Friend, who seemed to have this gift in a remarkable degree. I remember her once stopping in the middle of a sermon she was preaching at a week-day meeting to a congregation of entire strangers, and saying, "A young man has entered this room who has in his pocket some papers by means of which he is about to commit a great sin. If he will come to see me this afternoon at———(mentioning the house at which she was staying), I have a message from the Lord to give him that will show him a way out of his trouble." She then resumed her sermon where she had left off, and said nothing further of the incident. I was very much interested to follow this up, and I found a strange young man did in fact call on the preacher that afternoon and confess that he had a forged check in his pocket, which he was on his way to cash, when some influence, he could not tell what, had induced him to turn into the Meeting-house as he was passing. His name was not asked for nor given, but the message from the Lord was delivered, and the young man tore up the forged check in the preacher's presence, and promised to lead a new life. And some years afterwards the preacher met him and found that this promise had been fulfilled.

On another occasion, when this same preacher was staying in the country at the house of a cousin of mine, she came down to breakfast one morning and said that the Lord had revealed to her in the night that she was to take a message to a man living some miles off. No name had been given her, nor any indication as to the whereabouts of the man she was to see, but she told my cousin, that, if he would take her in his carriage, she was sure the Lord would show them in which direction to go. They set out therefore, and the preacher pointed out one road after another which they were to take, and, finally, when about six miles from home, and in a part of the country about which neither the preacher nor my cousin knew anything, she pointed to a house they saw in the distance, and said, "that is the house, and when we get there I shall find the man in the garden, and thou may wait for me at the gate." They accordingly stopped at this house, and, while my cousin waited, the preacher went straight through the grounds into the garden, and delivered her message to the man she found there. She told him he was contemplating a very wrong action which would bring great trouble upon himself and his family, but the Lord was willing to deliver him, and had sent her to open his eyes to the sin and the danger of what he had decided to do. The man was deeply impressed, and, after a little hesitation, confessed that all she had said was true, and that that very day had been the time when his plan was to have been carried out, but that now he dared not go on with it. He then and there gave it up, and said, after such a manifest token of God's interest in him, he would put the whole matter into His care, and would trust Him to manage it. And after events proved that this had been really done, and that all had turned out far better than he could have expected.

Were there space I could relate hundreds of similar incidents, but these will suffice. It will easily be understood, however, that, in the face of facts such as these, it is not to be wondered at that we were full of faith. Until I was married, a Minister was to me a person altogether removed from the ordinary ranks of men and women, a being almost from another sphere, with none of the common weaknesses of humanity, set apart for a Divine work, and endowed with almost Divine attributes. When I was a child I used to sit and watch them in "meeting" as they sat in long rows on the high benches facing the audience, the men on one side and women on the other, expecting every minute to see revealed the halo which I was sure must be encircling their heads, although invisible to me. And sometimes, when I got tired of waiting, I would screw up my eyes until I created a sort of shining circle around every object I looked at, and then tried to persuade myself that this was the invisible halo I was so longing to see.

As I grew older these fancies of course left me; but for many years a delightful mystery and awe still encircled the "gallery Friends" and the coming of a "travelling Minister" continued to fill me with eager and delicious expectations. Especially was this the case after my awakening at sixteen. In my diary I wrote in reference to the very Minister who had given that wonderful message to the young man, as follows:—

"Eleventh month, 29th, 1848. I heard today the most delightful news I have heard for a long time. The English Friends, *dear* Benjamin Seebohm and Robert Lindsay, are expected in town the next First Day. Oh! won't it be joyful! joyful! They will be at our First Day evening meeting. Hurrah! Oh! I am so glad I can hardly contain myself. I am very different from what I was when they were here last.

> Deeper than the gilded surface
>   Hath my wakeful vision seen,
> Further than the narrow present
>   Have my journeyings been.
> I have, midst life's empty visions,
>   Heard the solemn step of time,
> And the low mysterious voices
>   Of another clime.
> All the mystery of Being
>   Has upon my Spirit pressed;
> Thoughts which, like the Deluge wanderer
>   Find no place of rest."

I fully expected these inspired Friends to know by inward revelation all I had been going through, and of course hoped they would have a Divine message for me, direct from God. The longed for First Day came and I went to meeting with my brother, full of fearsome yet delicious anticipations. But alas! as was always the case with me, I was doomed to disappointment. Still it might come another time, and I lived in hope.

It was this constant expectation of a direct word from God that made the romance of my young life, and that was I feel sure, one of the secrets of the great hold Quakerism had on the young people of my day.

But, except for this inspirational preaching, we received from our society very little definite religious teaching of any kind. We had, as I have said, no Sunday-schools, and no Bible classes, and doctrines and dogmas were, to me at least, an absolutely unknown quantity. We had no Catechism and were not even taught the Ten Commandments, as they were felt to belong to the old Jewish dispensation which had passed away in Christ. I do not suppose that I was ever told so, but I had a distinct feeling as a child that the Ten Commandments, like the Lord's Prayer, were for "gay" and "worldly" ones. I felt somehow that they belonged only to the outside world (*i.e.,* all who were not Friends) who probably needed outward commandments to keep them good, while we Friends were to be good from deeper motives. For it was not that the moral training of the "Ten Commandments" had ceased to be binding, but that the Friends believed it was far more fully taught in the new commandments of the dispensation of Christ, which were to be written, not on tables of stone, nor even on the pages of a book, but upon the spiritual tablets of our hearts.

They believed that, because we were in Christ, we were to be controlled by a law from within and not by a law from without; and to them it was literally true that for people who were led of the Spirit, there "was no law." They taught that the fruit of the indwelling Spirit would necessarily be the fulfilling of the law, and that therefore no outward law would be needed; that, just as a man who is honest at heart needs no law to keep him from dishonesty, so, if a man is truly a Christian, he will need no law to make him act like a Christian ought to act. He will do it by the impulse of his inward life. The early Friends fully believed that if God has possession of the heart He will work in us both to will and to do of His own good pleasure, and that an outward law, therefore, would be a superfluity. We were consequently directed to yield ourselves to this inward Divine working, and to listen for the Voice of the Holy Spirit in our hearts; and we were taught that, when this Voice was heard, it must be implicitly and faithfully obeyed.

We were to expect to hear this "inward voice" at any or all times, and about all things; but were encouraged to look for it especially in our "meetings for worship" when the whole congregation were sitting in silence "before the Lord." Quaker meetings were always held on this basis of silent waiting, in order that in the silence, the Holy Spirit might have an opportunity of speaking directly to each individual soul. The Friends recognized the unseen but living presence of Christ in their meetings, and no individual was set apart to "conduct their service," or to be a mediator between their souls and their invisible Teacher. The silence might not be broken by any one, not even by an "acknowledged Minister," except under a sense of the direct and immediate guidance of the Spirit; but, under that guidance, any one, even the poorest washer-woman or the smallest child, might deliver the "message." This gave a mysterious and even romantic interest to our meetings, as we never knew what might happen, or who, even perhaps ourselves, might be "led" to take part.

I cannot say, however, that anything special ever came to me in any meeting. Now and then a sermon would be preached that seemed perhaps to apply to my case, but never strikingly enough to really impress me; and now and then it would happen that by some mysterious influence my heart would be "tendered," as it was termed, and I would feel for a little while as though God did after all care for me and would help me. But as a general thing my "meetings" were mostly passed in building air castles, an occupation that I felt to be very wrong, but which had an irresistible fascination for me. Curiously enough, these day dreams never took the form of love stories, as youthful air castles so generally do, I suppose because I had never been allowed to read novels, and never heard anything about falling in love. But I always made myself out to be something very wonderful and grand, and the admired of all beholders. Sometimes I was to be a preacher whose eloquence was to surpass the eloquence of all preachers since the world began; sometimes I was to be an inventor of more wonderful machines than ever had been invented before; but more often I was to be the most marvelous singer the world had ever known; and the "meetings" that stand out in my memory more distinctly than any other, were those of one special winter in my fourteenth year, when I endowed myself with an undreamed of gift for singing, that electrified everybody, and brought the world to my feet. Why I pitched on singing for my day dreams I cannot imagine, as it was a forbidden worldliness among the Quakers, and was something I scarcely ever heard, either in public or private; and I was myself so utterly devoid of any musical talent that during my whole life I have not been able to sing a note, or even to distinguish one tune from another. But so it was; and there I used to sit on the bench beside my mother, through many a long meeting, outwardly a demure little Quaker, but inwardly a great prima donna (not that I called myself that) with my whole foolish little heart swelling and bursting with the glory of my triumphs on the stage, which however was a place I had never even so much as seen!

Sometimes, however, my conscience would not permit me to indulge in my day dreams, and then my "meetings" would be filled with futile struggles against wandering thoughts, or with vain efforts to resist an uncontrollable desire to sleep, for to "sleep in meeting" was felt by all of us to be almost a crowning disgrace.

Whether on the whole those long, solemn meetings, with their great stretches of silence, and with sermons, when there were any, that made very little direct appeal to me, were or were not a valuable part of my religious training, I do not feel prepared to say, But one thing is certain, that, whether from the preaching in our meetings, or from the conversation of our elders, or from the atmosphere around us, there were certain strong impressions made upon me which stand out vividly in my memory.

Chapter 6

Quaker Guidance

The strongest impression made upon my young heart was the paramount privilege we as Quakers enjoyed in our knowledge of the "perceptible guidance" of the Holy Spirit, and the vital necessity of obedience to this guidance. It was fully believed by us young Friends that our "Society" was the sole depository of this knowledge; and although it was for the most part a great mystery to us, yet still we could not help feeling a certain pride in such a distinctive possession. That it was regarded by the Friends as a very real thing, was proved by the fact that anything which professed to be the result of this guidance was treated with the most profound respect and consideration. If even a child could say it felt a Divine "leading" in any direction, that leading was treated with loving consideration by the older Friends, and, unless it was manifestly improper, way was tenderly made for it to be carried out. For Friends believed their children were every one included among the lambs of the flock, and had the same privileges of hearing the voice of the Good Shepherd that their parents possessed.

A very striking illustration of his reverence for anything that was felt to be from Divine guidance occurred two hundred years ago in our own family history. An aunt of one of our great-grandfathers was a certain Elizabeth Haddon, who was the daughter of a wealthy Friend named John Haddon, living in Rotherhithe, now a suburb of London. John Haddon had purchased some land in New Jersey, intending to remove there with his family, and had even sent out mechanics who had built a suitable house and outbuildings. But meantime circumstances had made it necessary for him to remain in England. His young daughter Elizabeth, just eighteen, who believed she had felt a call to work in New Jersey, was greatly disappointed, but, as she prayed about it, she seemed to hear an inward voice telling her that she must take up the family burden and go over herself to the New World and develop the property there. She called her family together and told them of her impressions of duty. She was very young, and the country was unsettled, and her parents were frightened. But they were staunch Quakers, and they had always taught their children an implicit obedience to what the voice of the Lord might require, and they did not dare to oppose what their young daughter felt so strongly to be her duty, and, although in much fear and trembling, they made arrangements for her emigration.

This was in 1701. She found the country in a very rough state, but lived there long enough to see the whole neighborhood, largely through her own instrumentality, revolutionized into a most prosperous community, to which she was for many years an untold blessing. The town that sprang up near her home was called Haddonfield after her, and for many years our father had a country house not far off, where we entered into the fruits of our great-aunt's labors.

An American historian in relating her story says:—

"Among the many singular manifestations of strong faith and religious zeal, connected with the settlement of this country, few are more remarkable than the voluntary separation of this girl of eighteen from a wealthy home and all the associations of childhood, to go to a distant and unsettled country to fulfill what she considered a religious duty; and the humble self-sacrificing faith of the parents in giving up their beloved child with such reverent tenderness for the promptings of her own conscience, has in it something sublimely beautiful, if we look at it in its own pure light."

This absolute independence in all matters of felt duty has always seemed to me to be one of our greatest Quaker privileges. It left every individual free to serve God in the way that seemed right, without the often kindly meant but hindering interference of those around them. To say simply, "I feel it right to do so and so," invariably silenced all objections.

Nor was this only the case in spiritual matters, but in earthly matters as well, and it gave to each individual that position of independence which has always to my mind seemed one of the most vital of human needs. And I look upon the sense of personal ownership engendered by all this, as one of the most priceless of all the gifts that my Quaker inheritance has brought me.

I remember when I first waked up to the injustices of the position of women in the outside world, I was able to congratulate myself continually that it was so much better among "Friends"; and that not the most tyrannical "man Friend," even if he wanted to, would ever dare to curtail the liberty of his womankind, if only they could say they "felt a concern" for any course of action.

To interfere between any soul and its Divine Guide, except under a Divine constraint, was considered by the Friends to be one of the gravest wrongs that one person could inflict upon another; and in all my experience of Quakerism in my young days I have no recollection of its ever having been done, except by the Elders and Overseers. A Quaker "concern" was to my mind clothed with even more authority than the Bible, for the

Bible was God's voice of long ago, while the "concern" was His voice at the present moment, and, as such, was of far greater present importance. I do not suppose any one ever taught me definitely that this was the case, but the whole atmosphere around me, and the preaching I heard, was certainly calculated to exalt the "inward voice" and its communications above all other voices, and to make us feel that, since God spoke to us directly, we need not search into what He might say to any one outside of our sacred fold.

It might naturally be thought that this liberty in individual guidance would have led into extravagances, and in the early days of the society this sometimes happened. But in my time the Friends safeguarded their members from this danger by requiring all "concerns" or "leadings" that were at all out of the ordinary, to be brought before the Elders and Overseers, and judged by them in a solemn season of waiting upon God for His teaching. And, so convinced were all Friends that the collective voice of the Holy Spirit in meeting was of more authority than a private voice to an individual, that decisions arrived at under such circumstances were always accepted as final, and the conscience of the individual, whose "leading" was set aside, felt itself freed from the burden. It was an admirable safeguard, and during all my years of close association with the society I never knew of any instance of serious extravagance.

Apart from this teaching of the perceptible guidance of the Holy Spirit, nothing very definite or tangible was taught us. As far as I can remember we were never told we had to be "converted" or "born again," and my own impression was that these were things, which might be necessary for the "world's people," but were entirely unnecessary for us, who were birthright members of the Society of Friends, and were already born into the kingdom of God, and only needed to be exhorted to live up to our high calling. I believe this was because of one of the fundamental principles of Quakerism, which was a belief in the universal fatherhood of God, and a recognition of the fact that Christ had linked Himself on to humanity, and had embraced the whole world in His divine brotherhood, so that every soul that was born belonged to Him, and could claim sonship with the same Father. "My Father and your Father," He says, and the early Friends accepted this as true, and would have thought it misleading therefore to urge us to become what we already were. We were always preached to as "lambs of the flock," and as only needing to be obedient to the voice of the Good Shepherd, to whom we already belonged. The Friends did not shut their children out, but instead, with loving tenderness, shut them inside the heavenly fold; and all their teaching was to this effect.

For a little time, in my Plymouth Brethren days, I looked upon this as a dreadful heresy; but later on I learned the blessed fact, stated by Paul to the heathen idolaters at Athens, that we are all, the heathen even included, "God's offspring;" and I realized that, since He is our creator, He is of course our Father, and we equally of course are His children. And I learned to thank and bless the grand old Quakers who had made this discovery, since their teaching made it easy for me to throw aside the limiting, narrowing ideas I had at first adopted, and helped me to comprehend the glorious fact that in God we all "live and move and have our being," and that therefore no one can shut another out.

Chapter 7

QUAKER "QUERIES"

Next in importance to the impression made upon my young mind by this teaching regarding the perceptible guidance of the Holy Spirit, was the one made by "Friends' testimonies," as they were called, and the "Queries" that were founded upon them. These "Queries" were a series of questions in regard to the practice of Quakerism, which were solemnly asked and answered once a month in Monthly Meetings, appointed for the purpose of transacting the business of the society. There were eight of these "Queries," and they contained a splendid code of morals, calculated to develop a people of unflinching uprightness and honesty in all their dealings with their fellow-men, and of a grand self-restraint and self-denial in their private lives; and, much as I chafed at them as a child, I have never been able to forget the lessons they taught, and often to this day find myself guided by their precepts.

With such a monthly probing of conduct as these Queries compelled, it was almost a necessity that a high standard of righteousness should have become an integral part of a Quaker's life; and I feel it to have been an invaluable element of my own religious training.

Back of these Queries there was a body of "Friends' testimonies" from which the Queries had arisen, which although unwritten, except so far as they were expressed in the Queries, were absolutely binding upon every true Friend. I have often thought that they were in reality, though no one said so, our Quaker Ten Commandments, which we had put in the place of the Jewish ones. I certainly believed as a child that they were in fact the special commandments that had been given to us as Quakers, which differentiated us from the Christians around us, and made us the "peculiar people" we were proud to call ourselves. They were many of them very strict and severe, and to an outsider must often have seemed rather painful; but, as all the Quakers I knew had been brought up on them from infancy, they did not press as heavily upon us as might have been supposed. But they certainly did serve to keep Quaker feet walking in a narrow way, which way we believed to be the actual "strait gate and narrow way" spoken of in the Bible as the only path that "leadeth unto life." Every one of these "testimonies" had been, we were devoutly convinced, directly revealed by the Holy Spirit to the "early Friends"; and consequently, however unreasonable they might otherwise have seemed to us, we young Friends in my day reverenced them as the very oracles of God.

As these Queries seem to have almost entirely fallen into the background among the Quakers of late years, I will record them here, as a true exposition of the Quakerism of my young days.

"*First Query.*—Are all our religious meetings for worship and discipline duly attended; is the hour observed; and are Friends clear of sleeping, and of all other unbecoming behavior therein?

"*Second Query.*—Are love and unity maintained among you? Are tale-bearing and detraction discouraged? And where any differences arise, are endeavors used speedily to end them?

"Third Query.—Are Friends careful to bring up those under their direction, in plainness of speech, behavior and apparel; in frequently reading the Holy Scriptures, and to restrain them from reading pernicious books, and from the corrupt conversation of the world? And are they good examples in these respects themselves?

"Fourth Query.—Are Friends careful to discourage the unnecessary distillation and use of spiritous liquors, and the frequenting of taverns; to avoid places of diversion; and to keep in true moderation and temperance on the account of marriages, burials and all other occasions?

"Fifth Query.—Are poor Friends' necessities duly inspected, and they relieved or assisted in such business as they are capable of ? Do their children freely partake of learning to fit them for business; and are they and other Friends' children placed among Friends?

"Sixth Query.—Do you maintain a faithful testimony against oaths; an hireling ministry; bearing arms, training, and other military services; being concerned in any fraudulent or clandestine trade; buying or vending goods so imported; or prize goods; and against encouraging lotteries of any kind?

"Seventh Query.—Are Friends careful to live within the bounds of their circumstances, and to keep to moderation in their trade or business? Are they punctual to their promises, and just in the payment of their debts; and are such as give reasonable grounds for fear on these accounts, timely labored with for their preservation or recovery?

"*Eighth Query.*—Do you take due care regularly to deal with all offenders in the spirit of meekness, without partiality or unnecessary delay, in order for their help; and where such labor is ineffectual, to place judgment upon them, in the authority of truth?"

The reading of these Queries in our Monthly Meetings constituted a sort of monthly confessional for the whole society, and were seasons of solemn self-examination for both old and young. Each separate Meeting belonging to the "Monthly Meeting" sent in its own set of answers for this public confessional, and the consideration of these answers was called the "consideration of the state of society."

"Our meetings have all been duly attended by most of our members, but some Friends have not observed the hour."—"Mostly clear of unbecoming behavior, but some sleeping has been observed."—"Friends generally are careful to bring up their children in plainness of speech, behavior, and apparel, but more faithfulness in this respect is desirable."—"Our testimony against oaths and a hireling ministry, bearing arms, being concerned in any clandestine trade, and against encouraging lotteries, has been faithfully maintained by all our members." Such were some of the answers that linger in my memory.

It was the custom after each Query and answer had been read, for a time of silence to be observed in order to give Friends an opportunity to "relieve their minds" of any message that might have been given them concerning that special Query; and these opportunities were generally times of great searchings of heart with all who were present.

As I remember it, the one Query that was preached about the most frequently and the most fervently was the Third, concerning the testimony for "plainness of speech, behavior, and apparel, and against the vain fashions of the world." It was this testimony that did the most to make Quakers a "peculiar people," and that caused us young Quakers the worst of our heart burnings. I remember to this day the sufferings I used to undergo each month as I sat beside my mother and heard this Query read and preached about. My constant fear was lest it should make her more strict in trying to keep us from the "vain fashions of the world," which, in spite of our training, possessed a fascination we could not wholly conquer. As the Friend who was appointed to read the Queries approached this special one, I used to do my best to abstract my mind, and would even surreptitiously stop my ears, trying to cheat myself into thinking that, if I did not notice it, my mother would not either. But alas! as I recall those days, I must acknowledge that I was always doomed to disappointment, for, as I have said, the preaching about this particular Query was the most frequent and the most fervent, and in the end I, as well as my mother was always obliged to listen.

Two incidents of my childhood, connected with this Query, come up very vividly before me.

Our mother had brought us some white china crape shawls with lovely long fringes that seemed to us too beautiful for words, and we wore them with the greatest pride. But one day she came home from a meeting where the Queries had been read and answered, and told us she had felt in meeting that our long fringes were too "gay" for "Friends' children," and she believed it was her duty to cut them shorter. I can see it all today, as she carefully spread the shawls out on a large table, and laid a yardstick along the fringe at what she considered was the right length, and proceeded to cut off all the lovely beautiful extra lengths. It was like cutting into our very vitals, and I remember well how we pleaded and pleaded that the fatal yardstick might be slipped down just a little further. Our great fear was that our fringes would be shorter that the fringes of similar shawls that had been purchased at the same time for our most intimate friends, Hannah and Jane Scull, who were a little gayer than ourselves. To have their fringes, even so much as the tenth of an inch longer than ours, seemed to us a catastrophe not to be borne. I do not remember how it turned out in the end, but I shall never forget to my dying day the agonies of mind we went through in the process.

Another experience about dress left an indelible impression on my mind. The shape of sleeve that was considered "plain" in my day was what are called leg-of-mutton sleeves, and the sleeves of all our dresses were of this orthodox leg-of-mutton shape. But some benign influence, what it was we never understood, induced our mother one spring to let us have our sleeves made a little in the fashion, which happened at that time to be what was called Bishop sleeves, full at both the shoulder and the wrist. The fashion was for very large and full "Bishops" and our pride in them was immense. The dresses were our new spring school dresses, of a brown and white striped print, calico, we called it. They were finished while the weather was still very wintry-like, but so great was our desire to show off our fashionable sleeves to the astonished world, that nothing would do but we must put them on and go for a walk without coats; and no two prouder little girls were abroad in the whole world that morning that Hannah and Sally Whitall, as they walked along the streets of Philadelphia in their fashionable attire. I remember our younger sister Mary wanted to go with us, but her sleeves were still leg-of-mutton, and we felt it would take from the full effect, if one member of our party should display the despised sleeves, and we made her walk on the opposite side of the way. I can see her longing glances across the street now, as she admired our glory from afar. However, she had her revenge not long after, for ruffled panties (as we called drawers then) coming down to the feet, had come into fashion, and as our mother was making her a new set, they were made long and ruffled, while we still had to wear our plain hemmed ones, not showing below our dresses. And this time she also went out to walk to show her new panties, but, kinder than we had been, she invited us to accompany her. I am sorry to say, however, that old Adam in us resented her favored condition so strongly, that we refused to walk on the same side of the street with her, and scornfully crossed over to the other side, leaving her to walk alone, with all the glory taken out of her beautiful ruffled "panties" by our cruel scorn and unkindness.

The early Friends, in order to testify against the foolish changes of fashion among the "world's people" had, as far as possible, adhered to the style of dress that was being worn when they took their rise, and in a very few years this naturally grew peculiar, and finally became a sort of Quaker uniform, which all good Friends felt "led" to adopt. I say they adhered to the first style as far as possible, because moderate changes were inevitable from the fact that certain styles, when they ceased to be fashionable, dropped sooner or later out of the market, and could no longer be easily procured; and also because the views, even of the strictest, could not help being more or less modified by time and use.

The fact was that their "testimony" as to "plainness of apparel" was not a testimony against or for any special style of dress, but it was simply a testimony against following the "vain fashions of the world"; and by the time a style had become old-fashioned, and was going out, the Quakers would be prepared to adopt it.

I met lately in some extracts from an old diary the following curious illustration of this. In the time of Queen Elizabeth, before Quakers arose, it was the general fashion to wear green aprons as a part of a lady's church-going dress; but by the time the Quakers came on the scene this fashion had begun to die out, and starched white aprons were taking the place of green in the fashionable world. In order not to follow the changing fashions, Friends held on to the green aprons for their go-to-meeting dress, and their preachers preached against the fashionable white aprons as being of a "gay and polluting color." One old preacher, it is recorded, declared in one of his sermons, that the starch water used to stiffen these aprons was the "devil's water with which they needed to be sprinkled," and warned his hearers against its polluting use.

Curiously enough, this rooted Quaker objection to following the vain fashions of the world extended even to many useful inventions of which one would have supposed the practical good sense of the Friends would have seen the value. I remember that when sewing machines first came into vogue they were considered by the Friends exceedingly worldly. And, when I had made up my mind to buy one, I was obliged to make my purchase in secret, and to hide the machine in the most inaccessible room in my house, in order that no one might be grieved with my worldliness. Of course later on, when the Friends had got used to the innovation, sewing machines were to be seen in every well-ordered Quaker household; but for a long time I went about with a haunting sense of having fallen from grace, because of the worldly thing I had purchased.

The standard of plainness, therefore, necessarily varied from one generation to another. But whatever the standard might be, the "testimony" against the vain fashions of the world continued the same, and each generation felt the established costume of their day was of the nature of a Divine ordinance, especially patterned in Heaven itself.

This conviction of the sanctity of the "plain dress" arose largely, I believe, from the fact that all their own personal religion had come to them through this channel. The newly awakened Friend, whether young or old, was invariably confronted with the question of "becoming plain;" and the surrender of will involved in giving up to adopt the Quaker uniform always brought such peace and rest of soul, that it was almost inevitable they should consider the putting on of the "plain dress" as being the procuring cause of the blessing. This was especially the case with our own dear father. In his diary, under date of 1823 when he was just twenty-three years old, he writes:—

"While at home from my fifth voyage I believed it right to adopt the plain dress and language of Friends. While under the conviction of its being right, and fearing I should lose my situation if I did so, I met with Samuel Bettle, Sr., who, without knowing the distressed state of my mind, told me, if I was faithful to what I felt to be right, the Lord would make a way for me where there seemed no way; which indeed He did, giving me favor in the sight of my employer much to my comfort. Hearing of a ship as needing a chief mate, I borrowed a plain coat of my friend, James Cox, my own not being ready, and called to see the captain, telling him I could not 'Mr.' and 'Sir' him as was common. To which he replied kindly that it would only be a nine days' wonder, and at once engaged me as first mate. Thus my prayer was answered and a way made for me where I saw no way. Praised forever be the name of the Lord."

This was the turning point in his religious life, and it was followed by such an uplifting of soul, and such a sense of the love of God, that he was never able to dissociate them, and all his life believed, that, if any one else would adopt the same dress, the same blessing would follow. I believe he would freely have bestowed a "plain coat" as a gift upon anybody who would wear one; and nothing ever seemed to disturb his profound conviction that "plain coats" and "plain bonnets" had been shaped and patterned in Heaven. He even assured us once that he fully believed that the armies in Heaven, spoken of in Rev. 19:14, who followed the King of kings on white horses, all had on "plain coats!" He was a member of the Board of a Quaker college near Philadelphia, which required all its students to wear the "plain" straight collared coats. But in the hot summer weather, when the students were obliged to wear linen or seersucker coats on account of the heat, their thin straight collars refused to stand up, and wilted down with the heat. The question came before the Board as to whether, under such circumstances, they might not be allowed to wear turned down collars. Some of the Board were for yielding, but our dear father would not listen to this for a moment, but declared that, if there were no other way of making their collars stand, they must put whalebone in to stiffen them, for "stand they must." I believe however that the summer heats were too much for even his stalwart principles, and he was at last forced reluctantly to consent to the turned over collars.

I have no doubt the same thing occurs in other Denominations besides Friends. They have their own special forms and ceremonies, which are more or less incumbent upon their members, submission to which very often results in blessings of peace and rest of soul similar to those the Friends experienced when putting on the "plain dress;" and, like the Friends, many of them have no doubt supposed these forms or ceremonies to be the procuring cause of the blessings, and have in consequence exalted them into a place of sanctity, and have even believed them to have been ordained and patterned in heaven. I realized this very strongly not long ago when attending a Roman Catholic Mass in Italy. I was inclined to be critical over the gorgeous robes of the priests, saying to myself that the Lord could not possibly care for such things, when it flashed into my mind that after all there was no radical difference between a robe of crimson and gold, and a black coat with a straight collar, or between a Sister of Charity's quaint costume, and a sugar-scoop bonnet and a dove-colored shawl; and I saw that just as the Quakers of my childhood had been sure that their "plain" clothes were pleasing to God, so also these devoted priests were sure that their gorgeous robes were acceptable in the Divine sight. Each party believed they were obeying the Lord in regard to their dress, and their obedience to what they believed to be right was after all the essential point.

I have had no difficulty since then in feeling absolute Christian charity toward every honest form or ceremony, let it be as contrary to my own ideas as it may, for I realize that it is true that "the Lord seeth not as man seeth; for man looketh on the outward appearance, but the Lord looketh on the heart."

Chapter 8

THE "SUGAR-SCOOP" BONNET

One of the most prominent features of the "plainness of apparel" of my day was the bonnet worn by all good women Friends, which, from its shape, we young people irreverently called a "sugar-scoop," although it often seemed, to me at least, that we committed a sacrilege in daring to treat the sacred bonnet in such a fashion. For that it was sacred no young Quaker of my day would have dreamed of denying. A late writer, dealing with a little later date than my own, says concerning it:

"To one brought up 'within the fold' it is no light matter to approach so awful a subject as the Quaker bonnet. There was a solemnity about it that was born of terror. Whether it presided at the head of the 'women's meeting' or ventured in winter storms, protected in its satin or oilskin case under the Friendly umbrella, or even lay alone in splendid state upon the bed of the welcome guest; anywhere, everywhere, it was a solemn thing."[1]

Why this bonnet which was always made of a very delicate light silk, and was exceedingly expensive and difficult to make, and most uncomfortable to wear, should have been considered "plain," while a simple straw bonnet without trimming which would cost only a quarter as much, and would be infinitely more comfortable, should be considered "gay," is a mystery. But so it was, and whenever a "plain bonnet" was

[1]"The Evolution of the Quaker Dress," by A.S. Grummere.

spoken of, only a "sugar-scoop" was ever meant. The other articles of a woman Friend's "plain dress" in my day were a silk shawl of a soft dove color folded over a plain waisted, low-necked, dove-colored or brown dress, with folds of thin white muslin filling up the neck and crossed over the bosom, and a thin muslin cap of the same shape as the bonnet, tied under the chin with soft white ribbons, and always worn both indoors, and out under the "sugar-scoop." In cold weather they had large dove-colored cashmere shawls for outdoors, or cashmere Mother Hubbard cloaks pleated on to a yoke, with a silk-lined hood. These shawls were always folded with a point down the middle of the back and with three accurate folds at the neck immediately over the point, held by a stout pin. There was also a pin on each shoulder to hold the fullness steady, skillfully hidden to make it look as though the fullness held itself, and the shawl fell gracefully apart in front to reveal the crossed handkerchief of tulle or thin muslin that was crossed over the Quakerly bosom.

The "plain clothes" for the men were a cut-away coat with a straight clergyman's collar, and a broad-brimmed hat. The whole costume was very quaint, and, for the women Friends, very becoming, and I do not think I have ever seen sweeter faces anywhere than the placid, gentle faces inside these caps and bonnets; and I cannot but feel that the world is poorer for the disappearance of these quaint old costumes.

As a consequence of the fact that all Quakers both young and old were, as I have shown, treated as though they were "in the fold," and were therefore never exhorted to become converted in order to get in, the only thing we knew about, as indicating a change in any one's religious experience, was what was called "becoming serious" or "becoming plain," and this was always expressed outwardly by the adoption of the "plain dress" of the society.

The putting on of this "plain dress" was looked forward to by us young people as an inevitable fate that awaited all Quaker children, but a fate that was to be deferred by every known device as long as possible. The usual time for its happening in Philadelphia, where I lived, was at the spring "Yearly Meeting," which occurred in April, and at which time we all came out in our new spring clothes. It was then that the fate was most likely to descend upon its victims, and the young men and women of the society, who had "become serious," would feel it their duty to appear at "Yearly Meeting" in the sugar-scoop bonnets, or the straight collared coats and broad-brimmed hats, that were the outward badge of their inward change. I remember well how those of us upon whom the fate had not yet fallen, used to go to the first meeting of the "Yearly Meeting" early, and sit on benches where we could keep a good outlook on every one who came in, and watch to see which one of our friends and comrades had been snatched from our ranks to wear these distinguishing badges of having "become serious." Of all the wrestlings and agonizing that preceded this open confession of a change of heart we were only dimly aware, but there was enough solemnity and strangeness about the whole thing to make us feel that hence-forth our comrades belonged to another world from ours. And when, as often happened, this adopting of the peculiar Quaker garb was also accompanied by a few words spoken tremblingly in some Meeting by the young neophyte, we felt that the gulf between us could never be crossed until we too became the victims of a similar fate.

No words I could use could fully express the awful solemnity that, to my young mind at least, invested this fate. To "put on a plain bonnet," as it was expressed, seemed to me almost as much the end of all earthly human life as death would be.

After it, one could never again live as other people did. If one was young, one could never have any more fun, for it was evident that races could not be run, nor trees climbed, nor hay-mows scaled, in a dove-colored "sugar-scoop bonnet." If one was older, one could never care for earthly pleasures any more, but must care only for "Friends' meetings" and "Friends' testimonies" and "Friends' religious concerns," and must love to read the "Book of Discipline" and Barclay's "Apology" and "Friends' Religious Journals;" and must turn one's back forever upon all that was pleasant or pretty or attractive in life.

It can easily be conceived that since becoming serious meant inevitably to my mind the putting on of this awe-inspiring bonnet, it loomed before my fun-loving spirit as a fate to be unspeakably dreaded. Somehow I had gained the idea that our dear mother, in order faithfully to obey the Query about bringing up her children in "plainness of apparel," intended, when each one of her daughters reached the age of fifteen, to make them put on one of these bonnets. As a child she had herself been obliged to wear one almost from baby-hood. But even her carefully trained young heart had had its moments of rebellion, for she used to tell us, as a solemn warning, that when she was nine or ten years old the girls at school made such fun of her bonnet that she became most unwilling to wear it, but no entreaties could induce her parents to consent to her leaving it off. One morning, on her way to school, as she was crossing a lonely bridge over Woodbury creek, her dislike to her little "plain bonnet" grew so strong that she took it off and kicked it before her. All day the deed weighed heavily on her conscience, and as she came to that bridge on her return home from school in the dusk of the evening, she saw a dark shadow at little distance up the creek. To her excited imagination this shadow assumed the appearance of a threatening figure coming toward her with a fierce aspect. She firmly believed it was the Devil in person coming to snatch her to himself because of her wickedness, and, filled with terror, she flew home as fast as her trembling legs would carry her, promising in her childish heart never again to rebel against her "plain bonnet." We children were profoundly impressed with this story, and always regarded that special bridge with the most superstitious awe; and I can remember very well many a time racing across it in breathless speed, scarcely daring to breathe for fear I should evoke the awful spectre.

In the face of this experience of our mother's, I never for a moment dreamed that I could escape the fate of the "plain bonnet," and the horror with which as a child I watched my years creeping on one by one toward the fatal age of fifteen could not be described. But fortunately before I had reached that age, the subtle modification of ideas that affected the whole Society almost unconsciously, had affected our mother as well, and the dreaded "plain bonnets" never appeared on the scene. We had instead the simplest little straw cottage bonnets obtainable, but, compared with the "plain bonnets" we had so dreaded, they seemed so gay and worldly to our Quaker imagination, that we felt quite like "fashionable ladies," when we walked out with them on our heads, although I am convinced now that we must have looked like the primmest little Quaker maidens possible.

When the fate, as I call it, of the "plain bonnet" fell upon any young Friend, it was generally welcomed by the older Friends with a loving tenderness that made "the cross" less hard to bear; but sometimes it would descend upon a member of a family to whom it was most unwelcome. For there were degrees of plainness among us, some being "strict" Friends, or what were oftener called "solid" Friends, while others, who indulged more in the vain fashions of the world, were called "gay" Friends. In one such "gay" family which I knew, there was a bright, lively daughter named Elizabeth, of about my own age, who went through in her early girlhood what seems to me, in looking back upon it, a tragic experience. One day when the Query about "plainness of apparel" had been read, and the usual pause had followed, a travelling Minister arose and said in an impressive manner that she believed the Lord had given her a message for some young heart present, who was called upon to take up the cross and put on the "plain dress." For some reason the young Elizabeth was profoundly impressed, and an inward voice seemed to tell her the message was for her. She burst into a flood of tears, and at the close of the meeting one of the Elders, noticing her emotion, made her way to her side, and placing her hand upon her shoulder said solemnly, "Precious child, I believe the Lord has spoken to thee. Mayest thou be obedient to the heavenly vision." This confirmed the impression in the young Elizabeth's heart, and she went home bowed down with an awful sense of a Divine call which she felt she dared not resist.

But then began a fearful conflict. She knew her family would utterly disapprove, and she felt sure they would not give her the money to purchase the necessary articles for making the change of dress that she felt was required of her. She was afraid and ashamed to tell any one of what she was going through, and at last she decided she must try and make a "plain dress" for herself. She saved every penny of her allowance, and little by little gathered enough to purchase the cheapest materials she could find, and began at night alone in her room, after every one had gone to bed, to make with infinite labor and pains the required costume. She dared not ask for any instructions nor

any patterns, and night after night, with tears and sighs, she
worked at her unaccustomed task, until finally, in a rough and
imperfect fashion, the poor little costume was finished, and the
day came when she had to lay aside her "worldly" clothes, and
appear before her family dressed in the cap and handkerchief
and little drab shawl of the elderly Friends. What this cost her
she would never tell me, nor could she, even in middle ages,
speak of the reception she met with from her horrified family,
without tears of profound pity for the martyrdom she underwent. But she said that, whether she had done right or wrong,
she had at least been faithful to what she believed to be her duty,
and that this had brought her such infinite peace, and the radical
change in her life had been of such lasting benefit to her
character, that she never wanted to lay it aside, and until the day
of her death she still wore the same style of costume she had
adopted in such anguish of spirit as a girl.

Perhaps an extract from my diary, shortly after my awakening at sixteen, may give a little insight into the working of these
scruples upon the sensitive conscientious heart of another
young girl about my own age. She was a very special friend,
and was my confidante on all religious matters.

Under date of 11th mo. 13, 1849, I find the following:—

"A. has been spending a week with me, and I do not know
when I have enjoyed myself more. The spiritual communion
between us was perfect. I do not think we concealed any of our
feelings from each other. She told me of the mental suffering,
suffering greater than she could have believed, which preceded
the making known of God's will in her soul, and of the anguish
of spirit when that will was made known. She believed it was
required of her to give up immediately all her gay dress, to burn
her breastpins and her gold thimble, and many articles of

clothing, and even her dresses. It was a great trial, it seemed to her so like waste, and human nature shrank. And there was a still greater trial. She had done a large picture in monochromatic work, which her parents had had framed and hung in their parlor, and which they greatly admired. She felt she must take this picture and burn it also with the other things, frame and all. She knew how grieved her parents would be, and how silly it would look to her sister and brother, and the conflict was very great. But the reproofs of her Divine Guide were so heartrending that at last she could bear it no longer, and submitted. Her father and mother and sister were at Cape May at the time, or she said she could not have done it. When they returned she told them; and then, she said, it was impossible for her to describe the holy, heavenly calm which followed. She scarcely felt as if she was on earth. It seemed that she should never sin again, and the reward was worth far more than the suffering. How nobly she has acted. I fear I should have refused to obey, and would have borne any suffering rather than have made so great sacrifices. And now she has consented to put on a plain bonnet—a 'sugar-scoop,' as I call them, but though it is a great change and will be much talked about, she scarcely dreads it, so true does she find it, that God can make hard things easy and bitter things sweet. Could I take up the cross as she had done?"

That I personally must have been more or less affected by this experience of my friends is shown by an entry in my diary shortly afterwards.

"Eleventh month, 17, 1849. Sometimes today when I have been thinking about it, it has seemed to me almost as if it would be right for me to put on a plain sugar-scoop bonnet; but I hardly dare believe that so great a favor would be granted to me. It is strange, even to myself, that I have longed so for the time to come when I might make this sacrifice, though in truth it would be no sacrifice. People generally feel so averse to these bonnets, and I too did perhaps a year ago, but now I long for it so earnestly that I fear I cannot judge calmly and clearly about it; and gladly as I would make this and any other sacrifice which God might require, I know how awful it would be to run before I was sent, and to do what God had not required . . . It often seems to me that I cannot wait any longer, that I must do something to gain the salvation of my soul; and if God requires nothing, I must make offerings of my own. And yet, that I dare not do. Oh, I feel that I could love the cross and even the shame if only God would lay them upon me; but patience and quiet waiting are my duties now."

It is very evident from this extract that the martyr spirit had been aroused in me, and that I wanted to do something hard for the sake of my religion. But these feelings soon passed off, and the "sugar-scoop" bonnet I both dreaded and longed for never adorned my head. I was such a healthy young creature, and was so full of animal spirits, and so absorbed in the joys of my outward life, that my conscience was always very easily quieted; and for the most part I passed my girlhood unconscious of anything but those ordinary claims to the commonplace everyday duties of life, which my training and the compelling Quaker atmosphere around me made almost my second nature.

Chapter 9

THE "HAT TESTIMONY"

P art of the testimony to "plainness of apparel" was a testimony against what was called "hat honor." The Quakers felt that, since uncovering the head was the outward signification of their adoration toward God, it was not therefore right or fitting that it should be given to man. Barclay says, "He that uncovereth his head to the creature, what hath he reserved for the Creator?" Moreover, since it was considered a mark of special respect to certain people or certain places to take off the hat, Friends, who believed that all people were equally worthy of respect because all were children of one Father, and all places were equally holy because God's presence was everywhere, bore testimony to this belief by refusing to take off their hats to any person or in any place, except as comfort might require. Not even on entering a place of worship might this rule be relaxed, since to take off the hat under such circumstances would seemed to imply that God was more present inside that house than outside in the open air, and this was entirely contrary to the most fundamental Quaker ideas.

Prof. Wm. James in his most valuable book, "The Varieties of Religious Experience,"[1] speaking of the early Quakers and their peculiarities, says:—"Many of these peculiarities arose from their determination to have nothing to do with shams or pretenses, but to be true and sincere in all their dealings with God and with their fellow-men." George Fox believed that it was shown to him by the Lord that many of the conventional

[1] "The Varieties of Religious Experience," a study in human nature, by Wm. James, LL. D., published by Longmans, Green & Co.

customs of society were a lie and a sham. He says:—

"When the Lord sent me into the world, He forbade me to put off my hat to any, high or low; and I was required to 'thee' and 'thou' all men and women, without any respect to rich or poor, great or small. And as I traveled up and down, I was not to bid people 'Good-morning' or 'Good-evening'; neither might I bow or scrape with my leg to any one.... Oh! the scorn, heat, and fury that rose! Oh! the blows, punchings, beatings, and imprisonments, that we underwent for not putting off our hats to men!... But blessed be the Lord, many came to see the vanity of that custom of putting off hats to men, and felt the weight of Truth's testimony against it."

The whole body of the followers of George Fox received these revelations as made to him for their guidance as well as for his own, and renounced the worldly customs he condemned, as a sacrifice to Truth, and as the means of making their actions more perfectly in accord with the spirit they professed; and, until my time, this renunciation still continued, although I dare say many who made it had very vague ideas as to the why and wherefore of such peculiarities.

Some Friends in my young days even went so far as to look upon wearing the hat on all possible occasions, even at meals, as a sort of religious duty. On one occasion a young man I knew was walking with an "Elder" along the streets of Wilmington, Delaware, and the "Elder" was speaking to him about the importance of supporting Friends' testimonies on every occasion, and among other things spoke as follows:—

"I have noticed, my dear young friend, with great satisfaction, that thou are careful not to take off thy hat when meeting thy friends in the street, nor to remove it when entering the meeting house until thou hast taken thy seat. But I see room for even greater faithfulness in this respect, and I feel free to tell thee that I believe it is right for me to wear my hat at all times, except when I am in bed. I put it on the first thing on rising in the morning, nor do I feel at liberty to remove it until I have clothed myself in my night garment the last thing before getting into my bed at night."

This wearing of the hat was very often a source of much conflict and testing to such Quakers as were obliged, either socially or on account of business, to enter the presence of those who demanded this mark of respect. In the old Friends' Journals there are many accounts of the suffering caused by this "hat testimony." In the Journal of Thomas Ellwood, the friend of Milton, who became convinced of Friends' views, he tells of his father's violent antipathy to this "testimony," and says:—

"The sight of my hat upon my head when entering his presence made him so angry, that running upon me with both hands, he first violently snatched off my hat and threw it away; and then giving me some buffets on the head, he said, 'Sirrah, get you up to your chamber.'"

Another day he tells how he went to the dinner table with his hat on:—

"As soon as I came in, I observed by my father's countenance that my hat was still an offence to him: but when I was sitten down, and before I had eaten anything, he made me understand it more fully by saying to me, 'If you cannot content yourself to come to dinner without your Hise upon your head (so he called my hat) pray rise and go take your dinner somewhere else.' Upon those words I arose from the table, and went into the kitchen, where I stayed until the servants went to dinner, and then sat down contentedly with them."

Many years after Thomas Ellwood's experience, a wealthy English Friend, Joseph John Gurney, relates his own experience in 1810. He says:—

"I was engaged long beforehand to a dinner party. For three weeks before I was in agitation from the knowledge that I must enter the drawing-room with my hat on. From this sacrifice, strange and unaccountable as it may seem, I could not escape. In a Friend's attire and with my hat on, I entered the drawing-room at the dreaded moment, shook hands with the mistress of the house, went back into the hall, deposited my hat and returned. I went home in some degree of peace. I had afterwards the same thing to do at the bishop's. The result was that I found myself a decided Quaker, was perfectly understood to have assumed that character, and to dinner parties except in the family circle, I was asked no more."

Later still our own dear father had also something to undergo in this respect. On one occasion when he was hoping to be made captain of an important ship, and was to make his application to the owners, he went through great conflict of mind because he felt it his duty to enter their presence with his hat on, and he feared that this would prejudice them against him. But he was steadfast to what he believed to be his religious duty, and had a firm faith that the Lord would prosper him in so doing. He says in his diary:—

"Some of my friends thought my plain dress and language would stand in my way, but I told them to wait and see if I did not secure the position by the blessing of God, to whom I refer all my success in life. The ship 'New Jersey' was launched on the first of twelfth month, 1824, and, on the third, Whitton Evans, the owner conferred on me the command."

In reading a most interesting book lately called "The Testament of Ignatius Loyola," I was much interested in finding that this old saint of the sixteenth century shared in many of these early Quaker scruples. He says of himself that his custom had been in addressing people to omit all titles such as "Your Lordship," or "Your Reverence," devoutly holding this simplicity to have been the usage of Christ and His Apostles. Also he tells how he was tempted, for fear of the consequences, to relax this rule in the case of a certain captain, and says that, directly he recognized this to be a temptation, he thought, "Since so it is, I will not call him your Lordship, nor make him any reverence, nor will I pull off the cap from my head."

In fact in all ages of Christianity one of the ways in which an special devotedness has manifested itself has been in peculiarities of dress and address, and, except in the special testimony against all bright colors, which for some occult reason were considered to be worldly. Browns and drabs were unworldly, and most of our clothes rang the changes on these two colors. Sometimes a little green was allowed, and curiously enough a dark purple might now and then be indulged in, but red or blue or pink or yellow were entirely forbidden as being very gay. I even knew some very conscientious Friends who did not feel at liberty to have scarlet geraniums in their gardens, or a vase of scarlet flowers in their drawing-rooms.

After I had become an acknowledged religious teacher,

people in spiritual trouble often came to me for help. Among the rest there was one young Friend with a very scrupulous conscience, who came one day greatly troubled about scarlet geraniums. It appeared that she lived in one side of a pair of semi-detached houses in the suburbs of Philadelphia, with a little garden in front of both houses, containing an oval flower bed belonging to both, which she and her neighbor in the other half took turns each spring in filling with flowers. This year it was her turn, and wishing to please her neighbor, she had consulted her as to what flowers they should have. The neighbor expressed a preference for scarlet geraniums, and my friend was about to order them, when a sudden scruple seized her against allowing such gay flowers to adorn the garden in front of her house. She struggled and prayed about it, and the more she prayed the louder seemed the inward voice telling her it would not be right for her to have scarlet geraniums. But how to explain the matter to her neighbor, who knew nothing about Friends, she could not tell, and she was in great distress, and came to me for help.

I have always found that there is nothing more difficult to combat than scruples, and, although I tried very hard to convince my poor perplexed friend that there might be other matters in the Christian life more important than the color of the flowers in our gardens, and that perhaps the Lord would be more pleased by courtesy and kindness to her neighbor, than by any rigid rule as to the color of flowers, which color after all was of His own creation, and could not therefore be displeasing to Him, it was all in vain; and at last I was obliged to give her a piece of advice, to which I rather objected, and this was to "ask Josiah." Josiah was her husband, and I knew he had a fair amount of good common sense, and, although I did not as a general thing approve of letting husbands decide things for their wives, I felt it was in this case almost a necessity. And my opinion was justified, for "Josiah" wisely said he would take the burden of the scarlet geraniums on his shoulders, and he felt sure the Lord would not be displeased to see in front of their house flowers which He Himself had made.

Of course in the very nature of things, modifications of these extreme views were bound to creep in, and I have seen in my lifetime gradual changes, which as a child I should have thought it blasphemy even to image. As the young people of my generation, to whom these old testimonies were nothing more than mere "traditions of the elders," and not at all personal convictions of their own, grew to maturity, they insensibly dropped them, and the different Yearly Meetings gradually grew accustomed to changes that would once have bowed them to the earth with shame and sorrow.

English Friends, as far as I can recollect, were the first to yield; but the different American Yearly Meetings, all except ours in Philadelphia, were not far behind. We in Philadelphia held fast to our old customs as long as it was possible, but even we had to give way at last.

One of my sisters had married and settled in Baltimore Yearly Meeting, which was a Meeting that had accepted these changes far more rapidly than we had, and was considered by us in Philadelphia to be lamentably "gay." My sister had however taken with her the Philadelphia spirit, and, as her large family of daughters grew up, she tried hard to keep them to the Philadelphia standard of plainness. But it was all in vain, one innovation after another crept in, and she found herself powerless to prevent it. Fortunately she was blessed with a delicious sense of humor, and even in the midst of her struggles after plainness, she could not help seeing the funny side. She came to me one day to tell me of her difficulties, and to ask advice, and when she had laid it all before me, she suddenly jumped up with a roguish twinkle in her eye, and, holding up one foot in the air, she said, "Now, Hannah, please to Tell me where it will be safe for me to put my foot down. At one time I put it down at overskirts, but had to take it up again; then I put it down at artificial flowers in the children's hats, and again I had to lift it; then I put it down at rings on their fingers, and again it had to be lifted; and now I do not want to put it down again until I can be sure that I will not have to take it up. Does thee think, Hannah," she asked with a comically sober countenance, "that I might safely venture to put it down at nose rings?" This was too much for my gravity, and I burst into a laugh which my sister could not help joining, and somehow the air seemed cleared, and she decided that she could no longer engage in the fruitless effort to impart Philadelphia ideas into Baltimore, but would accept the inevitable modifications that could not fail to come, even in such a conservative body as Friends.

The simple truth was, as I have shown, that the aim of the Quakers was to avoid following the "vain fashions of the world," and they only adopted a new style when it had become old and was passing away, and Baltimore Friends got ready to do this a little sooner than Philadelphia Friends. One of my nieces from Baltimore tells me that she can remember well going to Philadelphia once to attend a party of her Philadelphia first cousins, and feeling horribly worldly and wicked because her dress was made more in the fashion than theirs.

How little all this can be understood by the young Quakers of the present day! But how tremendously real it all was to us.

Chapter 10

"PLAINNESS OF SPEECH"

The "plainness of speech" referred to in the Third Query meant primarily the use of "thee" and "thou" to a single person instead of the customary "you"; and it was this "testimony" that, in conjunction with the testimony about "plainness of apparel," especially marked us off as a peculiar people. To say "you" to a single person, whether to a Friend or to an outsider, was felt to be the extreme of insincerity and worldliness, and never once, until I was married, did I dare to transgress in this respect. Of course it made it very difficult for us to mingle much with the outside world, since they would be likely to stare and laugh at our quaint language.

The reason for this testimony was no doubt to be found in the absolute sincerity of the early Quakers, who felt it to be dishonest to use a plural pronoun to a single individual; and also in the fact that, when they started, it was the custom of the world to say "you" to a superior, and to say "thee" and "thou" only to inferiors, and the Quakers, who believed all men to be free and equal, and who believed this in a very practical way, could not brook such distinctions, and felt it right to address all classes alike.

Those "early Friends" were democrats in every fiber of their beings. And this was because of their profound conviction that of one blood God had made all the nations of the earth, and that all were equally His children. It was a grand foundation upon which to build their superstructure of morals, and it accounts for many things which might otherwise seem to have been foolish fads and fancies.

In Thomas Ellwood's autobiography he gives an account of the various things he felt called upon to give up when he was convinced of Quaker views, and among them we find the following reference to this matter of the plain language.

"Again the corrupt and unsound form of speaking in the plural number to a single person, you to one person instead of thou to one, which last manner of speech has always been used by God to men, and by men to God, as well as one to another, from the oldest records of time, till corrupt men for corrupt ends, in later and corrupt times, to flatter, fawn and work upon the senseless way of speaking *you* to one, which has since corrupted the modern languages, and hath greatly debased the spirits and depraved the manners of men;—this evil custom I had been as forward in as others, and this I was now called out of and required to cease from.

"These and many more evil customs which had sprung up in the night of darkness and general apostasy from the truth and true religion, were now, by the inshining of this pure ray of divine light in my conscience, gradually discovered to me to be what I ought to cease from, shun, and stand a witness against."

So strongly was this testimony as to the plain language pressed upon us, that during all my childhood I felt it would have been the height of insincerity and worldliness to say "you" to a single person; it seemed to me one of the "gayest" things I could have done. And even when I became a woman, and began to go more into the world, and found that there were good and true Christians who did not hesitate to use the forbidden word in their intercourse with one another, I still found it very difficult to frame my Quaker lips to utter it. Gradually however this difficulty vanished; and now, after seventy years, the "thee" and "thou" have become to me only the language of intimate friendship, and come to me instinctively and almost unconsciously the moment a friend really finds the way to my heart. In fact I judge of the state of my feelings towards a person by this test, and when I find myself addressing them as "thee" and "thou" I know I have begun to love them. And many of my friends, who have had no connection with Quakers, have caught the habit from me, and have themselves adopted the same dear words in our intercourse. My beloved Frances Willard was one of these, and she and I always thee'd and thou'd each other for many years before her death.

The same writer from whom I quoted before, tells in "A Boy's Religion" how he felt as a boy in regard to this "plainness of speech." He says:—

"I said 'thee' and 'thy' to everybody, and I would fully as soon have used profane words as have said 'you' or 'yours' to any one. I thought only 'Friends' went to Heaven, and so I supposed that the use of 'thee' and 'thy' was one of the main things which determined whether one would be let in or not. Nobody ever told me anything like this, and if I had asked any one at home about it, I should have had my views corrected. But for a number of years this was my settled faith.

"I pitied the poor neighbors who would never be let in, and I wondered why everybody did not 'join the meeting' and learn to say 'thee' and 'thy.' I had one little Gentile friend whom I could not bear to have 'lost,' and I went faithfully to work and taught him 'the plain language,' which he always used with me until he was ten or twelve years old, when the strain of the world got too heavy upon the little fellow!"

Another "testimony" connected with "plainness of speech," which was similarly the outcome of Quaker democracy, was against the use of "Mr." or "Mrs." or "Miss" in speaking to or of a person. These titles were considered to be a disobedience to the command of our Lord in Matt. 23:10, "Neither be ye called masters, for one is your master, even Christ." Moreover no genuine Quaker could consent to give a title to a rich man that was refused to a poor man; consequently they used their Christian names, without any prefix, to all alike; and always spoke of one another as Thomas, or Samuel, or Abigail, or Elizabeth, as the case might be. (We had no Reginalds, or Bertrands, or Ethels, or Evelyns, among us in those days!) Where a difference in age would seem to demand a little less familiarity, young people were expected to use the whole name, as Thomas Wistar, Abigail Evans, Samuel Bettle, Elizabeth Pitfield, and so on. This special testimony was often very inconvenient when dealing with the "world's people," and it caused many awkward dilemmas. Our dear father was very strict in regard to this matter, and could never be induced, no matter how inconvenient it might be, to use the gay "Mr." or "Mrs." I remember well the fun we sometimes had, after we were grown up, over his ingenious methods of extricating himself from difficulty when he did not know the first name of any one. He used to substitute for Mr. or Mrs. the word "Cummishilamus," and would say for instance "Cummishilamus Coleman" said or did so and so. When however he had to write the address on a letter, he could not of course use this word, and then he would turn to one of us and say, with a merry twinkle of his dear eyes,—"Come, Han, thee has no scruples, so thee may write the Mr. or Mrs. on this letter."

"Plainness of speech" also forbade our greeting our friends with good-morning or good-evening, or saying good-bye when parting from them. Good-bye was believed to be a corruption of God be with you, and, since God was always with you, it was a sort of unbelief to express a wish that He might be. And to say good-morning or good-evening, which was a form of wishing you might have a good morning or a good evening, was to express a doubt of the fact, known to every Quaker, that your mornings and your evenings must, in the order of Divine Providence, always be good. I grew up with a distinct feeling that it was very gay and worldly to use these expressions, and that the right, or in other words the "plain" thing to do was to greet my friends with, "How art thou?" or "How does thee do?" and to part from them with the simple word "Farewell." Though why "Farewell" was any more truthful than good-bye, even if good-bye did mean God be with you, I have never been able to understand.

In perfect consistence with the Quaker idea of the absolute equality of all human beings in the sight of God, "plainness of speech" forbade us to give the title of Saint to any of our departed fellow-Christians, and we were never allowed to use it, even as a prefix. We never for instance spoke of the Gospels as the Gospel according to St. Matthew, or St. Mark, or St. Luke, or St. John, but always said, "The Gospel according to Matthew," or Mark, or Luke, or John. I saw lately in an old diary kept by a Friend in the seventeenth century an account of one very conscientious Friend who felt a stop against using the prefix saint even in the names of places or streets, and who had great difficulty at one time in finding St. Mary Axe, because she dropped the Saint, and asked for it only as "Mary Axe Street," which no one understood.[1]

---

[1] *Friends' Examiner*, ninth month, 1902.

As a testimony against idol worship we were forbidden to call the months of the year and the days of the week by their heathen names, but were taught to keep to the "simplicity of truth" by calling them by numbers, as for instance, first month, second month, or first day, second day, etc. This was so universally observed in my circle that I do not think it ever entered my head to use the heathen names, and I remember I was greatly shocked when I came to England in 1873 to find that English Friends had given up the practice of using the numbers, and had gone back to the "heathen" names, and for a while I could hardly bring himself to feel they were really Friends at all. And even now, when I date my letters with these "heathen" names, I always feel somehow as though I were making a sort of forbidden excursion into the "gay world."

Chapter 11

FRIENDS' "TESTIMONIES" AGAINST FICTION, MUSIC, AND ART

Another point brought up in this same Third Query, which caused us great trouble was contained in the question whether Friends were careful to bring up their children in "frequently reading the Holy Scriptures, and to restrain them from reading pernicious books." All fiction of every kind was considered by the Friends of those days to be "pernicious," and on this point our mother was very strict, and we were not allowed to read even the most innocent and select Sunday-school stories. As to novels, the very word was felt to be wicked, and to this day I never use it without a momentarily instinctive feeling of lawlessness, as if I were deliberately doing something wrong.

As we grew older the line was naturally less strictly drawn; and when we became old enough to take the guidance of our lives a little more into our own hands, we would sometimes snatch a fearful joy from some story book loaned to us by one of our school friends. One of my most vivid recollections is of such an occasion, which was made all the more vivid to me because it was the first time I had dared to partake openly and boldly of the forbidden fruit.

It was one "First Day" afternoon when there seemed to be nothing going on. I had borrowed a book from one of my schoolmates which she had told me was "lovely," and I took this book, and stretched myself on the outside of my bed to read and eat at my leisure.

The story I read that day, under these delightful circumstances, seemed to give me the nearest approach to prefect bliss of anything I had ever before experienced, and it remains in my memory as one of the happiest days of my life. The book was "The Earl's Daughter," by Grace Aguilar, and to my young American and Quaker mind an earl was more like an archangel than a man, and to be an earl's daughter was almost akin to being a daughter of heaven. And to this day, in spite of all the disillusions that life has brought me about earls and their daughters, the old sense of grandeur that filled my soul with awe on the First Day afternoon so long ago, never fails to come back for at least a moment, when earls and countesses are mentioned in my presence.

But although I enjoyed this and other stories intensely, it was always with an uneasy conscience, and it took me fifty years to get rid of the feeling that to read anything fictitious was to commit a sin. My diary is full of the conflicts I went through on account of this, and, as I read them over, I cannot but feel a real pity for the hungry, ignorant young soul that was so tormented by the constant tendency to make a sin out of a perfectly innocent recreation. The thing that at last brought me deliverance was a sudden recognition of the fact that our Lord Himself constantly used parables, which were only another name for stories, to illustrate and enforce His teaching, and that therefore fiction was not in itself, as I had always thought, a synonym for sin, but that its sinfulness depended entirely upon the sort of fiction it was; and that often fiction might found to be an invaluable aid to virtue. But I have known many Friends who have been tormented by scruples on this point up to old age.

Music was another thing against which the Friends of my day had a very strong testimony. In a book of Discipline, published in Philadelphia in 1873, I have found the following passage in regard to it, which gives the Quaker idea concerning it.

"We would renewedly caution all our members against indulging in music, or having instruments of music in their houses, believing that the practice tends to promote a light and vain mind, and to disqualify for the serious thoughtfulness, which becomes an accountable being, hastening to his final reckoning. . . The spirit and language of the discipline forbid the use of music by Friends, without any exception in favor of that called sacred, and in order to produce harmonious action on this subject throughout the subordinate meetings, the yearly meeting instructs them that those members who indulge in the use of music, or who have musical instruments in their houses, bring themselves within the application of this second clause of the Discipline, viz.: 'And if any of our members fall into either of these practices, and are not prevailed with, by private labor to decline them, the monthly meeting to which the offenders belong should be informed thereof, and if they be not reclaimed by further labor, so as to condemn their misconduct to the satisfaction of the meeting, it should proceed to testify our disunity with them.'" 1873.

So strictly was the Discipline obeyed in this respect that I do not remember in my young days a single individual in our select circle who owned any sort of musical instrument, and above all a piano, which was considered the gayest of the gay. And when it chanced that I found myself in a strange room containing a piano, I always felt as if I were treading the very borders of hell. For many years after I was a woman I never heard any music anywhere that I did not have a secret half delicious sensation of tasting forbidden fruit. Even singing or whistling were frowned down upon. I remember once when a party of young Quakers were all together at Newport for a summer holiday, a dear old Friend called them into his room, and told them solemnly that he had been very much grieved to hear some of them whistling in the garden the day before, and he hoped they would not so transgress Friends' testimonies again.

That the Discipline in this matter was no dead letter is proved by the fact that when I was older and this testimony was more or less losing its power over the less "concerned" members, I knew of several instances where Friends, who, though otherwise exemplary, were not strict in the matter of music, were actually turned out of membership for having a piano in their houses. And as late as 1865 when we had presented our son Frank with a cottage organ (we did not dare to let it be a piano, as we felt organs were for some reason "plainer" than pianos), we were obliged to hide it in one of the top rooms of our house, in order to spare the feelings of our Quaker relations. I never shall forget my surprise when I first waked up to the fact that musical instruments were not only sanctioned in the Bible, but that we were actually commanded to use them. In reading the Psalms one day I could hardly believe my eyes when I came across Psalm 150 and read, "Praise ye the Lord. . . . Praise Him with the sound of the trumpet, praise Him with the psaltery and harp. Praise Him with the timbrel and dance: praise Him with stringed instruments and organs." I never heard any Friend explain how they got over this.

"Plainness" in my day also excluded pictures everywhere, except in books. No good Quakers would have any pictures on their walls, nor did they feel free to have their pictures taken.

Even daguerreotypes, when they came in, were considered "gay" by all the really good Friends. I believe they had an idea that pictures of oneself might tend to vanity. And for some occult reason it seemed to be felt that pictures or statuary were dangerous, as offering a temptation to idolatry. I certainly grew up believing that it was wicked to go to picture galleries, or to look at a statue. And I remember well, when I was about seventeen, breaking loose from all the traditions of my life, and going with a beating heart, as though on some perillously wicked excursion, into the Academy of Fine Arts in Philadelphia. There was a marble group there of Hero and Leander, and I am afraid Leander had not many clothes on, and I can see myself now, standing and looking at it with my heart in my mouth, and saying to myself, "I suppose now I shall go straight to hell, but I cannot help it. If I must go there, I must, but I *will* look at this statue." No words can express what a daring sinner I felt myself to be; and I remember distinctly that I was quite surprised to find myself safely outside that Academy, standing unharmed in Broad Street, without having experienced the swift judgments of an offended Creator.

I can see that marble group vividly even to this day, far more vividly than any statuary I have ever seen since; and although I do not suppose it was at all what would be called good art nowadays, yet to me it has always lived in my memory as the acme of all art, for it was my emancipation into the hitherto absolutely unknown art world. Nothing dreadful happened to me from looking at this, and I gradually gained courage for more, until at last I learned that a gift for art was as much a Divine bestowment as a gift for mathematics, and as such it could not be wrong to develop and exercise it. And gradually the Friends also have seemed to learn this, and those old scruples against art and music have almost entirely vanished from their midst.

Another testimony included in "plainness of apparel" in my young days was one against beards. It happened that when Friends' customs began to crystallize, smooth faces were universal; and, as a consequence, with the Friends' idea of not following the changing fashions, when beards began to be fashionable, Quakers kept on with their smooth faces. As the fashion for beards became more insistent, the Quakers took a firmer and firmer stand, until insensibly, without any real reason for it that I ever heard, it developed into a "religious testimony"; and when I was born into the Society it was one of the most stringent. I remember vividly the first time I saw a "preacher" wearing his beard. He was a visiting Friend from England, where they were less strict, and, in spite of the fact that I had a great reverence for English Friends, his beard seemed to me so evidently the mark of the evil one, that I felt it almost a sin to listen to his preaching. In several "strict" Meetings this same preacher was refused entrance to the "gallery" because of his beard; and I can remember well the great concern expressed by the Philadelphia Elders over this sad evidence of the "gradual encroachments of a worldly spirit in London Yearly Meeting."

This testimony against beards is shared, I believe, though probably on different grounds, by the Roman Catholic priests, and also by High Church clergymen of the Church of England. But the Friends meanwhile have dropped it, along with many others of the strict testimonies of my childhood. They still practice great moderation in their dress and address, and in the furnishing of their houses, and the ordering of their lives, but they have for the most part abandoned all idea of any special cut of clothes, or any stifling of natural gifts, either in literature, or art, or music, being a necessary passport to the favor of heaven. But one cannot but admire and reverence the sturdy adherence to what was felt to be a religious duty, even though it may seem to us a mistaken duty, which characterized those dear old saints.

Chapter 12

Quaker "Scruples"

The individual "scruples" resulting from the various "testimonies" of which I have spoken were practically endless, for each individual would of course interpret and apply them according to their own convictions of duty; and morbidly conscientious souls would be continually inventing new scruples, until life to some of them often became almost a torment. One of my friends, who had inherited a particularly morbid conscience, told me, after we were middle-aged women, that no words could express what she went through on this account when she was younger. She said that often it seemed impossible for her to get dressed and down-stairs in the morning because of the "scruples" that beset her about every article of her clothing, and that the only way she could sometimes manage it at all was by stuffing her ears with cotton, and repeating over, as fast as she could, extracts of poetry, so as to keep herself from hearing the inward voice that was continually urging her to fresh sacrifices.

In a diary kept by an old great-grandmother of our family in the years 1760 to 1762 there is a very quaint and vivid picture of the "scruples" which Quakerism of her day had engendered in an earnest but narrow-minded soul. In one place she writes as follows:—

"Solomon said of laughter, 'It is madness' and of mirth, 'What doeth it?' for even in laughter the heart is sorrowful and the end of that mirth is heaviness. I often think if I could be so fixed as never to laugh nor to smile, I should be one step better. It fills me with sorrow when I see people so full of laugh."

Again she writes bemoaning the lax condition of things among the Quakers of her day:—

"Oh! will there ever be a Nehemiah raised at our meeting? Oh! the fashions and running into them; the young men wearing of their hats set up behind; next it must be a ribbon to tie their hair behind. The girls in Pennsylvania have got their necks set off with a black ribbon—a sorrowful sight indeed. But what did that dear friend, Nicholas Davis, tell them—the old people had not done their duty, and that was the reason the young were no better. Six of those girls from Darby were here from John Hunt's. I thought they did not belong to Friends till I was informed they did. But I many times think what signifies my being concerned about fashions. Where is one Friend's child or children but some doddery fashion or another is on their backs or their heads? Here is this day Josiah Albason's son, all the son he has, with his hat close up behind."

Again under date of third month, 18, 1762, she writes:—

"Oh! lamentable is our case I think. I am so filled with sorrow many times about the wicked. Oh, I think could my eyes run down with tears always at the abominations of the times—so much excess of tobacco, and tea is as bad, so much of it, and they will pretend they can't do without it. And there is the calico. Oh! the speech, but where is our plainness? Ain't we like all the rest, be they who they will? What fashion have not the Quakers got? As William Hunt said, 'Oh! that we had many such as he, or enough such; there would be no calico among the Quakers, no, nor so many fashion-mongers.' I think tobacco, and tea, and calico may all be set down with the negroes, all one as bad as another."

Those extracts from my great-grandmother's diary show plainly that the scruples of one generation were not always the scruples of another; but in every case the spirit of self-denial was the same.

Another grandmother, nearer to me in time, whom I can well remember, felt a scruple against false teeth. They were just beginning to be used, and as she was toothless from old age, and had great difficulty in eating, my father had persuaded her to have a set made. But when they came home she told us that she "felt a stop" in her mind about wearing them, as they seemed to her to be of the vain fashions of the world. They were consequently put away in a drawer with her best silk shawl, and never saw the light again. I remember well how saintly we young people felt the dear old lady to be, as we watched her difficulty in eating, and her necessary refusal of so much that we thought good.

A dear friend who lived near us when I was a child, and who was a preacher in our Meeting, bought herself a new parlor carpet and had it laid down, and then became so afraid lest she had allowed pride to enter, that she felt "led" to have several wheelbarrow loads of rough stones dumped out upon it in order to take off its freshness. We children heard the story of it all with an awe not to be described, and from that time the preaching of this dear saint seemed to us like the voice of an angel from Heaven.

I cannot help contrasting here an experience of my own over a new carpet many years afterwards, when I had learned something of the life of faith, and knew the power of Christ to deliver. We had just bought a new Brussels carpet for our drawing-room, with delicate sprigs of flowers all over it, and I was very proud and pleased. Shortly after it was put down, my husband arranged to have a number of rough working-men come every Sunday morning to this very drawing-room for a Bible class. It was a great trial to me to have my carpet used in that way, and I was inclined to resent it, but I knew as a Christian I ought not to feel so, and yet I did not exactly see how to overcome the feeling. Some one happened to say to me about that time that there was always some passage in Scripture which would help you out of every difficulty. This impressed me, and once when I was praying about my carpet difficulty I said to myself, "Well, I am certain that there is no Scripture anywhere that says anything about drawing-room carpets;" when at that very moment there flashed into my mind the passage, "Take joyfully the spoiling of your goods." I immediately seized hold of that word of God as the Sword of the Spirit with which to conquer my enemy, and from that moment rather enjoyed seeing those rough men tramp over my new carpet. And I may say in conclusion that that carpet seemed as if it never would wear out. It lasted for years, until I was quite tired of the sight of it. I cannot help thinking mine was a better way than the rough stones of the dear old Friend.

After I had discovered this way of faith one of my friends who had suffered much from the Quaker "Scruples," gave me a striking analysis of the different methods of living the Christian life. She said, "I have noticed that there are three ways of getting to the other side of a spiritual mountain. Some people tunnel through by the sweat of their brows, and that is the Quaker way, and was for a long time my way. Some meander around the base of the mountain, going this way and that, but, because they always keep their faces turned towards the goal, they gradually, in spite of their meanderings, draw nearer and nearer to the other side; and this," she said, "was the way I adopted when I was worn out with my tunnelling. But now," she added, "here you are telling me that there is a third way, which is far better than either of the others, and that is the way of faith. You say that there are Christians who have found out that they can just flap the wings of faith and fly right over the mountain, and you declare that this is the way you adopt. I must confess that the people who adopt your way seem to get to the other side far more quickly and more easily than those who tunnel or those who meander, and I have decided to give up all tunnelling and all meandering, and to flap my wings too and to go over."

But the dear old saints, among whom my childhood and girlhood were passed, did not seem to know how to flap their wings; and for the most part they spent their lives in steadfast though weary tunnelling. But their faithfulness and self-sacrifice, even though I may feel it was in mistaken ways, seemed then and seems now to have been worthy of all honor. And the one strong overmastering impression that it all made upon my young heart was simply this—that, by hook or by crook, I had *got* to be good. No matter what lack of religious teaching there may have been in other directions among the Philadelphia Quakers, there was no lack here. The supreme and paramount necessity of being good—thoroughly and honestly and genuinely good—was in the very air we breathed, and almost in the very food we ate.

I confess that I sometimes chafed at this. The adventurous nature in me now and then pined for a chance to be naughty— to do something I ought not to do, or to leave undone something that was expected of me—but the limitations of my life made only very innocent naughtiness possible. And in looking back upon it now I am forced to admire the wonderful atmosphere of goodness that surrounded me with such a sure defense against the evil that would otherwise I feel certain, have been so enticing to a wild free nature like mine. For if any human being was ever born free I was. The one cry of my soul has always been for freedom. "Bonds that enslave and tyrannies that fetter" have always been my abhorrence, whether they were bonds of actual rules, or merely bonds of conventional custom. Had my parents made many rules, I should have been driven to disobey them, but the all enveloping atmosphere of goodness, in which they and their circle lived and moved, controlled and constrained my wayward spirit with such unconscious power, that I hardly knew I was being controlled, and had a blissful feeling that somehow I nearly always had my own way.

No one, who did not live in it, could I feel sure, conceive of the narrow range of life with which I was acquainted up to the age of eighteen. I never met anybody who lived in what was called "the gay world." My associates were only the staid, sober "Friends" of our little circle, and their carefully guarded children. I never, as I have said, was allowed to read any novels; and I had absolutely no opportunity of learning what life meant outside of our narrow Quaker fold. As to the sin of the world I had not the slightest inkling. Nobody every told me anything, not even the girls at school; or, if they did, I was too utterly ignorant and innocent to understand them; I venture to say that it would be perfectly impossible in the present day for a girl of eighteen to live in such an unreal world of ignorance as the one in which I lived, or to enter upon the responsibilities of life more absolutely unprepared to meet them.

My interior life up to the age of sixteen was of the simplest.

I believed what I was told, which however I have shown was very little, and troubled myself not one whit about the problems of the universe. My only conscious religious thoughts were an underlying fear of hell-fire, which now and then sprang into active life when any epidemic was abroad or any danger seemed to threaten. How I came to have this fear I cannot now remember, for the Quakers rarely touched on the future life in any way, either as regarded heaven or hell. Their one concern was as to the life of God in the soul of man now and here, and they believed that where this was realized and lived, the future could be safely left in the Divine care. But now and then I would get a sudden fright in regard to my future and would make tremendous resolutions about "being good" and would for a few hours really try to correct my faults. But such occasions were not very lasting, and I would soon relapse into the old unthinking ways.

As I have said, however, the atmosphere in which I lived was so impregnated with goodness that it was not easy even to think of anything naughty, much less to come to the point of actually doing it, and I believe I may fairly say that on the whole I was as good as a creature full of energy and high spirits, and with bouncing health, could be expected to be. But up to the age of sixteen I was simply a good animal. My spiritual nature was unawakened, and I had never consciously been made aware of the existence of my soul.

But a change was at hand, although I little knew it. My soul was awaking from its torpor, and, like the butterfly in the cocoon, was struggling to escape from the bonds that had hitherto held it in leash. My long search after God was about to begin.

Chapter 13

The Awakening

In the story of my religious life four epochs stand out clearly before me. The first one dawned as I have said when I was sixteen. In a dim mysterious way I began to be filled with vague longings after something that would satisfy my interior nature. In my diary of the autumn of 1848 I find records of these longings, and of a blind reaching out for something to fill what I called in the tragic language of youth "the aching void in my heart." In the midst of this I fell head over ears in love with one of the young teachers in the school I was attending, and her influence changed my life. I find a record in my diary of all the steps of my acquaintance with her—of my longings to speak to her and to beg for her love, and of my hesitation for fear of bothering her. I write about it as follows:—

"1848. Sixteen years old. This is an important time for me. Now is the forming time of my character. I feel as I never felt before. The great and solemn duties of life have, for the first time come before me. I was not born to be an idler, for I feel something within me, which tells me—

"'Life has imports more inspiring
    Than the fancies of thy youth;
It has hopes as high as heaven
    It has labor, it has truth.
It has wrongs that may be righted,

Noble deeds that may be done.
Its great battles are unfought
Its great triumphs are unwon.'

"Something which points onwards, far onwards into the
future, beyond this into a brighter, happier world, and tells me
of the glorious reward of those who fulfill their duties. I have
not felt this long:—three months ago I was a careless, happy
child. I am still a child, but an earnest reflecting one, no longer
careless or indifferent. How can I be so, when there is *so much*,
so very much to be thought about; and *so much* to be done?
What has caused this change? Then there was an aching void
in my heart. I felt a want of something, something I knew not
what, something indefinable which would cause me to sit
dreamily for hours and look into the sky, and watch the pale
stars or the moon, until my very being seemed merged into
theirs and I almost forgot I was on earth, while my thoughts
wandered far off to the pathless regions over which they
presided, and I would strive in vain to pierce the mysteries of
their existence. Study, I thought, would fill that void, but I
found I was mistaken. In such a state was my mind when, in
the beginning of ninth month we left our darling little cottage
home and returned to the city. If I had then met with one whom
I could have loved but whose principles were bad, I shudder to
think what would have been the consequences, for I am very
easily influenced by those I love. But my Heavenly Father was
willing to extend a little mercy toward me. He sent across my
path one in whom I found a *true friend*. She was a young girl
employed by Miss Maryanna as composition teacher named
Anna S—. I was prepared to love her even before I saw her,
for one whom I love had told me of her loveliness. For two
weeks after she first came to school I never spoke to her, I

believe, but once; and then I saw her looking for a book and handed one to her asking if that was the right one. I thought we never would get acquainted. I used to sit and watch her and wish I dare speak to her and kiss her, and this very longing made me particularly retiring. I would see her put her arms around other girls, and I would turn away in sorrow to think she would not do the same to me. At last one day, how well I remember it, I was standing at my desk when she came up and spoke about A. S. F. How happy I felt! How I longed to throw my arms around her neck and beg her to let me love her! My heart was all in a tumult, yet I answered her calmly and without emotion and she soon left me. However the ice was broken, we began to speak more frequently, and one morning she kissed me. That kiss was engraven on my heart. I felt that she loved me, and the thought was happiness. From that moment I have loved, nay almost idolized her. The aching void in my heart now is partly filled, for I have listened to her sentiments, I have seen her noble principles of action, and I have found that 'life is real, life is earnest,' and is not to be amusements. She has taught me, not in so many words but quietly, by her influence, that I have a mission to fulfill on earth, and straightway I must set to work to perform it. That henceforward I must struggle earnestly to become pure and holy and noble-hearted that I may be great in the world and perform faithfully my part in the great battle of life. Her influence has aroused me from my dream of childhood. In one short month I have become a woman. Oh! how blessed has her friendship been to me! I hope, earnestly hope I may not abuse the privilege."

A day or two later I wrote:—

"Every day I feel grateful to my Heavenly Father for

blessing me with such a friend as Anna. This is such an important period of my life. I tremble when I think of the awful responsibility resting upon me. My character is forming, and I have power to be what I choose. Oh, may I choose to be a good and noble woman! Today, as I walked along the street and thought of what might be my future destiny, it made me almost shrink. I may be destined for some great work. I feel that within me which tells me I could accomplish it. At any rate I shall do a great deal of good or evil. I *will* choose the former. Oh, my Father who art in Heaven, wilt Thou not assist me to advance in the path of self-conquest, which must be my first great battle. What a glorious triumph it will be if I succeed!"

According to my diary, every day now seemed to awaken my spiritual nature more and more, until at last a sort of climax arrived, and on 11th mo. 28th, 1848, I wrote:—

"An eventful day! Eventful I mean in my spiritual life. Today I have felt and thought enough for a year. My friend Anna read to us in class a book called 'Other Worlds,' and also 'Future Existence,' from the 'School Boy,' by Abbott. It was all interesting, and had an almost overpowering effect on me. As I listened to the accounts of those mighty worlds which are everywhere scattered around us, some of which are so distant that the rays of light from them which enter our eyes have left these stars six thousand years ago! As I reflected that these worlds were all moving on regularly, never disturbing each other, but all obedient to one mighty Creator, the grandeur of the thought was intense, and for a few minutes I felt as though the happiness of being born into a universe so limitless, so magnificent, so glorious, was too great. And as I heard of our future existence, of the glorious unimaginable happiness in store for us, of the perfect bliss of the good and holy, I inwardly thanked my Creator for placing me among beings whose anticipations were so happy. But then came the awful, the overwhelming thought that that eternity of endless bliss was only for the good, and the remembrance that I could have no share in it unless my heart was changed. Oh, I was almost too great to be borne. And these thoughts linger with me. Why is it?"

The impression made upon me by this glimpse, as it were, into the magnificence of the universe has never to this day left me. At the bottom of all my questionings about God there has always been a conviction of His illimitable power which nothing would ever be able to withstand. But for a long time, as will be seen, I thought of this power as being a selfish power, engaged, not on my side, but against me; and my one question for many years was as to how I could win the God who possessed it over to my side.

Chapter 14

ECLIPSE OF FAITH

This morbid self-introspection lasted, with variable degrees of earnestness, until the time of my marriage at nineteen. Nothing ever came of it, and in the nature of things, nothing ever could. It was a self-involved religion that had no relation whatever to any Divine facts. And I see now that it was a mercy my marriage, and the new life and wider interests into which I was introduced, more or less turned my attention in other directions, and made my religious emotions and feelings sink into the background for a time, so that my mind became free at a later period to take an entirely different view of the religious life.

I believe, however, that my experiences during these years have been valuable in one way, and that is in teaching me to avoid ever encouraging in the young people I have known any sort of a self-absorbed interior life. Self-absorption is always a temptation to young people, and if their religion is of a sort to add to this self-absorption, I feel that it is a serious mistake. If I had my way, the whole subject of feelings and emotions in the religious life would be absolutely ignored. Feelings there will be, doubtless, but they must not be in the least depended on, nor in any sense be taken as the test or gauge of one's religion. They ought to be left out of the calculation entirely. You may feel good or you may feel bad, but neither the good feeling nor the bad feeling affects the real thing. It may affect your comfort in the thing. If God loves you, it is of no account, as far as the fact goes, whether you feel that He loves you or do not feel it; although, as I say, it materially affects your comfort. Of course, if you really believe that He loves you, you cannot help being glad about it; but if you make your belief dependent upon your feelings of gladness, you are reversing God's order in the most hopeless kind of way. I like so much that story of Luther when the devil said to him: "Luther, do you feel that you are a child of God?" and Luther replied, "No, I do not *feel* it at all, but I *know* it. Get thee behind me, Satan."

During all the years when I was struggling over my feelings, I never succeeded in making them what I thought they ought to be; and as a consequence the religious part of my life was a misery to me. But after I had learned that the facts of religion were far more important than my feelings about these facts, and had consequently given up looking at my feelings, and sought only to discover the facts, I became always happy in my religious life, and had, without any effort, the very feelings of love to God, and of rest and peace and joy in my soul that before I had so vainly tried to work up. No words can express how vital I consider this point to be, nor how much, since I have found it out for myself, I have longed to make everybody else see it.

Many years after it had all become clear to me, one of my children came to me evidently in great perplexity and said, "Mother, how long does it take God to forgive you when you have been naughty?" "It does not take Him a minute," I replied. "Oh," she said, "I can't believe that. I think you have to feel sorry first for a good many days, and then you have to ask Him in a very pretty and nice way, and then perhaps He can forgive you." "But," I said, "daughter, the Bible says that if we confess our sins He is faithful and just to forgive us right straight off." "Well," she said, "I wouldn't believe that if fifty

Bibles said it, because I know that you have got to feel sorry for quite a good while, and then you have got to ask God in a very pretty way, and then you have got to wait till He is ready to forgive you."

I found the case was really serious, so, taking the child on my lap, I opened the Bible and made her read out loud the verse I had quoted, and then explained to her that God loved us so much that He sent His Son to die for us, and that, because of His love, He was always ready to forgive us the minute we asked Him, just as mothers were always ready to forgive their children as soon as the children wanted to be forgiven. At last the child was convinced, and putting her little hands together she said in a reverent little voice, "Dear Lord Jesus, I want you to forgive me this very minute for all my naughty, and I am certain sure you will, because you love me." And then she jumped down off my lap and ran away shouting merrily in childish glee.

My little girl was happy because she had found out a happy fact and believed it. But in her first way of looking at the matter she was only voicing the natural idea of the human heart. We all feel, as she did, that we must come to God with great doubt and timidity, as to a Being of whom we know but little, and whom we fear much; and that His favor depends altogether upon the beauty and suitableness of our emotions, and the ceremonious order of our approach. To come "boldly to the throne of grace to find mercy and obtain help in the time of need" is only possible to the soul that has been brought into a real acquaintance with the goodness of God.

During all the years however of which I speak, from the age of sixteen to twenty-six, I knew nothing of this. God was to me a far off, unapproachable Being, whom, in spite of all my eager and painful searching, I failed utterly to find. I had not the slightest conception of what the expression "God is love" meant. My idea of Him was that He was a stern and selfish task-master, who might perhaps, if one could only secure the sort of feelings and of conduct that would please Him, be induced to pay some little attention to the needs of His children, but who was for the most part so absorbed in thoughts of His own glory, and of the consideration and reverence due to Himself, that it was almost impossible, except by a superhuman degree of perfection, to win His regards. He seemed to me a supremely selfish Autocrat who held my fate in His hands, but who only cared for me in proportion to my power of adding to His honor and His glory. Of all His loving and beautiful unselfishness, which I was afterwards to discover, I had for all these years not the faintest glimpse.

Moreover, the only way I knew of by which one could know that this unapproachable Deity did condescend to turn even a slight ear to the cries of His children, was to have some sort of an interior feeling of it, and consequently, whenever I was religious at all, the whole energy of my spirit was spent, as I have said, in the effort to acquire in some occult way this necessary inward feeling. The sort of introspection I had imbibed from my Quaker teaching was calculated to lead to constant self-examination of the most difficult sort, because it was an examination, not so much into one's actions, as into one's emotions! And, considering what ticklish things our emotions are, and how much they depend upon the state of our health, or the state of the weather, or the influence of other minds, no more fatal occupation in my opinion can be indulged in than this sort of self-examination, and no more unreliable gauge could possibly be found as to one's spiritual condition than that afforded by one's own interior emotions. But the religion of my years between sixteen and twenty-six was nothing but a religion of trying to feel; and, as I was a very natural, healthy sort of being, my feelings were not likely to be very sentimental or pious; and the agonizing futile efforts that I have described to bring them up to the right religious pitch is something pitiful to consider.

My soul hungered after God, but I could not find Him. Even the comfort of prayer was denied me, for I had, as I have said, imbibed the idea that you could not pray acceptably unless you felt an inward sense of the Divine favor, and that any prayers offered without this sense were really a mockery, and even perhaps a sin. And, since this inward sense of God's favor was the very thing I was seeking to secure, and yet might not pray for until I first possessed it, I seemed tossed out helpless and forlorn into dreary darkness.

What the Bible said about God's love was altogether a secondary consideration to what I might feel about it; indeed, as far as I can recollect, I did not consider the Bible at all. "How do I feel?" not "What does God say?" was my daily cry. I was like a criminal in the presence of a judge, who, instead of being concerned as to how the judge felt about him, should spend all his efforts in trying to see how he felt about the judge.

A more ridiculous as well as pitiful attitude of soul one can hardly conceive of. And yet no one whom I approached on the subject seemed to know any better; and I floundered on in a despairing sort of way, afraid to give up my spiritual struggles lest I should be eternally damned, and yet realizing that they brought no help; and being continually tempted to upbraid God for being deaf to my cries.

I was like a man kneeling in a dark room and praying despairingly for light, ignorant of the fact that outside the sun was shining, and that it only needed to open the windows and light would pour in. In the very nature of things light, either in the physical world or the spiritual world, cannot be self-evolved. I had gone to work in entirely the wrong way. I was trying to feel before I knew; and, instead of basing my feelings upon my knowledge, I was seeking to base my knowledge upon my feelings.

It was just as if a man, wanting to travel to a certain place, should enter the first railway station he might come across, and, without making any inquiries, should take a seat in the first railway carriage at hand, and should then shut his eyes and try to feel whether he was in the right train or not. No man in his senses would do such an idiotic thing. And yet it was exactly this I was doing in my religious life. It never entered my head to try and find out the facts of religion. I did not even know there were any facts to find out. My relations with God seemed to me altogether a matter of my own feelings toward Him, and not in the least of His feelings toward me; and every religious energy I possessed was consequently directed toward getting up these necessary feelings.

Of course it was an impossible task, and, as time went on, and no right feelings would come for all my striving, I became more and more discouraged, and at last, when I was between twenty-three and twenty-four, I found myself being driven into absolute unbelief. I argued that, if there really was a God anywhere, some answer to all my long and earnest wrestling would surely have been vouchsafed to me; and that, since He made no sign, therefore He could not be.

Moreover, as I grew older, I had begun to learn something more of the awful condition of things in the world because of sin; and the manifest evidences I seemed to see of an imperfect creation in my own life and in the lives of others, where failure was generally the rule, and success only the exception, appeared to me incompatible with the idea of a wise and sensible

Creator, not to say a good One, such as I had been told I must believe in. And gradually the creation came to seem to me such a grievous failure that I felt driven to the conclusion that either it must have been a wicked God who had created us, or else we had not been created by God at all, but by some evil and malicious power opposed to Him.

In my diary under date of 11th mo. 5, 1855, I head my entry with the following ominous words:—

"The Eclipse of Faith."

"This last year has witnessed a great change in me. Every faculty of my nature has been thoroughly aroused. I have felt my mind expanding and have been cognizant of an actual and rapid mental growth. I pass from one phase of experience to another, leave behind me one standing place after another, and am now—where! Oh Christ, that I indeed knew where!

* * *

"An inevitable chain of reasoning on free will has loosened every foothold, and I know not where to rest, if indeed there *is* any rest. Without any apprehension on my part of the result, thoughts and reasonings have been slowly gathering around my faith, and dashing themselves against it, until at last, with a sudden shock, it has fallen; and I am lost!

"It has come to me like this. Benevolence certainly is a necessary attribute of the Almighty. His love, we are told, surpasses the love of an earthly parent far more than we can imagine. But it is utterly inconsistent with this to suppose that He can have any foreknowledge of the destiny of the human beings He creates. For of course, did He know, His benevolence would not allow Him to create any but beings destined to eternal happiness. Therefore He cannot be omniscient. Further if He were omnipotent, as we are told, He would have made such modifications of man's nature as would at least render the work of salvation less difficult and of far more frequent occurrence. Therefore He cannot be both all loving and also all powerful. Without either of these He ceases to be a God. Either He has set in motion a creating force which He can neither control nor end, and has performed His work in the first place so imperfectly and blindly that the results are grievously disastrous; or He has nothing to do with creation, and we are created by another and an evil Power.

* * *

"A further conclusion is forced upon me. Justice is another necessary attribute of a good God. But it were most utterly unjust that we now should be feeling the effects of Adam's fall, supposing there ever was such a thing. We are driven therefore from the possibility of a just Creator making independent beings suffer eternally for each other's sins. And on the other hand benevolence could not allow of the creation of innately wicked natures, while justice could not share in punishing them.

"There is no escape! A thousand questions rush in on every side. I am a sceptic!"

Chapter 15

A Renewed Search

This scepticism continued for over two years, and I had quite settled down to it and looked upon it as the normal condition of every thoughtful reasonable being. But the year 1858 was destined to see everything changed. Early in that year I had become acquainted with some very orthodox Christians who were full of the doctrines and dogmas of Christianity. As I have stated before, I knew absolutely nothing of doctrines. They had never come into my scheme of religion at all. I was immensely interested therefore in hearing about them, and began to wonder whether my unbelief might not have been caused by my utter ignorance of these very doctrines. Under date of April 25, 1858, I wrote in my diary:—

"The Bible talks of the necessity of being 'born again,' what *does* it mean? Is there really such a thing practically to be experienced? And is a belief in Jesus of Nazareth as the Saviour of the world necessary to it? Oh, how I long for settlement.... It may be that all my failures to find and walk in the right way arise from my rejection of Christ in the sense in which most Christians seem to receive Him, but I really cannot receive Him so. And besides, if their way *is* the truth, I must wait until my Divine Guide leads me into it; and certainly He is not leading me there now, but, it seems to me, further and further away.... My whole soul and intellect seem to shrink from the material orthodox view of the Gospel. It seems impossible for me to believe in the atoning merits of Christ's death. My mind revolts from anything so material as the thought that the outward death of His body, (which after all must necessarily have taken place in some way as a consequence of His humanity), could have had any atoning merits. Far more likely, if atonement was needed at all, was it His life that was the sacrifice. To put on humanity must indeed have been to Divinity a wonderful condescension, and bitter suffering; to put it off, no matter in what way, could be none whatever.

"But I may be wrong in my views. Only the Lord can teach me."

Again on May 18, 1858, I write:—

"I cannot help the feeling that I have attained to a higher form of Truth than the apostles had, and therefore I cannot pray 'Lord, I believe, help thou my unbelief' since I have no conviction of being in unbelief. I am not comfortable, however, in my belief or unbelief, whichever it may be, and yet I can see no way of escape. Last night at our Bible class I introduced the subject, hoping that my orthodox friends would be able to argue so conclusively on their side as to force me to a conviction in the orthodox form of faith. But I felt at the end that no argument could avail anything. If my belief is to be changed it will have to be by Divine power, and it would be indeed a being 'born again.' But it seems impossible to me."

Again on June 25, 1858, I wrote:—

"Cold and dead again and full of pride! The day will certainly come at last when it will be said of me as of Ephraim of old, 'She is wedded to her idols, let her alone!' My 'idol' now I fear is the pride of human reason which will not submit to become as a little child before it can enter the Kingdom of Heaven. . . . At present I am in great trouble because of my religious belief. I long to adopt the Orthodox creed, but cannot; and while on one hand it seems to me wicked that I cannot, at the same time it seems also wicked in me to try to do so, when a clearer light seems to have been granted me. If the truth is what Unitarians profess, I am afraid to know it. I dread the consequences. I shrink from the contempt and reproaches it would bring upon me. And yet at the same time there is perhaps something a little pleasing to the natural human pride and heroism to think of being called upon to take an independent stand for what I consider a higher form of truth. And yet I do not want to be independent of those I love. I am in a state of sad perplexity."

This perplexity increased and deepened, and I began at last to think it was dishonest not to speak it out to my friends, and was just about making up my mind to do so, when one day an event occurred that changed the whole current of my life.

And this brings me to the second epoch in my soul's history.

Chapter 16

RESTORATION OF BELIEF

It was in the year 1858 and I was twenty-six years old. I had just lost a precious little daughter five years old, and my heart was aching with sorrow. I could not endure to think that my darling had gone out alone into a Godless universe; and yet, no matter on which side I turned, there seemed no ray of light.

It happened that just at this time the religious world was being greatly stirred by the inauguration of daily noonday meetings, held from twelve to one, in the business part of the city, and crowded with business men. I had heard of these noonday meetings with a very languid interest, as I thought they were only another effort of a dying-out superstition to bolster up its cause. However, one day I happened to be near a place where one of these meetings was being held, and I thought I would go in and see what it was like. It was an impressive thing to see such crowds of busy men and women collected together at that hour in one of the busiest parts of the city, and I remember wondering vaguely what it could all be about. Then suddenly something happened to me. What it was or how it came I had no idea, but somehow an inner eye seemed to be opened in my soul, and I seemed to see that after all God was a fact—the bottom fact of all facts—and that the only thing to do was to find out all about Him. It was not a pious feeling, such as I had been looking for, but it was a conviction,—just such a conviction as comes to one when a mathematical problem is suddenly solved. One does not *feel* it is solved, but one knows it, and there can be no further question. I do not remember anything that was said. I do not even know that I heard anything. A tremendous revolution was going on within me that was of far profounder interest than anything the most eloquent preacher could have uttered. God was making Himself manifest as an actual existence, and my soul leaped up in an irresistible cry to know Him.

It was not that I felt myself to be a sinner needing salvation, or that I was troubled about my future destiny. It was not a personal question at all. It was simply and only that I had become aware of God, and that I felt I could not rest until I should know Him. I might be good or I might be bad; I might be going to hell—these things were outside the question. All I wanted was to become acquainted with the God of whom I had suddenly become aware.

How to set about it was the one absorbing question. I had no one I cared to ask, and it never occurred to me that prayer would help me. It seemed to me like the study of some new and wonderful branch of knowledge to which I must apply with all diligence, and I concluded that probably the Bible was the book I needed. "This book," I said to myself, "professes to teach me anything." I was going with my family to spend some weeks at the seashore, and I decided to take no books but the Bible, and to try and find out what it said about God. In my diary I wrote under date of July 16, 1858—

"I have brought my Bible to Atlantic City this summer with a determination to find out what its plan of salvation is. My own plans have failed utterly, now I will try God's if possible .... I am trying to believe Him simply as a little child. I have laid aside my preconceived notions of what He ought to do and say, and have come in simplicity to the Bible to see what He has done and said; and I *will* believe Him."

Some one had remarked once in my hearing that the book of Romans contained the clearest and fullest statements of Christian doctrine to be found in the Bible, and I set myself to read it. What I should have made out of it without any guidance I cannot say, but one day I mentioned to a lady, who was visiting us, how interested I was in trying to understand the teaching of the Book of Romans, but how difficult I found it, when she said she had a little book which had explained it to her, and asked if she might give it to me. I accepted it eagerly, and found it most enlightening. It set forth the plan of salvation as described in the third, fourth and fifth of Romans in a clear businesslike way that appealed to me strongly. It stated that mankind were all sinners, and all deserved punishment—that all had sinned and come short of the glory of God, and that there was none righteous, no not one; and it declared that therefore every mouth was stopped and all the world had become guilty before God (Rom. 3: 1-19). It went on to show that there was no escape from this except through the righteousness of Christ, which was "unto all and upon all them that believe"; and that Christ was our propitiation, through whom we obtained the "remission of sins that are past" (Rom. 3:20-26). And then it pointed out that by this process all boasting on our part was shut out, and we were justified before God not by anything we had done or could do, but by what our Divine Saviour had done for us (Rom. 3: 27-31). It declared that Christ was the substitute for sinners—that He had in their place borne the punishment they deserved, and that all we had to do in order to secure the full benefit of this substitution, was simply to believe in it, and accept the forgiveness so purchased.

Of course this was a very legal and businesslike interpretation of these passages, and was not at all the interpretation I should give to them now; but I want to tell, as truthfully as I can, the way things impressed me then. The very crudeness and outwardness of the interpretation made it easy for my ignorance to grasp it, and it struck me at the time as a most sensible and satisfactory arrangement. It was a "plan of salvation" that I could understand. There was nothing mystical or mysterious about it,—no straining after emotions, no looking out for experiences. It was all the work of Another done for me, and required nothing on my part but a simple common-sense understanding and belief.

Baldly stated it was as follows. We were all sinners, and therefore all deserved punishment. But Christ had taken our sins upon Himself and had borne the punishment in our stead, and therefore an angry God was propitiated, and was willing to forgive us and let us go free. Nothing could be more plain and simple. Even a child could understand it. It was all outside of oneself, and there need be no searchings within or rakings up of one's inward feelings to make things right with God. Christ had made them right, and we had nothing to do but to accept it all as a free gift from Him. Moreover, a God who could arrange such a simple plan as this, was understandable and get-at-able, and I began to think it must be true.

This all sounds very outward and very crude; but, after all, crude as it seems, there was behind it the great bottom fact that God was, somehow or other, in Christ reconciling the world unto Himself; and it was this vital fact of the reconciliation between God and man that had laid hold of me. And I believe it is this fact, however it my be expressed, that is the one essential thing in the outset of every satisfactory religious life. The soul must know that all is right between itself and God before it can try, with any heart, to worship and serve Him.

I had discovered this vital fact, and the religious life had begun for me with eager and enthusiastic delight.

In my diary I find in 1858 the following entries:—

"Restoration of Belief."

"August 20, 1858. Am I really coming to Christ? I ask myself this question with wonder and amazement. A month ago it seemed so utterly impossible. But I believe I am. It seems as if these truths in the New Testament have taken hold of my soul, and I cannot gainsay them. God only knows what the end will be.

"August 21, 1858. Many passages of Scripture have been impressed on my mind in my reading, and, having made up my mind simply to believe and not to reason or question, I *do* find myself inevitably brought to Christ as my Redeemer. My watchword for the last few weeks has been 'Thus saith the Lord' as a conclusive argument in every case.

"August 30, 1858. I am resting now simply on God's own record as the foundation of my hope. He says Jesus Christ is His well beloved Son, and I believe it. He says further that He gave His Son to be the propitiation for our sins, and I believe this also. He *is* my Saviour, not only my helper; and in His finished work I rest. Even my hard heart of unbelief can no longer refrain from crying out 'Lord, I believe. Help Thou my unbelief.'

"September 13, 1858. My heart is filled with the exceeding preciousness of Christ. And I am lost in wonder at the realization of His infinite mercy to me, who am so utterly unworthy of the least favor from His hands. How could He be so tender and so loving! I can write the words, 'It is all of free grace, but they only feebly convey the deep sense I have of the infinite freeness of this grace.' 'While we were yet sinners Christ died for us.' Could anything be more free than this? I have so long bewildered myself with trying to work out my own righteousness, and have found such weariness in it, that I feel as if I could never appreciate deeply enough the blessed rest there is for me in Christ. 'He was made sin for us who knew no sin, that we might be made the righteousness of God in Him.' No wonder the Apostle cried out from a full heart, 'Thanks be unto God for His unspeakable gift!'"

My diary is full of similar records, but these will suffice to tell of the wonderful discovery I had made. I want it to be clearly understood that it all came to me as a discovery, and in no sense as an attainment. I had been seeking after attainments in the past, but now I had lost all thought of any attainment of my own in the blaze of my discoveries of the salvation through Christ. It was no longer in the slightest degree a question of what I was or what I could do, but altogether a question of what God was and of what He had done. I seemed to have left myself, as myself, out of it entirely, and to care only to find out all I could about the work of Christ.

The thing that amazed me was how I could have lived so long in a world that contained the Bible, and never have found all this before. Why had nobody ever told me? How could people, who had found it out, have kept such a marvelous piece of good news to themselves? Certainly I could not keep it to myself, and I determined that no one whom I could reach should be left a day longer in ignorance, as far as I could help it. I began to buttonhole everybody, pulling them into corners and behind doors to tell them of the wonderful and delightful things I had discovered in the Bible about the salvation through the Lord Jesus Christ. It seemed to me the most magnificent piece of good news that any human being had ever had to tell, and I gloried in telling it.

So little however had I known of Christian ideas and Christian nomenclature, that I had not the least conception that what I had discovered made any difference in me personally, or that my belief in all this made me what they called a Christian. It only seemed to me that I had found out something delightful about God, which had filled me with happiness, and which I wanted everybody else to know. But that this discovery constituted what was called "conversion," or that I personally was different in any way from what I had been before, never entered my head.

One day, however, a "Plymouth Brother" friend, hearing me tell my story, exclaimed "Thank God, Mrs. Smith, that you have at last become a Christian." So little did I understand him, that I promptly replied, "Oh, no, I am not a Christian at all. I have only found out a wonderful piece of good news that I never knew before." "But," he persisted, "that very discovery makes you a Christian, for the Bible says that whoever believes this good news has passed from death unto life, and is born of God. *You* have just said that you believe it and rejoice in it, so of course *you* have passed from death unto life and are born of God." I thought for a moment, and I saw the logic of what he said. There was no escaping it. And with a sort of gasp I said, "Why, so I must be. Of course I believe this good news, and therefore of course I must be born of God. Well, I *am* glad."

From that moment the matter was settled, and not a doubt as to my being a child of God and the possessor of eternal life, has ever had the slightest power over me since. I rushed to my Bible to make myself sure there was no mistake, and I found it brimming over with this teaching. "He that believeth *hath*,"

"He that believeth *is*." There seemed to be nothing more to be said about it. Three passages especially struck me. 1 John 5:1, "Whosoever believeth that Jesus is the Christ is born of God;" and John 3:24, "Verily, verily I say unto you, He that heareth My word and believeth on Him that sent Me, hath everlasting life, and shall not come into condemnation, but is passed from death unto life;" and above all, John 20: 30, 31, "And many other signs truly did Jesus in the presence of His disciples, which are not written in this book: but these are written, that ye might believe that Jesus is the Christ, the Son of God; and that, believing, ye might have life through His name."

There seemed nothing more to be said. There were the things about Christ, written in the Bible, as clear as daylight, and I believed what was written with all my heart and soul, and therefore I could not doubt that I was one of those who had "life through His name." The question was settled without any further argument. It had nothing to do with how I felt, but only with what God had said. The logic seemed to me irresistible; and it not only convinced me then, but it has carried me triumphantly through every form of doubt as to my relations with God which has ever assailed me since. And I can recommend it as an infallible receipt to every doubter.

Of course at once, on having made this further discovery, of the fact that I was a Christian, I began to add it to the story I had already been telling, always ending my recital with the words— "And now, if you believe all this, you are a Christian, for the Bible says that he that believeth *is* born of God, and *has* eternal life."

I had got hold of that which is the necessary foundation of all religion, namely reconciliation with God, and had had my first glimpse of Him as He is revealed in the face of Jesus Christ. All my fear of Him had vanished. He loved me, He

forgave me, He was on my side, and all was right between us.
I had learned moreover that it was from the life and words of
Christ that my knowledge of God was to come, and not, as I had
always thought, from my own inward feelings; and my relief
was inexpressible.

I can see now, in looking back, that in many respects I had
only touched the surface of the spiritual realities hidden under
the doctrines I had so eagerly embraced. I was as yet only in
the beginning of things. But it was a beginning in the right
direction, and was the introduction to the "life more abundant"
which, as my story will show, was to come later. Meanwhile
I had got my first glimpse of the unselfishness of God. As yet
it was only a glimpse, but it was enough to make me radiantly
happy.

Chapter 17

THE ASSURANCE OF FAITH

I was so filled with enthusiasm over my discovery, that nothing else seemed to me of the slightest importance; and, as I have said, I attacked every friend I had on the subject, and insisted on knowing whether they too had found out the transcendent fact that their sins were all forgiven, and that they were the children of God. I simply *compelled* them to listen, whether they wanted to or not, for it seemed to me the most pitiful thing conceivable that anybody should fail to know it, while I was alive to tell it. And I must say that nearly every one I spoke to, partly perhaps because of their surprise at being attacked so vigorously, listened with eager interest, and sooner or later embraced the views I so enthusiastically declared. Very many of my friends of course really were already Christians, but had hardly dared to think themselves so; and to them my teaching brought the assurance of faith they so sorely needed.

In fact it seemed to me such a wonderful bit of good news, that I thought if I would go into the street and stand at the corners, and begin to tell it, everybody would open the doors and windows to listen to my story. I felt like a herald marching through the corridors of a prison, with a proclamation from the King, of free pardon to every prisoner. Paul's message in the Synagogue of the Jews at Antioch, when he spoke to them about Jesus, and said, "Be it known unto you therefore, men and brethren, that through this man is preached unto you the forgiveness of sins; and by Him all that believe are justified by the law of Moses," was my message; and the marvel to me was that every prisoner did not at once, on hearing it, open the door of his cell and walk out a free man. It seemed to me superlatively silly for any one, in the face of such a proclamation, to hesitate a single moment. Why should they worry about their sins, when God had so plainly declared that Christ had borne their sins in "His own body on the tree," and had taken them away forever? Why should they fear God's anger, when the Bible had assured us that "God was in Christ reconciling the world unto Himself, not imputing their trespasses unto them"? All these wretched doubts and fears seemed then, and have always seemed since, not only irreligious and a libel against the trustworthiness of God, but also as an evidence of a great lack of good sense. Either God is true or He is a liar. If I believe He is true, then good sense demands that I should accept His statements as the statements of facts, and should rest in them as facts.

One of the most helpful things to me at this time was a tract called "The Fox Hunter" by Caesar Malan. It was the clearest and most logical presentation of justification by faith that I have ever come across, and it proved to me beyond the possibility of question that the "assurance of faith" was at once the only biblical ground any one could take, and also the only common-sense ground as well. The foxes in this tract were doubts, and the hunter was the preacher who caught and killed them. And its whole teaching was, that if God *said* Christ had taken away our sins, then He certainly had done so, and they were of course gone, and it was not only folly but also presumption in us not to believe it.

I continually asked myself why every preacher did not tell out these facts clearly and fully so that no one could fail to understand them? And I felt this so strongly that, whenever I heard sermons that seemed to leave the matter uncertain, or confused, I thought nothing of going up to the preachers afterwards and expostulating with them, because they had not clearly preached the Gospel of Christ. I am convinced, in looking back now, that I must have made myself a general nuisance to our dear Quaker preachers, whose preaching I confess was not often in those days of this definite sort; but the truth was that what I had discovered seemed to me of such paramount and overwhelming importance, that no other consideration was worth a moment's notice. To be in a world full of sinners, who did not know that their sins were forgiven, and that they were the children of God, and who might know it, if only some one would tell them, seemed to me such a tremendous responsibility, that I felt compelled to tell it to every one I could reach. The dear quiet Friends could not understand such excessive, and, I dare say, unwise zeal, and my visits at any of their houses were fairly dreaded. Even my brothers-in-law were almost afraid to have me visit my own sisters, and in many ways I went through a sort of persecution, which no doubt I largely brought upon myself by my unadvised zeal, but which at the time seemed to me a martyrdom for the truth.

It is not often, I think, that the story of the Gospel comes so vividly to any one as it did to me. But from the fact that, as a Quaker, I had had no doctrinal teaching, all that I was learning about the salvation in Christ came in a perfect blaze of illumination. The Bible seemed fairly radiant with the "glad tidings of great joy," and I wondered why every one did not see it. As I knew literally nothing of Theology, and had never heard any theological terms, I took the whole Gospel story in the most common sense way possible, and believed it without any reservations. I often said I was like a prisoner who had come out of a dark underground cell into the light of ten thousand suns. And in spite of all the disapproval and opposition of the Elders and Overseers among the Quakers, and of my own family as well, my enthusiasm gained me a hearing, and nearly every friend I had came, sooner or later, into a knowledge of the truths I advocated, and more or less shared my rejoicing; so that gradually the opposition died down, and in the end, while the "solid Friends" could not fully endorse me, they at least left me free to continue my course unmolested.

No doubt the crudeness of my views was very patent to the more advanced spiritual Christians around me, and I feel sure now that a large part of the opposition I met with arose from this fact. But while I might wish my views had been more mature, I can never regret the enthusiasm that made me so eager to tell out to every one the best I knew.

And even the opposition was blessed to me, for it taught me some most invaluable lessons. I came across a book in those days, the name of which I regret to say I have forgotten, which helped me enormously. Its central thought was that one of the richest gifts a Christian could have was the gift of persecution, and that to be like the Master in being rejected of men, was the highest dignity to which a Christian could attain. It taught that he was the greatest Christian who was willing to take the lowest place, and that to become the chief of all could only be attained by becoming the servant of all. I was so impressed by this teaching that I tried to put it in practice; and, whenever I expected in any interview to meet with reproof or opposition, I would always beforehand pray fervently that I might receive it in a true Christian spirit. I was much helped, too, by a saying of Madame Guyon's, that she had learned to be thankful for every snub and mortification, because she had found that they helped to advance her in the spiritual life; and in time I learned something of the same lesson.

The special advantage I gained from the disapproval I met with was that it took a great deal of the conceit out of me. I had it so rubbed into me that I was only tolerated because of the kindness of my friends, that I really came at last to have a sort of instinctive feeling that I deserved nothing but snubs and reproaches, and that any unkindness that might be shown me was only my just desert. In fact I got into the habit of never expecting anything else, and ceased to think I had any rights that others ought not to ramble on. This habit of mind has given me the greatest liberty of spirit through all my life since, as I have never been obliged, as so many people seem to be, to stand up for my rights, and have in fact scarcely ever had the sense to see when I have been slighted. If one has no rights, their rights cannot be trampled on, and if one has no feelings, their feelings cannot be hurt. So deeply was this lesson engraved upon my soul by what I went through at the time of which I am speaking, that to this day I am always surprised at any kindness that is shown me, as at something entirely unexpected and undeserved. I do not know any lesson I have ever learned that has been so practically helpful than this lesson, learned from the opposition I met with in the early years of my Christian experience; although I have no doubt, as I have said, that I brought my trials largely upon myself, by my crudeness and my ignorance.

Crude and ignorant as I was, I had however, as I have said, got a firm grip on one magnificent foundation truth that nothing has ever been able to shake, and this was that God was in Christ reconciling the world unto Himself, not imputing their trespasses unto them. All was right between my soul and God. He was my Father, and I was His child, and I had nothing to fear. It was no matter that I had got hold of it in a crude sort of way. The thing was that I *had* got hold of it. There it was— the grand central fact of God's love and God's forgiveness, and my soul was at rest about this forever.

Chapter 18

THE ROMANCE OF THE RELIGIOUS LIFE

The disapproval of my own religious society, in these early stages of my new life, threw me very much under the influence of the Plymouth Brethren, who were at that time making quite a stir in Philadelphia, and whose clear teaching of doctrines, and especially of the doctrine of "justification by faith," was particularly congenial to my new way of looking at things. They were great Bible students, and I soon found under their teaching a fascinating interest in Bible study. It was all new ground to me, and I went into it with the greatest avidity. So delighted was I with the treasures I found in its pages, that at first my one fear was lest, as the Bible was such a short book, I should soon exhaust it, and come to the end of its delights, and I used to stint myself to small portions in order to spin it out the longer. But I soon found that this was not at all necessary, as the more I studied, the more I found there was to study, and each passage seemed to have a thousand continually unfolding meanings. The book was no larger than I thought, but it was infinitely deeper. It seemed to me something as if the truths in the Bible were covered with a multitude of skins, and as if, as I studied, one skin after another was peeled off, leaving the words the same, but the meaning of those words deeper and higher. I can never be thankful enough to the Plymouth Brethren for introducing me to the fascinations of Bible study.

It was a wonderful and delightful life I had now begun to live. I had begun to know God, and I was finding Him to be lovely and lovable beyond my fondest imaginings. The romance of my life had dawned. I cannot say how religion may have affected other people, but to me my religion has been all through a fascinating and ever unfolding romance. If for nothing else, I pity the poor unfortunate Agnostics of the present day for their missing of the most delightful of all romances. They can have nothing I am sure in all their lives to equal it. The nearest approach that I can think of to a like experience is the delight of exploring an unknown science, or a new field of mental research; but even that cannot equal, I am sure, the delights of exploring the Science of God. Imagine it for a moment. To have got on the track of a real acquaintance with the ways and character of God, the Creator of heavens and earth, and to be making continually fresh discoveries of new and delightful things about Him—what scientific research could be as entrancing? All that I had longed for and agonized over in my first awakening, was coming to me in clearest vision, day by day, and the ever recurring delight of new revelations and new ideas was more delicious than words could express. Then too the joy of telling it all to others, and the enormous satisfaction of seeing their faces lighten, and their hearts expand, as their souls made the same discoveries as my own. Ah, no one who has not experienced it, can know the fascination of it all!

I do not mean to say that I discovered everything at once, nor even that all I thought I had discovered proved to be permanent truth. My story, as I continue, will show that this was not the case. Like all novices in scientific research, I grasped many half truths, and came to many false conclusions. But the search of itself was delicious, and the finding out of one's mistakes far surpassed the mortification at having made them.

My soul had started on its voyage of discovery, and to

become acquainted with God was its unalterable and unceasing aim. I was as yet only at the beginning, but what a magnificent beginning it was. God was a reality, and He was my God. He had created me, and He loved me, and all was right between us. All care about my own future destiny had been removed from my shoulders. I could say with Paul, "I know whom I have believed, and am persuaded that He is able to keep that which I have committed unto Him against that day." I needed no longer to work *for* my soul's salvation, but only to work *out* the salvation that had been bestowed upon me. All the years of my self-introversion and self-examination were ended. Instead of my old fruitless searchings into my feelings and emotions for some tangible evidence of God's favor, the glorious news, declared in the Bible, that He so loved the world as to have sent His only begotten Son to save the world, absorbed every faculty.

It was no longer "How do I feel?" but always "What does God say?" And He said such delightful things, that to find them out became my supreme delight. I do not mean what He said to me personally in my heart, but what He had said to every human being in the Bible—the good news of salvation in the Lord Jesus Christ. Anything said to myself alone might be open to doubt, as to whether it was really myself who was meant, but anything said to the whole world could not help including me, and I greedily appropriated it all.

This went on for several years, during which I had a really glorious time. Between the joys of discovery on the one hand, and the joys of telling others about my discoveries on the other, my cup of the wine of life was full and overflowing. I had plenty of earthly trials, but somehow they were in the background compared to the fascinations of my religious life. Nothing that belonged only to the earthly life could really matter, when one's soul was daily tasting the blissful joy of reconciliation with God, and of being made a partaker of the glorious salvation of the Lord Jesus Christ.

And yet how little I knew, even of this, compared with what was to come!

Chapter 19

THE WAY OF ESCAPE

In 1865, family circumstances made it necessary for us to leave our delightful home in Germantown, and all our wide interests there, to live in a remote village in New Jersey, where we were almost entirely isolated from any congenial society. It was a pecuniary advantage to us, but was otherwise a very great trial, to me especially, and I confess that my spirit rebelled sorely at the change.

Little did I dream that it was here, in this very place, which seemed to me so isolated and desolate, that a glorious light was to dawn, and the fourth and crowning epoch of my religious life was to be ushered in.

It came about in this wise. I was, as I have said, very rebellious at my change of abode and of surroundings. But I had enough spiritual insight to know that this rebellion was wrong; that, since the change was a providential arrangement over which I had no control, the only right thing for me to do was to accept it cheerfully, and to say heartily, "Thy will be done," in regard to it. But although I scolded myself about it continually, I did not seem able to bring myself to the point of accepting God's will; and as a fact I did not really want to accept it. I felt that it was very hard lines for me to be obliged to leave my happy home in Germantown, and my sphere of usefulness there, to live in such a lonely far off place as Millville; and it seemed to me that God ought not to have allowed it, and that I had a right to grumble and fret. As a consequence I got into a most uncomfortable state of mind, where even my clear doctrines failed to help me, and I began at last to be afraid that I was going to lose every bit of religion I possessed.

In the face of a real need such as this, it was no satisfaction to know I was forgiven. I wanted more than forgiveness, I wanted deliverance. But how to get deliverance I could not conceive.

As we had a good many Mission preachers visiting us from time to time, I laid my case before several of them, and asked for help, but no one seemed able to tell me anything. Finally a very successful religious teacher came for a few days, and to him I poured out my trouble very fully, and begged him to suggest some way of deliverance. He took my case into serious consideration, and said he believed that what I needed was to undertake some Christian work, and that if I would start out the next morning and visit the poor people in the neighborhood, and see what I could do to help them, he thought I would find my spiritual life renewed, and all would be right. Accordingly the next day I proceeded to try the proposed remedy. But it did not take me long to find out what a futile remedy it was. In almost the first house I entered, I found a woman in the same sort of difficulty as my own, and sorely needing help, and I had no help to give. It seemed to me I was like a person trying to feed hungry people out of an empty bowl, and I saw that this was a silly and impossible thing to do. I went home more discouraged than ever, convinced, that, before I could help any one else, I must find some deliverance for myself.

There was a little dressmaker in the village who often came to sew for me; and, having so little society in the neighborhood, I would sometimes sit down and talk with her, as we sewed together. She seemed an unusually spiritually minded Christian, and I was much interested in her experiences. I found out that she held the view that there really was such a thing as victory over temptation, and that it was not necessary, as I had thought, to go on all your life sinning and repenting, but that a Christian might actually be delivered. She told me that among the Methodists there was a doctrine taught which they called the "Doctrine of Holiness," and that there was an experience called "sanctification" or the "second blessing" which brought you into a place of victory. I was immensely interested in all she had to say about it, and began to hope that perhaps I might here find the solution of my difficulties.

She told me there was a little meeting held in the village on Saturday evenings, where this doctrine was taught, and where people gave their experiences in regard to it, and urged me to attend it. I thought I might go some time, but I allowed things to interfere, feeling convinced that poor ignorant factory people could not have much to teach me. I had studied and taught the Bible a great deal, and had rather a high idea of my own religious attainments in that direction, and I felt that, if I should go to the meeting, I should probably have much more to teach them than they could possibly have to teach me.

At last, however, one evening, I made up my mind to give them the favor of my presence, and I confess a great favor I felt it to be. I went to the meeting, therefore, full of my own importance and my own superiority, and thought it very likely that I should astonish them by my great biblical knowledge. When I entered the meeting, a factory woman with a shawl over her head (she probably did not possess a bonnet), was speaking, and I heard her say these words: "My whole horizon used to be filled with this great big *Me* of mine, but when I got a sight of Christ as my perfect Saviour, this great big *Me* wilted down to nothing."

These words were a revelation to me. I realized that I knew nothing whatever of any such experience. My *"Me"* was very big and very self-assertive, and I could not imagine how it could, by any possibility, "wilt down into nothing." But a profound conviction came to me that this must be real Christianity, and that it was, perhaps, the very thing I was longing for. Needless to say, I did not undertake to do any teaching that night, but sat as a learner at the feet of these humble Christians, who knew but little of book learning, but whose souls were evidently taught by the Holy Spirit depths of spiritual truth of which I understood nothing. I began to attend the meeting regularly as a learner, and to embrace every opportunity possible to talk with those who understood this life. I found that the gist of it was exactly what Paul meant when he said, "Not I, but Christ," and that the victory I sought, was to come by ceasing to live my own life, and by letting the power of God "work in me to will and to do of His good pleasure."

In the diary under date of 10 mo., 18th, 1866, I say:—

"The Lord has been teaching me in many ways of late my utter weakness in the presence of temptation. I have grown much in knowledge, but I have not grown in grace, and I find that I have not actually any more power over sin than I had when I was first converted. This has not caused me to doubt the fact of my being a child of God, justified and forgiven, a possessor of eternal life and an heir of a heavenly inheritance. But, even while having this assurance, and never losing it, I have found that, while my heart condemns me, I cannot be happy; and I have been led to long for more holiness, for more power over sin, for more uninterrupted communion with God. But how to get at it I could not tell. Resolutions have proved utterly useless, and my own efforts have been all in vain. My prayers have been unanswered; and I have been ready a thousand times to give up in despair, and to conclude that it was not the will of God that I should ever attain to a victory over sin. And yet the Bible presents such a different picture of the Christian life,—'blameless, harmless, without rebuke,' with every temptation a 'way of escape,' 'purified,' 'conformed to the image of Christ,' 'holy as He is holy.'

"I find there are some Christians who say that by receiving Christ by faith for our sanctification, just as we received Him by faith for our justification, all this work that I long for is accomplished. That is, the *way* of accomplishing it is discovered. It is found out that the Bible teaches that the Lord can deliver from the power of sin as well as from its guilt, and the soul learns to trust Him to do it, and ceases to reply upon its own resolutions, or upon its own efforts after holiness, but commits the whole work of being kept from evil and delivered from temptation, to the Lord alone.

"I begin to see more clearly that the Lord is worthy of my most unlimited and boundless confidence; and perhaps this is the dawning of the light I have been groping for.

"It is a Methodist doctrine, and I have been used to hearing Methodists much objected to on account of it, but it seems to be the only thing that can supply *my* needs, and I feel impelled to try it."

Under date of 2 mo. 11th, 1867, I record my efforts to lay hold of this conquering faith, and add:—

"The present attitude of my soul is that of trusting in the Lord. And I have found it is a practical reality that He *does* deliver. When temptation comes, if I turn at once to Him, breathing this prayer, 'Lord, save me. I cannot save myself from this sin, but Thou canst and wilt,' He never fails me. Either He completely changes my feelings in the case, or He causes me to forget all about it, and my victory, or rather *His* victory, is entire. This is a secret of the Christian life that I never knew before.... But why have I not known it? Why has my course been such a halting, miserable one, when I might have lived in victory? What a striking proof I have been of the inherent legality and unbelief of the human heart, for, while trusting the Lord entirely and only for my justification, I have always been trusting myself for my sanctification.... I have depended upon my own efforts, my own resolutions, my own watchfulness, my own fervency, my own strivings, to accomplish the work of holy living. This was legality. It was as truly legality as if I had trusted to these things to save my soul in the first place. I was "frustrating' the grace of God as really in regard to my sanctification as those whom I have been used to condemn so utterly as legalists, were doing it in regard to their justification. I could easily see how they made the death of Christ of none effect by their legal strivings, but I was blind to the fact that I also was doing the same thing. Our strivings to be sure were with a different end in view, but it was still in both cases our own striving—in both it was self, and not Christ. 'For, if righteousness come by the law, then Christ is dead in vain.' But now how different it is! Now I commit my daily life to Him, as well as my future destiny, and I trust Him just as nakedly for the one as for the other. I am equally powerless in both cases. I can do nothing—not even I, the new man,—and if the Lord does not do it all, it will not be done. But oh! glorious truth, He *does* do it! When I trust Him He gives me deliverance from the power of sin as well as from its guilt. I can leave all in His care—my cares, my temptations, my growth, my service, my daily life moment by moment. Oh the rest and calm of a life like this!

". . . And this is the Methodist 'blessing of holiness.' Couched by them it is true in terms that I cannot altogether endorse, and held amid what seems to me a mixture of error, but still really and livingly experienced and enjoyed by them. I feel truly thankful to them for their testimony to its reality, and I realize that it is far better to *have* the experience, even if mixed with error, than to live without it, and be very doctrinally correct, as was my former case."

My diary at this date is full of the wonderful discoveries I was making, but these extracts will suffice. From this time the possibilities of faith opened out before me in a way I had never dreamed of. I saw that it was in very truth the victory that overcometh the world, and I marvelled at my blindness in never having discovered it before. For a third time a skin seemed to be peeled off the Bible, and it became again a new book to me.

> "The truth that was mine yesterday
>   Is larger truth today;
> Its face has aspect more divine
>   Its kingship fuller sway.
> For truth must grow, as ages roll,
> And God looms larger in the soul."

One day I was present at a meeting where the speaker read John 15, and the words "Without Me ye can do nothing" struck me with amazement. Hundreds of times before I had read and repeated these words, and had even preached from them. But now, so ablaze were they with wondrous meaning, that it almost seemed as if they must have been newly inserted in the

Bible since last I had opened it. Here was our Lord saying distinctly "Without Me ye can do nothing," and yet all the while I had been thinking I could and I must do so much! What sort of meaning had I been giving hitherto to this word "nothing"? I tried to remember, but all was a blank. I simply had not even noticed it.

Another day I came across in my reading that passage in the sixth of Matthew, where our Lord exhorts us to "take no thought for our life," on the ground that our Heavenly Father takes thought for us; and bases His assertion on the fact that, since God cares for the fowls of the air and the lilies of the field, He must necessarily do at least as much for His children who are, He Himself declares, of more value than many sparrows. I read the passage over and over with utter amazement. Could it really be true? Had it actually been in the Bible all these years? And, if it had, why had never I seen it? And yet as a fact not only had I seen it, but I had even known it by heart, and had many times repeated it. But in the only sense worth considering I never had seen it before. Now I saw; and, at the sight, cares, and worries, and fears, and anxieties, vanished like mists before the sun.

And it was the same with all the old familiar texts—they were literally illuminated with a new meaning. Every page of the Bible seemed to declare in trumpet tones the reality of a victorious and triumphant life to be lived by faith in the Lord Jesus Christ. My whole soul was afire with my discovery, and I could scarcely think or talk of anything else. I had found out something about the salvation of Christ of which I had never even dreamed, something that proved Him to be a far more complete Saviour than I could have conceived of.

I saw that He was not only my Saviour for the future, but He was also my all-sufficient Saviour for the present. He was my

Captain to fight my battles for me, in order that I need not fight them myself; He was my Burden-bearer to carry my burdens, in order that I might roll them off of my own weak shoulders; He was my Fortress to hide me from my enemies; my Shield to protect me; my Guide to lead me; my Comforter to console me; my Shepherd to care for me. No longer did I need to care for, and protect, and fight for myself. It was all in the hands of One who was mighty to save; and what could I do but trust Him?

No words can express the fullness and the all-sufficiency that I saw was stored up for me in the Lord.

I could not keep such glorious news to myself. Every one who came within the range of my influence was obliged to listen to my story.

One of the first to be told was the cousin whom I have mentioned a little way back, as being surprised at my teaching of the necessity of a continual bondage to sin, in spite of the fact that there was full forgiveness for all our sins, past, present, and to come. I seized the earliest opportunity I could find to have a visit from her, and, on her arrival, greeted her with the words, "Oh, Carrie, I have something so wonderful to tell you. We must not lose a minute before I begin."

As soon as we could get alone I poured out to her my new discovery, telling her I had found out that there was in Christ, not only forgiveness for sin, but also deliverance from its power, and that we need not any longer be the "slaves of sin," but might be more than conquerors through Him.

My cousin listened with amazed interest, her face growing more astonished and perplexed every minute, and when at last I paused to take breath, she burst out—"But Hannah, what *do* you mean? You have always told me that even although you were a child of God, you could not expect to be delivered from sin, or from worries, because the old Adam was too strong for you, and the new nature could not conquer the old. Why on earth," she asked with indignant remonstrance, "have you let me go on all this long time with that idea? When I was converted I fully expected to be delivered from sin, and from all worrying and unrest of soul, but when I talked to you about it, you said it was impossible in this life; and I thought of course you knew, and so I gave up all hope of it. And now here you say exactly the opposite. It certainly is very confusing, and I really do not know what to think."

I agreed with her that it was confusing, but that after all it had only been ignorance in the old days that had made possible such a false view of things as I had then taught, and that now I had discovered something far better in the gospel of Christ, and that all we had to do was to throw the old false view overboard, and accept the new truth that had been shown us. My cousin, who had all along had an instinct, in spite of all that was said, that the other way could not be the best the salvation of the Lord Jesus Christ had to offer, embraced with avidity this new teaching of deliverance from temptation through the Lord Jesus Christ, and carried it out far more faithfully than I did.

The practical working of my new discovery amazed me. I committed the whole matter of my rebellious spirit to the Lord, and told Him *I* could not conquer it, but that I believed *He* could conquer it for me; and then I stood aside, as it were, and left the battle to Him. And to my indescribable joy I found all my rebellion taken away, and such a spirit of peaceful acquiescence in the will of God put into its place, that the life which had before looked so utterly distasteful to me, began to look pleasant and even desirable. I found I could say "Thy will be done" heartily and with thankfulness. My discovery proved itself to be a practical success and I was enchanted.

In numberless ways I tested it and it never failed. One striking instance I remember vividly. I had been imposed upon in what I felt to be a most unjustifiable way, and in what I can see now, in looking back, was really unjustifiable, and I felt very much aggrieved, and was tempted to go into a fit of sulks and to show my displeasure by being sulky for a week or two. But, immediately, when the temptation came, a sight of the way of escape came also, and I rushed off to be alone somewhere that I might fight the battle out. I remember that I was so boiling over with provocation that I could not walk quietly, but fairly ran up to my bedroom, slamming the doors after me. When safe in the seclusion of my room, I kneeled down and said, "Lord, I am provoked, I want to be provoked, and I think I have cause for being provoked; but I know I ought not to be, and I want the victory. I hand this whole matter over to Thee. I cannot fight this battle. Thou must fight it for me. Jesus saves me now." I said these words out of a heart that seemed brimful of rebellion. According to all appearances I was declaring a lie when I said the Lord saved me, for I was not saved, and it did not look likely I could be. But by faith I laid hold of it, and declared even in the midst of turmoil that the Lord could and did save me now. The result was that immediately a summer morning of peace and happiness spread over me. All my resentment and provocation vanished, and I felt as happy as a bird in the sunshine at the thought of the very thing which before had made me so angry. My faith had laid hold of a divine fact. I had proved that God was able to deliver, and that He did deliver the soul that trusted Him. I realized that it was a wonderful truth that I had no need to fight my own battles, for the Lord fought for me, and I could hold my peace.

Many hundreds of similar battles have been fought and won for me since by the Captain of my Salvation, and the secret I learned then, of handing over the battle to the Lord, and leaving it in His hands, has never failed to work when I have acted on it. It has been to me over and over a practical illustration of Christ's words, "Be of good cheer, for I have overcome the world." *He* has overcome it when we will put the matter into His hands, and will stand aside and let Him fight. Never once, when I have done this, have I been disappointed; for it is blessedly true, although so few seem to know it, that He *is* able to save them to the uttermost that come unto God by Him, seeing He ever liveth to make intercession for them. He was able then, when the Epistle to the Hebrews was written, and He is able now; for He is not dead, but "ever liveth" to make intercession for us.

I had discovered that faith is the conquering law of the universe. God spake, and it was done, and, relying upon Him, we too may speak and it shall be done. A wonderful light streamed upon 1 John 5:14, 15. "And this is the confidence that we have in Him, that if we ask anything according to His will, He heareth us: and if we know that He hears us, whatever we ask, we know that we have the petitions that we desired of Him." I had always hitherto thought of this passage as one of those beautiful dreams of the Christian life that nobody, in their senses, supposed for a moment was meant to be realized in this world; but now I saw it was no dream, but was simply the statement of a Divine law, the law of faith; a law as certain in its action as the law of gravitation, if only one understood it.

Our Lord tells us over and over that according to our faith it shall be unto us, and actually asserts, without any limitations, that all things are possible to him that believeth; but I had never supposed this was anything more than a romance. Now I saw that He had been simply enunciating a law of the spiritual kingdom, which any one might try and prove for themselves.

I saw that faith links us to the Almighty power of God, and makes it possible for our weakness to draw down unfailing supplies of His strength; and there seemed no limit to its possibilities.

> "Faith, mighty faith, the promise sees
> And looks at that alone;
> Laughs at impossibilities,
> And cries, It shall be done."

I wish I could say that I have always since lived in the power of this divine law of faith. But one thing I can say, that whenever and wherever I have chosen to lay hold by faith of God's strength, it has always been made perfect in my weakness, and I have been able to say with the apostle, "In all these things we are more than conquerors through Him that loved us."

Chapter 20

A Discovery, not an Attainment

Again I want to make the fact clear that, just as it was before, what had come to me now was a discovery, and in no sense an attainment. I had not become a better woman than I was before, but I had found out that Christ was a better Saviour than I had thought He was. I was not one bit more able to conquer my temptations than I had been in the past, but I had discovered that He was able and willing to conquer them for me. I had no more wisdom or righteousness of my own than I had ever had, but I had found out that He could really and actually be made unto me, as the Apostle declared He would be, wisdom, and righteousness, and sanctification, and redemption.

I shall never forget the first time this declaration was proved to me to be, not only a pious saying, but a downright fact. Shortly after I had come to know something of the fullness of Christ's salvation, an occasion arose in my life when I realized I should have need of a very large amount of patience. An individual, who was especially antagonistic to me, was coming to spend two weeks at our house. She had always in the past been very provoking and irritating, and I felt, as the day drew near for her arrival that, if I behave to her in a really Christ-like way, I should need a far greater supply of patience than I usually possessed. As I was still new in the way of faith, I supposed I could only secure a sufficient supply by wrestling for it in prayer, and I decided, as my days were very busy ones, to devote a whole night before her arrival to the wrestling necessary to secure enough patience to last me throughout the two weeks of her stay. Therefore one night, after the rest of the family had retired, I shut myself up in my room, taking with me a plate of biscuits, which I had provided in case I should be hungry; and, kneeling down by my bed, I prepared myself for an all night conflict. I confess I felt rather like a martyr, for I had always found long times of prayer very fatiguing; but a stock of patience was a necessity, and I supposed this was the only way to get it. I seemed to picture it to myself something as if a great lump of patience was to be let down into my heart, from which I could break off a bit to use whenever the need should arise. But scarcely had my knees touched the floor when, like a flash, there came into my mind the declaration to which I have referred, "But of Him are ye in Christ Jesus, who of God is made unto us wisdom, and righteousness, and sanctification, and redemption; that, according as it is written, He that glorieth, let Him glory in the Lord." "Yes," I exclaimed inwardly, "and of course patience as well!" And I rose at once from my knees, with an absolute conviction that I did not in the least need, as I had thought, to lay in a big stock of patience to use during my friend's visit, but that I could simply, as the occasion arose, look to the Lord for a present supply for my present need. I seemed to see Christ as a great storehouse of supplies, from which I could draw whatever grace or strength I required; and I realized that it was utter folly for me to try and carry about with me stocks of grace, as it were in packages in my pocket, which, even if I could secure them, would be sure to be mislaid just when I needed them most.

It followed as a matter of course, that my faith was fully answered; and, although my friend was more aggravating than ever, the necessary patience was always supplied at every moment of her stay. And, what was even better than this special deliverance, I had learned the magnificent fact that inexhaustible storehouse of God's supplies lies always open to the needs and claims of His children. My patience in this case might be called an attainment by some, but I had not attained it, I had simply discovered a supply of patience in the Divine Storehouse, and by faith I had taken possession hour by hour of what that hour required.

When reduced to its final analysis, the discovery I had made was simply this, that there was stored up for me in Christ a perfect supply for all my needs, and that faith and faith only was the channel through which this supply could flow; that struggling, and wrestling, and worrying, and agonizing, cannot bring this supply, but that faith always will and always does. This seems a very simple discovery to have made, and one would suppose every child of God, who reads the Bible and believes it, would necessarily know it. But I for one did not know it, even after nine years of careful Bible study, and of earnest Christian striving, and when I did at last discover it, it revolutionized my life.

There was no mystery about it. It was not something added on to the gospel story, but was only the real meaning of the Gospel. Christ came, according to the Bible, to accomplish certain purposes; and the discovery I had made was simply that He might be depended on actually to accomplish these purposes. It goes without saying that, if this is the fact, then those who want these purposes accomplished, should hand them over to the One who has undertaken to do it; and to me this seemed then, and has seemed ever since, not any special religious attainment, but only good sound ordinary common sense.

When I call in a builder to build me a house, I do so because he knows how to build, and is able to accomplish it, while I neither know how nor am able. But I do not consider the fact of my putting the work into his hands as an attainment on my part, but only as a common-sense arrangement. If I am puzzled how to cross a roaring river, and discover a bridge, I do not call my action in crossing that bridge an attainment, but simply and only a most common-sense proceeding.

Consequently it always seems to me much nearer the truth to use the word gifts rather than the word attainments. Attainments imply work and effort on our part, and Christian graces are all a free gift from God. Those who are to "reign in life" are not those who attain to great heights of piety, but those who "receive abundance of grace, and of the gift of righteousness." He that spared not His own Son, but delivered Him up for us all, how shall He not with Him also freely give us all things? "Therefore let no man glory in men; for all things are yours; whether Paul or Apollos, or the world, or life, or death, or things present, or things to come; all are yours and ye are Christ's, and Christ is God's." To find out that all things are really ours, is not an attainment but a magnificent discovery, and the soul that makes it, would be amazingly lacking in common sense not to take possession of everything it needs.

It would take the pen of an angel to tell all that this discovery meant to me. But suffice it to say that life was transformed, and that where failure and defeat reigned before, victory and triumph became, whenever I chose to lay hold of them by faith, my daily and hourly portion. I was no longer the "slave of sin," compelled whether I would or no to obey it, but had entered into the "liberty wherewith Christ hath made us free," and did not need to be "entangled again with the old yoke of bondage." I thought I was happy before, but my happiness now was such as could not be described in words, and it often seemed to me that even Heaven itself could hardly have more to offer. But my joy was joy in the Lord, and not joy in myself, nor in any attainments of my own, for I had none. I understood what the prophet meant when he said, "Thus saith the Lord, let not the mighty man glory in his wisdom, neither let the mighty man glory in his might; let not the rich man glory in his riches: but let him that glorieth glory in this that he understandeth and knoweth Me, that I am the Lord which exercise loving kindness, judgment, and righteousness, in the earth; for in these things I delight, said the Lord."

I had no wisdom, nor might, nor riches to glory in, but I was learning to know the Lord, and in Him I could glory with all my heart.

"Where is boasting then?" asks the Apostle. And he answers in words that now at last I understood, "It is excluded. By what law? of works? Nay but by the law of faith." How can the soul boast of its attainments, when it has none; and how can it fail to make its boast in the Lord when He so freely bestows upon it the supply for all its needs? "For by grace are ye saved through faith; and that not of yourselves; it is the gift of God: not of works, lest any man should boast." "For they got not the land in possession by their own sword, neither did their own arm save them; but thy right hand, and thine arm, and the light of thy countenance, because thou hadst a favor unto them."

This was my experience, and with all my heart I could unite in the words of the Psalmist— "In God we boast all the day long, and praise Thy Name forever!"

Chapter 21

The Secret of a Happy Life

This new life I had entered upon has been called by several different names. The Methodists called it "The Second Blessing," or "The Blessing of Sanctification;" the Presbyterians called it "The Higher Life," or "The Life of Faith;" the Friends called it "The Life hid with Christ in God." But by whatever name it may be called, the truth at the bottom of each name is the same, and can be expressed in four little words, "Not I, but Christ." In every case it means that we abandon ourselves to the Lord for Him to work in us, both to will and to do of His good pleasure, that we take Him to be our Saviour from the power of sin as well as from its punishment, and that we trust Him to give us, according to His promise, grace to help in every time of need.

Personally I prefer to call it "The life of faith," as being more simple. But, in that book of mine, in which I have most fully set it forth, I have called it the "Secret of a Happy Life,"[1] for the reason that it was for so long a secret from myself, and because it is, I fear, still a secret from hundreds of God's children, who are groaning under the same grievous burdens as I once had to carry. It was not a secret in the sense that I had not discovered it. It was and is an open secret, spread wide out before all eyes in the Bible, if only I had had the spiritual discernment to see it.

"The secrets of the gods are from of old,

[1] Fleming H. Revell Company, 158th Fifth Ave., New York; James Nisbet & Co., L't'd, 21 Berners St., London.

Guarded forever, and forever told;—
Blabbed in all ears, but published in a tongue
Whose purport the gods only can unfold." [1]

An ox and a philosopher may look at the same field, but they will not see the same things there; and my eyes, before and after this glorious discovery, looked at the same Bible, and even read the same passages, but saw very different things. The Bible like nature lies open to all, but not all see it. The law of gravitation was working plainly before all men, but only Newton saw it. And similarly the law of faith was plainly shown in the Bible, although my eyes had failed to discern it. The forces we use in nature were not created by us, but only discovered. They existed as much before they were discovered as afterwards. And no discoverers of Nature's secrets have ever, I am sure, had greater delight in their discoveries, than I have had in my discovery of the "Secrets of God."

So great was my delight that I felt impelled to speak of it to everybody, and to compel every one to listen.

At first my husband, who was an earnest and successful Christian worker, felt somewhat frightened lest I might be rejoicing in some heresy that would do myself and others harm; and he continually fell back on the argument that the "old man" in us could never be entirely conquered in this life, but must always bring us more or less into bondage. One morning, when we were arguing the matter, I said, "Well, impossible or not, it is certainly in the Bible; and I would like to know what thee thinks of this passage in the sixth of Romans—'Knowing this, that our old man is crucified with Him, that the body of sin might be destroyed, that henceforth we should not serve sin.' What can this mean?" I said, "but that the body, that is, the power of sin, is really to be conquered, so that we no longer

1 Fleming H. Revell Company, 158th Fifth Ave., New York; James Nisbet & Co., L't'd, 21 Berners St., London.

need to serve sin?" Startled by the new light that seemed suddenly to shine out of these words, he exclaimed: "There is no such passage in the Bible." "Oh, yes, there is," I replied; and, turning to my Bible, I showed it to him. It was a passage with which, of course, he had been very familiar, but which now appeared to him with such an absolutely new meaning that he felt as if he had never seen it before. It brought conviction, however; and that time he did not rest until he had discovered the truth for himself.

His own account of this discovery, published in 1868, was as follows. After telling of the lack he had been feeling in his Christian life, he says:—

"I knew, however, that the Bible seemed to contemplate a better life for the Christian than this, and for some years the impression had been increasing upon my mind that there was some part of the truth of God that I had missed of finding. . . . I felt that in the truth, as I held it, there was a painful want of that spirit of love which is the uniting bond of the Church of Christ, and which the Scriptures declare is so much more and better than 'all knowledge' and 'all faith'; and I often expressed my growing conviction that there was some truth yet to break out of God's word that would fill our hearts with a love that could bear all things. So strong was this feeling that I had arranged for a meeting of some brethren, well versed in the Scriptures, to carefully examine together and in detail what part of God's word we had failed to receive and to teach. Circumstances delayed this meeting, but in the meantime, through an unlooked for channel, I was to receive the secret that was to teach me the joy of Christian liberty, and the power of true service. That was faith! Strange! that when I had so constantly taught faith as the appointed channel for the forgiveness of sins, I had failed to see that faith alone was also the means of deliverance from the inward power of sin. Not the sinner only, but the Christian also, must receive everything by faith.

"I met at this time some Christians whose inward life, as they described it, seemed to be very different from mine. They declared that practical sanctification was to be obtained, like justification, by simple faith; and that, like justification, it was to be realized in any moment in which our faith should be able to grasp it; and they declared further that they themselves had experienced it. The subject was continually brought to my attention, and over and over again proofs were brought from the Word, to which I professed to be, and verily thought I was, in such entire subjection. But I regarded the whole thing with a deep feeling of distress, for it seemed to me that what they were aiming after and professing to have attained was a perfection of the flesh, and *that* I knew was impossible. I scarcely know anything toward which I had such a deep-rooted prejudice, and I suffered many hours of anxiety in thinking over the sad consequences of this heresy which I saw creeping in among us. So determined was my opposition, that even familiar passages of Scripture, when quoted to prove that sanctification was by faith, and that it was possible to walk worthy of the Lord unto all pleasing, assumed such unfamiliar aspects that I could scarcely believe they were in the Bible at all.

"One morning, Rom. 6:6, was quoted to me with the remark that when God said of the believer that his 'old man is crucified with Christ that the body of sin might be destroyed, that henceforth we should not serve sin,' it certainly must mean something, and something too which would make it possible for a believer no longer to be the slave of sin. I was so astonished at the force of the words that I said at once and emphatically, 'That passage is not in the Bible,' although as a fact there were but few that were more familiar. And then, when forced to acknowledge that it was there, I took refuge in the plea that it was only judicial—that is, true in God's sight, but never actually true in the Christian's experience. But from that moment I began to wonder whether there might not be after all some truth in what they were teaching; and slowly I discovered that I had misapprehended their meaning. It was not a perfection in the flesh that they were talking of, but a death of the flesh, and a life of victory and triumph, and one well pleasing to God.

"'But is that *all* you mean?' I asked at one time, when this had been specially pressed upon me. 'That is nothing new. I have always known it.'

"'But have you *lived* it?' was the question asked.

"'Yes,' I replied, 'I have often lived so. Very often I have given myself up entirely unto the care of the Lord, and have realized that I was dead, and that He alone lived in me.'

"'You have realized this as an occasional experience,' was the answer to this, 'but have you realized it as a *life*? You say you have taken refuge in the Lord sometimes, but have you ever taken up your abode in Him?'

"I saw that I had not. My faith had been very intermittent in this respect. In circumstances of peculiar difficulty, or where I had had from any cause felt especially weak in myself, I had had resource to the Lord exclusively, and had always found Him at such times sufficient for my utmost need. But that this occasional experience might be and ought to be the experience of my whole life, I had never dreamed.

"'What would you think,' asked my friend, 'of people who should trust Christ in this intermittent way for the salvation of their souls;—who should one week realize their own powerlessness to do anything towards it, and should therefore trust it altogether and wholly to the Lord, but should the next week try to do it partly themselves, asking His help to make up what was lacking in their own efforts? Would not such a course seem to you utterly foolish and inconsistent? And yet is it not equally inconsistent, and equally dishonoring to the Lord, for you to trust Him for your daily living in this intermittent way, sometimes walking by faith, and sometimes by your own efforts?'

"I could not but acknowledge the truth of this, and the possibilities and blessedness of a life of continual faith began to dawn upon me."

Such was my husband's account of his discovery; and to my great joy we were both from this time forward of one accord in regard to it.

It was not that either he or I considered ourselves to have become sinless, or that we never met with any further failures. We had simply discovered the "Secret of victory," and knew that we were no longer the "slaves of sin" and therefore forced to yield to its mastery, but that we might, if we would, be made more than conquerors through our Lord Jesus Christ. But this did not mean that temptations ceased to come; and when we neglected to avail ourselves of the "Secret" we had discovered, and, instead of handing the battle over to the Lord, took it into our own hands as of old, failure inevitably followed.

But we had learned that it was really a fact that the Lord was both able and willing to deliver us out of every temptation, if we would but trust Him to do it; and we saw that our old idea that we were necessarily the "servants of sin" was contrary to the Scriptures, and was a libel on the completeness of the salvation of Christ, who had died on purpose to deliver us from its bondage. "For sin shall not have dominion over you: for you are not under the law, but under grace." And we had discovered further that faith and faith only was the road to victory, and that effort and wrestling were of no avail in this battle. Our part, we saw, was simply surrender and faith, and God's part was to do all the rest.

For a third time, as I have said, a skin was peeled off the Bible, and on every page we found the "secret of victory" set forth in letters of light. As before, the old texts took on a deeper and a fuller meaning. Take for instance the passage, "For whatsoever is born of God overcometh the world, and this is the victory that overcometh the world, even our faith. Who is he that overcometh the world but he that believeth that Jesus is the Son of God." This had been one of our favorite passages, but we had taken it to mean only a future overcoming, when death should be swallowed up in victory, and we should overcome the world by leaving it behind us. Now we saw that it meant a present overcoming of the world, by the power of a present faith, while still living in it.

Or take this passage, "Behold the Lamb of God that taketh away the sin of the world." This had meant to us heretofore the taking away of the future penalty of sin, but now we saw that it meant taking away its present power, so that we need no longer serve it or be a bond slave to it.

I might multiply innumerable instances of this unveiling of the Bible under our new light, but these will suffice. We had made a transforming discovery, and it filled our every thought.

It seemed to me such an amazing and delightful thing that, as I have said, I could not keep it to myself. Whenever I met any of my friends my first question would be, "How much time have you to spare, for I have something splendid to tell you." And I would at once proceed to pour out my tale of the great salvation I had discovered. To most of my friends it was as new and delightful as it had been to me, and many of them took hold of it at once as an experimental reality. But one of them, the friend who had been the means of my awakening at sixteen, and who had been my closest religious confidante ever since, after listening to my story, said, "But, Hannah, that is nothing new. I have always known it." "Then why," I asked in great indignation, "did you never tell me about it? Here have I been, as you must have known, struggling along all these years with my temptations, having a few victories perhaps, but a far greater number of defeats, and all the while you knew of a secret of victory and yet never told me. How could you be so unkind?" "But of course I thought you knew it," she replied. "It is what the Quakers have always taught. Their preaching is almost altogether about it. I thought every Christian knew it." "Well," I said, "every Christian does not know it, and very few, in fact, do know it. Most Christians believe that they are obliged, owing to the weakness of the flesh, to be the 'servants of sin' all their lives; and most of them think that in order to get any victory at all, they have got to fight and wrestle for it themselves; and they never see that the Bible declares that victory is given to faith and to faith only. I feel sure," I added, "that nearly all Christians believe, as I did, that they must do all the fighting themselves, but that, if defeat seems imminent, they can then ask the Lord to come to their help. But they do not in the least understand that what they are to do is to hand the battle over to Him in the very beginning, while they 'stand still and see the salvation of the Lord,' just as the children of Israel did at the Red Sea. Moses told the Israelites then that the Lord would fight for them, and they might hold their peace, and I think everybody who knows about it ought to tell people the same thing now. And," I added emphatically, as I bade my friend good-bye, "I for one mean to tell it wherever I can."

Consequently no one, whether old or young, whether an advanced Christian or a young beginner, to whom I dared speak, failed to hear the story, and, one after another, nearly all my friends accepted it and began to live in the power of it.

Among the rest was my own little daughter, who was at this time about seven or eight years old. She had begun to develop a spirit of great willfulness which I had found very hard to control. She herself recognized that it was wrong, and tried to conquer it, but she seemed somehow possessed. One day she came to me with a very puzzled air and said, "Mother, what *is* the reason I am so naughty? I know I am a little Christian girl, and I thought Christians were always good; but though I try as hard as I can to make myself good, I just can't help being naughty." I could sympathize with the child from my own experience, and I said, "I expect, darling, that the reason is just because you do try to make yourself good. We never can make ourselves good, let us try as hard as we may. Only our Heavenly Father can make us good, and we must just trust Him to do it. Whenever you feel tempted to be naughty, if you will tell Him all about it, and ask Him to make you good, and then will trust Him to do it, He will be sure to take all your naughty away." The child remained silent for a while, and then said thoughtfully, "Oh I did not know *that*. I always thought you had to put your will into it, and just do it yourself." And she walked thoughtfully away, having evidently got hold of an entirely new idea.

I very soon noticed a great change in her; all her willfulness seemed to have disappeared, and she was as biddable and gentle as a lamb. I said nothing, as I did not want to intrude roughly into delicate ground, but two or three days afterwards, as she was sitting on the floor of her nursery playing with her dolls, I heard her saying softly to herself, in a tone of subdued exultation, "Oh, I am so glad Heavenly Father is making me so good. It feels so nice to be good." Still I said nothing, but a few nights later, when I was tucking her up in bed she burst out with, "Oh, mother, aren't you glad Heavenly Father is making me so good? He is going to make me a great deal gooder, but aren't you glad He has made me as good as He has this far?" Then, as I hugged and kissed her, and rejoiced with her, she added solemnly, "Mother, do you tell everybody about this?" I replied that I tried to, but she was not satisfied, and said, "But, mother, you must not only try to, you must really do it every time you preach, for I expect there are lots of people like I was, who want to be good and don't know how, and you ought to tell every single person you meet." I have always taken this as a sort of Divine call for my work.

In fact, however, our hearts were so full of the subject that we needed no incentive to fulfill our little daughter's injunction, and everybody we knew did sooner or later hear our story. As a consequence a great stir was created in our own circle, and I may say all over the Church in America as well, and even in England. Inquiries began to come from all quarters as to what this new doctrine, taught by the Pearsall Smiths at Millville, New Jersey, could be; and very soon meetings and conferences began to be held in various places, many of which, are still held to this day, and are generally called "Meetings for the deepening of the Spiritual life." I shall hope to give a full account of this movement elsewhere.

Suffice it to say here that this discovery, which I have tried to set forth, was the beginning of a great revival in the spiritual life of the Church everywhere. It reached its culmination in the meetings held in 1873 and 1874 on the Continent, and at Oxford and Brighton, when thousands of Christians came from all quarters to hear the story; and the effects of which are still felt in numberless lives. I never go anywhere that I do not meet people who tell me that their whole lives were changed by what they learned at those meetings. It was not that they had found a new religion, but only that their old religion had become vital to them, and the things they had before thought they believed, had been made actual and living realities. They had *called* Christ their Saviour, but now they had learned to know that He really did save, and they had trusted Him to do it, and He had not failed them.

There had been nothing Sectarian in the teaching, and there had been no need for any one to change their Creed or their Denomination. In all Denominations, even where in other respects they may seem to hold widely diverging views, there have always been those who have understood and lived the life of faith, not only among the Methodists, but among the Quakers and among the Catholics as well, and in fact it is I believe at the bottom of the creeds of every Church. All that is needed therefore is for the members of each Church to give up merely *professing* their beliefs, and begin actually to *believe* them; and, in believing them, they will always find them to be true.

It is a blessed fact about the life of faith that, no matter what the Creed or what the Denomination, it fits into all, and the story is everywhere the same.

Chapter 22

HOLINESS CAMP MEETINGS

As may be imagined, we took every possible opportunity of learning all we could of the new truths we had discovered; and I must confess that, although we found, as I have said, that the Friends did actually teach it, yet it was among the Methodists we received the clearest light. The Methodists were very definite about it. They taught definitely that there were two experiences in the Christian life, the first being justification, and the second sanctification, and they urged Christians not to be satisfied with justification (i.e., forgiveness) merely, but also to seek sanctification or the "second blessing," as they called it, as well. I should not myself express the truth in this fashion now, but at that time I must acknowledge it was most helpful.

It was not, however, every Methodist who took this ground, as many thought it was too extreme. Those who did were called "Holiness Methodists," and it was from them we received the most help. They held "Holiness Meetings," for the express purpose of considering the subject, and it was our delight to attend these Meetings whenever we could. Especially did we enjoy their "Holiness Camp Meetings," which were held in the summer time in lonely forests or at seaside places. They were called "Meetings for the promotion of holiness," and were really great open air Conferences of Christians of all denominations, from all parts of the country, who were interested in the subject, and who would assemble at these Camp Meetings, living in tents under the trees, and spending a week or ten days in waiting upon God, and conferring together on the deep things of the Kingdom.

No words can express the wonderful power, and solemnity, and yet overwhelming joyfulness, of these meetings. We were there living in tents, entirely separated from all our usual occupations and cares, with nothing to do but to give ourselves up to the spiritual influences around us, and to open our hearts to what we believed to be the teachings of the Holy Spirit. Such a company of earnest Christians, all set on coming into a closer communion with God, could not fail to create a spiritual atmosphere of great intensity; and the thrilling experiences of spiritual joy that were told in every meeting, with the songs of praise resounding through the forest, and the happy faces of every one we met, were all something so out of the ordinary and so entrancing, that it often seemed almost as if we were on the very threshold of Heaven. I cannot help pitying every Christian who has known nothing of such seasons of pure delight. They were a sort of culmination of the grand spiritual romance which my religion has always been to me, and I count them among the most entrancing times of my life. To this day the sight of a camp chair, or of a tent under the trees, always brings back to me something of the old sense of supreme happiness that used to fill every hour of those delicious Camp Meetings.

A friend of ours who knew nothing of the special object of the Meetings, having heard that we were attending one of them, came unexpectedly to see what it was like. He arrived early in the morning, and on the way to our tent met the people returning from the early Prayer Meeting. He was profoundly impressed with their looks of peace and joy, and he said to us, "What is the matter with all these people, that their faces shine so? Nearly everybody I have seen on this Camp ground seems to have a shining face; but I met a few whose faces did not shine, and I want to know what is the difference." We told him as well as we could, that the "shining faces" were an index of hearts at rest in the Lord, while those whose faces did not shine had not yet learned the blessed secret. He listened to us with the deepest interest, and, when we had done, he said with conviction, "Well I am determined that I too will get a 'shining face,' and I will stay on this Camp ground until I do." And sure enough, in a few days his face too was shining with the joys of God's salvation.

I shall never forget the first time I was present at one of these Camp Meetings, and the first Prayer Meeting I attended. It was an early morning meeting in a tent. I knew nothing of Methodist Meetings, having never attended any except those little ones at Millville, and had no conception of the emotional atmosphere into which I had come. I found when I got into the meeting that I had forgotten my handkerchief, but having never in my life shed any tears in a meeting, I was not troubled. But in this meeting, the fountains of my being seemed to be broken up, and floods of delicious tears poured from my eyes. I was reduced to great straits, and was obliged surreptitiously to lift up my dress and use my white under-skirt to dry my tears. I have never since been to any meeting without at least two handkerchiefs safely tucked away in my pocket, although I believe I have never since been so overwhelmed with emotion, and I revelled in it.

As I left the tent where the meeting had been held, a Methodist "Holiness Sister," seeing my emotion, put her arm around me, and told me of her own experience in sanctification, and took me in hand to help me. Guided by her, I soon found myself in the way of getting the full benefit of all the exercises of the meetings. I found that they talked a great deal about what they called the "blessing of sanctification," and at every meeting we were urged to come forward to what they called the "altar" (which was really a bench set apart for the purpose) to seek for this "blessing." Just what the "blessing" was I did not understand, but it seemed to be something very tangible, which resulted from entire consecration and simple faith, and which made people rapturously happy. My "Holiness Sister" soon had me going forward to the "altar" to obtain this blessing. I was determined to get whatever there was to be had, and I was more and more fired with enthusiasm by the thrilling testimonies I continually heard on every hand from those who had received the "blessing," so that I was nothing loth to embrace every opportunity for going to the "altar" to seek it. In fact I enjoyed doing so immensely, for it seemed somehow to bring me to the delicious verge of unknown spiritual possibilities, that might at any moment reveal themselves.

Apart, however, from this treading as it were, on the threshold, no special "blessing" ever came to me from these visits to the "altar." I am not of an emotional nature, and none of the overpowering emotions I heard described, as constituting the "blessing," ever fell to my portion. But the grand truth that was taught at these Meetings, that the Lord Jesus Christ was a Saviour from the power of sin as well as a Saviour from the guilt of sin, became more and more real and effective to me; but of any blessing, as a blessing, apart from the truth, I realized nothing. A knowledge of the truth was all the blessing I ever received; and although at first I was somewhat disappointed, I came in time to see that a knowledge of the truth was all the "blessing" I needed. And I was gradually convinced that a large part of what was called "the blessing" was simply the emotional response of emotional natures to the discovery of a magnificent truth. To me it came with intellectual conviction and delight, but in both cases the truth was the same, and it was the truth, not the emotion, that set the soul free.

My husband, however, being of a more emotional nature than myself, did, at one of these Camp Meetings, receive the "blessing" in a true Methodist fashion. He came home full of a divine glow that seemed to affect everybody he met. He could not speak of the Camp Meeting without bringing tears to all our eyes, and it was very evident that he had gone through there a remarkable experience in his spiritual life. He said they had had one day a special meeting to pray for the "Baptism of the Spirit," and that after the meeting he had gone alone into a retired spot in the woods, to continue the prayer by himself. Suddenly, from head to foot he had been shaken with what seemed like a magnetic thrill of heavenly delight, and floods of glory seemed to pour through him, soul and body, with the inward assurance that this was the longed-for Baptism of the Holy Spirit. The whole world seemed transformed to him, every leaf and blade of grass quivered with exquisite color, and heaven seemed to open out before him as a present blissful possession. Everybody looked beautiful to him, for he seemed to see the Divine Spirit within each one, without regard to their outward seemings. This ecstasy lasted for several weeks, and was the beginning of a wonderful career of spiritual power and blessing.

I confess I was rather jealous that I did not receive a like "blessing," for I felt that I needed it quite as much as he did, and I renewed my efforts to obtain it. But it was all in vain; I never seemed to get out of the region of conviction into the region of emotion, and I found myself compelled to take all my experience intellectually and not emotionally. I became convinced at last that the reason of this difference between my experience and that of some others was not that they were peculiarly favored by God above me, but that their emotional natures received with these floods of emotional delight, the same truths that I received calmly, and with intellectual delight; the difference being, not in the experiences, but in the different natures of the recipients of that experience.

I have many times since noticed this difference in people's experiences; and I have also noticed that, very often the emotional experiences have not been as solid and permanent as the more intellectual ones. In the very nature of things emotions are more or less variable, while convictions, where they are really convictions, and are not purely notions or ideas, are permanent. Once convince a man that two and two make four, and no amount of dyspepsia or east wind can change his conviction; while everything that is only a matter of feeling, and not of conviction, is at the mercy of these and a thousand other untoward influences. I learned in time therefore not to seek emotions, but to seek only for convictions, and I found to my surprise and delight that my convictions brought me a far more stable and permanent joy than many of my more emotional friends seemed to experience. In the time of stress, with many of them, their emotions flagged, and even often vanished, and they had hard fights to prevent utter failure and despair, and some of them have been thankful at last to struggle back to the stable ground of conviction, which in their emotional days had seemed so barren and comfortless.

All this however took me many years in learning. But meanwhile the joy and power of the glorious secret we had discovered grew every year more and more practical; and more and more my soul learned to rest in absolute confidence on the keeping and saving power of the Lord. I must repeat what I have said elsewhere, that not for a moment do I mean that temptation ceased its attacks, or that we had reached what is sometimes called "sinless perfection." Temptations continued to arise, and sometimes failures befell. But we had discovered a "way to escape," and had learned that this way was the way of faith. We had found out that Christ was a Deliverer, not only from the future punishment for sin, but from the present power of sin, and we realized that we need no longer be the "slaves of sin." And just so far as we laid hold by faith of this deliverance, just so far were we delivered. We had not picked up holiness and put it into our pockets as a permanent and inalienable possession; but we had discovered the "high way" of holiness, and had learned the secret of walking therein. When we walked there, we had victory, when we tried other pathways, we found failure. It was simply this, that at last, after many years of "wilderness wandering," we had entered into the "promised land" and had found it true as was said to Israel of old that "every place the sole of your foot shall tread upon that have I given you." The whole land was ours, and it only needed for us to "go up and possess it."

We had discovered that the Bible stated a fact when it said, "And God is able to make all grace abound towards you; that ye, always having all sufficiency in all things, may abound to every good work." And we had proved in actual experience that God really *was* able, if only we were willing.

Christ had been revealed to us, not as our future Saviour only, but as our present and complete Saviour now and here, able to keep us from falling, and to deliver us out of the hands of all our enemies.

For myself I had now entered upon a region of romance before which the glory of all other romances paled into insignificance. It was like an exploration of the very courts of heaven itself. Every day was a fresh revelation. Words fail when I try to describe it. I often in my heart called it the "bird life," for I felt like a bird spreading its wings in a country all sunshine and greenness, and soaring upwards into the blue of an unfathomable sky. In the past, I had been a caged bird, happy in its cage because it knew nothing of the uncaged life outside. But now all barriers seemed removed, and my soul was set free to comprehend with all saints what is the breadth, and length, and depth, and height; and to know the love of Christ which passeth knowledge.

I thought, when I discovered the restitution of all things, that I had reached this comprehension, but I saw now wider breadths, and longer lengths, and deeper depths, and higher heights, than I had even conceived of then, and the love of Christ that seemed then to pass knowledge, became now an unfathomable abyss of delight.

I had found that God, just God alone, without anything else, was enough. Even the comfort of His promises paled before the comfort of Himself. What difference did it make if I could not find a promise to fit my case? I had found the Promiser, and He was infinitely more than all His promises.

I remember well how, when I was a child and found myself in any trouble or perplexity, the coming in of my father or my mother upon the scene would always bring me immediate relief. The moment I heard the voice of one of them calling my name, that very moment every burden dropped off and every fear vanished. I had got my father or my mother, and what more could I need. It was their simple presence that did it. They did not need to stand up and make a string of promises for my relief, nor detail to me the plans of deliverance. The mere fact of their presence was all the assurance I required that everything now would be all right for me,—must in fact be all right, because they were my parents, and I was their child. And how much more true must all this be in regard to our Heavenly

Father, who has all wisdom and all power, and whose very name is the God of Love. His presence is literally and truly all we need for everything. It would be enough for us, even if we had not a single promise nor a single revelation of His plans. How often in the Bible He has settled all the questions and fears of His people by the simple announcement, "I will be with thee." Who can doubt that in that announcement He meant to say that all His wisdom, and all His love, and all His omnipotent power, would therefore of course be engaged on their side?

I was married very young, and knew but little of housekeeping, and would naturally often find myself in bothers and snarls over my household duties, and not know what to do. And then sometimes, in the midst, I would hear the front door bell ring, and my mother's voice would ask, "Is Hannah at home?" And I would exclaim, with a sigh of infinite relief, "Oh, there is mother," and all my troubles would vanish as though they had never been. My mother was there, and would manage it all. And over and over again in my spiritual life the words, "Oh, there is God," have brought me a similar but far more blessed deliverance. With God present what can there be to fear? Since He has said, "I will never leave thee nor forsake thee," every heart that knows Him cannot but boldly say, "I will not fear what man can do unto me."

Every fear, every perplexity, every anxiety, find an all-satisfying answer in God—He Himself, what He is in nature and character. His ways, or His plans, or even His promises, we may misinterpret or misunderstand, but goodness of character we cannot mistake, and it is the character of God that is our resting-place. He can only act according to His character, and therefore what is His character is the one vital thing we need to know. If He is good, and unselfish, and loving, and wise, and just, and, with all this, omnipotent and omnipresent as well, then all must be ordered right for us. It cannot be otherwise. The seen thing may seem to be all wrong, but we know that the seen thing is very often not at all the true thing. What we are able to see is generally only a partial view and no partial view can be depended on. I may look at a partial view of a winding river, and declare it to be a lake, because no outlet can be *seen*. To witness the outward seeming of a parent's dealing with a child during the hour of lessons, or during the administration of medicine, or during the necessary discipline and training of a child's life, and to see no further than the outside, would give a very untrue idea of a parent's love. One must have, what George Macdonald calls, "eyes that can see below surfaces," if one is to do justice either to a good parent or to a good God. But when His utter unselfishness had been discovered, this interior eye is opened, all difficulties as to the apparent mysteries of His dealings are answered forever.

I can understand the joy with which the Psalmist reiterated over and over the goodness of the God of Israel. "Oh, give thanks unto the Lord, for He is good;" "Oh, trust in the Lord, for He is good;" "Oh that men would praise the Lord for His goodness;" "The earth is full of the goodness of the Lord;" "Come, taste and see that the Lord is good." Living all around Israel were nations whose gods were not good,—cruel gods, unjust gods, and, above all, selfish gods, who cared only for themselves and for their own glory, and who were sublimely indifferent to the welfare of their worshipers; and for the Israelites not to be afraid to contrast with these bad gods their own unselfish, and just God, and to be able to declare, without fear of contradiction, that He was a good God, must have given them triumphant delight. And I feel that it is no less of a triumph now, in the midst of a world that misunderstands and maligns Him, to be able, with absolute conviction and assurance to challenge every human being the world over to "Come, taste and see that the Lord is good."

Chapter 23

THE LOVELY WILL OF GOD

With my eyes thus opened to see the absolute goodness and unselfishness of God, I experienced a complete change of mind in regard to His will. In the past I had looked upon God's will as being against me, now I had found out that it was for me. I had thought it was something to be afraid of, now I saw it was something to be embraced with joy. Formerly it had seemed to me that His will was the terrible instrument of His severity, and that I must do all I could to avert its terrors from swooping down upon my devoted head. Now I saw that it was the instrument of His love, and could only bring upon me all that was kindest and best. I realized that of course it was impossible for the will of unselfish love to be anything but good and kind; and that, since He has all knowledge and all wisdom as well, it must, in the very nature of things, be the best thing the universe could contain; and that no greater bliss could come to any of us, than to have that lovely unselfish will perfectly done in us and for us.

To hide oneself in God's will seemed to me sometimes like hiding in an impregnable fortress of love and care, where no harm could reach me; and sometimes it seemed like a bed of softest down, upon which I could lie down in a delicious and undisturbed rest. I never can put into words all that I began to see of the loveliness, the tenderness, the unselfishness, the infinite goodness of the will of God! I fairly revelled in its sweetness.

It was not that life was to have no more trials, for this wise and loving will might see that trials were a necessary gift of love. Neither was it essential that we should be able to *see* the Divine hand in every trial, since my common sense told me that He must still be there, for a God who is omnipresent could not help being present somewhere, even in a trial, and, being in it, He would of course be there to help and bless.

We are not wise enough to judge as to things, whether they are really in their essence joys or sorrows, but the Lord knows; and, because He loves us with an unselfish and limitless love, He cannot fail to make the apparently hard, or cruel, or even wicked thing, work together for our best good. I say "cannot fail" simply because it is an unthinkable thing to suppose that such a God as ours could do otherwise.

It is no matter who starts our trial, whether man, or devil, or even our own foolish selves, if God permits it to reach us, He has by this permission made the trial His own, and will turn it for us into a chariot of love which will carry our souls to a place of blessing that we could not have reached in any other way. I saw that to the Christian who hides in the fortress of God's will, there can be no "second causes," for nothing can penetrate into that fortress unless the Divine Keeper of the fortress shall give it permission; and this permission, when given, means that He adopts it as being for our best good. Joseph was sold into Egypt by the wickedness of his brethren, but God made their wickedness the chariot that carried Joseph to his place of triumph over the Egyptians.

We may be certain therefore, more certain than we are that the sun will rise to-morrow, that God's will is the most lively thing the universe contains for us; and this, not because it always looks or seems the best, but because it cannot help being the best, since it is the will of infinite unselfishness and of infinite love.

I began to sing in my heart continually Faber's lovely hymn:—

"I worship Thee, sweet Will of God,
    And all Thy ways adore;
And every day I live it seems
    I love Thee more and more."

One verse in this hymn especially delighted me, because I so often found it practically true.

"I know not what it is to doubt,
    My heart is always gay;
I run no risks, for, come what will,
    Thou always hast Thy way."

The first time I realized it was as follows. It was three days after the birth of a darling little girl baby, for whom I had longed unspeakably, and who seemed to me the most ineffable treasure ever committed to mortal care. My nurse had been suddenly taken ill, and was obliged to leave, and we had been forced to get in a strange nurse whom I did not know, and whose looks I did not like. It was in the days when trained nurses were are less common than now, and I felt sure this one was unusually ignorant. I could hardly endure to have her touch my precious treasure, and yet I was not allowed to care for my darling myself.

It was winter time, and there was a blazing wood fire on the hearth in my sick room. On the first evening of her arrival, the nurse, after settling me in for the night, sat down close to fire taking my darling baby on her knees. Pretty soon she fell sound asleep, and I was awakened by her snores to see my darling lying perilously near the fire on her slanting lap, while her head nodded over it in what seemed to me like a drunken slumber. I tried in vain to awaken her, but my voice was feeble, and made no impression, and I expected every minute to see my darling baby roll off her lap into the fire. I could make no one hear, and I knew to get out of bed and go across the cold floor might seriously injure me. But my anxiety was so overpowering that I sat up in bed and was just trying to rise, when these words flashed into my mind—"I run no risks, for come what will Thou always hast Thy way." And with it came a conviction that my baby could not run any risks for she was safe in God's care. With an sense of infinite peace my head fell back on my pillow, and my soul sank back on the sweet and lovely will of God. I saw that my darling was cradled in the arms of Almighty love, and I went to sleep without care, and waked up to find her being comfortably tucked in beside me for her needed meal.

It was lovely beyond words to have had such a practical insight into the beauty and the blessedness of the Will of God!

I have had many such insights since, and I have learned to know beyond the shadow of doubt, that the will of God is the most delicious and delightful thing in the universe. And this, not because things always go as I want them to go, neither because of any extra piety on my part, but simply because my common sense tells me that the will of unselfish love could not be anything else but delightful. The reason heaven is heaven is because God's will is perfectly done there, and earth would necessarily be like heaven, if only His will could be perfectly done here.

I had been used to hear Christians talk about consecration to the will of God as being such a high religious attainment that only a few extra devout souls could hope to reach it. But with

my discovery of the infinite unselfishness of God, I came to
realize that consecration to Him was not an attainment but a
priceless privilege; and I cannot but feel sure that if people only
knew the loveliness of His will, not a devout few only, but
every single soul in the universe would rush eagerly to choose
it for every moment of their lives.

This seems to me to be not an extra degree of piety, but only
an extra degree of good common sense. If I were lost in a
trackless wilderness and could see no way out, and a skillful
guide should offer to lead me into safety, would I consider it a
hard thing to surrender myself into his hands, and to say "thy
will be done" to his guidance? And can it be a hard thing to
surrender myself to my Heavenly Guide, and to say "Thy will
be done" to His guidance? No, a thousand times no! Consecration, or as I prefer to call it, surrender to God, is the greatest
privilege offered to any soul in this life, and to say "Thy will
be done" is one of the most delightful things human lips are
allowed to utter.

An old writer has said that God's will is not a load to carry,
as so many think, but is a pillow to rest on, and I found this to
be true. My soul sank back upon it with a sweetness of
contented rest that no words can describe. At other times, to
say the words "Thy will be done" seemed to me like a
magnificent shout of victory, a sort of triumphant banner, flung
forth in the face of the whole universe, challenging it to
combat. So vividly did I realize this, that it drew from me the
only verse of poetry I was ever able to write, which, however
poor as poetry, was the heartfelt expression of a very real and
inspiring fact.

> "Thy wonderful, grand Will, my God,
>   With triumph now I make it mine,

And Love shall cry a joyous *Yes,*
To every dear command of thine."

But time would fail me to tell of all that my soul discovered when I discovered the goodness and unselfishness of God. To say that *He is enough* is to give an absolute and incontrovertible answer to every doubt and every question that has arisen or can arise. It may not seem to our consciousness that any prayers are answered, or any promises fulfilled, but what of that? Behind every prayer and behind every promise, there is God,—the bare God, if I may so express it; and, if He exists at all, we know He must be enough.

How often I had repeated the lines:—

"Thou, oh Christ, art all I want,
More than all in Thee I find."

But never until now had I known what they meant. They had seemed to express a beautiful sentiment, but now I saw that they simply stated a fact. I had begun to discover that He actually was all I needed; and that, even infinitely more than all, beyond what I could ask or think, was stored up for me in Him.

In a sense my search after God was ended, for I had discovered that He was enough!

I have had many blessed and lovely things to find out about Him since, but I had then reached Himself,—the real God, behind all the seemings, and my heart had entered into its rest. I had discovered that nothing else really matters,—neither creeds, nor ceremonies, nor doctrines, nor dogmas. GOD IS; GOD IS UNSELFISH; AND GOD IS ENOUGH!

Chapter 24

OLD AGE AND DEATH

And now that I am seventy years old, and life is rapidly passing from me, if I should be asked how my discovery of the unselfishness of God affects my feelings toward old age and death, I can only say, that, secure in the knowledge that God is, and that He is enough, I find old age delightful in the present, and death a delicious prospect for the future.

If it were not for Him, old age with its failing powers and its many infirmities could not but be a sad and wearisome time; but, with God, our lovely unselfish God, at the back of it, old age is simply a delightful resting-place. To be seventy gives one permission to stand aloof from the stress of life, and to lay down all burden of responsibility for carrying on the work of the world; and I rejoice in my immunity.

I have tried in my day to help bear the burdens of my own generation, and, now that that generation has almost passed away, I am more than happy to know that the responsibilities of the present generation do not rest upon me, but upon the shoulders of the younger and stronger spirits, who are called in the providence of God to bear them. I laugh to myself with pleasure at the thought, and quite enjoy the infirmities of age as they come upon me, and find it delightful to be laid aside from one thing after another, and to be at liberty to look on in a peaceful leisure at the younger wrestlers in the world's arena. I cannot say that their wrestling is always done in the way that seems best to my old eyes, but I admire the Divine order that evidently lays upon each generation its own work, to be done in its own way; and I am convinced that, whether it may seem to us for good or for ill, the generation that is passing must give place to the one that is coming, and must keep hands off from interfering. Advice we who are older may give, and the fruits of our experience, but we must be perfectly content to have our advice rejected by the younger generation, and our experience ignored. Were we willing for this, I am convinced the young would much more often be glad to profit by what is called the "wisdom of the old"; but, as it is, they are afraid to ask advice because they know they will be expected to follow it, whether it commends itself to them or not, and because they fear the old will feel hurt if they do not. Perfect freedom in asking advice can only exist along with perfect freedom not to follow that advice.

I am not of course referring to children, but to the adults of two generations, and I believe, as a general thing, the older generation, when it insists on its advice being taken, puts itself into the unenviable position of being very much in the way of the world's progress. It is found necessary in all lines of business nowadays to employ younger and younger workers, because the older workers are inclined to get into ruts, and are unwilling to be urged out of them. In this connection it is very striking to notice in the history of the Israelites how at the age of fifty they were, by the Divine order, retired from public service, whether in the Tabernacle or in the Army. "And from the age of fifty years they shall cease waiting upon the service thereof, and shall serve no more." It is manifest therefore that, if *they* were retired at fifty, one who is seventy, is at perfect liberty to stand aside from the world's work, and to enjoy that delicious sense of release from responsibility which is the happy privilege of old age.

We read a great deal about the old educating the young. We need just as much that the young should educate the old. I hear that there is a University in Brussels that carries out this idea. It is called the New University, and it is indeed new, for not only do the Professors hold classes for the pupils, but the pupils hold classes for the Professors; and I venture to predict that that University will produce results far beyond those of any other. It is not that I think the wisdom is all shut up in the young, but I am convinced that it is the divine plan that each generation shall have the guidance of its own era, and shall do its work in its own way. And any effort to upset this Divine order, efforts which I am sorry to say we old people are constantly being tempted to make, are sure to produce friction and to hinder progress.

People talk a great deal about the duties the young owe to the old, but I think it is far more important to consider the duties the old owe to the young. I do not of course say that the young owe us old people no duties, but at the age of seventy I have learned to see that the weight of preponderance is enormously on the other side, and that each generation owes to the succeeding one far more duty than the succeeding one owes to them. We brought the younger generation into the world, without consulting them, and we are bound therefore to sacrifice ourselves for their good. This is what the God who created us has done in the sacrifice of Christ, and I do not see that He could have done less. He has poured Himself out without stint for His children, and we must do the same for ours.

Having discovered the unselfishness of God, as every one who has lived to be seventy ought to have done, our attitude towards all around us, should be, up to our measure, one of a similar unselfishness. And surely this is what our Lord wants to teach us when He urges us to love our enemies, and to bless them that curse us, and do good to them that hate us; in order, He says, that we may be the children of our Father which is in Heaven, who Himself does these things. And He ends His words with the exhortation, "Be ye therefore perfect, even as your Father which is in Heaven is perfect." Our perfection therefore is to be the perfection of unselfish love; and, the older we are, the more fully we ought to know this and act on it.

Everything is safe when an unselfish love is guiding and controlling, and therefore my old heart is at rest, and I can lay down my arms with a happy confidence that, since God is in His Heaven, all must necessarily be right with His world, let the "seemings" be what they may. And I can peacefully wait to understand what seems mysterious now, until the glorious day of revelations, to which every hour brings me nearer.

It is to me a most comforting discovery, to have found out that God can manage His own universe Himself, and that He can do it even without my help. I never look at the sun, or the moon, or the stars, without a satisfying recognition of the fact that they are all the "work of His fingers," and that the management of them is His business and not mine, and give all things else, to His care, without a fear that the universe will be dislocated by my going. God is the Housekeeper of His own creation, and just as I should think it folly to worry myself over the housekeeping of my neighbors in Grosvenor Road, so does it seem to me even a greater folly to worry myself over the housekeeping of God. Therefore with an easy mind I can look forward to death, and the prospect of leaving this life and of entering into the larger and grander life beyond, is pure bliss to me. It is like having a new country, full of unknown marvels, to explore; and the knowledge that no one and nothing can hinder my going there, is a secret spring of joy in the bottom of my heart continually. Often and often, when some pleasant earthly plan is spoiled, I say to myself triumphantly, "Ah well, there is one thing about which I can never be disappointed, and that is dying. No one, not even an enemy, can deprive me of that!" Whenever I see a funeral I laugh inwardly at the fresh realization of the fact that such a happy fate lies before every one of us; and I hardly dare trust myself to try writing letters of condolence about the death of any one, for they are almost sure to turn into letters of congratulation at the happy escape of another prisoner from this earthly prison house.

In the different associations to which I belong my comrades never dare ask me to conduct a memorial service for our departed members, for fear I shall be tempted to give thanks for their release. Even for the going home of those I love, I can always rejoice, for it seems to me nothing but selfishness to let my loss outweigh their glorious gain.

I love Walt Whitman's matchless death song, and always want to send it to every dying friend:—

> "Joy, shipmate, joy.
> (Pleased to the soul at death, I cry.)
> Our life is closed, our life begins;
> The long, long anchorage we leave,
> The ship is clear at last, she leaps,
> She swiftly courses from the shore!
> Joy, shipmate, joy!"

This passing life with all its affairs, once apparently so important, fades into insignificance in face of the surpassing life beyond, and I am glad to be so nearly through with it. Its interest has gone for me; and I, who used to be so eager to see every new place, and to taste every new experience, care for them no longer. I have a most satisfactory feeling of being done with this earth. All places look alike to me, and all experiences seem tame in comparison with that which awaits me on the other side. As to what that is, I can only have vague ideas. I am like the butterfly, just preparing to slip out of its old cocoon, panting for the life outside, but with no experience to tell it what sort of a life that outside life will be. Only I believe with all my heart that the Apostle told the truth when he declared that, "Eye hath not seen, nor ear heard, neither have entered into the heart of man the things which God hath prepared for them that love Him." And what more delicious prospect could the soul have! I remember vividly my perfect delight many years ago in the prospect of exploring the unknown beauties of the Yellowstone Park, and of the Hoodoo Mountains in Wyoming Territory, a delight caused largely by the fact that they were unknown, and that therefore anything and everything seemed possible. But that delight was nothing compared to my delight now, in looking forward to the things which have not even entered my mind to conceive.

The one thing I do know about it is, that then will be fulfilled the prayer of our Lord, "Father, I will that they also, whom Thou hast given me, be with me where I am; that they may behold my glory which Thou hast given me." That glory is not the glory of dazzling light and golden brightness, as some might picture it, but it is the glory of unselfish love, than which there can be no greater. I have had a few faint glimpses of this glory now and here, and it has been enough to ravish my heart. But there I shall see Him as He is, in all the glory of an infinite unselfishness which no heart of man has ever been able to conceive; and I await the moment with joy.